Educational Delusions?

Educational Delusions?

*Why Choice Can Deepen Inequality
and How to Make Schools Fair*

———

Gary Orfield and Erica Frankenberg
and Associates

UNIVERSITY OF CALIFORNIA PRESS

Berkeley   Los Angeles   London

KH

University of California Press, one of the most distinguished university presses in the United States, enriches lives around the world by advancing scholarship in the humanities, social sciences, and natural sciences. Its activities are supported by the UC Press Foundation and by philanthropic contributions from individuals and institutions. For more information, visit www.ucpress.edu.

University of California Press
Berkeley and Los Angeles, California

University of California Press, Ltd.
London, England

Library of Congress Cataloging-in-Publication Data

Educational delusions? : why choice can deepen inequality and how to make schools fair / Gary Orfield and Erica Frankenberg and associates.
        p.   cm.
    Includes bibliographical references and index.
    ISBN 978-0-520-27473-0 (cloth : alk. paper)—ISBN 978-0-520-27474-7 (pbk. : alk. paper)
    1. School choice.   2. Educational equalization.   I. Orfield, Gary, editor of compilation.   II. Frankenberg, Erica, editor of compilation.
    LB1027.9.E395   2013
    379.2'6—dc23   2012040600

Manufactured in the United States of America

22   21   20   19   18   17   16   15   14   13
10   9   8   7   6   5   4   3   2   1

In keeping with a commitment to support environmentally responsible and sustainable printing practices, UC Press has printed this book on 50-pound Enterprise, a 30% post-consumer-waste, recycled, deinked fiber that is processed chlorine-free. It is acid-free and meets all ANSI/NISO (Z 39.48) requirements.

8/28/13

CONTENTS

ILLUSTRATIONS

FIGURES

TABLES

ACKNOWLEDGMENTS

Choice has been a major theme in civil rights policy since the 1960s. One of us, Erica Frankenberg, is the product of a good desegregated magnet school in Mobile, Alabama; the other, Gary Orfield, had his children attend a magnet school in Illinois and was deeply involved in the creation of new magnet schools in St. Louis and San Francisco, where federal courts appointed him as special master in each district's desegregation case. He was also one of the conveners of a faculty seminar at Harvard on choice and diversity, and a number of Civil Rights Project studies of desegregation and No Child Left Behind have discussed this issue. In fact, this book originated from a series of discussions after the February 2010 release of the Civil Rights Project report *Choice without Equity*, which describes the intense segregation of charter schools at a time when federal policy was strongly promoting them as a centerpiece of its reform agenda. Our study stimulated intense national debate. We concluded that as all states faced growing federal pressure to implement choice programs, it was time to bring together the latest research and to reflect on where the country is going and what issues a variety of experiences show need to be considered in making decisions about choice strategies.

We are especially grateful to Naomi Schneider at University of California Press, who saw that the issue of school choice from a civil rights perspective might have the makings of an important book. It has been a pleasure to work with her and the excellent staff at the press, who pressed us to explain, to document, and to condense the studies. Our intent was to produce a volume that would be accessible and based on clear evidence to help readers critically assess assumptions about school choice and the civil rights implications of the choices

ix

and decisions being made in their communities. Because much of the debate in this arena is ideologically driven, we grounded our examination in specific cases as a way to illustrate the relationships between policies and their effects on segregation and opportunity for poor and minority families, evidence from which readers could draw their own conclusions about school choice. The coverage of many of the topics we thought were important in such a volume—charter schools, magnet schools, and controlled choice plans—began as Civil Rights Project reports, but other chapters began as reports for other organizations, including the Institute for Race and Poverty at the University of Minnesota, the Charles Hamilton Houston Institute at Harvard University, and the Warren Institute at the University of California at Berkeley. Researchers at various universities wrote each of these reports. We reached out to these authors and to other colleagues. Happily, they all agreed to participate, even with a condensed editing timeline, and to make the chapters speak to the themes of the book and to be more accessible and consistent in tone. We have contextualized these individual studies with chapters on the history of choice and civil rights, the theoretical arguments for choice, and a conclusion suggesting strategies for choice more likely to realize civil rights objectives of access and equity for students of color.

Although we wrote most of the chapters in whole or in part, we were also honored to work with excellent scholars who each contributed important independent perspectives and conclusions. Each chapter clearly shows its authorship, as does the table of contents.

In addition to Naomi's suggestions, we appreciate those of two reviewers and of Carolyn Peele to clarify our meaning. Laurie Russman, Kyra Young, Tiffanie Lewis, and Jennifer Ayscue provided research and logistical support to help bring the manuscript to publication. Alison Tyler assisted with the proofreading.

The Civil Rights Project has focused on educational equity for sixteen years, during a time when school choice has rapidly grown and civil rights have receded. We think the growth of many contemporary forms of choice has occurred in such a manner as to harm the civil rights of students of color, low-income students, and limited-English students, along with their families, their teachers, and many of their communities. The growth of choice is also challenging the efforts of school districts in some areas to provide high-quality diverse educational opportunities. We strongly believe that at the beginning of the twenty-first century, schools remain a powerful tool for attaining individual opportunity and creating a thriving multiracial democratic society. It is clear that school choice is here to stay, and we hope this book furthers the conversation about how choice policies can both stop intensifying stratification and help us widen access to quality integrated educational experiences for all U.S. students. We have been inspired by people in communities across the nation who are constantly working to expand rights and lower barriers for students.

Finally, and in many ways most importantly, we want to acknowledge the understanding, support, and love we have received in such abundance from Patricia and Mark.

Gary Orfield and Erica Frankenberg

PART ONE

Introduction

Choice and Civil Rights

Forgetting History, Facing Consequences

Gary Orfield

The idea of school choice has a tangled history. It is an idea that has taken many shapes, under the banner of the same hopeful word, one that seems to have a simple positive meaning but embodies many contradictory possibilities. Choice has a thousand different faces, some treacherous, some benign. It includes the creation of charter and magnet schools, voluntary transfer programs under state and federal legislation, choice-based desegregation plans, transfer rights under No Child Left Behind (NCLB), and voucher programs. The distinctions and this history are important to understand because forgetting what has been learned about choice systems that failed means repeating mistakes and paying the costs. There is no reason to keep making that error.

The large-scale emergence of schools of choice is deeply related to the civil rights struggles of the second half of the twentieth century, on both the conservative and the liberal side. This book therefore brings civil rights back into the center of the debate about choice policies and alternatives, since both contemporary sides in the issue see offering better options to poor minority students as an essential goal of choice. The conclusions of a number of researchers suggest that although helping minority children is a central justification for choice proponents, ignoring the essential civil rights dimensions of choice plans risks compounding rather than remedying racial inequality.

WHAT IS EDUCATIONAL CHOICE?

School choice first arose as a major policy idea in southern states struggling over civil rights and was claimed by both liberals and conservatives. Much was learned through experiments in hundreds of communities about how different forms of choice worked. In recent decades, as the civil rights impulse has faded and its opponents have gained power, school choice has become increasingly separated from civil rights while being linked to different agendas. Yet the critical differences among types of choice have often been so obscured that few understand them. We need to sort out what we are talking about and connect the different plans to their consequences for students and our society. The stakes are high because educational inequality is intensifying while education is ever more critical in determining life chances, and the population of school-age children is becoming predominantly nonwhite.[1]

Choice is a very seductive idea. In a society with a powerful commitment to individual freedom, religious pluralism, democratic government, and a market economy, the idea of choice has many positive resonances. We choose our religion, we choose our spouse, we choose many aspects of our lifestyle, we select what we buy, and we want to believe that we can choose our future. What could be more American than the freedom to choose your own school, or even to create a school? Freedom, creativity, markets, competition, attacks on old bureaucracies—all of these match elements of American tradition and the spirit of an era that's cynical about government, disappointed in social reforms, and dominated by business ideas.[2] It hardly seems surprising that all of the five most recent presidents, both Republicans and Democrats, have embraced choice as a major solution for educational inequality and fostered it through public policy.[3] Not coincidentally, none of them has paid much attention to issues of discrimination.

President Barack Obama's administration actively used the economic disaster of the Great Recession of 2008–10 to strongly pressure states by offering desperately needed funds in exchange for policy changes, including a great expansion of charter schools in what it called the Race to the Top. There was little discussion of the fact that public school choice really isn't an American tradition, that only a handful of states had made large commitments to charter schools before the Obama administration encouraged them to do so, or that the evidence of charters' educational benefits was very weak. Education policy since Ronald Reagan has been based largely on standards and accountability, sanctions, and market competition, setting aside earlier concerns about poverty and race.[4]

What do the choice plans really mean? What do we know about the conditions under which choice provides clear benefits for the children and communities that most need them? Under what conditions is it likely to fail? What kinds of policies are needed to ensure racial equity and opportunity in choice programs? This book addresses all of these questions.

Our huge, diverse, and decentralized nation produces a wide variety of educational experiments and policies, whose impacts can be compared and from which important information can be gleaned. We have now had a half century of very different experiments with choice. Although it still plays a modest overall role in U.S. schools, it is growing rapidly and is heavily concentrated in districts with many of the nation's most disadvantaged students and most troubled public schools. Many choice advocates argue that it is the most important solution for the problems faced by millions of students in poor minority neighborhoods with segregated, high-poverty schools that fail to meet state and federal standards. Abigail and Stephen Thernstrom, in their book *No Excuses: Closing the Racial Gap in Learning,* see choice as central to a solution: "Unless more schools are freed from the constraints of the traditional public school system, the racial gap in academic achievement will not significantly narrow, we suspect." They say that since middle-class white families can choose their schools through the housing market, shouldn't poor black and Latino families have the same choice? Yet, it turns out, they want to offer those families not a choice to attend the schools in affluent suburban neighborhoods but instead just some choice, which is usually another segregated, impoverished school under a different management system. They say, "Every urban school should become a charter."[5] Civil rights advocates of choice often want a much broader kind of choice under very different rules.[6]

Too often choice has been assumed to be good in and of itself. In markets there are, of course, good and bad choices. And there are markets with strong rules of the game, as well as those in which deregulation leads to abuses. All of us who have lived through the Great Recession know that unregulated markets can produce very bad outcomes. At a time when there is a severe shortage of public resources in most states and communities, when poverty and racial isolation have grown, and when the consequences of educational failure have increased, it is critical to examine the evidence on how well various forms of choice are working, and for whom. It turns out that there is much less evidence in favor of some leading forms of choice than one might suppose from all of the enthusiastic advocacy for them.[7] If some forms of choice divert energy and money from more beneficial reforms or actually cause additional harm, we need to know about it.

Three Presidents Affirm Choice through Charters

One reason for the rapid expansion of choice, particularly in the form of charter schools, is broad bipartisan support. President Obama took the most assertive federal move in mandating this form of choice in states that had had few or no charters. While speaking at the National Urban League convention in 2009, he justified using emergency funds through his Race to the Top program to strongly press states to fund more charter schools.

> Now, in some cases [when schools fail], that's going to mean restarting the school under different management as a charter school—as an independent public school formed by parents, teachers, and civic leaders who've got broad leeway to innovate. And some people don't like charter schools. They say, well, that's going to take away money from other public schools that also need support. Charter schools aren't a magic bullet, but I want to give states and school districts the chance to try new

things. If a charter school works, then let's apply those lessons elsewhere. And if a charter school doesn't work, we'll hold it accountable; we'll shut it down.

So, no, I don't support all charter schools, but I do support good charter schools. . . . One school called Pickett went from just 14 percent of students being proficient in math to almost 70 percent. (Applause.) Now—and here's the kicker— at the same time academic performance improved, violence dropped by 80 per- cent—80 percent. And that's no coincidence. (Applause.)

Now, if Pickett can do it, every troubled school can do it. But that means we're going to have to shake some things up. Setting high standards, common standards, empowering students to meet them; partnering with our teachers to achieve excel- lence in the classroom; educating our children—all of them—to graduate ready for college, ready for a career, ready to make the most of their lives—none of this should be controversial.[8]

President Obama was suggesting that charter schools were better than regular public schools, that they were a "new thing," that deep educational problems could be solved by taking control from public schools and giving public funds to semiprivate local organizations, that success could be spread to many other schools, and that there was some kind of serious accountability in place for charter schools. He highlighted a few charters that had reported large gains and characterized charter schools as local, community-based efforts, even though there are growing firms deeply involved in managing many of them. He said that he was giving states "the chance" to expand charters, but he was actually strongly and successfully pressuring them by making this a precondition for competing for urgently needed federal funds to avoid massive cutbacks.[9]

Presidential support for charters has been bipartisan and enthusiastic for more than two decades. Obama's predecessor, President George W. Bush, praised choice and alternatives in his first State of the Union address, in 2001: "Schools will be given a reasonable chance to improve, and the support to do so. Yet if they don't, if they continue to fail, we must give parents and students different options: a better public school, a private school, tutoring, or a charter school. In the end, every child in a bad situation must be given a better choice, because when it comes to our children, failure is simply not an option."[10] Bush was carrying on themes developed by President Bill Clinton in his last State of the Union Address, in which he highlighted his support for expanding charter schools as a key edu- cational gain: "We know charter schools provide real public school choice. When I became President, there was just one independent public charter school in all America. Today, thanks to you, there are 1,700. I ask you now to help us meet our goal of 3,000 charter schools by next year."[11] Choice outside the public school system has been promoted as a major educational solution by leaders of widely differing political backgrounds. This movement is not the product of research showing that choice produces educational gains; that is usually simply assumed, even though research is, at best, mixed.[12] The debate is not about evidence—it is often about ideology.

No one who has looked at stagnant achievement scores and graduation rates or examined the reality of many public schools that serve communities of poor minority children can deny that these children deserve something far better than the schools they are assigned to.[13] There are many public schools that have been officially branded as failures for years under No Child Left Behind and state standards. They daily confront the personal and community consequences of concentrated poverty and often find it very hard to attract and hold the qualified, experienced teachers these students badly need. Accountability policies have documented the students' poor outcomes, but threats, sanctions, and many other reform ideas have failed to work. The achievement gaps have been virtually unchanged in the high-stakes testing and charter school era.[14]

The opportunity for students in these schools to enroll in much better schools would clearly be a benefit. Much of the publicity about charter schools assumes that they are the best way to provide such opportunities. Choice is attractive, usually does not cost much, and leaves those already satisfied with their schools undisturbed, just where they want to be. The politics and parent eagerness are not difficult to understand. Yet the questions remain: Do the common forms of choice help students learn more, graduate, go to college, become better citizens, or get good jobs? Are there better answers?

After half a century of unfulfilled pledges to fix the most troubled schools, we need to be sure that this is not another empty promise. Are we betting on something that has no net educational advantages and might even increase the already dramatic stratification of school systems that gives the best education to the most privileged families and segregated and inferior schools to the most disadvantaged? Markets and competition sound good, but a look at the kinds of grocery stores and health care services provided by the private market shows that competition has not provided quality in poor and minority communities equal to that available to middle-class neighborhoods, even with the substantial increases in their residents' buying power provided by food stamps and Medicaid.[15] Does school competition work any better? What kinds of choice are most effective?

Varieties of Choice

Analysts often say the devil is in the details when talking about whether or not a policy will work. Choice programs can differ in several fundamental aspects, producing major differences in the kinds of opportunities offered, who gets the best choices, and what the overall outcomes are. Choice can be within one school district or among school districts. It can be within public schools or between public and private schools. It can be open to all equally on the basis of interest, or choice schools can have admissions requirements, making the schools the choosers. It can have a plan for diversity or ignore the issue of segregation. Management can be nonprofit or for-profit. The program can provide free public transportation to chosen schools or require the family to provide its own transportation. It can offer genuinely beneficial choices of much better schools or limit choices to weak receiving schools. There can be good educational provisions for language-minority and special education children or there can be none. It can include subsidized lunches for poor kids or not. The receiving schools can feature strong professional faculties or inexperienced and untrained newcomers. The choice system can have strong outreach and counseling for all parents or limit its market to particular groups or neighborhoods. Special and unique magnet curricula may be offered or not.

All the combinations and permutations of these features mean that there are a great many kinds of choice and that the *kind* of choice offered matters greatly. Choice approaches cover the gamut from those likely to offer few benefits to children in poor communities to programs that could be of great value. In many voluntary transfer programs, few families understand their options, few transfer, and some transfer to even weaker schools. In Boston, however, thousands of families of color register their children years in advance for a limited chance to attend a strong suburban school system.[16] In many cities where students in schools that fail to meet standards have the right to transfer, only one or two in a hundred do so, in part because there are few schools that offer truly superior opportunities.[17] Choice is only meaningful as an educational reform strategy when better options are available and when the parents who need them know about them and are supported in making their decisions.

Is Choice an American Tradition?

Sometimes choice is discussed as if it were a basic American right, but it is not. Education is mandatory in the United States, it is a crime not to educate your children,[18] and the vast majority of American students have long been assigned to a particular public school, not asked to choose their own. School districts and state regulations were created with the goal of professionalizing teaching and assuring that all children received access to the essential curriculum. Public schools were designed to serve communities, not individuals, and students were legally required to go where assigned, unless they left the public system for a private school or homeschooling.

Educational choice within school districts is no more an American tradition than choice about police or fire service. We don't have competing bus or garbage services or park systems. Public agencies were created to do things that were seen as essential, providing common services meeting uniform standards, and their rules were meant to staff them professionally, avoiding patronage, nepotism, and the misappropriation of public funds. In many cities, educational administrative standards and professionalization followed scandals and serious inequalities in decentralized and politicized schools. Administrative control by state and local education agencies was long seen as a good thing. This is still how almost all major suburban school districts are run, and in those settings, no one is proposing to change it. Both choice and the other currently preferred interventions—high-stakes testing, accountability, and sanctions—are applied most extensively in poor nonwhite communities with schools highly segregated by race and poverty, while these same interventions are almost irrelevant in affluent communities, which leave the traditional system in place because they are not pressured by policies forcing schools with low scores to change. The presumption is that since things are so bad in poor communities of color, policy makers should be free to impose their experiments there. And because choice is primarily aimed at troubled, segregated, impoverished urban school systems, this suggests that it is not advisable in already successful areas. It is therefore all the more important to understand the different forms of choice, their impacts, and why what is seen as such an important reform—even a right—is usually targeted and limited in this way.

THE HISTORY OF CHOICE AS A MAJOR EDUCATIONAL POLICY

The Linkage of Choice and Desegregation

The initiative for educational choice is deeply wrapped up with struggles over race and the decline of our central cities and their school systems. Choice was traditionally a rare exception: there have been a few special schools within public school systems for many years and, of course, a tradition of vocational-technical schools that dates back to the early twentieth century. But the vast majority of U.S. students have always attended schools to which local officials assigned them. Special elite schools like Bronx Science in New York, Boston Latin, Lowell High School in San Francisco, and the North Carolina School of the Arts were not schools that families were free to choose; these schools used examinations, grades, and other methods to choose their own students from among those who applied. The same was true of gifted programs within regular schools.

Although choice advocates often trace their origins to the market theories of Milton Friedman, and some mention the War on Poverty's choice experiments in Alum Rock, California, the real beginning of choice as a serious force in U.S. schools traces back to the struggle over the enforcement of *Brown v. Board of Education* in the 1960s.[19] It first developed on a large scale as a strategy by recalcitrant school districts to respond to the legal demand by black families, backed by the U.S. Supreme Court in the 1954 *Brown* decision, for access to the

better schools provided only for white students. Supporters of school segregation initiated both choice plans designed to leave segregation almost completely
intact and voucher plans designed to permit white families and children to avoid
integration. In *Brown,* the court found the school systems segregated by law to
be "inherently unequal."[20] State laws mandating total segregation were now void
and change was needed.[21] A leading southern federal court ruled shortly after
Brown that the Constitution did not require desegregation of schools but instead
only some choice for some black students to transfer to white schools.[22] The
Supreme Court left most decisions about desegregation plans to the lower courts
for a generation. Until 1968 it did not define what kind of desegregation had to be
achieved. Meanwhile, the debate raged, and the southern position was that the
Constitution would be fully satisfied by providing a limited choice to transfer
for those students. No one thought that whites in the seventeen southern states
would chose to transfer to all-black schools, and they were right. Black students
who transferred to white schools often found themselves a small, isolated, and
unwelcome minority. A decade after *Brown,* 98 percent of black students were
still in all-black schools.[23]

Still, it became apparent that the South would not be permitted to blatantly
defy any compliance with *Brown.* Southern leaders searched for ways to hold
desegregation to a minimum, and the strategy known as freedom of choice was
adopted across the region. Separate school systems with their separate student
bodies and faculties would be kept as intact as possible. The black students who
tried to get into white schools had to run a gauntlet of procedural barriers and
their parents were often threatened within the community, and very few families
were willing to face these problems.[24] The historically black schools remained
absolutely segregated. Freedom of choice became, in reality, freedom to retain
segregation.

Under the 1964 Civil Rights Act, which required that recipients of federal
dollars end discrimination, in 1965 federal education officials set minimum civil
rights standards for choice, including (1) a clear chance for every family to make
choices each year, (2) a guarantee that these choices be honored, (3) a guarantee of
free transportation to receiving schools, (4) a prohibition on transfers that would
increase segregation, and (5) a requirement of fair treatment of new students in
receiving schools.[25] Federal authorities who evaluated the results of freedom of
choice in thousands of districts knew that real choice required strict preconditions. Though the result of these standards was a substantial acceleration of
desegregation, black schools were still untouched, faculties were still segregated,
and it became clear that much more would be needed to integrate the segregated school systems. In 1966 the federal government moved from a focus on
process to a focus on outcomes, requiring a set level of progress in integration

if choice was to be continued. Faculty desegregation was required. In 1968, the Office for Civil Rights simply set a deadline for the full integration of schools and faculties.[26] The federal courts similarly required actual desegregation rather than plans for choice. After the Lyndon Johnson administration started seriously enforcing Title VI of the 1964 Civil Rights Act, which prohibits discrimination in all institutions receiving federal funds, almost all southern districts began to desegregate, and the Fifth Circuit Court of Appeals in the Deep South adopted standards requiring comprehensive desegregation.[27] The Supreme Court, in its 1968 decision in *Green v. New Kent County,* held that constitutional requirements of full desegregation were not satisfied by a choice to transfer to white schools but required abolishing segregation "root and branch," something that choice systems almost always failed to do.[28] These policies soon meant that the South had the nation's most integrated schools for black students, a record that lasted until 2004.

Northern Choices: Open Enrollment and Optional Zones

Another choice-based approach was common in big-city school systems, especially for students located in diverse or racially changing areas. In northern and western U.S. cities with significant black and Latino school enrollments, segregation had also been the norm. It was accomplished mostly through housing segregation, locating schools to maximize racial separation, drawing school-attendance boundaries and adopting transfer policies that segregated students, and assigning teachers in a segregated way. Virtually every city ever examined by a federal court in a desegregation case—including Boston, Buffalo, Cincinnati, Cleveland, Indianapolis, Minneapolis, and Omaha—was found guilty of such pro-segregation practices.[29]

Although they claimed to be operating neighborhood schools, districts often drew boundaries along racial lines, ignoring the proximity of certain residences to particular schools, and changed the lines to preserve segregation as neighborhoods changed. Black or Latino children in overcrowded schools were regularly denied access to nearby white schools with space. As nonwhite populations in cities expanded, the Supreme Court struck down both laws that overtly segregated neighborhoods by race and laws that enforced restrictive covenants.[30] Minority communities expanded into sectors of previously white neighborhoods, leaving isolated pockets of whites inside minority neighborhoods and schools. To permit white students who happened to live in specified areas with heavily minority schools to transfer to white schools, many cities implemented optional attendance zones. Open-enrollment policies permitted families to transfer from those areas even if this increased segregation. These policies, of course, undermined integrated neighborhoods and sped the resegregation of their schools. Similar patterns occurred when unrestricted choice programs were adopted after the civil rights era.[31] Earlier, federal courts had found the dominant forms of choice across the United States to be fostering or maintaining unconstitutional segregation. Choice was a strategy strongly linked to segregation.

Vouchers for Segregation

The first significant use of vouchers by local officials came when Prince Edward County, Virginia, closed its entire school system in 1959 to prevent integration. The Virginia state legislature had enacted a law that called for the closing of any school that began integration and the governor had closed schools in several districts to prevent desegregation, actions that both federal and state courts eventually held to be illegal. This left the leaders of rural Prince Edward County facing the likelihood that some integration would be mandated in their district. In response they implemented their plan that completely shut down public schools in the county and provided private school vouchers. New private white academies promptly hired faculties made up almost completely of former public school teachers and resumed teaching whites. The black community lacked the money and power to create and fund its own schools, so the black children in the county went without schools for five years. When the case reached the Supreme Court, the justices ordered the reopening of the public schools.[32] During the oral argument on the case, Chief Justice Earl Warren responded to the county lawyer's arguments by saying that Prince Edward had provided African American children the "freedom to go through life without education."[33] One could argue, as the county's lawyers did, that there was no racial problem, since anyone could have a voucher for whatever private school where they could enroll. The fact that there was no school for blacks showed one of the great flaws of the market approach. The vouchers were perfectly effective in preserving segregation and took away the only option black students had. It turned out that the market had an absolute barrier and provided them with no replacement options, creating absolute inequality.

Two fundamental lessons of the early civil rights era were that producing integrated schools almost never happens by accident in highly segregated communities with deeply rooted racial and ethnic stereotypes and fears, and that unrestricted choice or voucher systems are more likely to compound than to remedy segregation and inequality. If the burden is put on the victims of segregation to change the situation and the involved institutions are absolved of any significant responsibility, very little will happen. This was why strict conditions about choice procedures, transportation, and related matters were put into operation in enforcing the Civil Rights Act and why mandatory desegregation orders were found to be necessary to actually integrate the schools in many communities.[34]

Magnet Schools:
Combining Educational Choice with Desegregation

In the mid-1970s, however, educators invented ways to use choice to produce diverse schools and to minimize the conflicts that often came at the beginning of mandatory desegregation. The most effective combination of choice, educational innovation, and desegregation came with the development of magnet schools. The Supreme Court confronted the nation's cities with a massive challenge in the mid-1970s. In *Keyes v. Denver* in 1973, it ruled that if civil rights plaintiffs could prove intentional segregation in substantial parts of a city, there should be a presumption that the entire city was illegally segregated, and the courts should issue an order to desegregate it.[35] It turned out that there was enough evidence to trigger such orders in virtually every city where a suit was filed.[36] The Denver case also ruled that Latino students were entitled to desegregation remedies. But the court's decision came too late, at a time when many central cities' schools were already heavily minority and had rapidly declining white enrollment as the white birthrate fell and many all-white suburbs were being built. This meant that full desegregation was not going to be possible within central cities—simply mandating that white students transfer to impoverished nonwhite schools was likely to speed their already well-advanced flight. The next year, in the Detroit (*Milliken v. Bradley*) case, the Supreme Court reviewed the finding of the lower courts that the only feasible remedy for intentional segregation would be a plan including the suburbs, which would increase the possibility for substantial desegregation, involve the region's strongest schools, and make white flight far less likely. When the court rejected this remedy 5–4, it left central cities facing massive problems.[37]

The top answer that emerged was magnet schools. Educational leaders in Milwaukee, Cincinnati, Buffalo, and elsewhere came up with the idea of using special schools with unique programs, combined with active recruitment, to increase integration. The plans included free transportation and policies that tried to guarantee a specific and stable level of desegregation. Senators John Glenn of Ohio and Daniel Patrick Moynihan of New York, both of whose states had city districts that were ordered to desegregate, succeeded in enacting a federal aid program, the Magnet School Assistance Act, which helped rapidly spread the magnet school idea across the country. Massachusetts was an early promoter of magnet schools.[38] One of the key conditions for receiving help was that the proposed school was part of a desegregation plan. Magnet programs expanded rapidly, even in the conservative 1980s, reaching 2,400 schools and more than a million students by 1991, and were highly concentrated in large cities.[39] Magnets came a generation before the charter schools of the 1990s and were (and remain) by far the nation's largest program of school choice. Magnets with civil rights policies provided answers to the segregating tendencies of unlimited choice while still greatly expanding parental choice and creating a level of integration that was broadly acceptable across racial lines. After the Reagan administration, however, these accomplishments received little attention.

Magnet schools have had a curious history, related to changing political and legal currents. They emerged and spread rapidly in the 1970s, when federal policy modestly subsidized and strongly encouraged them, but conservative administrations slashed the funds that supported them. Magnets were a singularly popular reform. There was great demand for the federal money set aside for them, and many districts financed their own, though they were slightly more expensive than regular schools because of the training and equipment needed to establish and operate distinctive educational programs. Federal funds were invaluable in covering the starting costs and special materials and training that many local school budgets could not. When funds were cut in the severe recession of the early 1980s, the momentum was broken.

Since both teachers and families were selecting these schools themselves and believed that they were getting something special, the problem in successful magnets often was dealing with disappointed people who wanted to enroll but could not. Another issue was that many magnet programs were opened within regular schools, which sometimes created apparent diversity in the school's enrollment statistics while hiding stratification and segregation within the school building.[40]

Many magnet programs began with first-come, first-served admissions, and parents waited all night out on the street before their district's magnet offices opened. Those in the front of the lines had information, social networks with information about schools and procedures, intense desire, and the time to do this. Many policies—such as locating the most desirable magnets in segregated black and Latino communities—were designed to offset such inequalities, to ensure integration, and to increase information dispersal to parents in disadvantaged areas. Lotteries replaced waiting lines. Magnets intentionally created highly differentiated opportunities to stimulate parent choice, including Montessori schools and their special pedagogy, schools that offered advanced intense instruction in science or developed talents in dance or drama, highly disciplined traditional academies, and many others. The great assets of magnet schools as a class were considerable. They were voluntary, they created educational innovation and excitement, and they were attractive to many middle-class parents in cities that had few desirable schools. Magnet schools often reported higher educational outcomes even after controlling for other differences between those who attended them and those who did not.[41]

Choice through magnets has had both benefits and costs. Although civil rights policies can make such choice far fairer than it would be otherwise, it still tends to foster differences. It generates unequal schools and creates tensions as well as providing opportunities. On the other hand, in central city school systems with poor reputations and little ability to reform themselves or hold middle-class families of any race, they have offered positive educational alternatives and helped avoid conflict that can come with mandatory desegregation. Strong magnets can also be widely admired and genuinely diverse schools in cities that had been written off. Even if a district had only islands of high prestige—a few desirable integrated schools that parents were eager for their children to attend—that was better than simply becoming a ghetto school system for poor families who had no choices. The Detroit Supreme Court decision left cities with no options for equitable, uniform, stable, and educationally valuable desegregation across the larger metropolitan communities. Many cities in decline since suburbanization began in the 1950s, wishing to do something to offset this trend, found magnets to be their best option. The extent to which the creative possibilities were fairly available to minority students, however, depended on the strength of the equity policies behind them.

The problem was that as magnets expanded and some became extremely desirable, as the courts dropped desegregation plans, and as the idea spread that race-conscious strategies were not needed, there were increasing attacks on the magnets' policy to set seats aside when necessary to guarantee diversity. Some parents who did not get their top choice sued. While the courts in the civil rights era subordinated such claims to the constitutional imperative of desegregation, increasingly conservative courts gave priority to individual rights, and the lessons of freedom of choice were forgotten. As the political climate and judicial appointments changed, there were more claims that the rights of white families had been limited. Under the 1991 *Oklahoma City v. Dowell* decision by the Supreme Court, many court orders incorporating magnet policies were dropped, and some school systems simply ended racial goals and desegregation controls, producing rapid resegregation in magnet schools.[42] Magnet schools had balanced the tendency toward stratification inherent in choice programs with a set of civil rights policies. When those were lifted, the pressures toward stratification were no longer offset.

Besides their desegregation policies, the other issue that the emerging conservatism had with magnet schools was that they were part of school systems with too many rules, even though many had a great deal of autonomy. Federal policy switched between the Jimmy Carter and Reagan administrations, from active encouragement of desegregated magnet schools to very limited financing of magnets and no support for desegregation goals and then to advocacy of charter schools. Presidents Reagan and George H. W. Bush presided over twelve years of anti–civil rights administrations. Even though many magnets had a great deal of autonomy, critics began to attack them for their desegregation rules and for being part of public school systems.

As the courts changed and diversity plans were dismantled, lawsuits challenged the right of schools to hold spaces for underrepresented groups, and some federal courts overturned those policies.[43] New magnet schools were sometimes created without desegregation plans, solely to offer special schools. Magnets that were born with desegregation plans and had been integrated often dropped their plans and became more segregated, though a substantial fraction did not, as discussed in chapter 5.

Throughout the magnet experience it has been apparent that parents with better information do better. Ironically, without civil rights policies in place they tend to do much better, increasing inequality. No matter how many strategies for fairness were devised, it was clear that parents who had better information about and understanding of what often became complex choice systems in large school districts were more likely to get their children into the best schools and that parents with less education, fewer connections, and less understanding of the impact of more competitive and integrated schools were less likely to make a choice or have their children accepted.[44]

Choice and competition for students, even for desirable ends such as lasting and substantial race and class desegregation, inevitably involve winners and losers among schools and reflect the unequal human capital and networks of different groups of parents. To the extent that these schools and programs are successful in becoming (or being perceived as) clearly superior, they can turn into not just means to an end but ends in themselves for ambitious parents, whose battles to get their children admitted sometimes challenge and defeat desegregation goals. Civil rights advocates understood the inherent problems of choice but also the great difficulty in finding ways to provide opportunities for minority children to access genuinely better schools while simultaneously attracting and holding more privileged families to produce the gains of class and racial integration. Given the difficult legal and policy constraints, magnets often became the best option if they could institute strong policies for equity.

Transfers and Controlled Choice

From the 1960s on a standard feature of a great many desegregation plans was the Majority to Minority (M to M) transfer plan, which permitted students to transfer only from a school where their race was the majority to one where it was the minority. In practice, this meant that black and Latino students transferred from segregated schools of their race to largely white schools. The numbers of such transfers were small, normally around 1 or 2 percent of those eligible. Another kind of transfer, beginning in the middle 1960s and spreading to only a few cities, was interdistrict transfer, usually from segregated central city schools to white suburban schools but sometimes to regional magnet schools in other districts serving the same metro area. Some of these plans have been very popular, but only those in St. Louis and Milwaukee reached numbers above a few thousand students, primarily because of the small number of suburban openings in most plans. And now both the St. Louis and Milwaukee programs have been reduced in scope in spite of substantial successes.[45]

The last of the major efforts to use choice for desegregation was called, appropriately enough, controlled choice. A fully developed controlled choice plan was first implemented in 1981, in Cambridge, Massachusetts, right across the Charles River from Boston, which had experienced tremendous conflict in its 1974 school integration plan, which mandated the transfer of students to schools across racial boundaries. Controlled choice was designed to move decisively away from both a neighborhood school system and a mandatory transfer plan by requiring parents to look across the district and rank their top school preferences. Because all parents with school-age children were required to participate, making a choice did not require special initiative or knowledge of the policy. Students were assigned to their highest-ranked school that was compatible with the city's desegregation goals. The great majority of families received one of their top choices, giving them a sense of control and minimizing conflict without abandoning integration goals.[46] There were, of course, some who did not get a top choice and protested the plan, but the number of involuntary assignments was much lower than in mandatory plans. There were a number of other provisions designed to ensure equity, such as an information center that parents were required or strongly encouraged to visit to receive information and counseling about their options (this was also often an element of desegregation and magnet plans).

Controlled choice encouraged competition among schools and addressed the normal exclusion of parents who did not choose from good transfer opportunities. Boston and a number of other districts subsequently implemented it.[47] This was the last of the choice plans that were designed with civil rights goals in mind. In districts that had controlled choice for a considerable period of time, parents' preferences for neighborhood schools declined sharply as they learned about other options. When the mandatory Boston court order was dropped after a more conservative Supreme Court authorized ending desegregation orders and there was a move to return to assigning students to their neighborhood school, strong opposition arose because a large majority of Bostonians saw these schools as weak, did not consider them a first choice, and did not want their children stuck in them.[48] As with magnet schools, the controlled choice experience showed that it was possible to use choice—with clear efforts to strengthen information dispersal and recruitment and put limits on segregative choices—to produce a good deal of integration with a minimum of community conflict and, at the same time, to create desirable schools.

FORGETTING THE LESSONS OF CHOICE PROGRAMS

If the central justification for choice in the late civil rights era was to create voluntary desegregation and equalize education through innovation, the choice programs that have come to the fore in a more conservative era have often been hailed not as means to an end but as solutions to failing urban schools without any reference to segregation or systemic barriers to choice. Conservatives who denied that the problem of failing schools was rooted in social inequality and systematically unequal schooling shifted the blame to families and school bureaucracies.[49] In contrast to civil rights advocates, who defined the central barriers to opportunity as racial discrimination, isolated poverty, and unequal education, the backers of newer plans—vouchers and charter schools—rested their claims on theories about the inherent inferiority of public schools run by large bureaucracies with strong teachers unions.[50] A school outside a public school system would, by its nature, be better. Bill Gates, whose foundation strongly supports charter schools, spoke to the National Charter Schools Conference in 2010, hailing the "great progress" of the movement and calling charters "the only schools that have the full opportunity to innovate" in a country where "the way we educate students . . . has not changed in generations." He said that public schools had received more funding over generations but had "poor results." The country needed "brand new approaches," and "that's the one thing charter schools do best." As in a market, "it's imperative that we take the risk to make change."[51]

Race and poverty were largely considered irrelevant, and many charter schools were intentionally established in impoverished minority neighborhoods, where families were desperate for any option and public schools were far less powerful than in the suburbs. Some were set up to serve only a particular racial or ethnic group, challenging basic elements of civil rights policy with the claim that they had special empathy for minority students, justifying segregation by race and poverty.[52] The operators of charter schools also claimed that educational entrepreneurs—such as themselves—could solve educational inequality using competition and freedom from bureaucracies and unions. They ignored the related facts that choice without civil rights controls would increase segregation and that segregated schools were systematically less successful, the realization of which had been central to the development of choice policy in the 1960s and 1970s. Segregation was simply accepted as a given and not seen as a serious limit to equal opportunity. Free markets and ending public regulation and the power of teachers' organizations would solve educational gaps.

From Magnets to Charters

Charter schools, invented in 1991, appealed to conservatives because of their autonomy and to moderate Democrats because they could help block the drive for vouchers, keeping funds in the public sector.[53] They had the advantages of little additional cost and none of the threat to the middle-class status quo that desegregation efforts posed, although the press often treated them as successful attacks on the status quo.[54] During the three Bush and two Clinton terms, as noted above, the priority in funding and advocacy shifted from magnets to charter schools, with funding for the former frozen during much of the George W. Bush administration. This continued under the Obama administration, in spite of the popularity of magnet schools and significant research showing that they resulted in gains on test scores even after controlling for the differences between their students and similar ones in regular public schools. In contrast, a series of major studies of charter schools conducted by the federal government, the Hoover Institute at Stanford, and other researchers showed no such advantage for charters, as discussed in chapters 6 and 7.[55]

Minnesota wrote charter schools into law in 1991, which, by coincidence, was the same year the Supreme Court authorized the termination of all kinds of school desegregation plans and segregation began to climb steadily across the country.[56] The first U.S. charter school opened in St. Paul, in 1992. The idea rapidly spread, and by the 2009–10 school year there were more than five thousand charter schools in the United States.[57]

The charter movement gained great popularity both because its basic assumptions were in tune with the times and because it avoided much of the political conflict produced by a long and futile fight over vouchers. Conservatives wanted choices outside the regular public schools and liberals wanted to protect the separation of church and state and avoid subsidizing private schools, four-fifths of which were religious. Charters were a new form of nonsectarian autonomous public school outside the established public school system, managed by nonprofit or for-profit groups. At first they represented a modest movement that strongly appealed to business executives and their foundations, which had started playing a large role in education policy, but nonetheless appeared to pose little threat to the regular system. One reason why this experiment seemed marginal was that research, even from conservative institutions such as the Bush administration's Department of Education and the Hoover Institution at Stanford, found no evidence of significant educational benefits in charters. In a period when conservatives placed enormous pressure on schools through test-driven accountability measures including No Child Left Behind and many state reforms, the failure to show benefits should have mattered greatly. NCLB produced a vast amount of data showing the poor performance of segregated impoverished schools, and many charters fell directly into that category and had similar outcomes.

As the charter movement grew, however, the owners and operators of these schools emerged as a highly organized and effective political lobby. Some talented and charismatic young educators had been attracted to the movement, and their schools were widely publicized. The charter drive received extensive philanthropic support, and the lobby was influential in a number of states and highly successful in Washington, most spectacularly in the Obama administration, some of whose top staff in the Department of Education were drawn from this movement. They wrote pro-charter priorities into the heart of the new policies for both NCLB accountability and the massive stimulus package designed to help pull the country out of the Great Recession. With the federal government in control of a vast amount of emergency money and school systems in desperate need of funds, the conditions were ideal for federal leverage to expand the charter movement. Most states rapidly yielded to the very strong incentives to lift state limits on charter school creation.[58]

Other factors favored charters. They often cost less than regular public schools and left completely untouched the well-regarded regular public schools of the middle and upper classes in the more affluent suburbs. They promised big successes without disturbing anyone but the vilified old bureaucracies and rigid unions, whose power had declined greatly by the mid-1990s as suburbia's demographic and political domination had increased. With some clearly excellent schools, limited accountability, and effective political mobilization, it did not matter much that the charter movement's educational outcomes were largely unimpressive.

Vouchers

Probably no major choice-based reform proposal in recent American history has generated a more passionate debate with fewer real consequences than the movement for school vouchers. It received a substantial impetus from a number of sources beginning in the 1960s. The federal War on Poverty sponsored an early experiment in a California district. One of the nation's most prominent sociologists, James Coleman, became a strong advocate for private schools, as did some other scholars.[59] The California law professors John Coons and Stephen Sugarman championed an expansive vision of vouchers with civil rights protections—an idea that the pure market proponents in the conservative movement did not adopt.[60] The Catholic hierarchy in the United States saw vouchers as an issue of basic fairness with regard to their system, which included schools in poor urban communities. They argued that millions of Catholics were taxed for a public system they did not use. This position, supported by many urban Democrats from Catholic areas in Congress, had destroyed President John F. Kennedy's effort to direct federal aid to education.[61] The business community also supported vouchers (for instance, a business leader in Indianapolis funded a private voucher program), and they became a major goal of the Republican Party, which has controlled the White House for five terms since 1980. After more than thirty years of active advocacy, many political battles, and the famous Supreme Court victory in *Zelman* (discussed below), however, only a tiny fraction of 1 percent of U.S. students use vouchers, and half of the areas where they were adopted had discontinued the policies by 2010. Their failure has revealed the limits of the choice movement.

Vouchers have spurred intense discussion since the 1980s, including the claim that opening up private schools, most of which are religious, to poor minority children would create more-integrated and better schooling opportunities. This was a successful argument in persuading the Supreme Court to permit vouchers to be used for religious schools in *Zelman v. Simmons-Harris*.[62] The decision allowed public subsidies to go to Cleveland-area religious schools willing to take transfer students from the city's public schools.

Unlike charter schools, vouchers have been a bitterly partisan issue. The support of five GOP presidents beginning with Richard Nixon, the national GOP, and many religious educators has had little impact. George W. Bush offered a typical statement of conservative support during his presidential campaign: "Let poor people choose their schools, like rich people do. Nowhere in the Constitution does it say that parents should not be able to choose where to send their children to school. Nowhere does it say that only people who can afford it should be able to choose to send their children to schools with quality academics and sound discipline, but poor people should not. We must say, clearly and emphatically, that the people who need help should not merely be passive recipients of a handout, but should have the freedom to choose where they receive services."[63] But vouchers have been defeated because of public opposition, the strength of public school and teacher organizations, and the lack of persuasive evidence that they would make a substantial difference for poor children or that there would be a good supply of high-quality spaces available at a reasonable cost if they were authorized. Since four-fifths of private schools are religious, voucher programs face serious legal barriers in the laws, including constitutions, of dozens of states that prohibit the use of public funds for sectarian institutions. (The *Zelman* decision made vouchers possible if states wanted them but did not overturn prohibitions against them in state law.)

When the conservatives were in power in the George W. Bush era, they persuaded Congress to adopt vouchers both in Washington DC, where Congress is often tempted to play city council and school board, and as part of the massive legislation to rebuild New Orleans after Hurricane Katrina. The exodus of families caused by the historic hurricane virtually wiped out the flooded city's public school system and gave voucher supporters in the Louisiana state government and the Bush administration a chance to work with billions of federal rebuilding dollars, as chapter 8 discusses.

Advocates of vouchers in other states thought that the public would embrace them in jurisdictions where decisions could be made by referenda, but they were wrong. Referendum campaigns to initiate voucher programs in California, Michigan, and Utah failed by large margins.

Voucher programs also came up against resistance in the courts. There was a fierce fight to create vouchers for needy students in severely inadequate schools in Florida, but the results were disappointing both educationally and legally. Florida scholars report that "in the most segregated districts the failing (F) schools or near-failing (D) schools enroll the great majority of each district's Black students. . . . However, few private schools have been willing to enroll students from the F schools."[64] This experience suggests that neither was there a good supply of options for the students—most of whom were black—in weak schools nor did all who were able to transfer find the choice a good one, since some quickly returned to public schools. The Florida Supreme Court ruled that the vouchers violated the state constitution, which forbade use of public funds for private schools, generating a battle to amend it.[65] In Wisconsin, civil rights lawyers challenged a voucher program for discriminating against handicapped students.[66] Voucher programs in general have faced problems because the schools were selecting students, not providing access to all equally, and recruitment and information requirements set by state law were minimal.

A major review of the evidence on vouchers by the economists Cecilia Elena Rouse and Lisa Barrow in 2008 concluded: "The best research to date finds relatively small achievement gains for students offered education vouchers, most of which are not statistically different from zero."[67]

Vouchers have no real significance in terms of impact on either segregation or educational opportunity, as many schools will not take them.[68] Further, many independent schools have tuitions far higher than the value of any proposed voucher. Even the theoretical value of voucher programs is limited because private schools educate only a tenth of U.S. students, and 82 percent of private school spaces are in religious schools created to provide appropriate religious education as well as regular instruction. This is unlikely to change, because the capital and other costs of creating large numbers of new schools are prohibitive.

So far U.S. voucher experiments have been limited, and there is no way to estimate what the impacts of a large expansion would be. Six significant programs have been initiated, but state courts overturned the Florida and Colorado laws, and Congress ended the Washington DC plan after Obama's election but reinstated it in 2011 as a part of a budget deal after conservatives took over the House of Representatives after the 2010 election. The best evidence on the possible impacts of large-scale voucher systems comes from countries that have experienced them, such as Chile and New Zealand. The experience of the former, which made a massive commitment to vouchers as a basic educational treatment, suggests that the impact would be to increase overall ethnic and class segregation.[69] In fact there were massive student protests in Chile in 2011 against educational stratification.[70]

After the 2010 U.S. elections, with the victory of conservatives in the House and in many state governments, the voucher issue came back on the education agenda not only in the agreement to renew the Washington DC program but also in a referendum scheduled for 2012 in Florida, a battle in Pennsylvania, and a variety of other initiatives. Although vouchers have had little impact in the United States to date, the movement supporting them has deep roots in the Milton Friedman theory of choice and is likely to be a recurring, if marginal, discussion. The charter school surge, which in some cases included converting financially troubled religious schools to charters, has taken most of the attention off the voucher issue. The latter turned out to be a sideshow of little practical importance, but the arguments it developed, particularly the attacks on school bureaucracies and teacher organizations, have become central parts of the charter movement. The most influential book of the voucher movement, John E. Chubb and Terry M. Moe's *Politics, Markets, and America's Schools,* blamed a conspiracy of bureaucracies and teachers' organizations for preserving the dysfunctional status quo, a theme echoed in a leading pro-charter book, Abigail and Stephan Thernstrom's *No Excuses.* The rhetoric of other pro-charter groups reflects this idea. The Walton Family Foundation (started by Helen Walton and her husband Sam, a Walmart cofounder), for example, which in 2010 gave $157 million to its education campaign focusing on charters, announced, "Our core strategy is to infuse competitive pressure into America's K-12 education system by increasing the quantity and quality of school choices available to parents, especially in low-income communities."[71]

The Spectacular Inconsistency of the Law on Choice

Educational issues in the United States often become legal issues. In a society founded by lawyers that has extremely powerful courts and strong ideologies of rights, this is not surprising. The U.S. Supreme Court has, however, taken wildly inconsistent positions on school choice, which has often resulted in confusion and erratic policy and reflects the ideological and partisan divisions within the country. Following *Brown,* the Supreme Court passively accepted "freedom of choice" for more than a decade, though it left segregation virtually untouched. By the middle 1960s, as the 1964 Civil Rights Act and other sweeping reforms were enacted to bring the power of the executive branch into the enforcement of desegregation, federal education officials recognized that choice plans were putting all the burden of change on nonwhite families. So they wrote civil rights protections into choice plans, telling school authorities that they would only accept plans that produced rapid gains in integration. These policies, backed by Justice Department lawsuits and the withholding of federal school funds from defiant districts, rapidly accelerated desegregation. They required, among other things, that all students be given a very clear opportunity to transfer each year, that all requests for transfer that increased integration be granted, that transfers increasing segregation be prohibited, that free transportation to receiving schools be provided, and that students be treated fairly in their schools. These requirements became standard in desegregation plans for decades to come.[72] Later, similar civil rights policies were central to the magnet school movement, which emerged as a way to voluntarily integrate urban schools.

Federal education and civil rights officials and the federal courts recognized that social pressure, harassment, and other factors often limited or blocked choice, which by itself fell far short of desegregating many schools that had always been operated on a discriminatory basis, including virtually all historically black schools. In a historic unanimous decision in 1968, *Green v. New Kent County,* the Supreme Court ruled that choice was not enough and that far-reaching mandatory measures were essential.

> "Freedom of choice" . . . is only a means to a constitutionally required end—the abolition of the system of segregation and its effects. If . . . it fails to undo segregation, other means must be used to achieve this end. The school officials have the continuing duty to take whatever action may be necessary to create a "unitary, nonracial system." Rather than further the dismantling of the dual system, the plan has operated simply to burden children and their parents with a responsibility which Brown II placed squarely on the School Board. The Board must be required to . . . fashion steps which promise realistically to convert promptly to a system without a "white" school and a "Negro" school, but just schools.[73]

The court concluded that choice could be a constitutional remedy for illegal segregation only under circumstances in which it actually worked. When it failed, as it did in the vast majority of cases, it had to be replaced by mandatory policies that produced integrated schools. The court also held in *Green* that choice plans that increased segregation were illegal, which often became grounds for findings by federal courts that cities in the North and the West, such as Boston, Cleveland, and Indianapolis, were violating the Constitution and had to implement districtwide desegregation plans.[74]

This did not mean that choice could not be used in a positive fashion. Courts approved voluntary race-conscious plans using choice in school districts that were not under court orders. Some of the earliest magnet schools were created in university communities that were voluntarily desegregating in the 1960s. The world's first touch-screen computer system, for instance, was tested in the Booker T. Washington school in Champaign, Illinois, an early illustration of the kinds of special offerings that can persuade families to make voluntary transfers. The devising and implementation of such plans had the triple advantage of taking desegregation battles out of the courts, involving educators, and enhancing local support. Early efforts of this sort appeared particularly in university communities, including Berkeley, California; Champaign, Evanston, and Urbana, Illinois;

and Boston, which had a voluntary interdistrict transfer plan, Metropolitan Council for Educational Opportunity (METCO).[75] Later, states such as Illinois, California, Minnesota, and Connecticut encouraged voluntary desegregation actions in school districts before those policies were dropped or gravely weakened decades after as the political tides changed.

The law consistently required systemic desegregation plans in districts with a history of discrimination until the Supreme Court's 1991 decision in the *Oklahoma City v. Dowell* case, which encouraged the termination of desegregation orders and did not require the maintenance of standards that would block resegregation in choice or magnet programs after a local court order ended.[76] Following *Dowell,* districts released from court orders were free to either abandon or continue applying civil rights controls to their choice programs. Those that dropped them often experienced rapid resegregation.[77] Some that maintained them were sued and lost, particularly in the Fourth Circuit Court of Appeals, which covers Maryland, Virginia, and the upper South and was the nation's most conservative appellate court in that period. In other words, race-conscious magnet plans were now being systematically attacked even when supported by local elected boards of education. The court-ordered dismantling of desegregation plans was under way, and the civil rights policies that had conditioned choice since the mid-1960s were quietly abandoned in some communities, prohibited by courts in others, and maintained elsewhere.

The Supreme Court's conservative majority, which was cutting back on desegregation and increasingly sensitive to claims that the rights of local whites were being violated, acted in the 2002 *Zelman* decision to address what it saw as the unfair situation of poor black children locked into Cleveland public schools (largely as a result of its 1974 decision protecting the suburbs from metropolitan desegregation plans) by authorizing vouchers for private religious schools. Few states were interested, since surveys consistently show that the large majority of Americans are satisfied with their own public schools and support public education. Conservatives next challenged the legality of civil rights enrollment controls in voluntary transfer and magnet plans. They argued that the absolute right of individuals to make choices in the education market must supersede what communities saw as the value of integrated schools.

In 2007, a transformed Supreme Court acted. Switching gears dramatically, it held in the 5–4 *Parents Involved* decision that the most common voluntary local desegregation efforts were no longer admirable efforts on behalf of integration but rather unconstitutional discrimination because they treated the choices of some individuals of different races differently when necessary to maintain diversity and avoid resegregation. The court now said that districts must end policies that blocked transfers or magnet applications that increased segregation, taking away a basic tool that federal civil rights officials and courts had found essential for decades.[78] Choice would have to be more like the freedom of choice and open enrollment plans of the early 1960s that had failed dramatically. Even before *Parents Involved*, nonracial choice plans had been producing rapid resegregation in cities that had ended integration policies in their magnet schools.[79] The Reagan administration's idea that taking account of race to intentionally integrate schools was just as bad as taking account of race to intentionally produce segregation was now the law of the land with the additional votes of two new justices who had worked in the Reagan Justice Department when it was struggling to end desegregation orders in the 1980s.

The chief justice and three supporters basically concluded that school segregation was no longer a problem and that doing anything aimed at integrating schools, even using a choice mechanism, violated the Constitution. They discussed none of the issues that had been so central in the *Green* decision. Four justices on the other side disagreed strongly with both the factual and the legal conclusions. In the middle, Justice Anthony Kennedy forbade race-based assignments but recognized that integration was important for schools and hoped that limited mandatory methods—which had failed in the past—would work now. His decision included no analysis of the history of freedom of choice. His controlling opinion said there was no need to "accept the status quo of racial isolation in schools" and affirmed that "this Nation has a moral and ethical obligation to fulfill its historic commitment to creating an integrated society that ensures equal opportunity for all of its children. A compelling interest exists in avoiding racial isolation."[80] But he took away critical tools for doing this.

The decision held the most common forms of voluntary desegregation plans to be unconstitutional. At the same time, it authorized far-more-contentious and less-effective plans that redrew attendance boundaries and paired schools. Boundary changes and pairing involved the mandatory reassignment of certain students, something that was much more explosive than the system of parental choice that it replaced. The legal scholar James Ryan commented that "the Court's decision makes it easier legally to leave segregated schools alone than to do something about them."[81] Harvard Law Dean Martha Minow noted that it meant that school authorities could only "try to produce racially integrated schools through . . . indirect means."[82] While many school systems were content to leave in place long-established and often popular magnet programs with integration policies, starting all over and trying to find an indirect and legal way to preserve some diversity was a major obstacle.

Justice John P. Stevens, the court's then-senior member, with a moderate Republican background, called the decision "a cruel irony" that took away long-accepted and workable remedies and "[rewrote] the history of one of this Court's most important decisions." The court, he said, previously had been "more faithful to *Brown* and more respectful of our precedent than it is today. It is my firm conviction that no Member of the Court that I joined in 1975 would have agreed with today's decision."[83] The kinds of choice that increased segregation were now legal and the kinds that had produced integration were prohibited, and the country was to abandon the goal of *Brown* or continue choice programs under policies that history had shown would probably produce increased segregation and inequality among schools.

The decision assumed that something else could be found, some indirect policy that would be color-blind but create diverse schools. Whether the policies that failed across the South and in many northern cities in the 1960s can work now is an important question in this book. The evidence on this point, from both new studies and previous research, is not optimistic.

Both the complexities of the different forms of choice and the extreme inconsistency of policy and law contribute to the deep confusion about this issue. When the Supreme Court shifts 180 degrees on the basic constitutional dimensions of choice and the administration of the first African American president forcefully pursues the rapid expansion of the most segregated sector of choice schools, charters, it is hardly surprising that citizens and educators are confused. A society with little historical memory may be in the midst of repeating the mistakes that led to the *Green* decision while forgetting the civil rights policies that conditioned and channeled choice for generations. The fact that a one-vote majority on the Supreme Court changed these fundamental assumptions means that this may not be the last shift. A bare-majority decision facing a bitter four-justice dissent is only as secure as that fifth vote.

The Obama administration's leading civil rights agencies issued guidance letters to schools across the country in December 2011 supporting the use of a variety of strategies to achieve integrated schooling without directly assigning students to schools on the basis of their race, which the Supreme Court had prohibited. The guidance also strongly affirmed the value of integrated schooling, which the Supreme Court had also affirmed.[84] This was the first major positive federal policy pronouncement on school integration since 2000 and reversed the policy of the George W. Bush administration, which had opposed any consideration of race. However, it is about purely voluntary actions by local education officials, who will still face complex challenges both in figuring out what approaches will work best given local conditions and in developing a constituency to support such a plan. The document's main importance was in telling educators both that integration is important and that the two involved central departments of the federal government, Education and Justice, will stand behind them if they take positive action to pursue integrated schools within the boundaries of the law.

Forgetting History, Repeating Old Mistakes?

The story of choice policies and the law on choice reflects the winds of political and social change in the nation. The evolution of choice as a serious component of American education began with a conservative strategy to preserve segregation and to provide an exit for white families from racially changing neighborhoods in northern cities. The Virginia voucher plan was undisguised racism. Across the South at the beginning of serious district-wide desegregation, local leaders set up "segregation academies," often with the support of local government. There was, of course, little willingness by the whites whose children left public schools to provide tax resources to adequately support the nonwhite public schools. New private schools expanded choice for whites while denying choice for blacks and undermined the schools that were their only option. In some communities, the abandonment or closing of public schools made the constitutional rights promised by the *Brown* decision a dead letter.

Civil rights law transformed choice by adding policies that worked better, but it still fell far short of substantially desegregating southern schools. At the peak of the integration effort, both federal civil rights officials and the U.S. Supreme Court basically rejected even choice with civil rights policies as hopelessly inadequate and implemented mandatory desegregation. When the Supreme Court ordered the desegregation of cities and then refused to include their suburbs, the cities responded with new forms of choice—magnet schools and controlled choice plans—increasing integration with what were often desirable educational options for parents of all races. This was supported by a small federal aid program and was highly popular in many cities, though there were always questions about its reach.

As a succession of conservative administrations succeeded in limiting civil rights policies, reconstructing the Supreme Court, and eliminating the federal funds that supported desegregation strategies, the social justice and integrationist theories of choice were replaced by market theory, which emphasizes the primacy of unconstrained individual choice and ignores external constraints on choice. This theory presumes that discrimination has ended, that race-conscious policies can no longer be justified, and that the real causes of educational failure are rooted in public school bureaucracies and unions—problems that could be solved by competition from private schools or semiprivate, publicly financed charter schools. The voucher and charter movements did not explicitly reject integration, and advocates of choice said it would increase real options for segregated minority families. Choice without civil rights protections expanded rapidly in charter schools. As their number increased, their striking segregation became apparent—were we repeating the errors of freedom of choice and open enrollment policies that had failed four decades earlier?

The Supreme Court's 2007 reversal left communities where choice had produced successful desegregated schools very discouraged. Some found new successful strategies; many simply gave up. Given the close division of the court and the recurrence of some of the results of the earlier color-blind choice approaches, one wonders whether this cycle is over or whether the effects of growing resegregation will one day become the basis for a new set of demands for connecting choice with civil rights. The Obama administration's civil rights guidance could be a first step in that direction.

THIS BOOK'S CONTRIBUTION

The basic goal of this book is to document the ways in which choice policies are playing out in a variety of contemporary communities and to relate those experiences and other research on choice and its history to basic questions of civil rights and the creation of real opportunities for black and Latino students locked into inferior, segregated schools, often in declining districts. The short answer is that for the dominant forms of choice at the center of the debate for the past three decades—charters and vouchers—there is no convincing evidence that color-blind choice makes any significant difference in student achievement. The currently dominant ideology of choice holds that any kind of choice is better than regular public schools by definition and considers school outcomes almost exclusively in terms of test scores. But this same ideology leads many away from looking at the high segregation of our schools and toward ignoring the increasingly powerful evidence of its educational damage for all students.

This book explores why choice policies have evolved as they have and whether choice provides access to more-diverse schools, with better-prepared classmates and teachers, schools that better reflect and prepare students for the highly diverse society in which they will live and work as adults. Since the 1970s this issue has been largely ignored in the debate over choice. As we forgot the lessons of the civil rights era, we tended to lose sight of its goals as well. This book puts them front and center.

Chapter 2 explores the basic arguments about choice both in market theory and in the very different integration theory, which derives from the civil rights experience. Both aim at the same goal, equalizing opportunity for the most-disadvantaged students, but their arguments have fundamentally different value and fact premises. This analysis provides a context for the case studies that follow.

The third chapter, by Erica Frankenberg, takes up a central challenge posed by the Supreme Court's major decision on voluntary desegregation programs in the 2007 *Parents Involved* case: because the court has prohibited the most common policies for preventing segregation in choice programs, must communities accept the resegregation of their schools that follows the dissolution of integration plans? Since policies using other variables, such as social class, in an indirect way to foster racial diversity have had limited success, this prohibition was a clear threat to that goal, and many districts overinterpreted the decision and assumed that they could not do anything that would work. But the Supreme Court majority actually said that school integration was still a compelling interest and explicitly authorized school systems to take some positive actions that were not about assigning individual students, such as redrawing attendance boundaries. Berkeley, a diverse district that has pursued integration for half a century, used computers to study and classify hundreds of mini-neighborhoods across the city by race as an important element in assigning students to schools. The policy—which focuses on neighborhoods, not individual students—worked and was upheld by the courts. It is an important example for other districts.

The way a community understands choice relates to its history and policies. In chapter 4, Barbara Shircliffe and Jennifer Morley's study of the Hillsborough County school district (including metropolitan Tampa, Florida) explores the impact of a long history of city-suburban desegregation on the way choice programs are framed. Because of that history—including the fact that the district is county-wide, encompassing cities and suburbs—Hillsborough possesses understanding and experiences that may help maintain some diversity even under a color-blind choice policy. This has been most difficult in Tampa, where substantial resegregation has occurred.

This book also analyzes the impacts of the two largest forms of choice now in operation in American schools—magnet schools and charter schools. In the decades since the civil rights era, as Genevieve Siegel-Hawley and Erica Frankenberg explain in chapter 5, the original goals of magnets have been modified and sometimes lost as the law and politics have changed. Yet they still constitute the nation's largest system of school choice, an important and popular option that national policy debates and funding priorities have nonetheless largely neglected for decades, not because of evidence that private and charter schools are better but because of the contemporary antagonism toward anything that is part of a public school system or has a union.

Since charter schools have been the most important manifestation of choice in the past two decades and have received far more governmental and private support than any other form, this book looks at them in three major chapters. Chapter 6, also by Frankenberg and Siegel-Hawley, shows how the lack of meaningful civil rights policies has made charter schools even more segregated than regular public schools, particularly for black students, and how, in spite of many claims to the contrary by the charter school movement and its advocates, there is no convincing evidence of any net educational advantage from charter schools. Though there are some outstanding charter schools that perform better than the average public school, there are more that perform worse, and, on average, there appears to be no significant difference in test scores between charter and public schools. Additionally, charter school research has virtually ignored many of the impacts of more-diverse schools. The study in chapter 7, by Myron Orfield, Baris Gumus-Dawes, and Thomas Luce, addresses the evolution of the charter school movement where it began, in the greater Minneapolis–St. Paul area. Chapter 8, by the same authors, looks at the rapid charterization of schools in the New Orleans area after Hurricane Katrina virtually wiped out the public school system there and conservatives in Washington DC and Baton Rouge took the opportunity to implement a massive experiment, using the leverage of billions of dollars of federal aid to rebuild the city. As president, both George W. Bush and Barack Obama have hailed some of the strongest charter schools in their visits to New Orleans, and the city provides a kind of test of what might happen under all-out charter school development. The results of this study raise challenging questions about the possible fragmentation and stratification of competing school systems within a single impoverished city as private schools that receive vouchers—and hence public funds—offer a variety of school programs while public schools become isolated, residual institutions. The researchers of chapters 7 and 8 find no convincing proof of educational gains but instead clear evidence that the charter schools have helped stratify, not diversify, the schools in the two areas. They also find nothing intrinsically superior about charter schools.

Determined to avoid the limits of publications that are content to merely describe problems, this book turns in its final set of chapters to the question of how we could use choice more effectively. Chapter 9 confronts the dilemma that inequality is rooted in metropolitan stratification but we are trying to deal with it through choices that are at either the neighborhood or the city level. The problems of segregation by race, class, and language and of unequal educational opportunity and achievement are starkly different in various parts of each metropolitan area. Policy discussions have largely ignored the metropolitan dimensions for decades, but there is powerful evidence favoring metropolitan-wide solutions, which produce more stable communities and more access to better schools for poor and minority students. There have been, however, some notable successes in metropolitan choice programs that deserve careful attention. Amy Stuart Wells and her coauthors explore those experiences and suggest ways that choice could be most effective across district lines. The link of housing to school options and the interaction of housing segregation with the fragmentation of metropolitan communities into many very different school districts are fundamental sources of unequal opportunity, and interdistrict policies are one of the only ways to overcome these forces.

Information availability is absolutely central to theories of markets, but research shows that the dispersal of information about choices is unequal in ways that further disadvantage minority and poor families. Any unequal distribution of information undermines the basic fairness of choice systems since it leads to the most-informed people—usually already otherwise advantaged—getting better opportunities. Jack Dougherty and his colleagues report in chapter 9 on a systematic effort in Hartford, Connecticut, to greatly raise the quality and accessibility of information about local schools. The project used the Web to improve information dispersal and worked against unequal internet access with special information and training sessions and access points. This chapter deepens understanding of information divides and the feasibility of interventions.

The current views of people in the Louisville (Jefferson Country, Kentucky) school district illuminate community desires in a metro district whose plan the U.S. Supreme Court struck down in 2007. Both parents and students told interviewers that they strongly favor continuing efforts to maintain diverse schools, in which both groups see important advantages. At the same time there are divisions over the effectiveness of the plan to achieve this and contradictions in some of the views, which express a simultaneous desire for choice, desegregation, and access to neighborhood schools. Chapter 11 explores the context in which district leaders must search for solutions.

The book concludes with a broader view of research on choice and diversity and the conditions for achieving and maximizing the potential benefits of diverse schools. It points to the possible contributions that can be made by federal and state actors, district- and school-level leaders, community and civil rights organizations, and external researchers. A central theme of the book is that the kind of choice offered and the terms under which it is implemented matter greatly in determining its consequences, and unless policy explicitly takes the race of students into account and has a goal of integration, it is likely to make segregation worse and opportunity more unequal. It would be a tragic outcome if a movement justified as an expansion of choices for the families that need them the most were to deepen separation and diminish opportunities. There is disturbing evidence that this is happening today. Yet there is a much richer and more beneficial practice of choice possible, deeply rooted in the experiences of the civil rights era, and there are ways to use its power for much more positive outcomes, for students, families, and our society.

NOTES

1. U.S. Census Bureau, *Statistical Abstract of the United States: 2012*, table 253.
2. Bartels, *Unequal Democracy: The Political Economy of the New Gilded Age.*
3. Henig, *Rethinking School Choice: The Limits of the Market Metaphor,* 231.
4. Schwartz et al., "Goals 2000 and the Standards Movement."
5. Thernstrom and Thernstrom, *No Excuses: Closing the Racial Gap in Learning,* 265.
6. Scott, "School Choice as a Civil Right: The Political Construction of a Claim and Implications for School Desegregation."

7. Dillon and Schemo, "Charter Schools Fall Short in Public Schools Matchup: U.S. Reports Findings of Study in 5 States."

8. *Washington Post*, "Obama Delivers Remarks on Education at National Urban League: Speech Transcript."

9. U.S. Department of Education, "President Obama, Secretary Duncan Announce Race to the Top."

10. Bush, first State of the Union address.

11. Clinton, eighth State of the Union address.

12. Carnoy et al., *The Charter School Dust-Up: Examining the Evidence on Enrollment and Achievement.*

13. National Center for Education Statistics, *NAEP 2008: Trends in Academic Progress, Reading 1971–2008, Mathematics 1973–2008*; Education Week, *Diplomas Count*, June 2011.

14. Fuller et al., *Is the No Child Left Behind Act Working?*

15. Prevention Institute for the Center for Health Improvement, "Nutrition Policy Profiles: Supermarket Access in Low-Income Communities."

16. Eaton, *The Other Boston Busing Story*, 4–6.

17. Sunderman, Kim, and Orfield, *NCLB Meets School Realities: Lessons from the Field.*

18. Apart from a very small proportion who are approved for homeschooling.

19. For more on Milton Friedman, see chapter 2. For Alum Rock, see Bridge and Blackman, *Family Choice in Schooling.*

20. *Brown v. Board of Education* (1954).

21. *Brown v. Board of Education* (1955).

22. *Briggs v. Elliott.*

23. G. Orfield, *The Reconstruction of Southern Education: The Schools and the 1964 Civil Rights Act*, 20.

24. U.S. Commission on Civil Rights, *Southern School Desegregation 1966–67.*

25. U.S. Office of Education, "General Statement of Policies," school desegregation guidelines, April 1965.

26. Orfield, *The Reconstruction of Southern Education.*

27. Bass, *Unlikely Heroes.*

28. *Green et al. v. County School Board of New Kent County, Virginia, et al.*

29. G. Orfield, *Must We Bus?: Segregated Schools and National Policy*, 19–24.

30. *Shelly v. Kraemer.*

31. Fossey, *School Choice in Massachusetts: Will It Help Schools Improve?*

32. *Griffin v. County School Board of Prince Edward County.*

33. *Griffin v. County School Board*, oral argument (in part 2 at www.oyez.org/cases/1960–1969/1963/1963_592/).

34. Lewis, *Portrait of a Decade: The Second American Revolution.*

35. *Keyes v. Denver School District No. 1.*

36. Center for National Policy Review, Catholic University Law School, *Why Must Northern School Systems Desegregate? A Summary of Federal Court Decisions in Recent Cases.*

37. *Milliken v. Bradley.*

38. Bureau of Equal Educational Opportunities, Massachusetts Department of Education, *Schools and Programs of Choice: Voluntary Desegregation in Massachusetts.*

39. Yu and Taylor, eds., *Difficult Choices: Do Magnet Schools Serve Children in Need?*, 9.

40. Betts et al., "Does School Choice Work? Effects on Student Integration and Achievement"; Bifulco, Cobb, and Bell, "Can Interdistrict Choice Boost Student Achievement? The Case of Con-

necticut's Interdistrict Magnet School Program"; Gamoran, "Student Achievement in Public Magnet, Public Comprehensive, and Private City High Schools."

41. Eaton, "Slipping toward Segregation"; Eaton and Crutcher, "Magnets, Media and Mirages."

42. *Board of Education of Oklahoma City Public Schools v. Dowell;* Boger and Orfield, eds., *School Resegregation, Must the South Turn Back?*

43. *Tuttle v. Arlington County School Board; Eisenberg v. Montgomery County Public Schools.*

44. Smrekar and Goldring, *School Choice in Urban America: Magnet Schools and the Pursuit of Equity;* Metz, *Different by Design.*

45. Wells and Crain, *Stepping Over the Color Line: African-American Students in White Suburban Schools;* Heaney and Uchitelle, *Unending Struggle: The Long Road to an Equal Education in St. Louis.*

46. Willie, Edwards, and Alves, *Student Diversity, Choice and School Improvement.*

47. Weaver, "Controlled Choice: An Alternative School Choice Plan."

48. Willie, Edwards, and Alves, *Student Diversity.*

49. Thernstrom and Thernstrom, *No Excuses.*

50. Chubb and Moe, *Politics, Markets, and America's Schools.*

51. Gates, remarks at the National Charter Schools Conference.

52. Frahm, "Charter Schools: A Debate over Integration and Education."

53. Nathan, *Charter Schools: Creating Hope and Opportunity for American Education.*

54. See, for example, the October 31, 1994, *Time* magazine cover, which read, "New Hope For Public Schools: In a grassroots revolt, parents and teachers are seizing control of public education."

55. Center for Research on Educational Outcomes, *Multiple Choice: Charter School Performance in Sixteen States.*

56. 1991 Omnibus K–12 Education Finance Bill (House File 700/Senate File 467, *Laws of Minnesota 1991,* chapter 265, article 9, section 3).

57. Center for Educational Reform, "National Charter School and Enrollment Statistics 2009, 2010."

58. Hess, "Race to the Top? The Promise—and Challenges—of Expanding the Reach of Charter Schools."

59. See, e.g., Coleman, Hoffer, and Kilgore, "Cognitive Outcomes in Public and Private Schools"; Bryk, Holland, and Lee, *Catholic Schools and the Common Good.*

60. Coons and Sugarman, *Education by Choice: The Case for Family Control.*

61. Price, "Race, Religion, and the Rules Committee: The Kennedy Aid-to-Education Bills."

62. *Zelman v. Simmons-Harris,* at 676–84 (Justice Thomas concurring).

63. Bush, "Cleveland Voucher Program."

64. Lee, Borman, and Tyson, "Florida's A+ Plan: Education Reform Policies and Student Outcomes," 149.

65. *Bush v. Holmes.*

66. DeFour, "ACLU Alleges Milwaukee Voucher Program Discriminates against Disabled Students."

67. Rouse and Barrow, "School Vouchers and Student Achievement: Recent Evidence, Remaining Questions."

68. Anrig, "An Idea Whose Time Has Gone: Conservatives Abandon Their Support for School Vouchers."

69. McEwan, Urquiola, and Vegas, "School Choice, Stratification, and Information on School Performance: Lessons from Chile."

70. Bodzin, "Chilean Students Taking to Streets against 'Pinochet's Education.'"

71. Walton Family Foundation, "Education Reform: Overview."

72. Orfield, *The Reconstruction of Southern Education.*

73. *Green et al. v. County School Board Of New Kent County, Virginia, et al.,* at 441–42.

74. Orfield, *Must We Bus?,* 21.

75. Sullivan and Stewart, *Now Is the Time: Integration in the Berkeley Schools.*

76. *Board of Education of Oklahoma City Public Schools v. Dowell.*

77. Reardon and Yun, "Integrating Neighborhoods, Segregating Schools: The Retreat from School Desegregation in the South, 1990–2000."

78. *Parents Involved in Community Schools v. Seattle School District No. 1.*

79. Mickelson, "The Incomplete Desegregation of the Charlotte-Mecklenburg Schools and Its Consequences."

80. *Parents Involved,* at 788–89 (Justice Kennedy concurring).

81. Ryan, *Five Miles Away, A World Apart: One City, Two Schools, and the Story of Educational Opportunity in Modern America,* 117.

82. Minow, *In Brown's Wake: Legacies of America's Educational Landmark,* 126.

83. *Parents Involved,* at 798–99 (Justice Stevens dissenting).

84. U.S. Department of Justice Civil Rights Division and U.S. Department of Education Office for Civil Rights, "Guidance on the Voluntary Use of Race to Achieve Diversity and Avoid Racial Isolation in Elementary and Secondary Schools."

Choice Theories and the Schools

Gary Orfield

School choice has become so important in American educational policy discussions because it resonates strongly with the basic beliefs of many Americans and with important aspects of American social and political ideology. Wealthy business leaders who insist on data rather than theories in their own businesses pour money into charter schools based on a simple faith that markets relying on individual choice have transformative power and that governmental regulations and unionized work forces are the only basic obstacles to educational equity. Eli Broad, the Los Angeles billionaire whose foundation has had a great impact on current educational policy debates and trained many current school superintendents and administrators, has often expressed the views that public schools should be closed down, that teachers' unions are a big problem, and that business principles could radically improve education. His foundation and the Gates Foundation contributed sixty million dollars to a 2008 public policy campaign to help shape the presidential debate, and their organizations have had large impacts on Barack Obama's education agenda.[1] They are applying their political ideology of sweeping deregulation to education reform even as the nation struggles to recover from the extremely destructive impacts of excessive deregulation of banking and financial institutions. Sometimes the groups they fund attack researchers who present data that challenge these assumptions, targeting them with emotional attacks that claim they do not care about minority or poor students. Often these foundations seem uninterested in research and certain that choice is a powerful educational treatment for inequality. For example, proponents define charter schools as good in and of themselves because they are not part of public school systems and further justify them by the fact that many parents enroll their children there—regardless of whether they actually improve educational outcomes. This broad free market theory of choice has a strong hold on current policy debates and is the central focus of this chapter.

There was a dramatic shift in theories about school choice in the 1970s and 1980s, directly reflecting changes in politics and law. The discussion changed from the use of choice as a tool for pursuing integration and diversity to the idea that choice itself was the treatment for educational inequality. This chapter explores the roots of these theories and some of the basic logical and factual questions about them. Obviously, in developing a policy it is important not only to have a theory about how it might work but also to critically examine the evidence about the theory's logic and the validity of its premises. Since any theory leading to a value judgment or action prescription must have both value and factual premises, both will be discussed here. This chapter begins with the dominant theory of the present generation and then looks back at the evolution of theories about the relationship between choice and equity, ending with a series of hypotheses about choice systems that the rest of the book explores.

It is important to note that both what I call the market theory of choice, which has been dominant in the past three decades, and integration theory, which emerged in the civil rights era, share a constantly expressed central goal or value: providing better educational opportunities for students in inferior neighborhood public schools. The fundamental differences between these two theories are in their factual premises and in the relative primacy they give to individual versus group and community goals.

The market and integration theories both have fervent supporters and fervent critics. Some opponents of choice are simply opposed to choice, seeing it as inconsistent with equality and a uniform set of educational offerings and describing it as a strategy to undermine teachers' rights and public schools more broadly. In many districts, students in regular schools and their parents complain of what they see as the preference given to magnets and charters. Jonathan Kozol, who has been a leading observer of U.S. schools for half a century, for example, points to the extreme stratification developing in Manhattan, where small "boutique" schools that serve elite populations are proliferating while a great many poor children attend weak schools.[2] These are issues well worth debating but are not the subject of this book, which is devoted to examining more closely the kinds of choice, not questions of whether school choice should exist. In our society—where extremely unequal schools perpetuate and even intensify severe inequalities in opportunities and income, no significant forces are working to ameliorate underlying economic inequalities that are the most extreme among modern democracies, and school reform agendas are usually limited and unsuccessful—making the right use of choice is very important. While interventionist civil rights and social policies have been defeated in recent decades, choice is still an open policy alternative, and the debate over divergent choice theories is a priority. This does not mean that a much broader agenda of social and economic reform is not necessary. It clearly is if we are to have a more just and equal society.

Some theorists and policy makers treat choice as highly beneficial exactly because it creates what they describe as a market, and they believe markets by their nature produce better results than government. Paul Peterson, for example, writes, "Public education in the United States seems incapable of self improvement," noting that expenditures have risen but test scores have changed little. He quotes another leading critic (and fellow Hoover Institute member), Eric Hanushek, who concludes that "productivity [the ratio of achievement gains to dollars spent] in schools has fallen by 2.5 to 3 percent per year."[3] Other theorists see choice as a two-edged sword. They favor certain kinds of choice not as ends in themselves but as means to correct inequality in education and rectify the clear inferiority of schools often educating minority and poor students. At the same time, they view unrestricted choice as a threat likely to compound inequalities and stratification. To them, choice is a potentially powerful tool for good or ill that must be channeled.

These contrasting beliefs and the theories that grow from them matter very much in policy decisions about choice. These different philosophies are based on divergent assumptions about the nature of markets, rights, government, race, and society but a shared conviction that predictable results will follow the adoption of certain kinds of policies. Because these assumptions are often decisive in motivating policy decisions and shaping the discourse about choice policies, it is important to examine them.

Though these theories arise from philosophical or ideological assumptions, the predictions that flow from them can be assessed though research. If data confirms the predictions, the theory is strengthened. But if the predicted results do not occur or very different results are found, the theory is undermined and the argument must be reformulated. A theory whose premises are disproved is not a reliable basis for policy, and a theory with contradictory premises needs clarification. This book is an effort to examine the conflicting propositions of these two outlooks and offer a theory that fits the observed facts, providing a basis for developing and implementing the most effective school choice policy.

AMERICA'S TRADITIONAL IDEOLOGY OF EDUCATION

Choice was virtually irrelevant to educational policy for the great bulk of U.S. history. The dominant ideology in American education from the mid-nineteenth century to the 1980s was that expanding the free, nonsectarian common school system and opening it to all would provide an equal opportunity for the improvement of all. Schools have been seen as a central institution for social mobility, for inculcating an understanding of national institutions and democracy, and for creating a common culture.[4] While they have always fallen short of these ideals, these goals have been widely shared. The struggles to open opportunity to minorities, women, the handicapped, non–English speakers, and others have always included a focus on full and fair access to schools. The claim that educational opportunity preserves the possibility of fair outcomes if students work hard enough has often justified the obvious conflicts between American belief in individualism, individual responsibility, and a real possibility of success, and the deep and persisting inequalities among groups.[5] U.S. society is therefore seen as morally good, not because it produces equality but because it provides a fair pathway to possible success for everyone. Each person is responsible for his or her own response to opportunities and success or failure in the market. When the educational system is challenged by critics, one response tends to be proposals for an expansion of opportunity.

Though U.S. public schools were remarkable in bringing together European immigrants (and later their children) from nations that differed profoundly in many dimensions, their record with nonwhites has been a massive disappointment. Indians, African Americans, and people of Mexican origin in the United States received little education until well into the twentieth century.[6] Rectifying this profound inequality has been a central issue in civil rights struggles.

For the two centuries after the first census in 1790, nonwhites constituted between 10 and 20 percent of the United States population, and the percentage of immigrants reached a historic low in the mid-twentieth century, before the 1965 immigration reform. Then the proportion of nonwhites exploded, particularly among the young, greatly raising the educational stakes.

The mid-1800s common school reforms that created public school systems were motivated by a belief that all students should be offered an adequate curriculum established by the state government. The idea of providing prescribed equal educational experiences was so strong that there was, in fact, a struggle in some parts of the country in the name of equal preparation to ban private religious education (the private sector of U.S. education has always been largely religious schools). In its classic 1925 decision in *Pierce v. Society of Sisters,* the Supreme Court rejected an Oregon initiative that required all children to attend public schools, ruling that the Fourteenth Amendment guaranteed the right to choose a private school. It held unanimously that "the fundamental liberty upon which all governments in this Union repose excludes any general power of the State to standardize its children by forcing them to accept instruction from public teachers only."[7]

More than 80 percent of private school students attend religious schools, but private schools educate only a small minority of American students—now about a tenth, down from a sixth in the mid-twentieth century. Even after the 2002

Supreme Court decision in *Zelman v. Simmons-Harris* breached the legal prohibition on public subsidizing of religious schools, there was little movement in the country to adopt school vouchers, and many states still forbid aid to religious schools.[8] Public schools operating under state law and the policies of state governments and local districts are clearly the dominant force in American education. As a result, the most consequential choice debates concern public schools.

From the mid-1800s, when they became widely established in the United States, until the 1960s, there was little provision for choice in public schools. All children were required to go to school, which was assigned by where they lived (and sometimes on the basis of their race), and they either went there or paid for a private school, which was also required to offer the basic state curriculum. In theory everyone was exposed to the same kind of educational opportunity. The common school ideology emphasized uniformity and universalism, at least for whites. Everyone was going to be introduced to the same basic learning by qualified teachers. There were decades of struggle to build systems of public education with adequate standards of teacher training and curriculum and to eliminate politics and partisanship in school operations across the country. Schools were seen as essential for the development and progress of communities and were expected to infuse millions of immigrants from divergent backgrounds with a shared culture and civic understanding.[9]

Until the mid-twentieth century, the federal government had almost no role in education policy, so the focal point for the development of public schools was state governments. Their efforts were highly uneven.[10] Additionally, in the mid-twentieth century seventeen states still had duplicate school systems serving the same areas, one for black and one for white students. Indian and Latino students also had separate schools or classrooms in some states. Linda Brown had to walk past a white school to a more distant black school, prompting her father to become the lead plaintiff in *Brown v. Board of Education,* which the Supreme Court decided by outlawing systems of schools intentionally segregated by race, generating decades of struggle.

Until the 1970s, most of the civil rights battle was about access to the same schools in the same neighborhoods. When it turned out that residential segregation in the increasingly urbanized South was producing segregated and unequal schools even without state segregation laws, the Supreme Court ordered mandatory desegregation across neighborhood boundaries in 1971.[11] It extended desegregation to northern and western cities in its 1973 *Keyes* decision but drew a line between city and suburban schools the very next year in *Milliken,* making desegregation impossible in many places with city school systems with few remaining white students.[12] Courts began dismantling desegregation orders seventeen years later, when the 1991 *Oklahoma City v. Dowell* decision allowed cities to have segregated neighborhood schools after a period of desegregation.[13]

Tasked with taking action against segregation, cities faced tension over the mandatory reassignment of students and teachers by courts, which led to a strong focus on new forms of race-conscious choice combining magnet programs with desegregation policies. Today, however, color-blind choice has become a central part of the discussion of educational reform, based on a theory that challenges the American tradition of public schools controlled by local elected boards and assumes that semiprivate schools are superior and unregulated individual choice will solve inequalities. As schools become ever more segregated by race and class and the links between segregation and inequality are more fully documented, the issue of segregation, of course, will not go away. The policy shift is often justified by claims that schools outside the public school bureaucracy will solve the problem because the need to compete makes them superior.

MARKET THEORY

The theory of school choice that has been most widely adopted in the past three decades in the United States, the market theory, argues that giving parents the right to chose schools for themselves and giving educators the opportunity to create or transform autonomous schools of choice will have a powerful educational impact.[14] The goal of this theory is equal opportunity to make a choice, assuming that parents know what is best and will equally understand and take advantage of broader opportunities without assistance. Obviously this theory starts with the individual, sees regulation by public agencies and legislatures as barriers to opportunity rather than guarantees of equal treatment, and assumes that a broad scope of individual choice will produce greater equity and higher levels of achievement.

The complicated part of this theory is that although the claim that choice will improve opportunities seems to be a factual premise subject to empirical investigation, it is also a central value premise in the broader theory of market economics and the political philosophy of individualism. That market competition creates value is a central premise of both the discipline of economics and conservative ideology, which therefore see markets as good by definition. Classical economics postulates that if both buyers and sellers are free to compete, there will be the most efficient outcomes, providing good products at good prices and strong incentives for improving them. In education the dominant version of this theory argues that if parents can choose to move their children, families and educators can create new schools exempt from regulation, they will not be trapped in inferior settings, and students will have much better opportunities. Children will be able to move out of settings where education reform rarely succeeds. The theory also holds that if educators are no longer limited (or protected) by school bureaucracies and union contracts, which by their very nature limit market competition, they will create new and better schools offering much richer opportunities, and those that do this the best will be rewarded with growing enrollments and public funds. According to this theory, rigid bureaucracies and self-aggrandizing unions, which conspire to block educational innovation and protect incompetence from the consequences of failure, are responsible for inferior schools, which consistently fail to meet standards.[15] Without competition, poor parents lacking money to buy themselves better alternatives through the housing market have nothing to bargain with because they have no ability to reject their local school. Teachers and administrators—as well as the unions and public school systems they're part of—can use their monopoly power to exploit helpless communities, protecting and enhancing their own status and resources regardless of the harm done to needy students.

In contrast, according to this theory, schools of choice have to be better to compete and survive.[16] And beyond their benefits to the parents who choose to transfer students to them and their contribution to breaking the chains of bureaucracy and teachers' organizations, the theory continues, these new schools—combined with the threat that parents will pull their children out of weak schools—will force traditional schools, which are locked in ineffectual bureaucratic cynicism, to transform themselves as their existence and budgets are threatened, thus improving education for the children whose parents do not choose to transfer them.

The market theory is not a zero-sum theory, where some lose and others win; it is an optimistic, positive-sum theory. It posits both the opportunity for strong individual benefits that motivate the choice process and, at no additional cost, competition pressures that will improve the schools not chosen. This is the application of Adam Smith's "invisible hand" to educational reform. Smith's ingenious insight, leading to the founding of modern economics, was to understand the ways in which individuals competing to buy and sell things in open markets, all seeking their own advantage, can, with no intention of doing so, increase overall efficiency and productiveness. The market rewards producers who are effective and efficient and destroys those who are not, thus encouraging growing efficiency and fair prices. It also brings together the information and energies of both buyers and sellers and directs profits to where they will be most productively invested. Smith explained:

> The invisible hand works without any awareness by the individual pursuit of profit. He [the individual buyer or seller] generally . . . neither intends to promote the public interest nor knows how much he is promoting it. . . . By directing that industry in such a manner as its produce may be of the greatest value, he intends only his own gain; and he is in this . . . led by an invisible hand to promote an end which was no part of his intention . . . . By pursuing his own interest, he frequently promotes that of the social more effectually than when he really intends to promote it.[17]

The dominant theory of educational choice is an effort to directly apply this classic view of economic markets to the operation of public school systems, where the invisible hand will do things public decisions cannot. Anyone who has seen the vast selection of goods and services generated by worldwide competition or examined the difficulties encountered in the centrally planned command economies of Communist countries has to concede that markets can accomplish some remarkable things. Likewise, bureaucratic planning is a very complex task that has often produced goods of poor quality. These economic experiences are central to the argument of the market theory of school choice. But they are, of course, about commodities and products, not schools. And in all advanced societies, markets are highly regulated to prevent dishonesty, to assure fair competition, and to ban products that would cause harm to their buyers. As Smith himself recognized, government has essential functions to perform in administering and facilitating commerce and providing education.[18] American conservatives tend to favor a more radical version of unregulated markets than did the founder of modern economics.

The Nobel Prize–winning economist Milton Freedman was a leading exponent of this theory of educational reform for half a century. Friedman, whose views have had an enormous impact on American conservatism, advocated school vouchers beginning in the 1950s, seeing them as equalizing opportunity through competition and choice. His statements were a mix of pure economic theory and a kind of antigovernment attitude that often flows directly from the basic premise that markets are inherently superior. "Our goal," he said, "is to have a system in which every family in the U.S. will be able to choose for itself the school to which its children go. . . . If we had that system of free choice we would also have a system of competition, innovation which would change the character of education."[19]

Calling the public school system "the single most Socialist industry in the U.S., leaving aside the military," he said it was "a monopoly" whose harm was "exacerbated by the fact that it has been largely taken over by teachers unions, the National Education Association and the American Federation of Teachers." He concluded that "reform has to come through competition from the outside and the only way you can get competition is by making it possible for parents to have the ability to choose." Competition would lead to "the same kind of change in the provision of education as you have had in industries like the computer industry, the television industry and other things."[20] Failing schools, in this view, are like failing factories.

Friedman argued that markets would be particularly helpful to the disadvantaged: "The people who live in Harlem or the slums or the corresponding areas in LA or San Francisco, they can go to the same stores, shop in the same stores everybody else can, they can buy the same automobiles, they can go to

[the] supermarket but they have very limited choice of schools. Everybody agrees that the schools in those areas are the worst[:] they are poor." He also noted that "those of us that are in the upper income classes have freedom of choice for our children in various ways[:] we can decide where to live and we can choose places to live that have good schools or . . . [pay] tuition at a private school. It seems to me utterly unfair that those opportunities should not be open to everybody at all levels of income."[21]

Though it was inconsistent with the tradition of American education, the market theory linked widely shared antigovernment and free enterprise values. In a society where there has been little educational progress for several decades and where increasing numbers of students are locked into schools where few succeed, it is easy to understand why this theory has great appeal both to business-oriented conservatives and to families with children in failing schools.[22] Since the civil rights era ended, almost all of the attention to choice policy has focused on the market theory, largely ignoring earlier theories relating inequality to exclusion and segregation. There was a change from presuming that inequality was based on social stratification and could only be remedied by a consciously integrationist use of choice (supported by other social policies to improve conditions for families) to assuming that inequality was caused by bureaucratic rigidity and the excessive power of teachers' organizations and could be changed simply by offering unregulated individual school choices.

Assumptions of the Market Theory

The classic assumptions in market economics, which specify the necessary preconditions for true markets working efficiently, have to be tested against what is known about the actual conditions of choice in urban American schools. The idea that markets are both fair and efficient in allocating resources and opportunities is based on the assumptions that (1) all potential customers have equal and accurate information, (2) there is broad competition among many suppliers and therefore a strong incentive for each to offer a better product, and (3) all buyers have an equal chance to buy. With many buyers and many sellers, and especially with simple, standardized, easily understood products like bushels of wheat or bales of cotton, sellers are forced to compete on price because no one has significant control of the overall market. If all these conditions exist, the theory holds, the better providers will prosper, the worst will fail, consumers will get better products at lower prices, results will be fair, and political forces and special connections will not matter. Under this theory applied to education, the previous monopolistic institutions (public schools) will have to compete for students and become better because otherwise they will lose per-student funding and staff.

Key assumptions of the market theory were clear in the Friedman argument. According to him, the basic problem with education for poor and minority families in Harlem and elsewhere was the "socialist" monopoly controlled by unions and bureaucracies, which stifled innovation in public schools. The cure was competition and "freedom of choice," which would make educational opportunity "open to everybody."[23] The union stranglehold would end and innovation would flourish.

John E. Chubb and Terry M. Moe's controversial and influential 1990 book, *Politics, Markets, and America's Schools,* purported to show statistically that public schools were systematically inferior to nonpublic schools and that this was because they were subject to the political control of elected officials. This book, which used data from a national longitudinal study, quickly became a leading justification for voucher supporters. Private school vouchers would mean that students and schools were matched by the informed market choices of parents, whose only real interest was good education for their children. Although many researchers harshly criticized the book, it became a sensation in the policy world, partly because of the extraordinary claims Chubb made, for example, in his article "America's Public Schools: Choice Is a Panacea."[24] The idea that there was a simple, choice-based way to accomplish what government had failed to do for generations had great appeal in an era of business dominance.

Though the arguments of Friedman, Chubb, and Moe aimed at supporting private schools and came before the invention of charter schools in 1991, they are widely cited by charter school leaders, many of whom believe they are offering the same kind of challenge to regular public schools. Charter schools enjoy strong support from business leaders who see them as entrepreneurial institutions creating a market and encouraging innovation. The foundations of the billionaires Bill Gates, Eli Broad, and the Walton family of the Walmart fortune, as well as the Wall Street private equity billionaire Theodore J. Forstmann, are just a few of the prominent supporters.[25]

Limits to the Market Theory

The fundamental problems with applying market theory to education are that the basic assumptions do not hold even in the realm of buying and selling much simpler products and services and that, even if they did, a market for schools has very complex products. The ideal model of unrestricted markets has a limited connection with reality. Almost all of the world's major successful market economies are heavily regulated to protect workers' and buyers' health and safety and to prevent anticompetitive trusts and financial conspiracies—in short, to prevent the major abuses that occur in uncontrolled markets. The goal of those selling goods is to make as large a profit as possible, and without regulation this can often be done in ways that mislead, endanger, or cheat customers, limit competition, or degrade the environment. The truth is that those who cheat will often make more profit, at least in the short run, and competition can produce a race to the bottom. The corporate structure, which offers huge compensation to executives who make short-term profits, often rewards the most rapacious behavior, which achieves quick results. It shields leadership from personal responsibility. Such massive prizes and minimal risks too often incentivize not the wisest and most ethical long-term investment but quite the opposite. When markets are deregulated, as were the banking and financial industries in the United States before the Great Recession, very profitable business can wreck the economy and threaten the entire world.[26] Markets can be a powerful force for better choices, but they can also be corrupted and distorted. Those without rules are risky and inefficient for everyone. How can you know that you are receiving the right amount of something if the weights are not regulated and checked, or that your money is safe in a bank if the bank is free to wildly speculate with its depositors' money? How could anyone reasonably buy a stock if companies could simply make up false business reports?

Getting the best results from competition requires enforcement of the rules of the game by government. When one uses the promise of private gains as the basic engine of change, one must channel that great force to produce real gains and limit harm. The drive for profits is a powerful motivator, and if it is possible to get more while doing less by cheating, the market will be corrupted. America's founders had no delusion that men were angels. That is why they designed a system of government full of limits, with institutions balancing and checking one another and with federal power offsetting the tendency toward local tyrannies.[27] It is ironic that the same ideology that assumes people are inherently inclined toward evil and corruption in politics and therefore need to be watched and limited somehow believes that people in markets are not subject to the same temptations. What we see in many discussions of school choice is a school produced by an ideal type of market instead of the real situation facing the most disadvantaged neighborhoods.

Examples abound about the necessity of limits on markets. Nuclear power produces a vast amount of electricity, but it can devastate the environment if not controlled properly. And while its profits are short term, it produces by-products with very long lives, thousands of years, whose cost to future generations must be considered. Everyone wants cheap flights, to cite another example, but very few people would want to fly through uncontrolled airspace in planes not regulated for safety. Modern capitalism is competition within rules of the game set by law and regulation. But those who favor school choice often strongly oppose regulation, having embraced a romantic version of markets.

The classic products of markets are objects, subject to regulation, not institutions that can capture their regulators. One of the differences between commodities markets and competition among schools is that the largest system of choice schools outside public control, charter schools, are not passive objects of choice produced by private markets but instead almost entirely government subsidized and very active politically, often succeeding in controlling the rules of the game to favor themselves.[28] They aren't really private anymore: any institution almost totally dependent on public dollars inevitably becomes quasi-public. And such institutions virtually inevitably organize lobbies whose objectives are to get more funds and minimize regulation, since their very survival depends upon a continuing flow of public dollars within a political process that distributes the permissions to create schools and decides on their funding.[29]

Market advocates assume that nonpublic institutions can remain independent from government and nonpolitical even when they are completely dependent upon public funds, forgetting the saying that is often called the golden rule of government: he who has the gold makes the rules. Government has vast leverage over the institutions it totally funds, which usually must win battles for appropriations every year. Whether the group is composed of scientists, green industries, or artists, if it depends on public dollars, it will organize associations to promote its mission and attempt to influence decisions about governmental resources. Totally dependent "private" institutions can become subject to many of the demands for accountability that public institutions face. Many "bureaucratic" rules have their origin in such demands. These groups must mobilize ideological and political support to protect themselves and to assure their continuity, and they typically do this through the creation of interest groups and lobbies. They may be private and nonpolitical in theory, but the logic of their situation makes them public and political in important ways.[30] The choice and charter lobbies are sometimes powerful enough to control the institutions that fund them, which is truly the antithesis of market competition.[31] This is doubtless a reason for the continued public funding of many charters with dismal or mediocre results. Such actions, of course, directly limit the power of market discipline.

The fact that voucher schools and charter schools have been able to secure public funding—often taken from public school systems that have many unmet needs—and to largely prevent effective regulation or sanctions reflects their political mobilization more than their educational benefits. Conservative support mobilized by the market metaphor has helped them to win policies that subsidize their expansion without demonstrating any academic advantages. Foundations and wealthy donors finance public relations and supplemental funding for the schools, and school founders and owners at the local and state levels mobilize to create powerful pressure groups.

It is impossible to explain school choice policy simply as a market mechanism, since charters have been able to define themselves in public as inherently good while avoiding the kinds of accountability and sanctions that public schools with similar achievement statistics often face. Market advocates are intensely critical of the political power of teachers' organizations but seemingly blind to the way the political power of charter schools severely limits market forces. In fact, they often fund charter school lobbies, frequently using foundations to reap tax subsidies while doing so.

Politics aside, there is a theoretical problem of equating efficiency with equity. Markets, by their nature, produce losers as well as winners, and market theory does nothing to guarantee equity of opportunity or outcomes, since many lose their resources in the long run even under perfect market conditions. The unequal rewards that come to the best producers and the losses of those who fail may drive competition and produce more efficiency, more bushels of corn, but they do nothing to assure that all buyers have an equal or even a sufficient supply of grain. Competition in true markets produces winners and losers—the creative destruction of capitalism. Some schools would succeed and grow, and others would lose everything. In a parallel way some students would make good (high-profit) decisions, and others would lose their school or even end up in a worse one. Creative destruction is supposed to result in more effective producers and lower prices but not to guarantee uniform standards or equality of outcomes for buyers.

A perfect market is not an empirical reality; it is a Platonic ideal type, like perfect honesty or perfect racial integration or a perfect defense policy. In reality, imperfections abound. The theory of perfect markets should be tempered by the skepticism about perfect governments that is so characteristic of American political philosophy. If we had a perfect democracy, all citizens would have an equal chance to participate, be treated equally by others, and confront no barriers, and all would willingly obey the decisions reached by the majority after full and fair consideration. But these ideal conditions do not exist in real societies. Power without limits is power that will be abused. James Madison sagely notes in the *Federalist Paper* number 51, written during the national debate over the adoption of the Constitution: "If men were angels, no government would be necessary. If angels were to govern men, neither external nor internal controls on government would be necessary."[32] Since neither of these has ever been the case, Madison argues, we need to regulate and limit each of the government's branches so it preserves freedom and can meet national needs but not harm its own citizens. One of the distinctive characteristics of American political philosophy is that it balances power with real constraints. In economic thought, however, particularly in times of business dominance, there is a tendency to assume that participants in markets will behave like angels rather than use whatever opportunities they have to maximize their interests, whether these reflect market ideals or not. It would be healthy if people applied the skeptical attitudes toward governmental power in political philosophy to markets and were more concerned about what actually happens rather than what the theory suggests. There are tremendous profits to be had in limiting competition, getting and exploiting inside information, and making people believe that products are more valuable than they are.

Further, in a perfect market, the theory argues, all potential buyers and sellers have an equal chance to participate. But if one group of competitors unfairly controls the rules of the game, they threaten the whole idea. If new schools outside the system can tap public school resources, attract the better students, send those with low scores or special needs back to public schools, avoid accountability, and create the belief that they are superior to regular public schools, a negative-sum game of increasing stratification and inequality can result, with the schools left behind demoralized and defunded. The students in public schools would be not beneficiaries of increased competition but the special victims of a distorted market. Something like this may well be happening in cities such as Detroit, which closed half of its public schools as students transferred to charters in other districts, and New Orleans.[33] Similar trends were apparent in other cities. Los Angeles School Board Member Tamar Galatzan in 2012 asked, concerning a wave of charters serving middle-class and white students in her part of the nation's second-largest district, "Will traditional public schools become a repository for the poor and the special education students of our city, with everyone else fleeing the traditional public school system? What does that mean for the future of California?"[34]

Even if, on average, the overall set of choices in a market improves, there is nothing to guarantee that the results for all groups of consumers will be more equal, or to prevent them from becoming more unequal. Indeed, in an arena—such as the real estate market—that has features of a true market, with a great many buyers and sellers and no one controlling much of the total market, some well-intentioned buyers lose everything, while some with a more shrewd sense of timing become rich, taking advantage of the losses of many others. Inequality is an essential product of market competition; in fact, it is a basic driving force. People with better information about and understanding of the system will get the best choices. This is why there have to be rules for markets to be fair: true information must be provided, competitors who cheat must be excluded, contracts must be enforced, and intimidation must be forbidden. Getting the balance right is a complex task.

Market theory is most directly applicable to the buying and selling of simple interchangeable products among thousands of independent producers and potential buyers and a simple and clear way to buy and sell the products. Under those circumstances, comparing prices is the only thing a consumer needs to do. Obviously, under modern economic conditions—with specialized and complex products, high entry costs, often limited competition, limited consumer understanding of differences, massive advertising designed to inflate the value of products, and a tremendous inequality of power between sellers and buyers—things are different.

The theory of market choice in schooling assumes that the customers (the parents) understand the different offerings and have meaningful choices. Unfortunately, this and other key parts of the theory don't hold in school choice. Schools are not a standardized or easily understood commodity. Even experts struggle to assess the real opportunities and impacts of individual schools. The only generally available information, test scores, mostly reflect out-of-school factors and can be manipulated in many ways.[35] Schooling is a highly complex commodity supplied in many forms, with high costs of entry into the market, and schools usually provide little useful comparative information to parents. How does an immigrant single mother who is not an English speaker, for example, acquire information and make good choices for the education of her children in a large city? (Twenty-one percent of U.S. children are growing up in homes where they speak a language other than English.)[36] What does choice mean in that context, and what forces influence choice or failure to choose? Is it fair that those who do not understand the system and do not choose often end up in the weakest schools, or that schools of choice often find ways to exclude the most expensive and low-scoring students?

There are rarely multiple suppliers of public schools in a given geographic area. Except in school districts with broad school choice programs and free transportation supporting them (conditions usually produced by desegregation plans), the options are seriously limited. Often there is only the neighborhood public school. Charter schools often do not offer either distinctive curricula or parent recruitment and transportation, so they may serve only a segmented market. Magnet and charter schools may have admissions criteria and may or may not provide free transportation. Schools in danger of losing students typically make few efforts to inform parents of transfer policies, if such exist. Such policies often don't provide for transportation anyway. Segregated and high-poverty neighborhoods might have a public school, a neighborhood charter school with equally low-scoring students and inexperienced teachers, and, in a few places, a voucher private school, all of which tend to be likewise segregated and impoverished. Many students with an unambiguous legal right to transfer, such as those in schools consistently failing to meet No Child Left Behind progress requirements, have few good choices, because most of their districts have few high-performing schools of any type.[37]

Two of the most important limits on the school market are jurisdictional boundaries and lack of transportation, both of which radically curtail choice. Metropolitan regions are the natural market area for most economic decisions in a society where more than four-fifths of the population lives in or near cities. No one hesitates to cross a municipal boundary when shopping, when buying a home, when seeking entertainment, or in many other aspects of life. In fact, a massive part of advertising is to inform people about their opportunities and to draw them across those borders. In all but a handful of choice plans, however, school district lines become absolute walls, which separate the students most in need of strong schools from the vast majority of schools with the most resources, the best teachers, and the strongest curricula and paths to success in college.

Districts with significantly stronger schools often don't provide free transportation, which limits choice on the basis of income and wealth, reinforcing inequalities. In these areas, families without the resources to provide their own transportation can only watch as better-off children enjoy them. The school choice theories and policies that have been dominant since 1980 almost totally ignore these very real market barriers. A choice system that cuts off the vast majority of the strongest schools from the children who need them most and instead preserves them for students with many types of home advantages is not a market system in any meaningful sense. Many critics who agree with Milton Friedman's complaint that poor students do not have the same chance as affluent students to access better schools strongly oppose policies that would enable many of these students to enroll in the schools in the critics' own suburban districts. It is a curious fact that market models are rarely applied to the mainstream schools in the predominantly middle-class suburban communities where many of their advocates live. If markets create such gains, why do affluent areas not also seek to use them? Why do suburban communities wall off their schools and prosecute parents from other jurisdictions who try to access them? In fact, most such communities not only provide no choice in schools but also do everything possible to limit their housing market in ways that exclude families who are not affluent but might wish to send their children to these neighborhoods' schools.[38] Suburban districts simply assign children to the nearest school, and their schools, of course, report high achievement, graduation, and college-going statistics. Suburban housing and land-use policies, which exclude affordable and subsidized housing while taking no significant action against housing discrimination, produce dramatic contradictions with market theories. Though school opportunity is tied to housing, there is no metropolitan housing development market, and local land-use and zoning regulations forbid builders from producing affordable rental housing for families in most areas with excellent schools—facts that are also almost completely ignored in choice discussions.[39] Yet it is clear that subsidized housing, for example, has long been and continues to be developed in ways that exacerbate school segregation and unequal educational opportunity.[40]

The fact that individual municipalities have the right to exclude students from other school districts is the basic but overlooked cause of school inequality. Suburbs with strong schools often use their housing and building-code policies to exclude all but the upper-income fraction of families. Few of these communities have serious policies to deal with the continuing housing discrimination, documented in housing market audits, against nonwhite families who have enough income to live there. These policies give affluent suburban communities the advantages of access to the economy of the metro region while shifting many of the costs back to the cities and denying city students access to their schools. When Milton Friedman, Abigail Thernstrom, and many others argue that choice should provide poor children with the same opportunities their own children receive, they don't really mean the same middle- and upper-class suburban schools connected to good colleges; they mean the choice of a charter or a voucher school that serves other poor minority children. They certainly don't discuss the extreme control of the housing market, which prevents any of the children they express sympathy for from living in suburban communities where good public schools already exist. They use the market metaphor selectively. Claiming that unequal schools reflect individual choice and not systemic problems can shift the blame from a general system of racial and class segregation to the "antimarket" teachers' organizations and school districts that resist charter schools.

It could be argued that suburban residents don't need schools of choice because they can choose their schools through the housing market. There is, of course, some truth to this. White and Asian families with substantial incomes can, of course, exercise broad choice in where they live and what school district they have access to. Being able to choose housing, to get favorable loans, and to live in a costly community is linked to improved schooling opportunity. The frequent use of school test scores in marketing housing is a reflection of widespread concern for at least one aspect of school quality in housing searches.[41] (Interestingly enough, there is also evidence that whites are moving to whiter areas, regardless of school quality.)[42] Given the other forces that affect housing searches even for the middle class, however—such as amount of equity, previous location, job and institutional commitments, transit and freeway locations, location of relatives, and ability to obtain mortgages—even families with the ability to choose often confront limitations accessing strong schools. And from 2007 to 2012, a severe housing market crisis locked millions of families in place regardless of their desires, stuck in underwater mortgages on residences they cannot afford to sell. But in spite of these limits on choosing schools through housing decisions, there is a striking disinterest in and even hostility toward the expansion of charter schools in many suburban communities. The reality is that these communities tend to be satisfied with their schools and often see charters as threatening the financial base of a healthy and desirable system. Federal policy squarely focuses intense external pressure to expand charters on places with low-scoring schools, which include most segregated low-income schools. There is very little external pressure on affluent suburban communities to create them. We force poor communities to implement forms of choice their school officials do not want because of the belief of others that it will be good for them since choice is inherently superior. In the communities where business leaders, policy makers, and other advocates often live, however, there is little choice.

The truncated school choices for city residents are very different from what an actual market would offer. Often, in paying more attention to the theory than to the situation on the ground, advocates treat the choice that is available (such as a neighborhood charter school not significantly different from the local public school) as a major solution. To call this a market and to suggest that these choices are somehow similar or equal to what affluent families get through their choice of communities is to stretch the market metaphor to the breaking point. What is valuable about a market is real choices, among all available goods, at prices that are lowered by widespread competition. What we have in school choice programs today is limited choice, little information for parents, and an unsupported theory that any nonpublic school will produce educational gains simply because it is nonpublic. The fact that parents seek this limited choice is taken as evidence that choice is better, and data to the contrary is ignored.

Market theory assumes that people know what they are buying and make decisions based on comparisons of offerings from many providers. If people do not know what they are buying or have false information, markets are inefficient. Theorists of school choice often simply assume that parents have good knowledge and that their decisions show that the chosen schools are better. The actual state of parental knowledge and how it relates to school quality are, of course, researchable questions. What we know is troubling. Empirical studies show that rates of both knowledge about and the use of choice programs strongly skew toward the more educated, the more affluent, and the better-connected families.[43] This pattern is stark and clear. If unequal knowledge reflects family inequalities, choice can become a mechanism to reinforce rather than overcome stratification.

The school choice market theory assumes that educational quality will be the basis of choice. But if the chooser has little valid information, this cannot be true. Additionally, it is clear that white families often make choices not on educational information but on issues such as race, a major nonmarket factor that, if not dealt with, will increase the already severe racial separation in unequal schools and undermine the stability of integrated schools and neighborhoods.[44] The fact that unrestricted choice led to white families leaving integrated areas half a century ago was a major reason why civil rights policies restricted choices that increased segregation. When whites leave or stop moving into a neighborhood, resegregation is often rapid and usually triggers a similar change in school population, producing a situation where families who accept or prefer stable integration lose that choice. When desegregation policies were dropped, the result was frequently rapid resegregation of the choice schools.[45]

Another question in market theory is whether all potential customers are treated equally. In an ideal market, anyone who can pay the market price (in the school market, anyone whose tuition costs can be covered by private funding or per-student public funding) is treated equally. Often in school choice situations, however, there are additional requirements or screening methods for students, or a lack of information intelligible to, for instance, non-English-speaking parents, which introduce nonmarket factors and may screen out the most disadvantaged students.

Classic microeconomic theory focuses overwhelmingly on individuals and choice. It assumes that choices reflect a rational comparison of services and result in good and efficient outcomes, and it pays little attention to impacts on communities and institutions or to barriers to real choice. Recent awards of Nobel Prizes in Economics to scholars in behavioral economics who believe that it is important to understand how people actually make choices rather than to assume rationality reflect contemporary challenges to these assumptions.[46] Much of this book is devoted to explorations of these assumptions and to research that is essential to either sustain or challenge the premises of both market and integration theories. If something is to be done to change the opportunities of the children whom both theories purport to serve, it is important to move the discussion from dogma to experience.

INTEGRATION THEORY

Integration experiences provide a very different theory of choice, which shares the market theory's stated goal of improving education for disadvantaged students but sees the root of inequality not in schools' governance structure but in social and economic stratification perpetuated by schools that are segregated by race, class, and language. It sees choice not as an end in itself or as a substantive educational treatment but as one important means, if properly regulated, to accomplish something more basic. Choice in this theory is a noncoercive framework of policies using incentives and other mechanisms to enforce minority rights in a broadly acceptable way and attain the benefits of substantial, lasting desegregation. It was implemented on a large scale a generation before the current market theory became dominant. Integration's basic goal is to get highly disadvantaged and isolated students into classrooms and schools with higher-achieving students and teachers while allowing for as much family choice for all groups as is compatible with this aim, and many schools were designed on these principles to elicit choices through superior educational offerings and have been enthusiastically chosen across racial lines for generations. This theory assumes, as the Supreme Court concluded in *Brown* and subsequent research has confirmed, that segregated schools are "inherently unequal" in a society with a history of racial exclusion and subordination and deeply rooted practices and beliefs that perpetuate them.

One of the properties of markets is that under some circumstances, each individual trying to maximize his or her own benefit can result in no one getting to have what a great many would prefer. The economist Thomas Schelling has explored this dilemma for a variety of activities, such as residential integration.[47] It is clear, for example, that nearly everyone in a city on a sea would like to have the option to walk and swim along the beach without paying an entrance fee, but no individual would have the incentive to pay to acquire and maintain a free public beach, so the likely outcome is that the vast majority will have no access to something that almost everyone would prefer. This is, in fact, a central reason why government is necessary: to resolve the conflict between the aggregate impact of individual choices and the common needs that no individual or group of individuals acting separately can fulfill. Given the facts that the spread of segregation is deeply rooted in features of the housing markets, that most people would accept stably integrated but not racially transitional neighborhoods, and that there are different preferences for level of integration, the market is unlikely to provide the option that most people in diverse communities would prefer but is likely to produce neighborhood resegregation in a changing neighborhood and decline in the absence of policies to limit market forces.[48] In that case, almost no one gets what he wants.

When the options are all well-integrated schools, many choices are acceptable to people of various racial, social, and ethnic groups. In most choice plans that are part of desegregation strategies, the great majority of families get their first or second choice, so controversy is often limited. Without desegregation standards and controls, individual schools tend to resegregate, and the intense demand for the remaining handful of well-integrated, well-performing schools produces many losers, a good deal of conflict, and lost support for the public schools. In the integration theory, the use of choice and the creation of educational options diminish community conflict while expanding opportunity. Magnet schools, for example, often accomplished voluntary integration and were oversubscribed, so they had to use lotteries (with desegregation guidelines) to deal fairly with excessive demand.[49] Integration theory sees controls on choice as a precondition for fostering lasting integration, by blocking the segregative effect of neighborhood change, and views unrestricted choice as an instrument of resegregation that undermines the kinds of choices most people would prefer. By limiting individual choices, the system provides better options for most people and the community.

Since choice for integration, unlike pure market approaches, often requires change in the schools of privileged groups, opening them to some less-privileged families, it is far more controversial than market approaches. Families who believe they have an absolute right to their first choice are angry when they do not get it. Choice in the integration context is basically a tool to try to replace conflicts over student assignments with situations of mutual advantage by offering tangible educational incentives to powerful groups of parents while also subordinating their choices to a common goal. In the integration theory, the basic sources of school inequality are not bureaucracies and unions but the underlying social inequalities that separate and unequal schooling by race and class reinforce. The policy goal in this theory is to create diverse schools where formerly excluded, disadvantaged students learn more by being in contact with better-prepared and more privileged students and teachers, and privileged students lose nothing in achievement and gain in many other ways.[50] The broadened curricula that come from some forms of curriculum-driven choice, such as magnet schools, are important side benefits. But the main goal is bringing students and teachers to integrated schools in a positive way. The belief is that this has the potential to help transform the students' life chances and the community's race relations.

It is relatively easy to ask practical questions about the sweeping claims of Milton Friedman's market theory, but it is also not difficult to point out practical limits to the integration theory in the current legal and political context. The Supreme Court's 1974 decision in *Milliken v. Bradley* drew a strong legal wall between central cities, where millions of black and Latino students attend failing schools almost totally segregated by race and poverty, and the better suburbs, where most white students and strong schools are. This decision also had the unanticipated consequence of making regional approaches to the rapid resegregation of a growing number of suburban school districts very difficult, if not illegal. Many suburbs that strongly opposed regional solutions a generation ago now need them to prevent resegregation, but there are no tools to achieve them. This means that there are critical limits on the possibility of integration under current law.

A second key restriction is that achieving the maximum benefits of integration theory requires not merely getting students into more diverse schools but also avoiding classroom segregation and ensuring equal treatment within the schools. Typically, however, choice plans focus simply on getting students into more advantaged schools and not on changing schools and faculty in ways that would maximize benefits, such as integrating faculty and providing appropriate training for teachers in techniques to create equal-status interaction, which research across the world shows facilitates successful intergroup relationships.[51] Faculty should also be taught to understand and respect the diversity of children's backgrounds and assure they feel welcome and receive fair treatment. Decades of research have documented that such conditions are necessary for maximizing gains.[52] Changing the internal operation of schools and the beliefs and practices of teachers requires serious help. The Reagan Administration canceled the Emergency School Aid Act, the major federal desegregation assistance program, in 1981 in spite of evidence of its substantial educational and race relations benefits.[53] This generation's policy debates have ignored the challenge of creating successful diverse classrooms with teachers who can work well across lines of race/ethnicity.

American political philosophy and ideology are closely linked to legal developments. The integration theory of choice developed out of the experience of attempting to realize the goals set forth in *Brown v. Board of Education* and civil rights law. The Supreme Court's later decisions, which in 1991 led to the ending of most large mandatory desegregation plans and in 2007 forbid the most common forms of voluntary desegregation, have eliminated most of the infrastructure for pursuing the policies of the integration theory and forced school districts committed to diverse schools to come up with new approaches.[54] After legitimating race-conscious plans for decades, the court has now adopted a much more individualist approach and says that most of these plans are unconstitutional. The parents who brought the cases against voluntary plans devised by local school boards claimed that the primary right in choice plans must be individual choice, even if it resegregates the schools. The Supreme Court agreed, holding in *Parents Involved in Community Schools v. Seattle School District No. 1* that no student could be given or denied an assignment on the basis of his or her race in a voluntary desegregation plan. In his concurring opinion, Justice Anthony Kennedy adopted the goals of the integration theory, calling integration a compelling interest, but forbade the means that had worked to achieve it; he did not reconcile this contradiction.[55]

Current legal limits block integration choice approaches in a number of settings. This does not mean, however, that it is impossible to devise policies that would produce considerably more integration and make the desegregation that does exist, often because of blacks and Latinos moving into previously all-white suburban communities, more successful and stable. Nor do these legal barriers prevent discussing what would be necessary to seriously pursue the integration theory in the future or examining the settings in which desegregation across city-suburban lines was implemented. And districts that have never desegregated or that commit new forms of discrimination are still liable to court-ordered integration plans.

A 5–4 Supreme Court decision does not mean that the legal battles are permanently settled: a number of school districts are seeking indirect ways to preserve diverse schools, and theories have long lives. Even as Friedman could develop his theory at a time when there was no significant support for it, theories of integration can be further developed and perhaps pursued in indirect ways now—and more directly in the future if the law changes back.

The premise underlying the integration theory is that inequality of opportunity is linked to social stratification, which means that normally the most-privileged students receive the best schooling opportunities and historically excluded populations receive the worst. This theory draws from both the historic record of unequal opportunity in racially and economically stratified schools and evidence of the impact of peer groups on educational success articulated in the 1966 Coleman report and many other studies of schooling.[56] A peer group's family and community background and the distribution of qualified and experienced teachers and challenging classes strongly shape a school's impact. Family influences are more powerful for middle-class students with resources and education, while school is more decisive for students isolated in families and neighborhoods with far less social capital. This theory says that schools as they have normally been organized tend to reflect and perpetuate the relative status of their students.[57] Changing this outcome requires getting disadvantaged students access to the strongest and most-respected schools.[58] Integrationist choice plans aim to do that by creating win-win situations in which both privileged and disadvantaged students gain in a variety of ways.

Desegregation, however it is accomplished, is powerful because it connects students from excluded groups to the information and opportunity networks that exist in better schools and that greatly enhance their prospects for later success in mainstream institutions and relationships.[59] Choice systems that produce magnet schools with authentically distinctive curricula not only enrich the system's educational offerings and capacity to meet the needs of individual children, whatever their race, but also help keep middle-class families in urban communities and retain their support for public schools.[60] Ironically, the very success of this strategy sometimes gives birth to attacks on desegregation policies. The intense parental demand for access to excellent magnets originally created to produce integration can lead to struggles over their admissions methods. Since an important part of the attraction of these schools is that they are stably integrated, successful attacks abetted by conservative courts following an intensely individualist theory of opportunity can kill the goose that laid the golden egg. Stable integration is a clearly positive attribute for most families but rarely happens by accident, and removal of the controls that create and maintain it in schools usually means that no one can have what a great many want.

But integration theory goes beyond the creation of a diverse student body, also emphasizing the importance of an integrated faculty, multicultural curriculum, and equal-status treatment in all aspects of school operation. It is about producing stably integrated and equitable institutions in a segregated and unequal society and sees schools as critical not only for educational opportunity but in preparing young people to effectively live, work, and be citizens in a highly diverse society.[61] In a society with no racial majority, these skills will be important for white children also.[62] This is a theory of deep institutional change.

Integration theory also includes elements of competition, but of a different kind than those in market theory. The basic idea is that students learn from one another, that contact and competition with high-achieving students stimulate learning, and that teachers operate at a higher level when there are more well-prepared students in a class. Educators in general prefer to teach well-prepared groups of students in well-regarded and well-supported schools.[63] Accountability

systems, which tend to brand as failures and sanction a great many schools serving minority and poor communities, only speed the departure of the teachers
who can find jobs elsewhere.[64] Schools with a critical mass of privileged students
offer more competitive courses and tend to provide a clear, default path to college. If desegregation is implemented well, the impacts on children's lives can be
substantial and they can face and learn to deal with the kind of experiences they
will encounter in today's diverse colleges.

Integregation theory is much more, of course, than an educational reform
strategy, though it is that as well. It has a broader social goal: to change the beliefs
sustaining prejudice and discrimination and to help both students of color and
white students function more effectively and fairly in a diverse society, most
of whose children will not be white. This theory is strongly connected to the
creation and maintenance of diverse neighborhoods, since racial change and
resegegation are much more likely in communities with segregated or resegregating schools than in communities with good integrated schools. Choice, with
appropriate regulations, is a way to attain these diverse neighborhoods.

Is Integration Impossible? The White Flight Hypothesis

Some argue that integration is attractive in theory but impossible to achieve in
reality because whites will simply leave the school district and a desegregation
plan will just accelerate their departure. This argument has its source in James
Coleman, Sara Kelly, and John Moore's famous 1975 study of white flight, which
triggered a tidal wave of research and instantly became part of court battles
across the country.[65] It followed the first years of mandatory urban desegregation,
in the early 1970s, when courts suddenly implemented massive involuntary reas-
signments of students and teachers in almost all of the cities in the South and several big northern cities. The research claiming large effects was almost exclusively
about black-white settings that were in the early stages of kinds of plans that
have not been implemented for more than three decades. Most of this research is
unrelated to situations of choice-based desegregation plans in multiracial cities.

The agreed-upon results of many studies include the following:[66] (1) White
flight, which basically reflects housing patterns, exists since it began long before
there was desegregation and continues after desegregation efforts end, and exists
in places where that were never desegregated. It began in earnest with the construction of massive suburban development marketed only to whites. (2) It usually accelerates significantly for a time at the beginning of new mandatory plans
limited to central cities. (3) The highest and most stable desegregation comes
in metropolitan-wide mandatory plans. We also know that whites, Asians, and
middle-class African Americans and Latinos have all relocated to suburbs in
most metropolitan areas, leading to the resegregation of city neighborhoods and
schools, and that whites still have a tendency to move away from concentrations

of black students.[67] Such trends are ongoing in growing sectors of suburban rings, which are experiencing soaring nonwhite enrollment growth and typically have no desegregation plans.

The truth is that diverse neighborhood schools have had a tendency toward resegregation for generations, since the housing market offers what many whites see as a choice only between resegregating schools and overwhelmingly white middle-class schools in more segregated outlying white areas. Both conditions and attitudes are changing, however. Black-white residential segregation has been declining for at least two decades, and there are now multiracial communities in which the largest minority group is Latino.[68] The question is whether we can slow the transitions from diverse to segregated communities and increase the number of communities with lasting integration. Many communities now use magnet schools, the nation's largest system of choice, as part of an effort to hold and expand white, Asian, and middle-class enrollment in diverse schools.

Ironically, research clearly shows that the most dramatic school desegregation plans—those which included central cities and their suburban rings and produced the deepest and longest-lasting desegregation by integrating all the schools, many for a third of a century—were often well accepted by locals (see chapter 11) and had a clear tendency to increase stable residential desegregation.[69] In other words, individual choice in the face of a segregated and discriminatory housing market produces widespread instability and resegregation, denying even many middle-class minorities the opportunity to attend good schools, while drastic desegregation mandates create more positive school and housing conditions, lasting neighborhood integration, and neighborhood economic and social desirability. Unfortunately, the courts have severely undermined the possibility of implementing the most successful solutions, which is why educators and civil rights groups are struggling to figure out what forms of choice plans will work today to guarantee substantial and lasting diversity in school enrollments, in spite of all the limits inherent in boundaries, districts, and the inability to directly consider individual students' race. Color-blind choice plans permit whites to transfer out of integrated communities and into more-segregated white communities, speeding white flight just like the urban open-enrollment plans of the 1960s (see chapter 1). There are no easy or comprehensive solutions available within the existing constraints, but doing nothing is no solution. And some forms of choice do provide important educational and social alternatives.

Markets and Integration: The Dimensions of Difference

In the market theory, equality comes simply from giving students in weak public schools a choice to go to some school (in practice, usually a segregated charter school) that is outside their local public school system and is governed differently. The governance structure is expected to produce the educational benefit.

In integregation theory, the idea is, as much as possible, to give students from segregated, high-poverty neighborhoods access to predominantly white and Asian schools, which, research shows, are likely to be better in crucial respects.[70] In the market theory, choice itself is the educational treatment. In the integration theory, choice is one strategy to decrease conflict and increase voluntary participation in programs that intentionally cross lines of race and class to foster successful integration. Its goals are community-wide.

Although these two theories have fundamentally different philosophic and intellectual roots, they both contain testable assumptions about the nature of social and educational realities. The market theory derives from economic theory's ideal type of markets and basically believes that people operate as autonomous individuals and that the sum of individual choices will provide better opportunities for all; therefore, no systemic limitations on choice are needed to produce good outcomes. The integration theory is strongly rooted in sociology and law and is based on a philosophy that recognizes that the social order is highly stratified and discriminatory on the basis of race and ethnicity and that the effects of a long history of overt discrimination are still powerful. It sees individuals as deeply limited by isolation and unequal knowledge and views positive governmental action to use choice with integration requirements as a key part of a solution.

Three decades ago there was a profound shift from following the integration theory to following the market theory in formulating choice policy and programs. We can now examine the evidence on the assumptions and outcomes of each theory to determine the best way to use choice to accomplish the goal affirmed by both sets of advocates—improving the education of disadvantaged students in obviously unequal schools. Though both theories support programs called school choice, they rest on divergent and incompatible assumptions.

CONCLUSION

Often choice is described as something that is simple or clear, but it can have profoundly different meanings and results. It seems like such an easy-to-understand and positive concept, but the vast differences among theories of choice are often lost in superficial claims.

The currently dominant market choice theory is based on unexamined assumptions derived from a simplified version of an economic model that does not exist in any society. Such a theory can raise important propositions, but only good research can evaluate whether they are true and whether the theory works. Market theory can be understood largely as a subset of the belief in unregulated markets and the ideology that any institution that is not subject to public control is likely to be better by its very nature than one that is. It follows that creating more nonpublic schools will somehow transform all educational outcomes, without regard to what programs they implement. The fact that many interests and leaders powerfully support these beliefs does not make them true.

Policy discussions in recent decades have largely forgotten integration theory, though it was developed as the result of experience with different kinds of choice in many hundreds of school districts. But the fact that something is ignored for a time does not make it untrue.

Exploring the validity of differing assumptions about choice is central to this book. Its analysis accepts the claim that the schools available to many students in segregated urban settings are shamefully inadequate and that choice mechanisms must be part of the solution. We created this book in good measure out of concern that the movement from the integration theory to the market theory of choice happened without an adequate examination of either their premises or their results. This book is not antichoice and does not see either of these approaches as a panacea for educational equality. It does, however, critically examine the evidence in a number of contemporary contexts and in its final chapter offers a policy framework on the basis of what it sees as the most compelling evidence about using choice to increase school equity.

Choice is meant to disrupt the status quo and is defended as a great creator of opportunity and positive change, but fundamentally different theories and philosophies are at war under its broad umbrella. Praising choice in abstract terms is affirming something that has many contradictory realities and consequences without thinking through the many different kinds of processes that can either open opportunity or increase stratification. Not all choice mechanisms are good. Some may cause additional harm. Depending on the nature of the choice offered and the validity of the assumptions on which it rests, something may sound good but turn out to be deeply disappointing, or what looks like a simple pathway to opportunity may turn out to be a complex path with many turns and dangers but also with the possibility of real gains. Much of the discussion of choice issues has been painfully shallow, full of vague concepts and unsupported claims. By the end of this book we hope that people will know what they are talking about when they speak of educational choices, and what assumptions underlie their arguments. We hope that thoughtful consideration of the studies in the chapters that follow and a critical understanding of often unexamined theories about how choice can help or harm profoundly excluded families will enrich the debate. We assume that both sides in this debate are sincere in their desire to help the millions of children who do not have a fair chance at education—which is often their only chance for social mobility—and hope that this book can help us move from good intentions to better results.

NOTES

1. Warner, "Why Are the Rich So Interested in Public-School Reform?"; Riley, "'We're in the Venture Philanthrophy Business.'"

2. Kozol, *The Shame of the Nation: The Restoration of Apartheid Schooling in America.*

3. Peterson, "School Choice: A Report Card."

4. Welter, *Popular Education and Democratic Thought in America.*

5. Hochschild and Scovronick, *The American Dream and the Public Schools.*

6. Weinberg, *A Chance to Learn: A History of Race and Education in the United States.*

7. *Pierce v. Society of Sisters of the Holy Names of Jesus and Mary,* at 534–35.

8. *Zelman v. Simmons-Harris*; Anrig, "An Idea Whose Time Has Gone: Conservatives Abandon Their Support for School Vouchers."

9. Weiss, ed., American Education and the European Immigrant: 1840–1940; Lieberson, *A Piece of the Pie: Blacks and White Immigrants since 1880.*

10. Folger and Nam, *Education of the American Population,* 152–55.

11. *Swann v. Charlotte-Mecklenburg.*

12. *Milliken v. Bradley.*

13. *Board of Education of Oklahoma City Public Schools v. Dowell.*

14. See, for example, Thernstrom and Thernstrom, *No Excuses: Closing the Racial Gap in Learning*; Carter, *No Excuses: Lessons from 21 High-Performing, High-Poverty Schools.*

15. Chubb and Moe, *Politics, Markets, and America's Schools.*

16. Ibid.

17. Smith, *An Inquiry into the Nature and Causes of the Wealth of Nations,* 194.

18. He himself was appointed a customs official in Edinburgh at the age of fifty-five. Ibid., vi.

19. Friedman Foundation for Educational Choice, "Milton Friedman on Vouchers."

20. Ibid.

21. Ibid.

22. Godwin and Kemerer, *School Choice Tradeoffs: Liberty, Equity and Diversity,* 232–34.

23. Friedman, who lived in one of the most hypersegregated housing markets, Chicago's South Side, ignored these markets that treated families of different races with the same incomes in extremely unequal ways. Friedman Foundation for Educational Choice, "Milton Friedman on Vouchers."

24. Critics pointed out, for example, that there were inadequate measures for key variables and that, at best, the public-private difference explained a very small part of the variance in test scores. Fundamental difficulties in the comparisons include a serious problem of selection bias: by their nature, choosing a different school and persisting in transferring a child distinguish parents who do these things from those who do not, whether or not they have the same income and race. There are often unmeasured but important differences in motivation, organization, etc., among parents who make choices in a complex system, and those differences are likely to impact student achievement. Further, schools of choice exercise varying types of control in selecting their students and dropping those who do not conform, something that is far less possible in regular public schools, and they are less likely to have to deal with students and teachers who don't want to be there. In any case, and even ignoring these unmeasured differences, a raging debate over two decades has produced no compelling evidence of any academic achievement benefits of private schools. Henig, *Rethinking School Choice: The Limits of the Market Metaphor*; Cookson, *School Choice: The Struggle for the Soul of American Education.*

25. See, e.g., Bill Gates, remarks at the National Charter Schools Conference; Walton Family Foundation, "Education Reform: Overview."

26. Ritholtz and Task, *Bailout Nation: How Greed and Easy Money Corrupted Wall Street and Shook the World Economy*.

27. Madison, Jay, and Hamilton, *Federalist Papers* nos. 10 and 48.

28. See, for example, Solochek, "Critics Say Florida Lawmakers Are Too Cozy with Charter Schools."

29. The Center for Responsive Politics reports that a number of charter schools and related organizations are formally registered as federal lobbies. See the search result at www.opensecrets.org/lobby/lookup.php?type=c&q=charter+school (accessed December 21, 2011).

30. Ripley and Franklin, *Congress, the Bureaucracy, and Public Policy*; ibid., "Interest Groups and the Policy Making Process: Sources of Countervailing Power in America."

31. See, for example, Kimberley, "Hedge Fund–Funded Charter School Lobby Buys Elections, Destroys Education."

32. Madison, Jay, and Hamilton, *Federalist Paper* no. 51.

33. Associated Press, "State Orders Detroit to Close Half Its Schools."

34. Galatzan, "A Wave of Affiliated Charters: What Does It Mean?"

35. Koretz, *Measuring Up: What Educational Testing Really Tells Us*.

36. Federal Interagency Forum on Child and Family Statistics, "Language Spoken at Home and Difficulty Speaking English."

37. Sunderman, Kim, and Orfield, *NCLB Meets School Realities: Lessons from the Field*, 39–56.

38. Rury and Saatcioglu, "Suburban Advantage: Opportunity Hoarding and Secondary Attainment in the Postwar Metropolitan North."

39. Ihlanfeldt, "Exclusionary Land-Use Regulations within Suburban Communities: A Review of the Evidence and Policy Prescriptions."

40. Pfeiffer, *The Opportunity Illusion: Subsidized Housing and Failing Schools in California*.

41. Wells et al., *Both Sides Now: The Story of Desegregation's Graduates*.

42. Clotfelter, *After Brown: The Rise and Retreat of School Desegregation*.

43. Fuller, Elmore, and Orfield, eds., *Who Chooses? Who Loses?: Culture, Institutions, and the Unequal Effects of School Choice*; see also chapters 10 and 11.

44. Clotfelter, *After Brown*; Holme, "Buying Homes, Buying Schools: School Choice and the Social Construction of School Quality"; Charles, "Can We Live Together? Racial Preferences and Neighborhood Outcomes."

45. Reardon and Yun, "Integrating Neighborhoods, Segregating Schools."

46. Daniel Kahneman, for example, received the Nobel Prize in Economics in 2002. His work includes studies on the limits of rationality in choice, such as Kahneman and Tversky, eds., *Choices, Values and Frames*.

47. Schelling, *Micromotives and Macrobehavior*.

48. Massey and Denton, *American Apartheid: Segregation and the Making of the Underclass*; Bobo, Schuman, and Steeh, "Changing Racial Attitudes toward Residential Integration."

49. Goldring and Smrekar, "Magnet Schools: Reform and Race in Urban Education," 13–15.

50. This goal was reported in 1966 in Coleman et al., *Equality of Educational Opportunity*, and in scores of subsequent studies, e.g., Schofield, "Review of Research on School Desegregation's Impact on Elementary and Secondary School Students"; Rumberger and Palardy, "Does Resegregation Matter?: The Impact of Social Composition on Academic Achievement in Southern High Schools."

51. Pettigrew and Tropp, *When Groups Meet: The Dynamics of Intergroup Contact*.

52. Frankenberg and Orfield, eds., *Lessons in Integration: Realizing the Promise of Racial Diversity in American Schools*.

53. The Omnibus Budget Reconciliation Act of 1981 eliminated the ESAA, which often funded

Robert Slavin's extensively documented Student Team Learning program. See G. Orfield, *Congressional Power;* Slavin, *Student Team Learning: A Practical Guide to Cooperative Learning.*

54. *Board of Education of Oklahoma City Public Schools v. Dowell; Parents Involved in Community Schools v. Seattle School District No. 1.*

55. *Parents Involved,* at 788–89 (Justice Kennedy concurring). See also chapter 1.

56. Coleman et al., *Equality of Educational Opportunity;* Linn and Welner, eds., *Race-Conscious Policies for Assigning Students to Schools: Social Science Research and the Supreme Court Cases;* Brief Amicus Curiae of the 553 Social Scientists in Support of Respondents in *Parents Involved in Community Schools v. Seattle School District No. 1 et al.* and *Crystal D. Meredith v. Jefferson County Board of Education et al.;* Mickelson, "Twenty-First Century Social Science Research on School Diversity and Educational Outcomes."

57. Rumberger and Palardy, "Does Segregation Still Matter? The Impact of Social Composition on Academic Achievement in High School."

58. Bowles and Gintis, *Schooling in Capitalist America: Education Reform and the Contradictions of Economic Life.*

59. Wells and Crain, "Perpetuation Theory and the Long-Term Effects of School Desegregation"; Granovetter, *The Strength of Weak Ties.*

60. The Supreme Court discussed these issues as the basis for upholding affirmative action in the context of higher education in its 2003 decision in *Grutter v. Bollinger;* see also G. Orfield and Kurlaender, eds., *Diversity Challenged: Evidence on the Impact of Affirmative Action,* 111–219.

61. Frankenberg, "America's Diverse, Racially Changing Schools and Their Teachers."

62. Yen, "Census Shows Whites Lose US Majority among Babies."

63. Sunderman, Kim, and Orfield, *NCLB Meets School Realities,* 81–104.

64. Wells and Crain, "Perpetuation Theory and the Long-Term Effects of School Desegregation"; G. Orfield and Kurlaender, eds., *Diversity Challenged;* G. Orfield and Lee, *Why Segregation Matters: Poverty and Educational Inequality;* G. Orfield and Reardon, "Race, Poverty, and Inequality."

65. Coleman, Kelly, and Moore, *Trends in School Segregation, 1968–1973.* A number of scholars at a symposium that Coleman attended soon after this book's publication challenged its claims. See Orfield, *Symposium on School Desegregation and White Flight.*

66. See, e.g., Orfield, G., "Segregated Housing and School Resegregation," 314–18.

67. Frankenberg and Orfield, eds., *The Resegregation of Suburban Schools: A Hidden Crisis in American Education;* Clotfelter, *After Brown.*

68. Roberts, "Segregation Curtailed in U.S. Cities, Study Finds."

69. Siegel-Hawley, "City Lines, County Lines, Color Lines: An Analysis of School and Housing Segregation in Four Southern Metropolitan Areas, 1990–2010."

70. Orfield and Lee, *Why Segregation Matters.*

PART TWO

School Districts' Use of Choice to Further Diversity

3

The Promise of Choice

Berkeley's Innovative Integration Plan

Erica Frankenberg

Since the 1960s, the Berkeley Unified School District (BUSD) in Berkeley, California, has voluntarily committed to integrating its schools. It provided the first major test of a city struggling to find a successful integration strategy that would survive court challenges after the Supreme Court forbade many kinds of voluntary desegregation plans in 2007.[1] In contrast to many other districts, which either let their desegregation standards in choice plans lapse or tried to substitute desegregation based only on socioeconomic status, which has typically not produced a high level of racial desegregation, Berkeley invented a method that used a sophisticated analysis of neighborhood characteristics, including race, for student assignment and successfully defended it in California's courts. Berkeley's experience suggests a possible route for combining choice and integration in many school districts.[2]

Now on its third major integration plan guiding student assignments, Berkeley has maintained a commitment to diverse schools, even as legal options and political considerations around school integration have shifted and the district's population has changed. Its current student assignment plan is a controlled choice plan. It seeks to provide parental choice while allowing the district to manage the choices in a way that furthers its goal of diversity. Educational choice has proliferated as a way of giving parents more input into where their children attend school and, as a result, of generating support for public education.[3] Proponents have suggested that an additional benefit of controlled choice plans is that they cause schools that are chosen by fewer families to seek to improve.[4]

Berkeley is well known for its liberal, multiracial population, yet it is home to neighborhoods that are deeply segregated by race/ethnicity and socioeconomic status. Despite this, the city's public schools each reflect the district's multiracial student population, thanks to the district's innovative integration plan, adopted in 2004, which centers on a unique, multifaceted conceptualization of neighborhood diversity. This plan sought to provide equitable schooling choices for families and to integrate the district's eleven elementary schools by race, household income, and family educational background. As the district implemented the plan, it adopted procedures to ensure that its choice-based system did not advantage any group of families in the district while actively promoting school equity to make all schools attractive choices.

For four decades, BUSD has striven to integrate its schools in the absence of consent decrees or court orders requiring desegregation. Its success is particularly notable given its location in an area of Northern California that includes San Francisco and San Jose, two districts with expired consent decree desegregation plans, high segregation, and wavering commitments to furthering race-conscious desegregation.[5] Unlike these and other districts across the nation that have struggled and resisted complying with state and federal court orders, Berkeley chose integration. Beginning in 1968, under the leadership of Superintendent Neil Sullivan, it began voluntarily pursuing mandated school integration to mitigate the city's segregated housing patterns, which produced racially segregated schools: predominantly African American/nonwhite and low income on the west side of the city and white and affluent on the east side, patterns that continue to this day.

Berkeley is an important case study because of its multiracial diversity and the deep racial polarization of its neighborhoods, two conditions that pose unique challenges for school integration. Since the 1960s, diversity in BUSD has become more complex with the increase of nonblack students of color. As the country grows more racially diverse and both racial and economic segregation continue to deepen, understanding BUSD's student assignment plan is important for communities whose districts may be transitioning from being primarily biracial to having three or more racial or ethnic groups of students.

THE BERKELEY UNIFIED SCHOOL DISTRICT

The Berkeley Unified School District is coterminous with Berkeley's city boundaries. It currently serves approximately nine thousand students in eleven elementary schools, three middle schools, one comprehensive high school, and one small continuation high school; there are no charter schools. The district enjoys extensive financial support from the citizens of Berkeley. For several decades, BUSD has had relatively stable enrollment, educating between eight and ten thousand students per year. The district has considerable economic, linguistic, and academic diversity; more than 40% of students receive free or reduced-price lunch, and one-eighth are classified as Limited English Proficient. The district has long-standing racial/ethnic gaps in achievement and dropout rates.

Berkeley is a midsize city with just over one hundred thousand residents. It is relatively compact, only 10.5 square miles, which allows for the easy transport of students from anywhere within the district for desegregation purposes, and is home to the University of California's Berkeley campus, one of the leading public universities in the country. The university enrolls nearly thirty-five thousand undergraduate and graduate students and has a major influence on the city. The San Francisco Bay Area is one of the nation's most expensive housing markets, and housing prices in Berkeley reflect this, but as in many university cities, more than half of its available housing units are renter occupied, and the vast majority of rental units are subject to the city's rent stabilization ordinance.[6]

City Demographics

Berkeley has grown increasingly diverse since its first desegregation efforts in the late 1960s. In particular, there has been an increase in the percentage of Asian, Hispanic, and multiracial residents. A majority of Berkeley residents remain non-Hispanic white, and the percentage of white residents has slightly increased since 2000. Asians constitute the second-largest group, at nearly 18%, likely due to the large Asian population at UC Berkeley. Latinos are another 10% of the population. The Asian and Latino populations have steadily grown in size and proportion since 1970, while the number of non-Hispanic blacks has fallen precipitously since 1990 as affluent blacks have moved out to diverse suburbs and increasing housing costs have squeezed out working-class blacks. African Americans were nearly one-quarter of all residents in 1970 but constituted just over 10% of the population in 2007.

As one would expect in a city with a highly selective and prestigious university, Berkeley's residents, on the whole, are highly educated and wealthy, but vast differences exist among racial/ethnic groups. Nearly two-thirds of adults have college degrees or higher, and only 8% lack a high school diploma. However, just 40% of Latino and 20% of African American residents have at least bachelor's degree, and 4 in 10 black and Latino residents have a high school diploma or less. One-third of all Berkeley families have incomes of $100,000 or more, including nearly half of all white families (compared to just 8% of African American and 15% of Latino families). Only 12% of families with children live below the poverty line, though this figure is disproportionately higher for black and Latino families.

Residential Segregation

The residential segregation of Berkeley—and its relationship to racially isolated schools—is one of the reasons BUSD adopted its school desegregation plan during the 1960s. Although racial residential segregation in Berkeley declined between 1980 and 2000, for some groups it still remains high. In general, whites and Asians have become more integrated with one another, while blacks and Hispanics are largely separate from these groups.

In 2000, clear separation existed in Berkeley. White and Asian youth are concentrated on the east side (north and south of the university campus), and the northeast Berkeley Hills section is heavily white and affluent. African Americans and Latinos are largely concentrated on the west side and to the south, adjacent to Oakland. There is remarkably little overlap between block groups that have the highest concentrations of white/Asian and African American / Latino school-age residents.[7] Latinos and Asians are not as highly concentrated as blacks and whites. Neighborhoods with higher concentrations of high-income families are in northeast and, to a lesser extent, southeast Berkeley, both areas with concentrations of white students. Areas with lower median income include those immediately adjacent to the university, which may house students with little to no current income and few children, and the southwestern part of Berkeley bordering Oakland.

In other words, BUSD and the city of Berkeley are highly diverse and have maintained an unusual stability of diversity for four decades. But alongside this considerable racial/ethnic diversity is persistent and substantial residential segregation. The inequality in household income and educational attainment among different racial/ethnic groups necessitates a school integration plan to prevent schools from being segregated by race and class.

BERKELEY SCHOOL DESEGREGATION EFFORTS
IN A CHANGING CLIMATE

The current desegregation plan is the latest in a series of innovative efforts. In the 1960s, Berkeley became one of the first urban school districts to voluntarily desegregate its schools. While BUSD's first major desegregation effort involved mandatory student assignment, as did many plans of that era, its current plan incorporates a substantial use of family choice as well as important features to ensure that choice does not lead to segregation by race or socioeconomic status. The community's commitment to maintaining integrated schools despite neighborhood segregation has remained constant as the legal, demographic, and educational context have shifted.

In the mid-1960s, following complaints by the National Association for the Advancement of Colored People and a district report documenting de facto segregation, BUSD implemented a voluntary transfer program between paired elementary schools and redistricted its middle schools to promote racial integration. Then-superintendent Neil Sullivan and the school board led this effort, prompting a recall campaign targeting those who supported integration, but a sizable majority of voters sided with them, which further strengthened the district's resolve.[8] Over the next two years, 250 black elementary school students voluntarily bused to schools in East Berkeley. A subsequent task force noted that among the limitations of the plan was the fact that nonwhite students overwhelmingly bore the burden of busing.[9] After 1968, when the board implemented a new plan that had four attendance zones and paired predominantly white and predominantly black elementary schools, more than one-third of elementary students bused to schools.[10]

Controlled Choice

The district's commitment to school desegregation and mandatory assignment to elementary schools remained in place for decades. But by the early 1980s the racial imbalance had grown and many white families were opting out of the district because the grade configuration of the schools meant students had to transition to a new school four times between kindergarten and twelfth grade.[11] Finally, a 1992 bond measure that supported upgrading school facilities forced the district to reevaluate the capacities of all of its schools and who they were serving.[12]

Educational choice was growing in popularity across the country—as were magnet schools—as a possible avenue for "natural" desegregation through parental choice. Many Berkeley community members expressed concern over introducing a choice system to BUSD, noting the inequalities among residents in time and resources for making informed choices.[13] In late 1993, however, the school board voted to phase out the two-way mandatory busing plan and implement a controlled choice integration plan. The district recognized that schools needed to be strengthened to encourage families to choose outside their neighborhood.[14] The new plan divided the district into three elementary school zones (Northwest, Central, Southeast), each of which incorporated part of both the hills and the flats. The zones were created by mapping the entire city into 445 planning areas that are four to eight city blocks in size and geolocating student residential patterns by race/ethnicity. The goal of the plan was to give each elementary school a distribution of race/ethnicity (defined as white, black, and other) that reflected its zone's racial/ethnic distribution within plus or minus 5 percentage points. Families ranked up to three elementary schools within their zone, but the final decision resided with the district, which considered choice, sibling, and zone priorities as well as the race/ethnicity of individual students. In the first round of assignments, for the 1995–96 academic year, nearly 90% of families received their first choice.[15]

The Current BUSD Student Assignment Plan

In 2000, the school district explored revising its student assignment policy to go beyond race/ethnicity and include measures of socioeconomic status. Noting that residential segregation within Berkeley remained entrenched, the district convened a Student Assignment Advisory Committee (SAAC) to explore diversifying schools through the use of neighborhood demographics including family income, home sale values, and the percentage of households headed by single females. Committee member, parent, and computer mapping specialist Bruce Wicinas, who had developed a customized software program to create the zones for the prior plan, facilitated the SAAC's new simulations, but the board did not act on its proposals. After a lawsuit challenging the controlled choice plan was filed, three former members of the SAAC resumed their efforts to refine the integration plan based on neighborhood demographics.

The new plan was similar to the existing plan in that it retained the three elementary school zones, the two middle school zones, and parental choice. It differed from the 1994 plan in one fundamental way: rather than considering the race/ethnicity of individual students, it took account of the racial/ethnic, economic, and educational diversity of each student's neighborhood so that schools reflected zone-wide diversity in these factors. The new plan did not receive universal support from the community; in fact, protestors stood outside the board meeting objecting to the dilution of race in student assignment.[16] However, the school board approved the policy change and put the new plan in place in the 2004–5 academic year. At the same time, it also restated the district's forty-year commitment to racial/ethnic desegregation and explained the need to consider parental education and household income in assignment to reduce racial and socioeconomic isolation in schools.[17]

A New Measure of Diversity.   The new plan assigns each of the 445 planning areas a "composite diversity category" of 1, 2, or 3. To calculate this, BUSD uses U.S. Census and district data, evenly weighing (1) household incomes; (2) the education attainment of adults aged twenty-five years and older; and (3) the percentage of elementary students of color. In general, planning areas designated as category 3 have low percentages of nonwhite elementary school students and higher than average household incomes and levels of education among adults. Category 1 planning areas are typically the opposite, and those in category 2 are, in general, in between. All students living in a particular planning area are assigned that area's diversity category regardless of their household's socioeconomic characteristics.

Choice Priorities.   Families are allowed to rank up to three schools and three Spanish dual-immersion and/or bilingual education programs for assignment. After placing all enrolled elementary students in the school they currently attend, the district prioritizes applicants as follows:

1. Berkeley residents who are siblings of any current student attending the school who will continue in attendance for the upcoming year
2. Berkeley residents living within the attendance zone
3. Berkeley residents living outside the attendance zone

These priorities apply to all applicants regardless of whether they are new to the district or are currently enrolled students requesting a transfer.[18] The district assigns students to dual-immersion and bilingual programs, then to general programs. BUSD's software considers students' diversity categories as it assigns them by priority category. The 2004 plan primarily applies to the elementary schools, although the same principles hold for assignment to Berkeley High School's four small schools and two programs.

The goal of the student assignment plan is for all grade levels at each elementary school to reflect (within 5–10 percentage points) the zone-wide distribution of diversity codes. The manager of the Admissions Office determines grade level capacities at each school and calculates each attendance zone's probable diversity category distribution based on multiyear averages of applicant pools and enrollment to estimate the proportion of students from each diversity code to be enrolled at each grade level at each school. Every zone has a different distribution of the three diversity codes; as such, the diversity category distribution at each school will vary depending on the zone it is in. In fall 2007, a total of 198 kindergartners enrolled in Northwest Zone schools. Of these, 52% lived in planning areas with composite diversity code 1, while 26% and 22% lived in planning areas that were coded 2 and 3, respectively. Each of the kindergarten classes at the three schools in the Northwest Zone reflected this distribution within 5–10 percentage points. The same was true for the schools located in the Central and Southeast Zones: the diversity of their per-class kindergarten enrollment was, in most cases, very similar to their zone-wide diversity.

DOES BUSD HAVE RACIALLY AND ECONOMICALLY INTEGRATED SCHOOLS?

Achieving racially and economically diverse schools is a two-part process for districts: they must attract and hold a diverse study body and distribute enrollment relatively evenly across schools. A choice plan relies, in part, on producing schools that are attractive to eligible students and their families, and schools that follow a desegregation policy based on choice must be able to attract a diverse range of students. Hence this chapter explores participation in public schools by Berkeley residents and assesses the racial and economic integration of BUSD schools.

There are a number of schooling options in Berkeley and its surrounding cities for local families to choose from, including traditional public schools, charter schools, private schools, and homeschooling. According to 2007 estimates, 77% of Berkeley residents enrolled in K–12 attend public schools, while 23% attend private schools, rates that have remained fairly consistent since 1990. Private school usage among Berkeley residents is higher than the 15% rate of the larger San Francisco metropolitan area. As of 2000, there were striking differences in the usage of public schools by race/ethnicity in Berkeley. In particular, 62% of non-Hispanic white students attended public schools, while more than 80% of Latino and more than 90% of black students did. This suggests that BUSD was not attracting white students at the rate of students of color in 2000. However, the majority of school-age residents from every racial/ethnic group in Berkeley report attending public schools.

Because the goal of Berkeley's plan is for each elementary school to achieve diversity (as measured by the diversity categories) that reflects zone-wide diversity, we assess whether its schools are (a) racially/ethnically diverse and (b) economically diverse. If all elementary schools were integrated, each would have similar racial and economic compositions within 5–10 percentage points of the composition of the district elementary school student population. Despite the neighborhood segregation described above, there is substantial diversity across the district's elementary schools in particular, to which the 2004 plan explicitly pertains.

The current Berkeley integration plan was implemented for the entering kindergarten class in 2004–5, so elementary schools in 2008–9 had one grade level of students who were admitted under the previous assignment plan. In general, BUSD's elementary schools appear integrated when using the 10 percentage point criteria. In 2008–9 there were no schools where Asians and whites deviated from their proportional share of students and just one where African Americans did so. There were two schools (both with Spanish dual-immersion programs) where Latinos varied more than 10 percentage points from their representation among all elementary school students (see table 3.1).

The number of schools where groups' representation differed from that among all elementary school students increased for all four groups using the stricter criteria of 5 percentage points. The white and Asian student populations differed by more than 5 percentage points in one school each from their percentage among all elementary students. By contrast, black and Latino student composition deviated from their share of elementary students in four and seven schools, respectively. Variation in Latino school level percentage is the largest, from one school with less than one-tenth of students who were Latino to another where Latinos constituted more than one-third of all students. All four racial/ethnic groups were within 5% of their share of the composition of the entire BUSD elementary student body in three of the eleven schools: Jefferson, Emerson, and Cragmont.[19]

There are similar patterns in economic integration. In 2007–8, 48% of elementary school students were receiving free or reduced-price lunches. Whereas the

TABLE 3.1 Deviation from system-wide racial and economic composition in BUSD
among elementary schools, 2008–9

	Asian/ Pacific Islander	Black	Latino	White	Low income
Percentage of elementary school students	7.6	19.4	21.5	30.4	48.0

Number of schools where representation
  deviates 10 percentage points or more from
  that in the district
	0	1	2	0	2

Number of schools where representation
  deviates 5 percentage points or more from
  that in the district
	1	4	7	1	6

NOTE: There are eleven elementary schools in BUSD. American Indians/Alaskan Natives are 0.3% of the district enrollment; 20.9% of respondents gave either multiple responses or no response (percentages sum to more than 100 because of rounding). The low-income percentage is from 2007–8.
SOURCE: California Department of Education Data Quest.

percentage of low-income students varied by 10 percentage points or more from all elementary school students in just two schools, that number increases to six when applying the 5 percentage point criterion. In one school nearly 60% of students were from low-income families, while in another that percentage was only 35%. Two of the three schools where all racial/ethnic groups were properly balanced were out of economic balance, having lower percentages of low-income students than the district did. BUSD's student assignment plan is not as effective in diversifying by socioeconomic status as it is in integrating most racial groups.

There is a rich diversity of students in BUSD's schools, demonstrating the district's attractiveness to Berkeley residents of all backgrounds. While integration varies by racial group, in general it is fairly high across the district. In elementary schools, less variation exists among white and Asian students, while black and Latino students are disproportionately enrolled in a few schools. These patterns of deviation from the system-wide averages have remained relatively constant over the past few years. Despite these disparities, it is a remarkable achievement to come relatively close to district averages using only choice mechanisms and non-individual measures of race and income.

There is more disparity between schools when examining student poverty than race/ethnicity. This might affect how parents perceive and choose schools. For example, they might not want to send their children to schools with particularly high numbers of low-income students. In choice-based systems, schools that are somewhat imbalanced may become more so over time.[20] These trends will be important to monitor to ensure that schools that differ from the system-wide average do not diverge further. Can BUSD's policies and procedures mitigate such stratifying effects?

IMPLEMENTING THE BUSD INTEGRATION PLAN: ENSURING THAT CHOICE DOESN'T STRATIFY

Berkeley's history of commitment to voluntary desegregation—in a metropolitan area that has witnessed considerable disagreement about court-ordered desegregation policies—has undoubtedly contributed to its current racial integration. A few key components of BUSD's plan help it maintain racially diverse schools.

First, the district has in place a series of practices, described below, to try to counteract the often stratifying effects of educational choice policies. The entirety of the current plan—not simply the criteria by which choices are granted—is important for creating and sustaining Berkeley's racial diversity. Second, the three zones that cut across the entire district remain identical to those of the prior plan, but an added layer of diversity codes distinguishes the 2004 plan from its predecessor.

The Mechanics of the Plan

An abundance of research has documented the unequal resources—including information, motivation, and resources—of families of different racial/ethnic groups and social classes as they engage in school choice. Whether navigating a system with multiple requirements, deadlines, and options or forming different choice sets, families engage seemingly neutral systems of school choice with different opportunities to learn about the available options.[21] If districts that offer school choice are unmindful of these differences, they run the risk of perpetuating the very inequities that the integration policy was designed to address. There are several ways BUSD proactively addresses disparities in participation and information dispersal. In addition to describing the mechanics of the plan, we will analyze the choices of and outcomes for the 659 families that participated in round 1 of the kindergarten student assignment process for 2008–9.[22]

Enrollment season begins in early fall each year, almost a year in advance of when the assignments take effect. In fall, the district reaches out to families to encourage them to participate in the choice system, learn about their options, and submit their school rankings by the round 1 assignment deadline, typically in February. All families new to the district and current elementary school students requesting a transfer must submit a Parental Preference Form, available in both English and Spanish, which asks about preschool experience, home language, highest parental education level, student ethnicity, and the current enrollment of any siblings in a BUSD elementary school. The form also describes the assignment system's priorities (e.g., sibling preference, in-zone schools, out-of-zone schools) and explains that transportation is provided for all elementary students to schools within their zone that are, as of fall 2009, more than 1.5 miles from their home.[23]

The BUSD Admissions Office works with the elementary schools to help inform families about all schools and programs. Families can determine their zone by visiting the office or the district's website, which includes extensive information on the integration plan. The office also organizes an annual Kindergarten Fair in early fall where each elementary school hosts a booth staffed by school administrators and parent volunteers and where staff from the district's central office share information on transportation and district-wide programs. Elementary schools are open for visitors two mornings per week during December and January. In addition, each hosts a Kindergarten Night in January when families can visit the school and meet teachers and principals. The manager of the Admissions Office also visits district-run preschools and local Head Start programs to notify the city's low-income families of the choice system and school visitation options.

This analysis of estimated family participation rates in the first round of the student assignment system for the 2008–9 school year suggests that the district could improve its efforts. The 659 applications it received for kindergarten placement by the first-round deadline accounted for approximately 76% of all kindergartners who enrolled in BUSD in fall 2008. African Americans and Latinos are less likely than whites to participate in round 1, although those who do participate are very likely to enroll. Of the fifty-eight self-identified African American students whose families participated in round 1, most (fifty-two) enrolled in BUSD that fall. However, according to official district enrollment statistics, there were 110 African American kindergartners enrolled in BUSD in fall 2008, suggesting that just 47% of African Americans participated in round 1. The figures for Latinos and whites are 69% and 91%, respectively. This may reflect mobility that is typical in a university city, or the need for improving the district's efforts to reach these families.

Families can rank up to three schools within their attendance zone. The vast majority of families choosing a kindergarten in round 1 listed three schools on their form, while less than 11% chose just one, and the majority chose a school within their zone as their first choice (see table 3.2). Although students receive a lower priority in assignment and no transportation to schools outside their attendance zone, 39% of families chose at least one school outside their zone, and 13% picked an out-of-zone school as their first choice.[24] There were distinct patterns by race/ethnicity and parental education. Similar proportions of whites and African Americans chose three schools on their Parental Preference Forms, but fewer Latinos did so. Likewise, families with lower educational attainment were more likely than families with more education to list fewer than three schools. More than one-quarter of Latino families listed a school outside their zone as their first choice, as did 28% of parents with high school diplomas or less, even though doing so results in a lower-priority assignment. Both of these

TABLE 3.2 Requests for kindergarten made by families in round 1, 2008–9

	Number of Schools Requested				Other Requests	
					Spanish-English dual immersion	First-choice school outside home zone
	Three	Two	One	None		
Total	78.2%	9.7%	10.9%	1.2%	32.5%	13.4%
Race/ethnicity						
White	83.3	7.3	9.1	0.4	30.6	10.3
Latino	58.6	17.2	20.2	4.0	43.4	25.5
African American	84.5	6.9	8.6	0.0	32.8	21.2
Asian/Other	80.4	5.9	13.7	0.0	11.8	12.0
Multiracial	83.0	9.2	6.5	1.3	39.2	7.4
Highest education level within household						
College graduate or greater	81.9	7.1	9.9	1.1	32.0	10.8
Some college	79.8	13.9	6.3	0.0	34.2	16.9
High school graduate or less	65.4	16.1	14.8	3.7	35.8	28.4

NOTE: Percentages may sum to more than 100 because of rounding.

choices make it more likely that students will be assigned to a school they did not select. On the other hand, Latinos chose dual-immersion schools at the highest rate among all racial/ethnic groups, which is not surprising in a state that has eliminated most other forms of bilingual education.

Families are notified of their assignments by early March. For the 2008–9 year, 76% received their first-choice school or dual-immersion program, 8% received their second choice, 9% received their third choice, and 7% were assigned to a school they did not choose. The district's goal is to assign students whose choices cannot be accommodated to a school within their zone. It requires students to register at their assigned school within one month, during which time families can file a hardship appeal or request their children to be wait-listed at an unlimited number of schools.

The district's practice of making phone calls to families that have not yet reserved their seats after round 1 of assignments helps to reach parents who may not have received the initial letter of assignment for various reasons, including mobility. Offered spaces are taken back if families do not secure their seats by the deadline. As spaces open up, students move off wait lists. The district holds a second lottery round of assignments in late May for families that missed round 1 or are requesting a transfer. The same instructions as those in round 1 apply regarding confirming or declining placement offers and joining school wait lists. In mid-August, district staff call incoming kindergarten families to confirm their enrollment and potentially move students off wait lists. Among all round 1 students who matriculated in fall 2008, 8% enrolled at a school different from the one they were initially assigned to.

The district has several small but significant additional practices to ensure that the plan's implementation meets its diversity goals. First, it makes adjustments to capacities by setting aside a small fraction of seats (in 2008 less than 10% of the total) in some schools or programs. The manager of the Admissions Office determines if this is necessary before conducting round 1 by comparing the diversity code distribution of each grade level–specific program and school applicant pool with the historical diversity code distribution of the school's zone. If, for example, a diversity category is significantly underrepresented among the applicant pool of some grade level of a school in comparison with the estimated zone-wide diversity target, the manager will accordingly adjust round 1 capacities for that school and level, using the set-aside seats. This also assists the district in balancing the student population.

The management of wait lists is also crucial. Families may request their children to be wait-listed for an unlimited number of schools and programs other than the one they were assigned to. As spaces become available, the Admissions Office places students into schools according to both the set of priority categories it uses during round 1 and the effect on schools' diversity, rather than managing the wait lists on a first come, first served basis, which might favor more advantaged families that have the flexibility and resources to comply with requirements that may involve visiting the school district or standing in long lines. This is another practice that advances the district's diversity goals by recognizing potentially unequal opportunities.

Promoting School-Site Equity

One of BUSD's integration goals is promoting school-site equity, partially to ensure equal opportunity for all students but also to demonstrate to families that their child will get a good education even if their first choice cannot be satisfied. In so doing, the district explicitly links school-site equity to a successful choice system. Moreover, although the student assignment plan is based on choice, the district does not encourage its elementary schools to compete with one another. Families, however, approach school choice with many factors in mind beyond a general program of study, including extracurricular offerings, test scores, building facilities, and school and class size.[25]

Indicators of school-site equity are observable across BUSD: for instance, all elementary schools have libraries and fee-based after-school care and enrichment classes. Perhaps particularly important for low-income families, the district has a universal breakfast program for all students regardless of household income. Average class size appears similar across all schools.

One of the most important resources a school has is its teaching force. Whereas most research concludes that teachers tend to leave schools with higher percentages of students of color and that such segregated minority schools have more novice teachers, our analysis shows that BUSD teacher distribution does not reflect such patterns.[26] The elementary school with the lowest percentage of white students (John Muir) had the highest average amount of teaching experience and was one of two schools without any novice teachers. By contrast, some of the elementary schools with the highest percentages of white students had higher percentages of novice teachers. It is also remarkable to see the extent of teacher stability given the San Francisco Bay Area's expensive housing market. Other research has shown that teachers are far more likely to remain in stably integrated schools, such as those fostered by the Berkeley plan, than in resegregated schools.[27]

Racial diversity of teachers is another important component of the district's plan and has long been part of desegregation efforts in districts across the country.[28] Our analysis of faculty diversity suggests that while there is considerable variation across BUSD schools (elementary schools range from 47% to nearly 80% of teachers who are white), there does not seem to be a particularly strong relationship between the percentage of white students and the percentage of white teachers, as is often the case elsewhere.[29] Of the four elementary schools with the highest shares of white teachers, two had the lowest percentages of white students, while the other two had the highest percentages of white students. On this important measure, at least, there is evidence of BUSD's equity across school sites.

At the same time, differences across school sites exist that could influence choice and the decision to matriculate. First, there are variations in building facilities despite the district's commitment to equity among facilities. Second, some schools are smaller than others, with little room for expansion given the city's density. Finally, test scores on California's school accountability measure, the Academic Performance Index, vary across schools.

Are Berkeley Families Convinced That All Schools Are Equal?

For any controlled choice plan to succeed, all schools must be regarded as good options so that students will matriculate into the school district even if they do not receive their first choice and so that there is demand for all schools. To assess these things, we must examine choice and matriculation patterns by school, including matriculation rates by choice received. If all schools are regarded as good, we expect to find few if any that are over- or underchosen by families within their zones, and similar matriculation rates across schools and families of different racial/ethnic and parental educational backgrounds regardless of choice received. We used the diversity distributions of fall 2007 kindergarten enrollment for this analysis.

TABLE 3.3 Berkeley elementary school seats, first-choice requests,
and matriculation rates for round 1 of kindergarten placement, 2008–9

	Number of kindergarten seats	Number of first-choice requests from zone	Ratio of seats to requests	Share of first-choice requests from zone (%)	Matriculation rate of assigned students (%)
Northwest Zone					
Jefferson	40	73	1.8	34	86.0
Rosa Parks	40	40	1.0	19	66.0
Thousand Oaks	60	78	1.3	36	88.7
Central Zone					
Cragmont	60	92	1.5	37	81.0
Oxford	60	55	0.9	22	87.9
Berkeley Arts Magnet	60	22	0.4	9	65.1
Washington	60	32	0.5	13	62.7
Southeast Zone					
Malcolm X	60	62	1.0	34	97.0
John Muir	40	24	0.6	13	75.9
Emerson	40	60	1.5	32	78.4
LeConte	20	23	1.2	12	64.0

Schools that are overchosen receive a number of requests from at least two diversity code categories of applicants that are overrepresented in comparison with their zone diversity distribution targets. Each zone has at least one under-chosen school, as measured by the first-choice requests it receives from families in its zone. These schools also typically have lower matriculation rates among students who were assigned to them (see table 3.3). Of the three Northwest Zone schools, one (Rosa Parks) is undersubscribed: it received just 19% of the first-choice requests from zone families, and it was underchosen by families in two out of three diversity codes; its matriculation rate was also lower than those of the other two schools in the zone. The Central Zone has four schools, two of which combined (Berkeley Arts Magnet and Washington) received just 22% of first-choice requests from Central Zone families; these two schools also had lower matriculation rates than the other two Central Zone schools (Cragmont and Oxford). Likewise, the Southeast Zone has four schools, two schools of which combined (John Muir and LeConte) received just 25% of first-choice requests from families in that zone, but only LeConte had comparatively low matriculation rates. In contrast, while both Emerson and Malcolm X account for 66% of all first-choice requests of Southeast Zone families, Malcolm X received most of its requests from families living in diversity code 1 planning areas and fewer from diversity codes 2 and 3 than the district's goals required.

As explained above, the majority of families who participated in round 1 received their first-choice school or dual-immersion program (76%), while 7% were assigned to a school they did not choose. There was slight variation in choice outcomes by race/ethnicity and parental education, with the percentages of whites and families headed by parents with college degrees or higher receiving their first choice more similar to the overall total (74% and 75%, respectively). In contrast, Latinos (87%), African Americans (81%), and families whose parents had high school diplomas or less (79%) were more likely to receive their first choice.[30]

Choice received is related to matriculation into the district, but this too varies by race/ethnicity. The vast majority of students matriculate into the district: 84% of those from families that received their first choice compared with 67% of those from families that did not. Latinos and African Americans were more likely to matriculate than whites regardless of choice received. Considering the vast socio-economic differences between whites, Latinos, and African Americans in Berkeley, these results are not surprising. The generally higher incomes of whites afford them alternatives to public schools. However, the majority of whites and families headed by college-educated adults did matriculate regardless of choice received.

In brief, there is mixed evidence that BUSD has convinced its resident families that all elementary schools in the district are equal. Some schools are clearly overchosen, while some are underchosen, with corresponding matriculation rates among those who are assigned to them. Likewise, the children of families that do not receive their first choice are less likely to matriculate into the district than those of families that do receive their first choice, yet the fact that the majority of all groups matriculate is positive. This plan creates a powerful incentive to improve underchosen schools.

The Aftermath of Parents Involved: Combining Choice with Zones

One tool that has been used for decades to assign students to schools—for both diversity and other purposes—is attendance zones. In desegregation plans, zones are drawn to encompass a mix of races/ethnicities. In its 1971 *Swann* decision, the U.S. Supreme Court suggested that school districts should use noncontiguous zones, combining two areas of a district that are not geographically proximate, to desegregate.[31] In *Parents Involved in Community Schools,* it also affirmed the use of attendance zones in both the court-ordered and the voluntary integration plans to promote racial diversity in Louisville, Kentucky. This decision did, however, prohibit certain uses of individual students' race to determine whether their choice of school would be granted.[32]

Berkeley's plan incorporates geography at two levels. It creates small planning areas and assigns a diversity code to each that applies to all the students within. In addition, it divides the district into three zones, each containing a handful of schools. In assigning students to schools, the plan first considers zone residence, then diversity code. Thus, living within the zone of a school provides an advantage in getting assigned to that school.

The 2004 plan retained the three zones drawn for the previous plan. In determining those zones, the district had sought to evenly divide the existing capacity in the elementary schools and the size of the population and to reflect Berkeley's racial composition. Significant residential segregation and the challenge of working around the UC Berkeley campus on the district's east side complicated this task. Eventually, the district designed three roughly equivalent zones. In addition to the logistical challenges, political pressures often accompany rezoning, which is perhaps why they have not been revised. Carrying them over from the previous plan also meant less change for the district and its families. In its description of the 2004 plan, BUSD said that it will monitor the boundaries to make sure that population shifts do not create zones with unequal populations or school capacities.[33] As this book goes to press, there is another round of discussions about possbile modifications. Communities continue to change, and so must plans.

CONCLUSION

School districts voluntarily pursuing integration face demographic, legal (at both federal and state levels), and economic challenges. Berkeley's schools remain integrated through a voluntary choice system that recognizes the value of diversity, helps stabilize the community, and gives the great majority of residents good options. Other communities, including Louisville, Kentucky, looking to prevent resegregation have already replicated this model. Importantly, its choice-based integration policies have been successfully defended against legal challenges.

In 1996, California voters passed Proposition 209, which prohibits the discriminatory or preferential use of race and ethnicity in public schools, among other arenas. A 2003 lawsuit challenging BUSD's student assignment plan by alleging violation of Proposition 209 prompted the district to consider and ultimately adopt the new assignment plan in 2004 even though the court ruled in its favor. In 2006 the Pacific Legal Foundation sued BUSD over its voluntary desegregation plan, alleging that the use of race/ethnicity as one of three factors in calculating the composite diversity code of each residential planning area violated Proposition 209. In 2007 the trial court ruled in favor of the district. The California Appellate Court upheld this decision and ruled unanimously that the assignment policy did not violate Proposition 209 because "every student within a given neighborhood receives the same treatment, regardless of his or her individual race" and "regardless of whether his or her own personal attributes (household income and education levels, and race) match the general attributes of the planning area in which the student lives."[34] The California Supreme Court denied the petitioners' appeal on June 10, 2009.

This chapter documents the struggles of a medium-size school district with an issue it has been working on for forty years. Despite real challenges of racial/economic polarization in the community, Berkeley has figured out a set of policies that create diverse schools. The city's demographics have been more stable than those of much of the country during the past decade, including many districts with neighborhood schools. Its recent experience runs counter to people's expectation of white flight when an integration plan is implemented. The city's integration plan may even have helped stabilize the district's demographics despite a highly expensive housing market.

An important aspect of BUSD's success has been understanding that to create integrated schools using a choice-based assignment policy, there must also be improved and equal educational options, which is also sound education policy. Policy discussions often frame better schools and integration as trade-offs, but the Berkeley experience suggests that they are not mutually exclusive. The denial of such framing is perhaps easier in a city like Berkeley, whose activist population has supported the district's decades-long commitment to far-reaching efforts to combat residential segregation that, without policy intervention, would lead to school segregation.

The Berkeley plan is not a panacea. Such plans address within-district segregation but not the extremely high levels of between-district segregation. Still, if they can stem residential transition and create stably diverse communities, perhaps over time the racial/ethnic differences across school district boundary lines will lessen. The residential mobility of a university city like Berkeley poses challenges for its plan, which is closely linked to residential demographics. Will the district adjust its plan after the 2010 Census data becomes available? In particular, analyzing how the three zones compare in terms of school-age population and capacity is important, since they have remained the same for fifteen years. Changing zone boundaries is often politically contentious and can be particularly difficult in districts experiencing significant population change as they try to maintain diversity.

The 2007 U.S. Supreme Court *Parents Involved* decision was portrayed as dramatically limiting or ending voluntary integration.[35] But the court acknowledged that there are compelling reasons to voluntarily pursue integration: to prevent racial isolation and to create diverse schools. Berkeley is an important example of how school districts can pursue these goals without relying on individual racial classifications. The facts reviewed above would suggest that BUSD's policies and procedures fall squarely within the parameters set by the courts. Smart, committed educators in Berkeley with an understanding of the law have adopted an integration plan that combines an assignment strategy using zones at two levels, educational reform to improve and equalize all schools so they are attractive to community residents, and outreach as a way to counter uneven resources among families.

NOTES

This chapter is drawn from a longer report about Berkeley. See Chavez and Frankenberg, "Integration Defended: Berkeley Unified's Strategy to Maintain School Diversity."

1. *Parents Involved in Community Schools v. Seattle School District No. 1.*

2. Jefferson County, Kentucky, was one district that followed Berkeley's lead. See chapter 11.

3. Harris, "Lost Learning, Forgotten Promises: A National Analysis of School Racial Segregation, Student Achievement, and 'Controlled Choice' Plans."

4. Willie and Alves, *Controlled Choice: A New Approach to School Desegregated Education and School Improvement*, 8–9.

5. Biegel, "Court-Mandated Education Reform: The San Francisco Experience and the Shaping of Educational Policy after *Seattle-Louisville* and *Brian Ho v. SFUSD*"; Koski and Oakes, "Equal Educational Opportunity, School Reform, and the Courts: A Study of the Desegregation Litigation in San Jose."

6. City of Berkeley Planning and Development Department, "City of Berkeley 2009–2014 Housing Element," ch. 5: "Objectives, Policies and Actions."

7. A census block group has between six hundred and three thousand residents and is smaller than a census tract, which is roughly equivalent to and more commonly known as a neighborhood.

8. For more on Superintendent Sullivan's efforts, see Sullivan and Stewart, *Now Is the Time: Integration in the Berkeley Schools.*

9. Berkeley Unified School District, *Integration of the Berkeley Elementary Schools: A Report to the Superintendent.*

10. Sullivan and Stewart, *Now Is the Time.*

11. Students went to schools in the hills or the central part of the district for grades K–3 and switched to schools in the south or the east of the district for grades 4–6.

12. Holtz, "Berkeley Hopes to Woo Whites to City Schools"; Slater, "The Integration Calypso."

13. See chapter 10 for how access to information about choice can be unequal.

14. Herscher, "Berkeley Plans to Overhaul Public Schools"; Olszewski, "Integration Phase-Out in Berkeley Schools: Neighborhoods Prepare for End of System."

15. Olszewski, "School Choice Delivers in Berkeley: Most Children Get Into the Campuses Parents Had Picked."

16. Hernandez, "Berkeley Schools Redraw Plan for Integration."

17. Berkeley Unified School District, "Information on Berkeley Unified's Student Assignment Plan: BUSD Student Assignment Plan/Policy."

18. Requests for interdistrict transfers are typically fulfilled in August just prior to the start of school. In 2007–8 there were 677 requests to transfer or remain a transfer student in the district, of which approximately 500 were granted. Unless otherwise noted, subsequent figures are from data provided by BUSD.

19. Each of these schools was the most highly chosen in its zone for the 2008–9 kindergarten cohort, suggesting that the plan is most successful at integrating students where demand is highest.

20. Amicus Curiae Brief of the American Psychological Association in Support of Respondents in *Parents Involved in Community Schools v. Seattle School District No. 1 et al.* and *Crystal D. Meredith v. Jefferson County Board of Education et al.*

21. Fuller, Elmore, and Orfield, eds., *Who Chooses? Who Loses?*; Hamilton and Guin, "Understanding How Families Choose Schools"; Bell, "Real Options: The Role of Choice Sets in the Selection of Schools."

22. California does not require kindergarten attendance. The California Teacher's Association

estimates that 80% of first graders attended kindergarten ("Why Isn't Kindergarten Mandatory in California?").

23. Bhattacharjee, "Budget Cuts Result in Reduced School Bus Services."

24. According to district staff, many families list the school that is closest to their home as their first choice even if it is not in their zone, which lowers their priority.

25. Hamilton and Guin, "Understanding How Families Choose Schools"; see also chapter 10.

26. Freeman, Scafidi, and Sjoquist, "Racial Segregation in Georgia Public Schools, 1994–2001: Trends, Causes and Impact on Teacher Quality"; Lankford, Loeb, and Wyckoff, "Teacher Sorting and the Plight of Urban Schools: A Descriptive Analysis"; Clotfelter, Ladd, and Vigdor, "Teacher-Student Matching and the Assessment of Teacher Effectiveness."

27. Frankenberg, "America's Diverse, Racially Changing Schools and Their Teachers."

28. *Green et al. v. County School Board of New Kent County, Virginia, et al.*

29. Frankenberg, "The Segregation of American Teachers."

30. This is at least partially because whites are overrepresented in diversity code 3 planning areas. Any member of a group overrepresented in a diversity category is less likely to receive their first choice, especially of an overchosen school, given the district's goal of having enrollments that reflect zone-wide diversity at each school.

31. *Swann v. Charlotte-Mecklenburg.*

32. *Parents Involved in Community Schools v. Seattle School District No. 1.*

33. Berkeley Unified School District, "Information on Berkeley Unified's Student Assignment Plan."

34. *American Civil Rights Foundation v. Berkeley Unified School District.*

35. For reactions to the decision, see Frankenberg and Le, "The Post–*Parents Involved* Challenge: Confronting Extralegal Obstacles to Integration," 1015–21.

4

Valuing Diversity and Hoping for the Best

Choice in Metro Tampa

Barbara Shircliffe and Jennifer Morley

Serving Metro Tampa, the Hillsborough County Public Schools (HCPS) district has relied heavily on choice policies for the past two decades, and school leaders still express a significant commitment to using choice to promote school diversity even though the desegregation plan that led to the creation of many of the choice options has ended. After implementing a comprehensive desegregation plan following the Supreme Court's 1971 *Swann v. Charlotte-Mecklenburg* decision authorizing the use of busing, this large system had few segregated schools for decades, while continuing to grow rapidly. The district was known for its historically positive leadership in pairing schools in mostly white suburban areas with those in predominately black city areas. In addition, it designed magnet programs explicitly to produce desegregated schools. HCPS was credited with achieving one of the highest rates of pupil integration in the large metropolitan districts of the South, even surpassing Charlotte-Mecklenburg, North Carolina.[1] In 1978, the *Washington Post* dubbed Hillsborough County as desegregation's "quiet success."[2] Years later, Drew Days, the chief civil rights official of the Jimmy Carter administration and a Yale law professor, described the county's effort to desegregate schools as "ahead of its time."[3] HCPS leaders embraced choice as the primary means to maintain a desegregated school system. Their district is a good place to think about the difference that generations of desegregation may make in the operation of choice programs.

Despite HCPS's desegregation legacy, in 2000 the county school board approved a controlled choice plan amid a contentious legal struggle over whether district officials had done all they could to create integrated schools. The local chapter of the National Association for the Advancement of Colored People

(NAACP) and the NAACP Legal Defense and Educational Fund (LDF), groups that had always been at the center of southern desegregation efforts, believed that the district had failed to maintain good faith in operating schools on a desegregated basis and wanted judicial intervention. In 1998 the district judge overseeing the case agreed, prompting school officials to file an appeal.[4] Throughout the litigation, HCPS officials insisted that school choice within demographically diverse regions and zones, well-placed themed programs, and transportation to certain choice options, including magnets, would promote voluntary desegregation, but they rejected racial limits, used in other controlled choice plans. The NAACP and the LDF argued that without provisions to guarantee racially balanced schools, parental choice would grossly accelerate resegregation. In much harsher language, the president of the local NAACP branch publically denounced choice as a bad idea that would "create all black schools and all white schools . . . taking us back to pre-1954."[5] In 2000 the school board voted, however, to approve the plan, with the only African American board member casting the dissenting vote. Four months later the Court of Appeals overruled the lower court, and court-ordered desegregation was dropped, leaving the key decisions about the future to the HCPS's board.[6] The controversy reflected the multiple meanings of choice and the equity implications of what type of program is pursued.

This chapter examines the Tampa story to consider whether school choice policies promote or undermine school desegregation. In Tampa, school choice has not brought about a return to rigid segregation. Yet findings indicate that choice without desegregation controls is extremely limited in reducing segregation and socioeconomic isolation. As the NAACP and the LDF predicted, since the implementation of the controlled choice plan in 2004, the number of high-poverty and predominately black and Latino schools has increased—despite the concerted use of magnets and attractors (programs in such fields as computer science, science, technology, engineering, and mathematics) to lure middle-class and white children to public schools in predominately low-income minority areas and despite district officials' hopes that African American parents residing in the city would opt to send their children to suburban schools. As segregation has increased in the city, the number of racially diverse schools elsewhere has grown for reasons that seem to have little to do with choice policy. For instance, of the county's twenty-three racially balanced elementary schools (as of 2009–10), all but one (a magnet) are located in suburban growth areas within and outside Tampa, raising questions about the future of desegregation in the outer rings.[7] School authorities and local communities must also face the issue of whether this diversity will be lasting or transitional, like the often temporary diversity of racially changing city neighborhoods.

Decision making in Tampa took place in the larger context of the national retreat from desegregation policies and the trend toward using market-based solutions to address "failing" public schools and the achievement gap. The current choice movement favors voucher programs and charter schools legislated and created with no incentives to increase racial or socioeconomic diversity.[8] Five years before the passage of No Child Left Behind (NCLB), state-driven educational reform in Florida introduced school accountability and mandated school choice. We consider how this national and state policy context has shaped HCPS's commitment to expanding magnets and choice options, for instance, in rural and suburban areas experiencing large-scale racial change, even if these programs are not meeting integration goals. We suggest that the performance-based accountability agenda has absorbed the equity potential of certain choice options, diluting the latter for the benefit of the former. Although the language of diversity remains, it appears that school choice options, including magnets, are serving other purposes. For one, choice has aided HCPS's efforts at managing growth, which is increasingly important after Florida's voters passed a 2002 constitutional amendment mandating reduced class sizes. When enrollment relies more on choice than on neighborhood, some of the problems of overcrowded areas can be dealt with much more easily. Second, choice has brought millions of dollars of federal resources into public schooling and the local economy. Third, choice and magnet programs have helped boost the test scores of schools deemed failures under Florida's accountability system. It is important to stress that racially balanced suburban schools also perform well under the accountability system, in contrast to most, but not all, of the resegregated low-income black and Latino schools. Yet within many racially balanced and desegregated schools, in spite of gains, racial achievement gaps persist, particularly for low-income and African American students, indicating, as John Diamond asserts, that "race continues to provide structural, institutional, and symbolic advantages to some groups and disadvantages to others regardless of the racial composition of schools."[9]

SITE AND DATA COLLECTION

With more than 250 schools (including 36 charters) enrolling 194,000 pupils, HCPS is the eighth-largest district in the nation. Like those of many large metropolitan areas, its enrollment has recently (as of 2003) shifted so that white (non-Latino) children are no longer a majority, reflecting the demographic transformation sweeping across the Sunbelt. In the past decade, Hillsborough County's white public school population has declined from 50% to 41%, while the Latino public school population has increased from 21% to 34%. In 2010, of the students enrolled in HCPS, roughly 5% were classified as multiracial, 3% as Asian, and less than 0.5% as American Indian.

As a large countywide school district, HCPS encompasses rural, suburban, and urban communities within the Tampa metropolitan area. All Florida metros have single countywide districts, putting them in a better position to avoid resegregation than the fragmented metropolitan school districts in many parts of the country, where city-suburban desegregation is impossible because of the legal limits the Supreme Court placed on boundary crossing in its 1974 *Milliken* decision.[10] Research shows that countywide school systems often had less white flight during desegregation—since white parents could not move to separate suburban districts to avoid integration—and provide greater equity in local school resources.[11]

The analysis that follows is based on in-depth interviews with school and civil rights leaders conducted when the HCPS controlled choice plan was being drafted (1998–2002) and six years (2009–10) after its implementation. In addition to interviews, we use school demographic and achievement data and court and district documents to assess the outcomes with respect to student diversity and school achievement.[12] But first we provide background on the transition from desegregation to choice in HCPS.

MOVING TO CHOICE IN THE DESEGREGATION PLAN

Debates about the future of desegregation in Tampa came to a head during the 1990s, when the school integration movement experienced major setbacks across the country. In 1991 the Supreme Court, changed by conservative appointments, directed lower courts to end supervision once the courts determined that the segregated "dual school system" established under Jim Crow laws had been replaced by a "unitary school system" in which the vestiges of past segregation had been eliminated "to the extent practicable."[13] Once the courts declared a district unitary, it could, if it wished, reinstate a neighborhood school system, even one certain to be highly segregated. During the next decade many major urban desegregation plans in the South were terminated. At that time, unlike other districts that had gained relief from a court oversight, HCPS had experienced neither rapid white flight nor financial instability. The district had implemented a comprehensive busing plan during the 1971–72 academic year without violence, and white flight from its public schools was minimal. As result of this plan, the populations of most, but not all, schools were balanced. *Balanced* was defined as roughly 20% black and 80% white (a category that included Latinos, Asians, and American Indians). Like HCPS, school boards across the South implemented busing plans following the Supreme Court's 1971 decision in the *Swann* case. During the 1970s there was an increase in the level of integration of black students with white students in Tampa, one of the largest in the South. By 1980 the typical black student in the district was in a school with 72% white students, an increase of 37 percentage points over the population of white students in the typical black student's school in the 1970s.[14] These data do not tell the whole story, however, because in desegregation planning most of the children from Tampa's signficant historic Latino community (which had been centered around the cigar industry and farming) were classified as whites and often used to desegregate black schools. The original desegregation case, *Manning v. School Board of Hillsborough County,* did not consider Latinos as part of the plaintiff class, and the more recent increase in the Latino population came after civil rights initiatives had dissipated.[15]

Despite being seen as a model for metropolitan desegregation, HCPS experienced patterns of resegregation in several schools during the 1970s. The federal district judge did not require school officials to maintain a particular race ratio for each school, and, amid spreading housing segregation, there was a gradual increase in the number of segregated schools. Over these years, HCPS's school board approved decisions—boundary changes and attendance modifications— that addressed racial imbalance, yet such "changes were infrequent and were made in conjunction with some other factors" and not solely for the purpose of preventing resegregation.[16]

Under the 1971 desegregation plan, parents could seek to transfer their child to a school where his or her race was a minority through the Majority to Minority (M to M) program. District officials never viewed M to M as a viable desegregation tool, as few applied and it was difficult to develop a transportation program based on a small number of applicants. For the most part, they saw the spread of segregated schooling as a natural by-product of residential change. By 1990, twenty-six schools had black or white enrollments exceeding the designated ratio, and thirteen were more than 40% black.

HCPS's first initiative to expand choice under the mandatory desegregation plan began in the late 1980s. The impetus for altering the plan was largely rooted in dissatisfaction with the grade configuration. In 1971, to achieve the court-recommended guideline while pacifying white suburban parents, all schools in predominately black urban areas were converted into single-grade (sixth or seventh) centers or junior highs. Schools in the predominately white suburban areas served largely elementary and senior high school grades. This meant that both white and black students who wanted to or had to attend public schools had little choice but to enroll in schools outside their neighborhood. Subsequently, it was not uncommon for children to attend five different schools while residing in the same home. The plan also meant disproportionate busing of African American children. Not surprisingly, throughout the 1970s and 1980s, African American parents expressed concerns about small children traveling to schools outside their neighborhood and out of the reach of their parents, who often worked long hours and lacked transportation. Although white parents perhaps held similar concerns, their children were transported outside their area for only two of the twelve years (sixth and seventh grade).

In 1991 the district judge approved a consent agreement between the district and civil rights attorneys to modify the plan. The Middle School Plan (also called the Cluster Plan) took seven years to implement, during which time the county established four elementary school magnets, five middle school magnets, and magnet programs at four high schools. Under the Cluster Plan, the district continued to bus children for the purposes of desegregation. Half of the elementary schools, a little over a third of newly created middle schools, and nearly half of high schools had satellites, noncontiguous attendance areas from which students were assigned to promote racial balance.

The implementation of the revised plan was not without controversy. In 1994 the LDF filed a complaint that the district was in violation of the district court's 1971 order and the 1991 consent decree because several schools were "racially identifiable," defined as more than 40% black or less than 10% white. A federal judge took the very unusual step of directing a review of the case to see whether or not it could be dropped. Though federal judges never initiated desegregation on their own motion, a number of them have closed down plans without either party requesting this, a rare kind of judicial activism.[17] In Tampa the judge ordered hearings before a magistrate to determine if HCPS had achieved unitary status. In 1997 the federal magistrate recommended the district be declared unitary. However, the district judge disagreed and in 1998 refused to release HCPS from court supervision regarding the persistence of pupil segregation in several schools.[18] With the issue now in play, the school board appealed this ruling while also involving stakeholders including the LDF and the local NAACP branch in developing a plan for "acquiring and maintaining unitary status."[19]

While HCPS's case was under appeal, the movement to expand choice options, including charter schools and vouchers for private schools, was driving the legislative educational agenda in Florida. Most observers noted that throughout the 1980s and 1990s, the "political and judicial tide" was ushering in a new era of voluntary desegregation under the choice umbrella.[20] The Florida legislature passed a charter school law in 1996 and the following year required all county school districts to develop controlled choice plans.[21] In this context, it is not surprising that HCPS looked to choice as a mechanism for moving from mandatory to voluntary desegregation.

Controlled choice with expanded magnet programs and other school attractors emerged as a key feature of HCPS's plan to achieve unitary status.[22] Controlled choice had been invented in 1980 in Cambridge, Massachusetts, to avoid the mandatory reassignment of students in the city across the Charles River from Boston, where there had been intense racial conflict during the desegregation of the 1970s. Under this system all families were required to rank their top several choices of schools, and everyone was given their highest choice that was compatible with school diversity. In other words, if a school was equally attractive to African American, Latino, and white parents, then it would be fully integrated through choices. If not enough students of a certain ethnicity chose to go, some people of that ethnicity who had the school as a lower choice would be assigned there. Likewise, if too many people chose the school, some of them would be assigned to a lower choice. But the great majority of students received one of their highest-ranked choices. Using this plan, Cambridge achieved a relatively high level of desegregation with very little conflict. Later, in the 1990s, it responded to changes in the law by managing enrollments primarily to assure social class diversity.

To develop their own controlled choice plan, HCPS school officials formed a planning group and an at-large advisory committee while continuing to hold discussions with the LDF and the local NAACP chapter. They also solicited the involvement of Dr. Gordon Foster, the director of the Miami Desegregation Center, as a consultant and surveyed parents to identify the types of magnet programs that had the most promise for attracting enrollment. To get citizen feedback about various other aspects of the proposed plan, school officials organized community meetings throughout the district. They proposed dividing the district into seven geographical regions (suburban and rural areas) feeding into zones (central city areas). Students living in regions could select schools within their region and associated zone (with transportation provided to underenrolled schools or to transfers that would create more racial balance) or outside their region (with transportation provided only to magnet schools) at the beginning of elementary, middle, and high school.[23] Children residing in zones could opt for transfer any year to a suburban school in the region associated with their zone. However, the only students who had to choose a school under this plan were those who were being bused for desegregation. Most of these children were African Americans who resided in the zones. "Choice attractors" were defined as "special programs placed at selected schools in order to draw students from a particular area into a particular area." "Dedicated Magnets" had "small proximity areas around each school for neighborhood students," who had priority acceptance, while "the rest of the seats are filled from countywide applicants."[24]

Hillsborough's branch of the NAACP opposed the plan and withdrew from the planning process, hoping this would lead the district judge to order choice controls that the LDF had advocated. Branch president Sam Horton was one of the most outspoken critics of school choice as a means of voluntary desegregation. He was concerned that the proposed controlled choice plan would lead to resegregation if parents chose neighborhood schools. He put little faith in the efficacy of magnet schools as a desegregation tool. For Horton, who was a school principal during the 1971 desegregation process, "choice" smacked of the days of school board recalcitrance toward integration in the decades following *Brown v.*

Board of Education. During the 1960s, school boards used "freedom of choice" plans to maintain segregated schools: School officials would assign students on a segregated basis and thereafter permit parents to request that their children be transferred elsewhere. School boards then denied requests made on behalf of African American children to transfer to white schools.[25]

Although HCPS's leadership had used freedom of choice to resist desegregation during the 1960s, following the Supreme Court's decision in *Swann,* a shift occurred, and it, like many other school districts, began focusing on making desegregated schools attractive to white parents. With this shift, new leadership was needed, and in 1967 Hillsborough County's school board appointed its first nonelected superintendent, Raymond Shelton, a Nebraskan, who believed desegregation would improve public education. A former district director who joined the HCPS in the early 1970s explained recently: "I believe the public school system over a period of thirty years, through osmosis if nothing else, accepted the value of diversity in public education; the diehard 1950–1960 administrators were leaving the system and being replaced by administrators like me who believed in diversity and felt that the desegregation plan was a way to fix a broken school system."[26] Nevertheless, the split between school officials and the NAACP over establishing choice controls still reflected vastly different views about the school board's obligation to create racially balanced schools. Decades of mandatory school desegregation did not create racially integrated neighborhoods in the manner or to the extent that many had hoped. For example, between 1970 and 1990 the number of census tracks in the HCPS district with 95% or more black population declined from seven to two. Yet the number of census tracks with 50% or more black population increased.[27] In the past two decades most of the changes in the region's residential diversity have occurred in growth areas in unincorporated Hillsborough County and not in central city neighborhoods or Tampa's elite enclaves. School leaders have attributed resegregation to demographic shifts in residential patterns they believed were beyond the board's control.

Under a controlled choice plan, school officials can take a variety of factors into consideration in granting and denying choice placements to achieve racial balance. However, HCPS officials saw little point in adopting race ratios for choice given that they believed doing so would be illegal once the county was released from court oversight (in fact, many years were to pass before the Supreme Court ruled some forms of racially targeted voluntary plans illegal in the 2007 *Parents Involved* decision).[28] Early in the planning process, the assistant superintendent for administration stated that "race ratios have not been ruled out" but cautioned that "legal experts" advised that "a plan that included race-conscious rules would likely be vulnerable to court challenges down the road."[29] In 1999 a lawsuit was filed against Hillsborough and other counties for setting dual criteria for admitting white and minority children into gifted programs in response to a 1991 directive from the Florida Department of Education (FDOE) to address the underrepresentation of black, Latino, and low-income children in such programs. In 1999 the FDOE settled this lawsuit by agreeing to eliminate race as a factor in gifted placement, leading to a decrease in the representation of blacks and Latinos in gifted classes, a problem that persists into the current century.

HCPS leaders did not see abandoning desegregation controls as forsaking the goals of diversity. Unlike in places like Berkeley, school leadership in HCPS did not want to tier choices to prevent or deny transfer requests that might result in resegregation. The growth in magnet enrollment in HCPS since 1991, according to school officials, demonstrated that choice options had appeal. As the former district director commented, through magnet programs and special assignment, 20% of HCPS's school population "had been on choice for ten years" before 2001, proving that "choice works."[30] School leaders were hoping that a history of desegregated schooling plus strategically placed magnet and attractor programs based on community input would influence individual choices in such a way as to produce integration.

AFTER UNITARY STATUS

Although HCPS was declared unitary in 2001, it did not implement its controlled choice plan until three years later. Funded by a $10 million federal grant, the plan has confronted major problems and overall has not curtailed resegregation. District officials spent nearly half a million dollars on marketing during the plan's first year only to find, as one who helped supervise the process recalled, that "well after we came out of court-ordered deseg[regation] and got ready to implement our choice plan . . . a lot of the schools were at their capacity, so we could not offer them up for choice."[31] Offering choices without capacity threatened the process. The problem grew between 1999 and 2003, when HCPS's school population soared by nearly 14%, picking up 22,275 new students (under state policy at the time, a school was not considered at capacity until it had 120% enrollment, and new school construction outlays were on a five-year cycle).

An issue of greater concern was that many African American parents residing in the city wanted their children to attend schools in their neighborhoods. School officials had hoped that the children who had been bused for desegregation—about eight thousand students, mostly African Americans residing in the city—would opt to continue attending their suburban schools. But the parents of about half of these children chose neighborhood assignments, and at the time, there were not enough seats in city schools for them.[32] During the 1990s, when HCPS converted many of the city's single-grade centers into elementary and middle school magnets, only a small surrounding area was designated priority attendance, while the rest of the enrollment was drawn district-wide. A district administrator explained, "You had a lot of students in the core of the city that had no schools to go to if they did not participate in choice, so if they did not participate in choice and there was no neighborhood school for them to go to, then what are you going to do with them?" In response, school officials quickly converted two urban elementary schools with available space into K–8 facilities to provide seats for these children, which the administrator acknowledged "did not go so well."[33] That black parents in the city did not wish to "choose out" to suburban schools partially frustrated the plan's capacity to create racially balanced schools.

Beyond these initial problems, the increase in segregation, which began prior to choice, accelerated in subsequent years, particularly in central city schools. In 1999 nine regular elementary schools were classified as 90% or more nonwhite.[34] Prior to the plan's implementation in 2003–4, sixteen elementary schools fell within this category. In 2008–9 the number of elementary schools with 10% or less white student enrollment climbed to twenty-three. Of these, twenty-one are designated as urban and all are high poverty. The only integrated school left in the city of Tampa, in the heart of the district, is a magnet school.

These patterns of segregation reflect the geographic distribution and the changing demographics of the public school population, particularly the rapid growth in the proportion of Latinos and the gradual decline in the number of white students. In 2009 41.3% of the HCPS school population was classified as white, 28.2% as Latino, 21.7% as black, and 3.1% as Asian. In addition, most public school children (52.3%) attend suburban schools, while 22.5% and 20% are enrolled in urban and rural schools respectively.[35] Of HCPS's white students, 62% attend suburban schools, while only 8.4% are enrolled in urban schools. Among the district's black students, 37.7% attend suburban schools and 44.7% attend urban schools. Almost half of the district's Latino students are enrolled in suburban schools, and a little over 26% attend urban schools. Therefore, black students constitute the largest percentage (44.7%) of children attending urban public schools, while only 15.5% of students enrolled in urban public schools are white. It is clear that schools will remain segregated unless suburban and urban communities become more integrated or school policies provide incentives for suburban-urban school transfers.

According to 2009–10 school-level demographic data, only 23 of the county's 141 (K–5) elementary schools were balanced (defined as having no more than a 10% deviation from countywide demographics for blacks, Latinos, whites, and Asians). As mentioned, in 2009–10 the only balanced central city elementary school was a magnet, but it was the only magnet school that falls into this category. That year, the county's eight other K–5 magnets had an overrepresentation of blacks and an underrepresentation of whites, while two had an overrepresentation of blacks and Asians and an underrepresentation of whites. Comparing the levels of racial segregation between magnet schools and charter schools, another choice option with no diversity goals, is difficult because the grade structure of these schools differs significantly.[36] Under the 1991 consent decree, the district agreed to limit black enrollment in magnet schools to 40%. As of 2008–9, of the county's nine elementary magnets, only one was balanced with respect to black, white, and Latino students. However, only two of the nine would be considered racially isolated, defined as less than 10% white. White enrollment in most magnets ranged from 10% to 25%.

Keeping magnet schools desegregated requires continually recruiting both white and nonwhite students. District officials regularly discuss the lack of white student enrollment in magnet programs. Moreover, one district administrator mentioned the idea that magnet schools have a tipping point leading to racial turnover to explain why they remain predominately nonwhite: "If you pump[ed] them [low-income African American and Latino children] into the magnet schools that [had] room available, then you shifted the balance, and . . . as you had a higher portion of lower-socioeconomic African Americans, it pushed the suburban students out: they wouldn't go." Reflecting the irony of choice as a strategy to promote integrated schooling, he continued, "I think if you go to a school that has too many people that are not like you and you can choose to go someplace else, even within your neighborhood, you are going to do that."[37] This was a basic reason for using racial controls of enrollment for magnet schools. When the controls lift and everyone is free to go after uncontrolled individual choices, everyone can lose the opportunity to attend a diverse school.

Much of the current racial diversity in HCPS schools is a result of racial transition in parts of suburbia and school officials' moving children from a few overcrowded urban schools to suburban ones in response to Florida's Class Size Amendment. As previously discussed, all but one of the county's twenty-three most racially balanced elementary schools are in suburban areas. Eight of these schools were not balanced prior to the implementation of choice. Ten of these schools are Title I, with high concentrations of low-income students.[38]

The emergence of diversity in suburban schools relates in good measure to the migration of nonwhite families to population centers outside Tampa. As of 2008–9, blacks constituted 15.5% of all students enrolled in suburban public schools. As stated earlier, 37.7% of all black children go to public schools in suburban areas. Nevertheless, black students are overrepresented in urban schools, where they are 44.7% of all children enrolled. Four of the county's balanced elementary schools are in Brandon, a formerly rural town that developed in the 1980s into one of Tampa's megasuburban communities. In 1988 a local reporter speculated that had Brandon become a separate municipality, it would have been the fifteenth-largest city in Florida.[39] Another four balanced elementary schools are in a suburban area that also experienced rapid growth, namely New Tampa. If the racial balance in these suburban schools is a temporary product of a changing neighborhood rather than a reflection of a stably integrated community, the diversity may be transient. Defining a stable community has become extremely difficult because people have not been able to move due to the foreclosure crisis and the Great Recession.[40] As of 2011, Florida had a quarter of the nation's foreclosures.

Integration, Segregation, and Accountability

Florida has a uniquely obtrusive school accountability system, which includes grading schools from A to D and F using the Florida Comprehensive Assessment Test (FCAT). The test contains reading and mathematics portions, each with a possible student score scaled from 1 through 5 (5 being highest). The test also includes a writing segment that is graded from 1 to 6 (6 being highest). Elementary and middle schools are graded using FCAT scores only. School grades are calculated by combining the percentage of students in each scale score category with computations involving student learning gains (reflecting adequate yearly progress, or AYP). Schools have a possible 800 points, and getting fewer than 395 points means a grade of F. High school grades are 50% based on this formula and include other components such as graduation rate, accelerated coursework completion, and the postsecondary readiness of students (as measured by the ACT, SAT, or Common Placement Test).[41]

Using a grade as the sole measure of assessing the successes and failings of a particular school has many limitations, especially since research shows that grades are more strongly linked to student characteristics than to school programs.[42] Yet these grades are heavily publicized in Florida and used as proxies to inform public perceptions of school quality, so they are therefore pertinent to the discussion of school choice. A pilot study of HCPS schools conducted by Charles Willie, Ralph Edwards, and Michael Alves in 1999–2000 indicated that more-racially-balanced schools were likelier to earn an A.[43] To look at the relation between school demographics and grades under Florida's accountability system today (using 2009–10 data), we classified as imbalanced any school that deviated at least 10% from district-wide proportions of minorities or students eligible for free or reduced-price lunch (FRL). We found that there is a connection between school grades and levels of race and socioeconomic segregation. Of the seventy-two regular elementary schools, including magnets, to earn As, white and/or Asian students were overrepresented in 56% (forty schools), Latino students in 19% (fourteen), and black students in only 5.5% (four). All eight of the county's D and F elementary schools have an overrepresentation of black students. These schools, not surprisingly, also have a high percentage of students on FRL.[44]

As mentioned earlier, magnet schools are predominately nonwhite, with an overrepresentation of black students and a significant number of Latino and Asian students. They perform better in Florida's accountability system than do nearby traditional public schools. For example, of the four schools with an overrepresentation of African American students to earn an A, all but one are magnets. Only one K–5 magnet school earned less than a B in 2009–10. In comparison, of the nine nearby public elementary schools, only one earned an A. Among the rest, one earned a B, three earned Cs, two earned Ds, and two earned Fs. Given these results, magnet schools may offer more in the way of benefits even if they do not attract large numbers of white children. The backgrounds of students and families that select magnets over neighborhood schools may, of course, influence the higher school-wide achievement of magnets. It is likely that magnets attract more socially mobile parents, who, by virtue of choosing them, are actively engaged in their children's schooling.

It is important to note that none of the twenty-three balanced schools (most in suburban areas) earned less than an A, and nearly half are Title I. One might conclude that imbalanced magnet schools perform close to balanced traditional schools and much better than segregated low-income neighborhood schools. Magnet schools tend to have a lower percentage of students on FRL than nearby neighborhood schools, but their rates are still high. All of the district's elementary magnets except one have from 56% to 94% of students on FRL, with 79% the average. (The nine nearby traditional schools' rates range from 85% to 98%, with 96% the average.) Therefore, magnet programs may be promoting socioeconomic diversity even if they do not create racially balanced schools. The question remains whether choice is addressing the educational needs of students if it creates more segregated schools.

Looking to the Future

HCPS leaders' efforts to reverse resegregation through the use of magnet programs and other choice options remain frustrated, suggesting a need to explore alternatives. Though considerable diversity remains since the district was declared unitary in 2001, it is declining, and the number of segregated high-poverty schools is up sharply. A long history of desegregation and the past two decades of choice-based voluntary programs may have slowed the resegregation process.

Like many school districts, HCPS implemented controlled choice to maintain a unitary system while transitioning out from under court supervision. However, its version did not include desegregation controls that advocates insisted were essential. Hillsborough's local NAACP chapter denounced the plan, and the LDF took issue with school officials' resistance to using race ratios to guide choice placements. However, once HCPS was released from court supervision in 2001, the NAACP and the LDF no longer had legal standing to challenge the plan. The district has nevertheless retained a triracial Choice Advisory Committee, with representatives appointed by the school board, the NAACP, and the Hispanic Services Council, an organization dedicated to promoting integration, in part through bilingual and bicultural education.[45]

The extent to which controlled choice, including magnets, has reduced the pace of school resegregation is difficult to gauge. Racial segregation among HCPS schools has increased since the implementation of the controlled choice plan in 2004, yet with population growth and new school construction the number of demographically balanced schools has slightly increased as well. Most of the county's racially balanced elementary schools are in growth areas outside Tampa, and only one is a magnet. Furthermore, the district has continued to make decisions that increase racial balance in suburban schools, such as using noncontiguous zoning. Yet a district official who is responsible for drawing school boundaries explained that achieving student diversity is not the "driving force" of pupil assignment, as it was under court-ordered desegregation.[46]

District officials openly acknowledged that the number of high-poverty and high-minority schools has increased since the implementation of choice in 2004. One district head suggested that choice has played a part in but does not tell the entire story of the growth in high-poverty schools in the county. An administrator in charge of federal programs explained, "In around 2000, 2001, 2002, we had about eight or nine schools in our district that were above 90% poverty, and currently we have almost thirty-three." He attributes some of the increase to the "choice process . . . overnight allow[ing] parents back into their neighborhood schools, if that's what they choose." This administrator observed that as low-income parents have opted for nearby schools in predominately poor residential areas, the number of high-poverty schools has increased. The economic downturn, which caused more families to file for FRL, also increased the number of high-poverty schools. Since the implementation of choice in 2004, the district has "gained another ten or thirteen schools" with 90% or more students eligible for FRL.[47] Many of these schools are outside the urban core, in suburban and rural areas that have experienced rapid growth, an increase in Latino population, and the effects of the current economic downturn. The district has targeted schools in these areas for magnet programs.

CONCLUSION

The abandoning of civil rights strategies in favor of choice and privatization at the federal and state levels has set the South (and the rest of the nation) on a gradual path toward strongly increased stratification and inequality. Although, as Amy Stuart Wells and Robert Crain note, voluntary desegregation has proved more effective than the freedom of choice plans of the 1960s, the Supreme Court has made it more difficult by limiting some integration methods available to school districts.[48] The Tampa story suggests that school choice without methods to produce socioeconomic integration—even with considerable investment in magnet programs, transportation, and school attractors—may do little to counter trends toward resegregation. Moreover, the county's long history with desegregation has not seemed to lead to class- or color-blind school or housing choices, particularly among affluent residents. Rather, class and racial interests continue to structure behaviors around residential and school choice in ways that undermine educational equity.[49]

Since they implemented controlled choice in 2004, HCPS officials acknowledge, there has been an increase in predominately minority and high-poverty schools, as in other areas in the South since desegregation plans have been dissolved.[50] Although they are attentive to and deeply concerned about increasing segregation, district officials in Hillsborough nevertheless installed a color-blind choice system, as they believed they must in light of *Parents Involved*. HCPS's controlled choice plan has had limited results in promoting school diversity. For one thing, significant numbers of parents have not passed over neighborhood schools in favor of options meant to promote diversity. Magnet students represent roughly 15% of the county's student population. In the 2009–10 academic year, 13,708 students were enrolled in magnet programs, 696 students were given priority acceptance because they lived in magnet attendance areas, and 480 students were enrolled at Rampello, a magnet school that draws parents who work in downtown Tampa. In contrast, although about half that of magnets, enrollment in charter schools—which Florida law has allowed for and encouraged the creation of since 1996—has grown much more rapidly in the past ten years.

Despite the fact that only slightly more than 20% of district students participate in choice programs, HCPS has a strong commitment to choice. Most of these students are not enrolled in the county's magnet programs. Nevertheless, district-level administrative personnel often mentioned choice and particularly magnet programs in interviews, reinforcing the rhetorical institutionalization of diversity despite the fact that choice programs have not been successful as a desegregation tool. For example, despite an increase in the number of high-poverty schools, a federal program administrator defended the choice process with hopeful comments: "I think as a whole as we have really developed in this district our choice process, and we have, I feel like [there is] a great amount of diversity in many more of our schools than maybe what we had before, based on that choice process. You know, we are looking at every single child as, 'we've got to do something to help them.' "[51]

The increase in high-poverty schools and related achievement disparities has led some to advocate for choice controls that place poverty caps on schools.[52] HCPS has not yet embraced such measures. For school officials, choice provides an important means of creating diversity, and in its absence—a complete neighborhood system with no transportation options, magnet programs, or attractors—HCPS's schools would be even more segregated. If desegregation is no longer the driving force of school choice, it is important to reflect on what is and how choice is serving other district goals that a return to a neighborhood system would not meet, such as garnering resources, managing growth, and raising school-wide achievement at certain schools.

Choice provides flexibility in growth management. Under choice in a rapidly expanding school district, seats can be filled before new construction begins, and schools with waning enrollment can be opened up to choice options, maximizing overall capacity. This process has created some stability, even given Florida's tremendous growth in the past decades and the implementation of the state's Class Size Amendment. Choice programs also help school districts obtain federal and state funds. As mentioned above, HCPS received $10 million in federal funding to implement choice and $750,000 in state funding to "mentor other school districts" that subsequently adopted choice plans. As one supervisor commented in 2004, "Over the next five years, Hillsborough Choice will add $11 million to the local economy."[53] In 2007 the district received $20 million through Voluntary Public School Choice (VPSC) and the Magnet School Assistant Program, to cover five years of expanding attractors and promoting desegregation. More recently it received another $11 million under VPSC. Federal programs supporting magnets and choice provide districts with additional resources, particularly funds for transportation, quality teaching incentives, classroom technology, and curriculum development. There are also grants to aid magnets in optimizing physical space in underutilized schools. As discussed above, converting high-poverty traditional public schools into magnets has boosted school achievement under Florida's accountability system, reducing the number of failing schools. Magnet schools may be attracting more socioeconomically diverse, if not more white, students to low-income city neighborhoods. The data, while limited, suggest that social integration (defined more broadly than the presence of white children) has merits for creating successful schools. A main limitation of magnets is that they are not intended to create system-wide integration, so it is critical to consider how segregated nonmagnet schools could benefit from enhancements and incentives for socioeconomic integration.

Under a neighborhood system and in the absence of HCPS's choice plan, school leaders believe, the district's schools would have experienced more racial and socioeconomic segregation. The Supreme Court's 2007 *Parents Involved* decision created obstacles to positive integrative action. Districts can no longer assign children to schools solely on the basis of race, but they can pursue desegregation through boundary changes and site selection with reference to students' poverty status, language background, or neighborhood, for instance.[54] Unlike a number of other districts, HCPS has not adopted socioeconomic integration as a policy. However, noncontiguous zoning and magnets in Hillsborough have hinted at the possibilities offered by embracing such a strategy to foster diversity. Given the steady increase in the county's Latino population, establishing dual-language schools and programs, in particular, may help promote diversity, as evidence shows has happened elsewhere.[55] In addition, Tampa and the surrounding communities' rich multicultural heritage and strong social capital within black and Latino communities should be used to enrich the curriculum of suburban schools. These avenues can provide solid directions for Hillsborough and other districts committed to finding ways to make choice and magnet schools achieve the goal of promoting student diversity.

NOTES

The data presented, the statements made, and the views expressed are solely the responsibility of the authors.

1. Douglas, *Reading, Writing and Race: The Desegregation of Charlotte's Schools,* 246.

2. Sinclair, "Desegregation's Quiet Success," 1A.

3. Days, "The Other Desegregation Story: Eradicating the Dual School System in Hillsborough County, Florida."

4. *Manning v. School Board of Hillsborough County* (1998).

5. Schweitzer, "Critics Scorn New Desegregation Plan."

6. *Manning v. School Board of Hillsborough County* (2001).

7. In this chapter, racially balanced schools are defined as those with no ethnic subgroups deviating more than 10% from countywide school demographics.

8. For an assessment of both progressive and unlawful choice legacies, see Forman, "The Secret History of School Choice: How Progressives Got Here First."

9. Diamond, "Still Separate and Unequal: Examining Race, Opportunity, and School Achievement in 'Integrated' Suburbs."

10. *Milliken v. Bradley.*

11. Logan, Oakley, and Stowell, "School Segregation in Metropolitan Regions: The Impacts of Policy Choices on Public Education"; Lankford and Wyckoff, "Why Are Schools Racially Segregated? Implications for School Choice Policies."

12. HCPS provided all district demographic data cited in this chapter. All achievement data was accessed through the website of the Florida Department of Education's Division of Accountability, Research and Measurement, www.fldoe.org/arm/.

13. *Board of Education of Oklahoma City Public Schools v. Dowell.*

14. Orfield, *Public School Desegregation in the United States, 1968–1980.*

15. Bowman, "Pursuing Educational Opportunities for Latino and Latina Students."

16. "Report and Recommendation," *Manning v. School Board,* 20.

17. Parker, "The Future of School Desegregation."

18. *Manning v. School Board* (1998).

19. Hillsborough County Public Schools, "School District of Hillsborough County Plan Development for Acquiring and Maintaining Unity Status." The school board decided to appeal, in part, because the federal magistrate had recommended that the district be released from court supervision.

20. Wells and Crain, "Where School Desegregation and Choice Policies Collide: Voluntary Transfer Plans and Controlled Choice," 60.

21. Florida Statutes, Section 228.056, "Charter Schools"; ibid., Section 228.057, "Public School Parental Choice."

22. In HCPS's planning documents, "Choice / Controlled Choice Open Enrollment" was defined as any program that "allow[ed] parents to choose schools their children will attend within pre-

established parameters or boundaries established by the School Board" ("Tools for Maintaining Integrated School Systems").

23. Hillsborough County Public Schools, "School District of Hillsborough County Plan Development for Acquiring and Maintaining Unity Status."

24. Ibid., 97.

25. Greenberg, *Crusaders in the Courts: Legal Battles of the Civil Rights Movement,* 268.

26. Interview with School Choice Office administrator, Tampa, Florida, October 9, 2009. All interviews cited in this chapter were conducted in confidentiality, and the names of the interviewees are withheld by mutual agreement.

27. "Report and Recommendation," *Manning v. School Board,* 20.

28. Schweitzer, "Distrust Surrounds School Vote"; *Parents Involved in Community Schools v. Seattle School District No. 1.*

29. Schweitzer, "Critics Scorn New Desegregation Plan."

30. Interview with School Choice Office administrator.

31. Ave, "Few Pick Schools, So Far"; interview with school boundaries district administrator, Tampa, Florida, June 16, 2010.

32. Ave, "East Tampa Magnet Schools May Close."

33. Interview with school boundaries district administrator.

34. "Regular" elementary schools were the 141 K–5 facilities not including charters.

35. There are 9,715 students enrolled in public schools that do not have a geographic code, representing 5% of the public school population.

36. Greene, "Choosing Integration," 36.

37. Interview with school boundaries district administrator.

38. Title I is a federal aid program that assists schools with a high number of low-income students.

39. Proctor, "Brandon Deserves to Vote on Its Future."

40. Harrington and Cameron, "Pockets of Severe Poverty Intensify and Spread around the Tampa Bay Area."

41. Florida Department of Education, "Grading Florida's Public Schools, 2009–10."

42. See Salganik, "Apples and Apples: Comparing Performance Indicators for Places with Similar Demographic Characteristics," for a discussion of the political and methodological limitations in comparing performance even among schools with similar demographics.

43. Willie, Edwards, and Alves, *Student Diversity, Choice and School Improvement,* 106.

44. Borman et al., "Accountability in a Post-desegregation Era: The Continuing Significance of Racial Segregation in Florida's Schools."

45. See www.hispanicservicescouncil.org/history.php.

46. Interview with school boundaries district administrator.

47. Interview with federal programs district administrator, Tampa, Florida, November 20, 2009.

48. Wells and Crain, "Where School Desegregation and Choice Policies Collide."

49. Brantlinger, *Dividing Classes: How the Middle Class Negotiates and Rationalizes School Advantage.*

50. Boger and Orfield, eds., *School Resegregation: Must the South Turn Back?*

51. Interview with federal programs district administrator.

52. Kahlenberg, *All Together Now: Creating Middle Class Schools through Public School Choice.*

53. Minutes of the School Support Committee, April 26, 2004, City of Temple Terrace, Florida.

54. *Parents Involved in Community Schools v. Seattle School District No. 1,* (Justice Kennedy concurring).

55. Gándara, "Latinos, Language, and Segregation," 271–73.

5

Designing Choice

Magnet School Structures and Racial Diversity

Genevieve Siegel-Hawley and Erica Frankenberg

Magnet schools represent the first mainstream policy effort to combine school choice with the pursuit of racial diversity.[1] During the 1970s, as urban districts around the country grappled with the implementation of *Brown v. Board of Education*'s mandate, pioneering educators in Milwaukee, Cincinnati, Buffalo, and other communities sought to create educationally distinctive schools that would produce significant voluntary desegregation. When magnets first emerged as a major model of choice, almost all were designed as part of desegregation plans. Most of the start-up costs were thus funded through desegregation court orders or special federal desegregation aid money. Today, the unique features of magnet programs (such as innovative curricula and teaching methods) continue to attract a wide, diverse group of families across traditional attendance zones to schools typically located in urban cores. To ensure that all families have access to magnet programs, many also offer important civil rights protections, including open enrollment, outreach, and transportation.[2] Fundamental to the design of magnet schools is, of course, the fact that both students and teachers choose to learn and work within them. They are the largest set of schools of choice today.

Over the years, magnets have played a role in both furthering integration efforts and fostering the growth of public school choice. Yet after 1991, when the Supreme Court began to reverse desegregation policy and as charter schools made their debut as a choice framework, attention began to turn away from magnet schools—and many magnet schools began to turn away from desegregation goals.[3] Nonetheless, they have been an extremely important experiment in urban desegregation strategy, and their accomplishments deserve close attention.

Today the term *magnet school* encompasses a wide variety of educational settings. Beyond two broad, general characteristics—the provision of something that is educationally unique from what other public schools offer and a non-reliance on traditional attendance zones—magnet programs have considerably different designs.[4] The sector includes whole-school programs, smaller magnets housed within a host school, magnets with competitive or noncompetitive entrance requirements, and magnets with or without racial diversity guidelines. This varied group of schools can thus give important insight into the conditions and structures that promote diversity within educational choice systems.

Recognizing their different contexts and conditions, this chapter seeks to develop a deeper understanding of contemporary magnet school trends. We look specifically at the characteristics of student enrollment to understand whether magnets are more or less racially, socioeconomically, or linguistically diverse than regular public schools and charter schools. This chapter also draws upon two surveys of magnet schools to describe the relationship between the racial composition and the design and structure of these programs. We find that certain characteristics, such as the presence of desegregation goals or the provision of free transportation, are associated with more integrated magnet environments and higher levels of parent demand. We argue that magnet programs, when carefully designed, continue to offer a critical example of school choice used to promote diversity.

THE BACKGROUND AND CONTEXT
OF MAGNET SCHOOLS

In 1976, Congress amended the Emergency School Aid Act (ESAA) by initiating a federal grant program, known as the Magnet Schools Assistance Program (MSAP), for districts interested in opening magnet schools to further desegregation goals.[5] One year later, on the heels of several extensive court-ordered desegregation plans, Congress passed an amendment placing severe restrictions on federal agencies' ability to prescribe busing as a remedy for segregation.[6] This action, compounded by the Supreme Court's 1974 retreat from authorizing comprehensive city-suburban desegregation, prompted liberal factions to support magnet schools as one of the few remaining desegregation strategies that appeared politically viable.[7] Progressive magnet supporters were also joined by many conservatives, including President Ronald Reagan, who touted the virtues of school choice—in part because of the market-based implications of offering alternatives to public schools.[8]

Following their inception, magnet schools rapidly multiplied. In the early 1990s more than 232 school districts contained magnet schools.[9] A decade later the U.S. Department of Education (ED) estimated that more than half of all large urban school systems had used or continued to use magnets as a tool for desegregation.[10]

The Shifting Purpose of Magnet Schools

ED has conducted three broad reviews of magnet programs established with the help of ESAA funding or MSAP grants. The first two evaluations (importantly, these pertained only to magnet schools receiving federal funding, a subset of all programs in the magnet sector) examined the extent to which MSAP awardees specifically designated desegregation as a goal of their programs. By the time of the third and final ED study, which did not research desegregation goals, the George W. Bush administration's Justice Department was pressing for the dissolution of desegregation plans. While the narrowing of research goals did not necessarily mean that the magnet programs themselves were no longer establishing desegregation goals, ED's failure to examine what had been a key focus of the first two reports is indicative of changing values.

More specifically, the first ED report, released in 1983, found that more than 60% of the magnets studied were "fully desegregated," with the remainder still reporting substantial racial and ethnic diversity.[11] Subsequent reviews occurred after the Supreme Court authorized the termination of desegregation plans in the 1990s. The next evaluation, published in 1996, found less encouraging results: only 42% of federally funded magnet programs were operating under obvious desegregation guidelines.[12] And last, the most recent magnet study, issued by ED in 2003, found that 57% of newly founded magnet programs were making progress in combating racial isolation, while another 43% were experiencing an increase in segregation.[13] It explicitly cited the use of race-neutral admissions criteria as a possible explanation for the fact that more than two-fifths of 1998 MSAP awardees reported rising levels of racial isolation.[14]

Taken together, these ED evaluations reinforce two key points: (1) magnet programs by no means guarantee integrated schooling and in some cases may produce just the opposite; and (2) many magnets are being established today without explicit goals for desegregation. Additionally, in the years since the last federal evaluation of magnet programs, the Supreme Court's 2007 Parents Involved decision has created additional obstacles to using race to produce integrated magnet schools under many cities' existing voluntary integration policies.

With desegregation goals changing, and constrained by judicial rulings and the standards and accountability movement, magnets have experienced increased pressure to raise students' academic performance. Indeed, for each renewal of MSAP funding, magnet programs were expected to serve as beacons of innovation, reform, or high academic standards, in addition to preventing racial isolation.[15] As we see in the following section, magnet programs have been relatively successful in improving academic outcomes, but the addition of these extra educational goals may have complicated efforts to foster racial diversity.

The grant eligibility requirements shifted in the most recent round of federal

MSAP funding—the first since the *Parents Involved* decision. Under the Bush administration, MSAP applicants were required to propose race-neutral means of reducing or eliminating racial isolation. According to ED's evaluation during that period, using race-neutral criteria dampened MSAP grantees' ability to reduce or eliminate racial isolation.[16] In contrast, Barack Obama's ED recently proposed a new interim rule to allow districts more flexibility to design plans that will comply with *Parents Involved* (notably, its holding that the pursuit of diversity should not be binary white-nonwhite or black-nonblack) and reduce minority isolation. The rule says that ED will evaluate the reduction or elimination of minority isolation in magnet and feeder schools in a case-by-case manner that takes into account the particular circumstances of the district.[17] While this flexibility is intended to help districts, it may result in confusion. Without clear guidance at the federal level, communities must wrestle with how to define a reduction of racial isolation in their local context.

The courts recently declared unitary (i.e., ended judicial oversight of school desegregation in) a number of districts awarded 2010–13 MSAP grants, perhaps suggesting that ED values supporting the continuation of diversity efforts through a boost to area magnet programs. Magnets are central to desegregation policy in other school districts awarded grants in the most recent cycle (e.g., Los Angeles Unified; Hartford, Connecticut; several countywide districts in Florida). Further, a survey of sixty-four magnet school directors indicates that MSAP awardees from this cycle were substantially more likely than those from the previous, Bush-era cycle to report the presence at their school of diversity goals and outreach efforts—two important civil rights considerations.[18] Each of these developments may signal a federal reaffirmation of the original goal of magnet schools: voluntary integration.

Benefits of Magnet Programs

A number of studies have pointed to important academic gains for children attending magnet schools. In 1996 Professor Adam Gamoran at the University of Wisconsin at Madison published one of the more widely disseminated of these reports.[19] It remains one of the few large-scale, national studies of magnet school effects. It was based on a sample of urban students from the federal National Educational Longitudinal Survey (NELS) and sought to estimate differences in tenth grade achievement for students attending magnet schools, regular public schools, Catholic schools, and secular private schools. The author controlled for an extensive list of family background characteristics in addition to looking at the different types of high schools. Significantly, the analysis showed that magnet schools were more effective in raising student achievement in reading and social studies than regular public, Catholic, or secular private schools. It also found that magnet students made faster achievement gains in most subjects—with the exception of mathematics—than students in other types of schools.

This report supported the finding of the first ED study on the integrating potential of magnets (mentioned previously) that more than 80% of magnets surveyed had higher average achievement scores than the district average for regular public schools.[20] A follow-up summary of the 1983 ED report highlighted four school districts where, after controlling for differences in student backgrounds, magnet programs had positive effects on achievement test scores.[21] More recent research based on magnet programs in San Diego found that acceptance to a magnet high school via lottery was associated with positive gains in math achievement two and three years into the program.[22]

On the other hand, several other studies attempting to control for selection biases found no significant differences in student achievement between magnet high schools and comprehensive high schools.[23] Similarly, an older case study of magnet programs in Prince George's County, Maryland, found that evidence of heightened magnet student achievement may have been overstated because of the district's reliance on outdated testing measures. The authors concluded that changes in the testing regimen and a lack of program evaluations meant that evidence of enhanced achievement in the county's magnet schools was unreliable and invalid.[24]

Connecticut's interdistrict magnet programs offer the most current evidence of the link between magnet school attendance and higher academic achievement. As part of its compliance with a statewide desegregation case, Connecticut has established more than fifty interdistrict magnet schools in metropolitan Hartford, New Haven, and Waterbury. These schools draw students from multiple districts with the intent of providing racially diverse educational settings. Through a comparison of magnet lottery winners and losers, an analysis of student achievement in interdistrict magnets found that these schools had positive effects on reading and math scores. Among middle school students from Hartford, the effects were largest for those at magnet schools with forty percentage points fewer minority students than the regular schools they would have attended otherwise. A second iteration of the study based on the same set of programs examined outcomes beyond student achievement and found that magnet school students generally reported more positive academic attitudes and behaviors than students in nonmagnet schools.[25]

Finally, a 2011 study validated the "magnetic" mechanism at the heart of the magnet concept using a sophisticated econometric analysis that tracked longitudinal outcomes for a magnet program in a midsize urban district. Researchers concluded that "magnet programs are effective tools for attracting and retaining households and students."[26] By carefully analyzing the impact of winning or losing school lotteries on families' decisions to stay in or leave a school district, the researchers found that magnet programs retained significant groups of white students from higher-income and more-highly-educated communities. This, of course, was one of the major early goals of magnet schools and is important for educational performance, since the retention of more affluent families and high-achieving students has positive influences (e.g., increased graduation and postsecondary aspirations) on these students' peer groups.[27] These families also benefit the economic health of the cities whose magnet programs attract them. The study additionally found that magnet elementary schools reported fewer offenses and suspensions and that high school magnet students had better attendance rates than their nonmagnet peers.[28]

By their very design, magnets offer educational opportunities and experiences outside traditional curricula. Yet one of the ironic aspects of magnet school evaluation is that it is commonly limited to math and reading scores. If a student becomes fluent in another language, learns how to operate a commercial enterprise, develops a deep understanding of history or government, or learns to sensitively perform a role from Shakespeare, that counts for nothing in traditional evaluations. This means that virtually all appraisals of the educational effects of magnets ignore the very aspects that make the programs magnetic.

In sum, most research to date suggests that important benefits are associated with attending magnet schools. More research is needed to fully comprehend academic and nonacademic outcomes for magnet students. It is worth noting here, though, that broader studies of racially diverse schools have generally showed positive academic and social outcomes for students. Racially diverse learning environments have been linked to enhanced classroom discussion, more advanced social and historical thinking, greater commitment to increasing racial understanding, improved racial and cultural awareness, and higher levels of student persistence.[29] Diverse schools have also been associated with improved academic achievement for black students, accompanied by no decline in scores for white students.[30] Beyond the K–12 schooling experience, integrated school environments eventually translate into loftier educational and career aspirations for students, an enhanced awareness of the process involved in attaining such goals, and superior social networks.[31] Given that racial diversity has long been an important—and at times guiding—principle for magnet schools, it stands to reason that documentation of the benefits of racially diverse schools may also apply to magnet programs.

MAGNET SCHOOL STUDENTS

In 2008–9, more than two and a half million students enrolled in magnet schools across the nation, up from just over two million students four years earlier.[32]

TABLE 5.1 Magnet versus nonmagnet district enrollment patterns by race, 2008–9

Racial/ethnic or other student group	Percentage of enrollment in districts with at least one magnet school	Percentage of enrollment in districts with no magnet or charter schools	Percentage point difference
White	35.2	60.8	25.6
Black	30.7	12.5	-18.2
Latino	27.3	20.7	-6.6
Asian	6.1	4.5	-1.6
American Indian	0.6	1.5	0.9
FRL eligible	54.7	42.0	-12.7

NOTES: There were a total of 11,080,715 students in districts with at least one magnet school, and 36,939,492 students in districts with no magnet or charter schools. Percentages may sum to less than 100 because of rounding.
SOURCE: National Center for Education Statistics, Common Core of Data, 2008–9

Magnet programs enrolled more than twice the number of students served by charter schools, making them by far the largest sector of choice schools.

Black students made up more than 30% of students attending magnet and charter schools in 2008–9, compared to roughly 15% of students attending regular public schools. Latino students made up a larger percentage of the magnet enrollment (29.0%) than either the charter enrollment (25.4%) or the regular public school enrollment (21.8%). Both choice sectors served a far smaller percentage of white students than regular public schools (56.6%), though charter schools (38.3%) enrolled considerably higher shares of white students than magnet programs (30.3%).

In 2008–9, low-income students (those eligible for free and reduced-priced lunch, a rough proxy for relative poverty) made up roughly 45% of regular public and charter school enrollment but 56% of magnet school enrollment. These substantial differences suggest that magnet programs are not necessarily creaming more advantaged students from regular public schools. The same pattern holds true even after accounting for the fact that magnet schools are typically in districts with higher shares of low-income students.

The enrollment patterns of magnets are related to their primarily urban locations. Many originated in desegregation orders, which, outside the South, were almost solely limited to central cities and excluded outlying suburbs. Table 5.1 compares the average racial composition of a school district containing at least one magnet program to that of a district without any magnet or charter schools. It shows that on average, districts containing at least one magnet school enroll substantially higher percentages of black and Latino students—and much smaller percentages of white students—than districts without magnet schools. Districts with magnet schools also reported a much higher enrollment of low-income students. History plays into these patterns. Many magnet schools were traditionally in disadvantaged central city neighborhoods and were freed from the restrictions of attendance zone boundaries to help disentangle residential segregation from school segregation.[33]

SEGREGATION AND MAGNET SCHOOL DESIGN: EVIDENCE FROM TWO SURVEYS

Magnet schools vary widely in both design and structure. Some maintain a commitment to their historical mission to help desegregate students, while others do not. Programs may focus on different themes or emphases, such as certain learning techniques or foreign language acquisition. Magnets can be either housed within a host school or established as whole-school programs. Some magnet schools have competitive entrance requirements, but others emphasize noncompetitive admissions processes. Many, but not all, magnet programs conduct outreach and provide free transportation. The diversity among this group of schools can thus offer important insights into the conditions and structures that promote diversity within magnet programs.

In the following sections, we examine the ways in which many of these design characteristics relate to the racial composition of magnet schools. Several terms are used to describe school racial contexts, including "racially isolated minority schools," "racially isolated white schools," and "one-race schools."[34] A racially isolated minority school is one where more than 80% of the students are black or Latino, while "racially isolated white school" describes those where less than 20% of students are from underrepresented backgrounds. "One-race school" describes a similar, but more extreme, situation, in which 90%–100% of students are from the same racial or ethnic group.[35] The existence of these types of isolation in magnet schools should be considered in conjunction with the fact that most magnets are in central cities (as noted in the above section). Many regular public schools in similar locations are also struggling with patterns of intense racial and socioeconomic isolation.

Survey Samples

To explore the different ways in which the structure or design of magnet schools relates to the composition of their student bodies, we analyzed selected questions from the federal National Center for Education Statistics' Schools and Staffing Survey ("Schools and Staffing"), last conducted in 2007–8. We examined the restricted-use version of responses to the Schools and Staffing school and teacher questionnaires related to magnet school design, admissions requirements, and teachers.[36] We supplemented this data with Magnet Schools of America (MSA) survey responses obtained from a sampling of magnet administrators, teachers, and district officials.

The Schools and Staffing sample included just over 7,000 regular public schools, educating more than 4.3 million students. Within the larger sample were 506 magnet schools enrolling approximately 500,000 students. We limited the analysis to only regular or special emphasis schools, for a final sample of 449 magnet schools and 6,482 nonmagnet schools. Where noted, we further restricted magnet schools to whole-school magnets (192 schools serving 121,565 students). Schools and Staffing data for school-within-a-school magnets includes all students attending the school—including those who are enrolled in the regular public school housing the magnet—so removing school-within-a-school magnets from the analysis in certain sections allowed for a more accurate understanding of the trends. Both magnet and nonmagnet schools in the Schools and Staffing data set report disproportionately higher shares of white students and lower percentages of poor students than the corresponding averages in the federal public school universe.

In addition to the Schools and Staffing sample, we used a nineteen-item survey instrument covering a range of issues related to racial integration and diversity efforts in magnet schools and programs. It included a number of questions not asked of the federal Schools and Staffing sample. The survey was disseminated at the annual MSA conference in April 2008 in Chattanooga, Tennessee. Though this was not a random sample of the magnet community, following the conference, 236 completed, anonymous surveys were forwarded to the researchers. Survey respondents had the option of identifying the name of their school or district.[37] This information allowed for a comparison of respondents' perceptions of the racial integration of their school(s) to both their self-reported estimates of racial and socioeconomic composition and, when possible, to federal data.

Among those who reported their district identification, MSA sample respondents came from more than sixty districts and from every region across the country. The magnet schools with which they were associated combined to educate approximately four hundred thousand students. The majority of survey respondents were teachers (34.7%), followed by principals and assistant principals (24.2%) and magnet coordinators (15.7%). Although there was considerable variation among school and district student body composition, respondents reported, on average, that their magnet school student populations were 31% white and 63.5% low income (as measured by free and reduced-price lunch status). These numbers closely approximate federal data figures.

Using both survey samples helped us better understand the extent to which students and schools may differ across a variety of magnet contexts and furthered our analysis of the ways in which school structures, such as admissions requirements or program focus, relate to student body composition. Though each of the samples presented some limitations, together they provide the best feasible understanding of magnet school trends and issues. There remains, of course, an obvious need for more extensive research on magnet programs.

Desegregation and Other Goals

The legal, political, and educational landscape has changed dramatically over the four decades that magnet schools have been in existence. Given that many were created as a tool to further desegregation, we examined the extent to which programs still operate under desegregation goals, as well as how a shift away from such goals may have impacted integration levels.

Among the Schools and Staffing respondents, roughly one-third of magnet programs were designed explicitly to integrate students and reduce racial isolation. These schools had higher enrollments of black, Latino, and Limited English Proficient (LEP) students and those qualifying for free and reduced-priced lunch (FRL) than magnet schools without such a focus.

Mirroring trends reported in the Schools and Staffing data set, nearly one-third of magnet programs in the MSA sample reported that they still had desegregation goals—either under court order, under ED's Office for Civil Rights (OCR) agreements, or because of local voluntary action. Yet the combined share of MSA respondents whose magnet schools no longer or never had desegregation goals was more than 40%. Another 12% reported that they had already changed or were in the process of changing to race-neutral enrollment factors (i.e., poverty status or geography). In short, results from the MSA sample suggest that magnet desegregation goals have considerably shifted.

The presence of desegregation goals related to patterns of racial isolation. In the MSA sample, more than three-quarters of schools with desegregation goals were either substantially integrated under the current policy or were experiencing a gradual increase in levels of integration. In the other direction, according to Schools and Staffing respondents, a much higher percentage of magnet schools without a desegregation focus were racially isolated white schools. At the same time, however, considerably higher shares of magnet schools with a racial focus were racially isolated minority schools, compared to non–racially focused schools. Schools and Staffing survey responses thus suggest two trends: magnets without desegregation goals may be more likely to become segregated white schools, while magnets with diversity goals may attract larger shares of minority students.

According to the 2008 MSA sample, just over 35% of magnet schools that had changed or were in the process of changing to race-neutral goals reported a decline in integration levels. Schools with shifting goals also constituted the lowest share of substantially integrated magnets. These patterns indicate that abandoning desegregation goals may not be compatible with maintaining stable integration, at least among this set of schools, though there was a fair amount of variation within the group. Such variation would be expected depending on the types of goals they were switching to (e.g., those that promoted more integration) and how long ago the goals had changed, among other factors.

Magnet Program Focus

Magnet programs are often designed with a special programmatic emphasis.[38] According to the Schools and Staffing sample, magnets that emphasized a certain kind of instructional approach (e.g., Montessori) and those that did not reported roughly equivalent shares of students from different racial, socioeconomic, and linguistic backgrounds.[39] Black students were the slight exception to this generalization, representing 22% of the enrollment at magnets emphasizing an instructional approach, compared to 26% at non–instructional approach magnets.

Magnet programs focused on foreign languages were more likely to enroll disparate shares of student subgroups than magnets focused on specific instructional approaches or gifted and talented programs. For example, LEP and Latino students were much more likely to enroll in magnets focusing on foreign language acquisition.

Magnets specializing in challenging courses also had disparities. Low-income students made up 38% of Advanced Placement–focused magnet enrollment, compared to 49% in magnet schools without an AP focus. LEP-identified students were also less likely to enroll in AP-themed magnets. Similar trends appeared in whole-school magnets: those with an emphasis on AP courses enrolled disproportionately low shares of black students and low-income students and higher shares of white students than whole-school magnets without an AP focus.

Magnet Structure

Magnet programs traditionally follow one of two configurations. Some are established as schools unto themselves, and districts tend to assign these programs their own campuses. For this reason, schools such as these are often referred to as "whole-school magnets." The second type are those within a traditionally zoned school. Some students there attend the magnet program with a special theme, while others go to the same school for nonthemed education. This is referred to here as "a school-within-a-school magnet."

According to data from Schools and Staffing sample respondents, racial makeup varies considerably between whole-school magnet programs and school-within-a-school magnets. School-wide, in comparison to within-school, magnet programs attract a higher share of black students and low-income students. By contrast, within-school programs attract more Latinos and LEP students, with Latino students making up 25% of the enrollment in within-school magnets and

16% of whole-school magnet students. These disparate numbers may stem from within-school magnet programs that have a bilingual focus.

Among Schools and Staffing respondents, school-wide magnet programs report only a slightly higher percentage of racially isolated minority schools than within-school magnets. At the same time, a higher percentage of school-wide magnet programs are racially isolated white schools.

Patterns of racial isolation among whole-school and school-within-a school magnets varied much more substantially within the MSA sample.[40] Two-thirds of whole-school magnets (66.1%) reported substantial integration or a gradual increase in integration levels. By contrast, only half of the school-within-a-school magnets were similarly integrated. Further, 16.6% of school-within-a-school magnets reported being one-race schools, suggesting that they are less effective than whole-school magnets (6.1% of which reported being one-race) in creating racially diverse schools.

Admissions Criteria

Early desegregation plans specified that student assignment to all schools, including magnets, should be based purely on interest, not ability.[41] As a result, most magnet programs originally did not employ admissions criteria. Yet magnet schools today often consider a variety of factors in selecting students for enrollment, particularly if demand exceeds the number of available seats. These factors might include recommendations, special needs, interviews or an audition, academic record, or testing results.

We examined both survey samples to investigate whether a relationship exists between integration levels and the use of selected types of competitive admissions criteria.[42] Our findings from the Schools and Staffing sample indicated that the close to one-third of magnet schools with some type of admissions requirement attracted more racially diverse students. These schools had lower percentages of white students and considerably higher shares of black students. Yet after limiting our analysis to school-wide magnet programs, we found that those with admissions requirements were considerably less likely than those without to enroll FRL-eligible students.

Specific types of competitive admissions criteria were linked to differing racial contexts in magnet schools. Some magnets, for example, consider the results of either standardized tests or other tests adopted by the school in the admissions process. Black, Latino, low-income, and LEP students were less likely to enroll in magnets employing admissions tests. Meanwhile, magnets in the Schools and Staffing sample using a nonstandardized admissions test reported twice the share of Asian students than magnets with different admissions requirements.

Magnet school respondents in the Schools and Staffing sample that used an interview as part of the admissions process enrolled high shares of Latino and low-income students and lower shares of white students than magnets without interviews.[43] Those that considered recommendations as part of the admissions process had higher shares of black students (39%, compared to 31% in schools not using recommendations) and slightly higher shares of low-income students.

MSA survey respondents reported more distinctive competitive entrance criteria trends. In general, higher percentages of schools using essays and interviews reported substantial integration or increasing integration during the past decade. By contrast, magnet schools using test scores or auditions experienced lower levels of integration.

We also examined MSA survey findings for reported integration levels at magnet schools with noncompetitive admissions criteria, like a lottery or open enrollment. These supported the conclusion that non–competitive admissions schools are more integrated. For example, fewer programs using a lottery were one-race schools than magnets using virtually every type of competitive admissions criteria. Respondents from open enrollment magnets reported the highest share of substantially integrated schools and some of the lowest shares of schools with decreasing levels of integration.

In sum, magnet school admissions policies were associated with diversity levels in different ways. Respondents from the Schools and Staffing sample suggested that magnet schools with some type of admissions requirement attracted more racially diverse students. But looking specifically at the different types of requirements, MSA respondents reported that magnet programs using competitive admissions criteria, especially auditions, test scores, and grade point averages, were less likely to be integrated than those using interviews and essays. MSA respondents from magnet schools employing lotteries or open enrollment procedures reported the highest levels of integration.

Widening Access: Outreach and Transportation

Outreach to families and communities is an important component in providing all children equal access to magnet school opportunities.[44] Students cannot attend a magnet school if they do not know about the program. Outreach may take the form of information sessions or fairs at different locations in the community, a parent information center, the work of district employees dedicated to this task, and publications promoting awareness, among other efforts.[45]

The vast majority of respondents in the MSA sample reported that their school(s) had some type of outreach.[46] Interestingly, while all types of outreach were related to higher levels of increasing integration than those of schools without outreach, outreach was also connected to disproportionately high levels of decreasing integration. These trends may reflect two scenarios: (1) some magnet programs might have chosen to engage in outreach efforts because they were experiencing a decrease in integration, and (2) magnet schools' outreach efforts may have helped to increase levels of integration. Of course, it is also possible that outreach efforts had been in place but were not successful in attracting a racially diverse group of students.

The first legal requirement of free transportation for students granted transfers to increase racial diversity appeared in the 1965 Department of Health, Education, and Welfare (the precursor to ED) school desegregation guidelines, which explained what was necessary for district compliance with the 1964 Civil Rights Act.[47] Free transportation has therefore long been considered one of the ways to help ensure that all students are able to attend a program of choice, regardless of family situation, language, socioeconomic status, or racial/ethnic isolation.[48] In recent years, however, a number of school districts around the country have either cut or considered cutting transportation to magnet schools because of financial constraints imposed by the Great Recession.[49]

In the MSA survey—conducted just prior to the recession—we asked about the provision of transportation to magnet schools.[50] We found that white students make up nearly 33% of the student body in the average magnet program offering free transportation, compared to 23% in magnets that do not provide free transportation. Respondents also reported that nearly 12% of schools that did not provide free transportation to their students were largely one race, nearly double the percentage of one-race schools that did provide transportation (6.4%).

PARENTAL DEMAND FOR MAGNET SCHOOLS

Family demand for programs and schools is fundamental to any school choice policy, and demand from a wide variety of families is necessary to ensure diversity. Historically, parents have had considerable interest in magnet schools; for example, one analysis found that three-quarters of districts with magnet schools had more demand than available seats.[51] Yet in almost any complex choice system, there are some options that generate more demand than others. In the case of magnet schools, some programs are more magnetic in attracting students. They may also experience varying levels of demand across racial and socioeconomic groups, since families may have different preferences for such factors as a school's theme, reputation, or location.

The MSA survey sought to quantify some of these trends by drawing a distinction between the demand for magnets from all groups versus the demand from some groups. The vast majority of survey respondents indicated that demand for magnet schools had increased in the past decade. However, while almost half reported that demand had increased among all groups, another 19% reported that it had increased among only some groups, suggesting that some magnet schools in this sample were having trouble attracting a broad range of parents.

In this sample, increased demand for magnet programs among all groups was associated with stable or rising integration levels and the presence of desegregation goals. These patterns may suggest that parents value the emphasis that many magnets have traditionally placed on creating racially diverse school environments. Additionally, school-within-a-school magnets tended to be related to strong demand in the MSA sample (61.1% of within-school magnet respondents reported increasing demand among all groups of parents, compared to 45.5% of whole-school magnet respondents), as was special outreach.

TEACHERS IN MAGNET SCHOOLS

The racial composition of public school faculties continues to lag behind that of student enrollment. Overall, white teachers constitute roughly 86% of the teaching force, even though white students make up 55% of the nation's school enrollment.[52]

In addition to offering more-diverse learning environments, magnet programs generally employ more racially diverse faculties than nonmagnet schools. Only 75% of magnet school teachers in the Schools and Staffing sample identified as white. Further, the percentage of black teachers in magnet schools (13%) was more than twice the share of black teachers in nonmagnet schools (6%). Magnet schools also report a higher share of Hispanic teachers (9%, compared to 5% in nonmagnets). Still, as in regular public schools, the diversity of teachers in magnets lags behind that of their students.

Magnet school faculties are more racially diverse than those of nonmagnet schools in every region of the country, but the South has particularly high shares of both black and Latino magnet teachers. Just 66% of southern magnet school teachers were white, compared to 80% in the region's nonmagnet schools. Nearly one-fourth of southern magnet school teachers were black and another one-tenth were Hispanic. While the shares of black and Latino teachers were lower than those of same-race magnet students in the region (40% and 19%, respectively), the South far outpaces other regions of the country in magnet school faculty diversity. This may be the result of a deliberate aim to create more-diverse faculties along with diverse student bodies, perhaps stemming from earlier desegregation plans.

The MSA sample supplemented these findings with evidence regarding the training and stability of magnet teachers. MSA respondents reported that, on the whole, magnet programs provided teachers with little to no training for racially diverse classrooms. Of respondents reporting no training, the highest number were at largely one-race schools. The dearth of training in these environments is troubling, given the reported levels of nonwhite students and white faculty at these schools.

Substantially integrated magnet schools in the MSA sample were associated with significantly lower rates of teacher turnover than schools in the surrounding area. Conversely, one-race magnet schools were the least likely to report low rates of teacher turnover.

CONCLUSION

Magnet schools offer a compelling example of school choice structured explicitly to encourage racial integration. However, in conjunction with broader policy shifts, recent dedication to fostering diversity in magnet schools has wavered.

At their best, magnet schools have provided special curricular offerings along with very good parent information, free transportation for interested students, desegregation standards for student body composition, outreach to eligible students, and selection methods relying on student interest rather than screening tests. Magnet school settings have also contained integrated staffs of teachers drawn by interest and strengthened by training and curricular materials.

In contrast to other forms of choice, magnet schools began as part of a strategy to accommodate parental preferences while accomplishing broader district goals of remedying segregation and promoting racial diversity. Unfortunately, increasing judicial reluctance over the past two decades to support race-conscious desegregation efforts (even when voluntarily adopted by school boards), in combination with the continued persistence of residential segregation and the growth of other forms of public school choice, has created a difficult climate for magnet schools.

In the midst of dramatic federal support for the burgeoning charter school movement, policy discussions have waned regarding the role that magnet schools have played in creating innovative, racially diverse schools and in combining parental choice with explicit goals and structures to attain that diversity. Magnet schools and, more specifically, their desegregation objectives have been overlooked, symptomatic of the movement away from desegregation in all public schools.

The Schools and Staffing and MSA surveys showed that the presence of desegregation goals, outreach and transportation policies, admissions practices, and school focus and structure were all related to enrollment demographics in magnets. The existence of diversity goals was associated with more-diverse magnet environments, though both surveys indicated that just a third of magnets still operate under such policies. Programs conducting outreach to diverse communities were more strongly associated with higher levels of racial integration, as were schools providing free transportation to all students.

This chapter also demonstrates the importance of maintaining racially diverse schools, since lower teacher turnover and higher rates of demand among all groups were associated with the MSA sample's integrated magnet programs. We also found more racial diversity in magnet faculties than in nonmagnet faculties, though the former still reflect the overall disconnect between student and teacher composition in all public schools. In particular, the share of black teachers in magnet schools was more than twice that in nonmagnet schools. Such patterns may result from a deliberate aim to create more-diverse faculties—typical of prior desegregation plans—when schools are also focused on creating diverse student bodies.

As the trend toward increased family choice in public schooling steadily grows, and as students experience intensifying segregation, it is important to understand how to structure choice to promote integration. The findings from this chapter—which suggest ways of increasing diversity among both students and teachers—are applicable to all forms of educational choice.

Magnet schools grew out of an urgent search for some means of combining desegregation and educational innovation to retain middle-class families that had been rapidly leaving central cities. The magnet school movement created some incredibly successful systems and programs. It recent years, though, its original desegregation aim has become unfocused. It is critical that we extend contemporary research on magnet schools, provide more assistance for cities wishing to create or improve magnet systems, and help devise strategies to legally maintain diversity under the *Parents Involved* ruling.

NOTES

1. In the first portion of this chapter, we use *diversity* broadly to refer to students from a variety of racial and socioeconomic backgrounds learning together in an educational setting. We do so recognizing that the definition of *diversity* may vary by district and region. In subsequent sections, however, we provide specific parameters for terms like *segregation* and *integration*.

2. Frankenberg and Siegel-Hawley, *The Forgotten Choice: Magnet Schools in a Changing Landscape;* Goldring and Smrekar, "Magnet Schools and the Pursuit of Racial Balance."

3. Frankenberg and Le, "The Post–*Parents Involved* Challenge: Confronting Extralegal Obstacles to Integration"; Steele and Eaton, "Reducing, Eliminating, and Preventing Minority Isolation in American Schools: The Impact of the Magnet Schools Assistance Program."

4. Metz, *Different by Design: The Context and Character of Three Magnet Schools.*

5. ESAA was established in 1972 to help school districts implement desegregation more broadly. For further information on ESAA and MSAP, see Orfield, *Must We Bus?: Segregated Schools and National Policy,* 245–46, 429–33.

6. Raffel, *Historical Dictionary of School Segregation and Desegregation: The American Experience.*

7. Frankenberg and Le, "The Post–*Parents Involved* Challenge," 1049.

8. Chubb and Moe, *Politics, Markets, and America's Schools.*

9. Goldring and Smrekar, "Magnet Schools: Reform and Race in Urban Education."

10. Goldring and Smrekar, "Magnet Schools and the Pursuit of Racial Balance."

11. Blank et al., *Survey of Magnet Schools: Analyzing a Model for Quality Integrated Education.*

12. Steele and Eaton, "Reducing, Eliminating, and Preventing Minority Isolation in American Schools."

13. The 2003 report covered MSAP grantees from 1998 to 2001. While the first two ED studies assessed the effectiveness of magnets in reducing or eliminating minority isolation as it related to the desegregation goals of each program, the 2003 report did not include a direct assessment of desegregation goals. Christenson et al., *Evaluation of the Magnet Schools Assistance Program, 1998 Grantees;* Brief Amicus Curiae of the American Civil Liberties Union et al. in Support of Respondents, *Seattle/Louisville.*

14. Christenson et al., *Evaluation of the Magnet Schools Assistance Program, 77.*

15. Frankenberg and Le, "The Post–*Parents Involved* Challenge," 1056–59.

16. Christenson et al., *Evaluation of the Magnet Schools Assistance Program, 77*; Brief Amicus Curiae of the American Civil Liberties Union et al.

17. U.S. Department of Education, "Magnet Schools Assistance Program." The department also removed earlier references to specific white-nonwhite student percentages in assessing the extent to which the racial impacts of voluntary plans on the district's other schools are acceptable under Title VI (which prohibits agencies receiving federal funding from discriminating on the basis of race, color, or national origin).

18. This March 2011 online survey, disseminated by Magnet Schools of America, is drawn from Siegel-Hawley and Frankenberg, "Reviving Magnet Schools: Strengthening a Successful School Choice Option."

19. Gamoran, "Student Achievement in Public Magnet, Public Comprehensive, and Private City High Schools."

20. Blank et al., *Survey of Magnet Schools.*

21. Blank, *Educational Effects of Magnet High Schools.*

22. Betts, Zau, and Rice, *Determinants of Student Achievement: New Evidence from San Diego.*

23. Cullen, Jacob and Levitt, "The Impact of School Choice on Student Outcomes: An Analysis of the Chicago Public Schools"; Ballou, Goldring, and Liu, "Magnet Schools and Student Achievement."

24. Eaton and Crutcher, "Magnets, Media, and Mirages," 280–84.

25. Bifulco, Cobb, and Bell, "Can Interdistrict Choice Boost Student Achievement? The Case of Connecticut's Interdistrict Magnet School Program."

26. Engberg et al., "Bounding the Treatment Effects of Education Programs That Have Lotteried Admission and Selective Attrition."

27. Rumberger and Palardy, "Does Segregation Still Matter? The Impact of Social Composition on Academic Achievement in High School."

28. Engberg et al., "Bounding the Treatment Effects of Education Programs."

29. Millem, "The Educational Benefits of Diversity: Evidence from Multiple Sectors."

30. Braddock, "Looking Back: The Effects of Court-Ordered Desegregation."

31. powell, "Towards an 'Integrated' Theory of Integration"; Wells, "The 'Consequences' of School Desegregation: The Mismatch between the Research and the Rationale."

32. References to 2005–6 National Center for Education Statistics enrollment data in this section are based on tables 1–4 in Frankenberg and Siegel-Hawley, *The Forgotten Choice: Magnet Schools in a Changing Landscape.*

33. Goldring and Smrekar, "Magnet Schools: Reform and Race."

34. G. Orfield, Siegel-Hawley, and Kucsera, *Divided We Fail: Segregated and Unequal Schools in the Southland.*

35. Frankenberg and Siegel-Hawley, *The Forgotten Choice.*

36. The authors would like to thank Jia Wang, who did the analysis of magnet school responses from the Schools and Staffing Survey.

37. This was not a required question, a decision made with the intention that, without reporting this information, respondents might give more candid responses.

38. Goldring and Smrekar, "Magnet Schools: Reform and Race."

39. This question was only asked of Schools and Staffing respondents; the MSA survey did not include a section on the focus of magnet schools.

40. Whole-school magnets constituted the largest number by far of schools participating in the MSA survey (70.2%). A 1994 ED evaluation estimated that 58% of magnet schools were whole school and 38% were school within a school. See Steele and Levine, "Educational Innovations in Multiracial Contexts: The Growth of Magnet Schools in American Education."

41. See, e.g., court-ordered or Department of Health, Education, and Welfare (now ED) / OCR agreements.

42. Respondents were allowed to select as many criteria as they wanted, because many schools use more than one factor for admissions. While some magnet schools may employ competitive admissions criteria, it should be noted that recipients of MSAP funding are not allowed to. They can, however, use lotteries to allocate seats in cases where student demand exceeds capacity.

43. These patterns did not hold, or there were minuscule differences, for nonmagnet schools that used interviews and recommendations.

44. Wells and Crain, *Stepping Over the Color Line: African-American Students in White Suburban Schools;* Fuller, Elmore, and Orfield, eds., *Who Chooses? Who Loses?: Culture, Institutions, and the Unequal Effects of School Choice.*

45. Cookson, *School Choice: The Struggle for the Soul of America Education;* Glenn, McLaughlin, and Salganik, *Parent Information for School Choice: The Case for Massachusetts.*

46. Schools and Staffing sample respondents were not asked about outreach methods.

47. Orfield, *The Reconstruction of Southern Education: The Schools and the 1964 Civil Rights Act.* These guidelines became particularly important after the 1965 passage of the Elementary and Secondary Education Act, which increased federal funding for schools but contained a provision allowing for the withholding of money from districts not in desegregation compliance.

48. Wells, "African-American Students' View of School Choice."

49. Frankenberg, Siegel-Hawley, and Tefera, "School Integration Efforts Three Years after *Parents Involved.*"

50. Schools and Staffing sample respondents did not answer questions concerning the provision of transportation.

51. Blank, Levine, and Steele, "After Fifteen Years: Magnet Schools in Urban Education."

52. Frankenberg, "The Demographic Context of Urban Schools and Districts."

PART THREE

Charter Schools and Stratification

6

A Segregating Choice?

An Overview of Charter School Policy, Enrollment Trends, and Segregation

Erica Frankenberg and Genevieve Siegel-Hawley

The expansion of charter schools has been championed by every presidential administration since that of George H. W. Bush, under whom the first such schools were founded. These administrations have supported charters by escalating financial allocations for them and using the presidential bully pulpit to promote their virtues.[1] Given such high levels of federal support, it is not surprising that charter school numbers have exploded over the past two decades, although nationally and in every state, charter schools still serve only a small fraction of the public school enrollment.

In an extraordinary intervention in state education policy making, the Barack Obama administration used leverage created by a national economic crisis to make badly needed emergency funding dependent on the alteration of state laws and policies that excluded or limited the number of charter schools. Thirteen states—including some that eventually did not win Race to the Top funding—promptly changed their policies, essentially making what had been an educational approach of real significance in only a handful of states into a national movement.[2] The Obama administration also focused attention on converting traditional public schools into charters as a solution in its "turnaround" policy for the nation's most troubled Title I schools. It committed billions of dollars through the Title I School Improvement Grants to transform the five thousand lowest-performing schools using one of four reform strategies; the "restart" strategy allowed schools to be converted from public to charter. Since there is no research-based consensus that charters are educationally superior, this forceful policy appears to reflect an ideological position. Undoubtedly, the newest fiscal incentives for states to increase the number of charter schools will only fuel their expansion in the years to come.

Supporters of charter schools cite a number of arguments that have helped the movement gain traction among education stakeholders. Like proponents of other forms of choice, charter school advocates argue that forcing all schools to compete for students will lead to more experimentation and ultimately better outcomes. In an era of skepticism about government, charter schools' autonomy from local school districts may also attract supporters. Some—though certainly not all—civil rights and minority groups support charter schools, arguing that black and Latino students in urban areas with underperforming schools deserve the same opportunity to choose that wealthy and white families exercise when they move to suburban communities with better schools.

The discourse about charter schools' success has largely focused on narrow measures of individual student outcomes. Most of the research on charter schools has examined whether they foster higher student achievement than traditional schools.[3] Less examined has been the extent to which students in charter schools persist to graduation; studies in different cities and states report mixed findings.[4] We also do not fully know about rates of attrition from charter schools or how those trends may impact comparisons to public schools, which must serve all students. One recent study put attrition from charter schools in Chicago in one year at 11%.[5] And there are, of course, many goals of schooling that should be examined in any publicly funded school.

What is common across the justifications for charter schools and the discussion of their "success" is a focus on how they may improve individual outcomes without consideration of larger concerns about how these schools or family choices affect the education of all students. Charter schools draw money and people from public school districts, increasingly segmenting these resources into smaller units, which may become more homogeneous over time.[6] This means not only that resources leave the district instead of benefitting a larger portion of the population than is served by a single charter school but also, because of increased homogeneity, that students are not exposed to others from different backgrounds than their own. Further, it stands to reason that families who choose charter schools will be less invested in the success of the public school district.[7] We see the ultimate realization of this trend in several cities. As more charter schools have opened in Detroit (it had more than seventy in 2008–9), half of its public schools have closed and class size has increased. Likewise, in spring 2012 the Philadelphia school district, facing massive budget cuts and an increasing charter school presence, announced it would disband by 2017.

Charters are the most rapidly growing sector of schools of choice, expanding largely without regard to many of the civil rights safeguards connected with earlier types of school choice. This chapter focuses on the access to and segregation in charter schools of students from different racial, class, and language groups. These factors certainly relate to student achievement, including educational attainment, but we will forgo a consideration of student performance in charters. Decades of research demonstrate the inequality of segregated minority schools and the benefits for all students who attend racially diverse schools.[8]

Despite early suggestions that charter schools could be places of integration because they were not limited by school district boundaries, the emerging research consensus is that, in fact, students are more segregated in charter schools than in public schools, which are also experiencing increasing segregation. Minority concentration is extremely high in charter schools, particularly of African American students. In some instances, charter schools are pockets of white isolation.[9] Because of state legislation about how and where they can be established and who can attend them, most studies of segregation in charter schools concentrate on one state, metropolitan area, or district. Opinions differ as to how to best compare charter and public school segregation, but patterns of racial isolation in charter schools hold across contexts and methods of analysis.[10]

This chapter explains the policy context within which charter schools operate and examines the extent to which they show evidence of oversight for civil rights protections. We then describe patterns of access to charter schools and school-level segregation by race, class, and language. We conclude by discussing the implications of these findings and how policies might restore civil rights considerations into this rapidly expanding sector of school choice.

THE FEDERAL AND STATE POLICY CONTEXT OF CHARTER SCHOOLS

Federal Charter School Policy: Little Civil Rights Guidance

In the past sixty years the vast majority of challenges to segregation have come in federal court, through the enforcement of the 14th Amendment's equal protection clause or the 1964 Civil Rights Act's prohibition on discrimination in school systems receiving federal aid. The actions of the executive and legislative branches of the federal government were important in enforcing these decisions in the face of resistance from recalcitrant states and districts.[11]

As recipients of federal funds, charter schools must, of course, abide by federal requirements that prohibit discrimination on the basis of race, but federal civil rights policy explicitly pertaining to charter schools is relatively nonexistent. In one of the few examples of federal leadership on charter schools and civil rights, at the end of the Bill Clinton administration in May 2000, the Department of Education's Office of Civil Rights (OCR) issued nonbinding guidance describing, among other topics, how charter schools should recruit and admit students of different racial backgrounds. During the first term of the George W. Bush administration this guidance was archived, meaning that it no longer reflects the official position of the Department of Education. It had not been reinstated as of three years into the Obama administration.[12]

Currently, federal policy guidance on civil rights in charter schools pertains to those funded by the Public Charter Schools Program (CSP). This guidance, released by the George W. Bush Department of Education, requires recipients of CSP funds to use a lottery in admissions decisions if there are more applicants than available spaces. However, this requirement allows for flexibility that might advantage some groups of students over others. For example, charter schools may weight the lottery and, potentially more significantly, set minimum criteria that aspiring students must meet to join the pool of eligible applicants. If schools require academic credentials, such as certain grade point averages or standardized test scores, they may advantage students who attended more rigorous schools or, given the achievement gap, white or wealthier students. Likewise, if a condition for admission is that a student's family must commit a certain number of hours to participating at the school, that will likely eliminate many students whose parents have inflexible work schedules. Either of these scenarios would allow schools to use a lottery—even without weighting—but could result in a student body with more limited representation of disadvantaged groups than that of a school without minimum criteria. The guidance for CSP recipients also includes requirements for outreach, but they are vague enough that the outreach may not be fully effective in contacting diverse groups of potential students; for example, the guidance requires outreach to all members of a community, but *community* could be defined as a neighborhood or in other narrow ways.[13]

State Policy on Civil Rights and Charter Schools

By 2007–8, forty states and the District of Columbia had passed legislation authorizing the creation of charter schools. Differences in legislation wording, time in existence, and local contexts mean that what charter schools look like—and how they operate—in each state varies widely. In Missouri, for example, they can only be established in Kansas City and St. Louis. Ohio also limits the districts in which charter schools can be established. State charter school legislation also has provisions relating to student diversity, and other policies may impact charter school enrollment.

We classify the District of Columbia and the forty states that allow charter schools into the following major categories describing their charter legislation as it relates to diversity:

1. Has a general nondiscrimination provision

2. Requires that establishing a charter school will not interfere with an existing desegregation plan or OCR agreement
3. Includes some type of affirmative step to create diverse schools, such as a plan to achieve a racially diverse enrollment or requiring charter schools to reflect the composition of the surrounding district.[14]

Some states require both compliance with desegregation orders and more affirmative steps for diversity and are classified in both categories. In general, the very presence of three different kinds of legislation relating to charter school diversity signals a lack of cohesive guidance and regulation.

Our analysis illustrates the variation in charter diversity policies among states. Just sixteen states fall under the strongest, "more affirmative steps" category.[15] Fifteen others simply require that charters comply with existing desegregation plans. Finally, another thirteen have provisions containing a general nondiscrimination clause similar to what is embedded in federal legislation, in essence offering only a vague and likely difficult to enforce commitment to integration in charter schools.[16]

The second group of states has legislation requiring compliance with existing desegregation plans. Language in this type of legislation is comparable to the Supreme Court's *Wright et al. v. Council of the City of Emporia et al.* obligation for public school districts created while a desegregation plan was in place not to interfere with such compliance efforts. As more desegregation plans come to an end, however, this category of state legislation may have less impact on charter schools.[17]

The third category can be more far-reaching, though it varies in terms of whether states require or allow affirmative efforts.[18] We find that ten of the sixteen states in this category (or one-quarter of all states with charter legislation) require affirmative diversity actions of all charter schools. The other six states either require affirmative steps of some schools and districts or simply permit such actions.

The types of affirmative steps fall into two broad classes. Ten states specify that charter schools should have a plan to recruit a diverse group of students; several of these states, in fact, require that charter petitions delineate specific recruitment or outreach efforts in order to be approved. The second class requires or permits charter schools to have enrollments that reflect the population of the surrounding district or community. Since it discusses schools' racial composition, states with this kind of legislation are more likely to be in legal jeopardy after *Parents Involved in Community Schools v. Seattle.* Of these, Nevada and South Carolina have the most specific laws—Nevada specifies that charter school enrollment should be within ten percentage points of the overall racial composition of the district, and South Carolina specifies twenty percentage points—but each state's legislation also provides for flexibility in meeting these targets. Yet if charter schools find a way to achieve these goals without considering the race of individual students, it is probable that such goals will still be deemed permissible under *Parents Involved*.[19]

The lack of federal guidance on charter school diversity and the importance of avoiding racial isolation in charter schools may have helped contribute to the array of different directives at the state level. State legislation may thus reflect a federal reluctance to regulate charter segregation levels as the focus on school racial isolation has waned.[20]

Aside from diversity requirements and nondiscrimination obligations, there are other, seemingly race-neutral decisions about charter schools that could have significant consequences for their ability to attract a diverse student enrollment. For instance, the lack of legislation extending charter transportation across district lines undercuts one of the sector's integrative strengths: the opportunity to attract a diverse student body across such boundaries. Since most school segregation today exists between districts, charters represent an important opportunity to override the lines dividing school systems.[21]

Charter legislation related to location, district type, transportation, and funding may indirectly relate to racial diversity. If charters are incentivized or required to locate in predominately poor, nonwhite areas—some states only permit the establishment of charter schools in central city districts—they are likely to disproportionately serve disadvantaged populations, especially if free transportation is not available. And if state-funding formulas encourage charters to reach out to disadvantaged students or to give priority to students in academically failing schools, the likelihood that they will attract a racially or socioeconomically diverse population further diminishes.

In conclusion, state legislation relating to diversity in charter schools varies widely across the forty-one jurisdictions that allow them. Indeed, on every topic outlined above, state guidance is a complex array of legislation. This may reflect the dearth of federal leadership on integration in charter schools, but on their own, states have not come up with a streamlined approach to either promoting racial diversity or avoiding racial isolation in charters. And while this review of the legislation suggests that a number of states have at least considered ways to promote diversity in the charter sector, there is no guarantee that the confusing variety of laws produces adequate results.

Civil Rights Compliance

The courts are one venue for enforcing civil rights requirements in charter schools. In *Wright v. Emporia*, the U. S. Supreme Court prohibited the formation of a new school district that it judged would impede an existing district's ability to desegregate. Because creating a charter school is similar to creating a splinter school district, federal courts could look to the effects of a proposed school on enforcing existing desegregation orders.[22] Following the Supreme Court's guidance in that decision, more recent federal court decisions require charter schools to show that they will comply with existing desegregation orders and not negatively affect desegregation.[23]

OCR also plays an important role in enforcing the civil rights of students in all schools, including charters, through compliance reviews and by investigating complaints it receives. These rights include protection from racial discrimination and disparities that are prohibited by Title VI of the 1964 Civil Rights Act. OCR has stepped in to monitor the relationship between a charter school and an ongoing desegregation order. The Beaufort County (South Carolina) school board approved a charter for Riverview Charter School in December 2008, which was conditional on the school's compliance with an existing desegregation decree. In summer 2009, after an OCR investigation found that Riverview was out of compliance—its share of white students was more than thirty percentage points higher than the district's—the school signed an agreement with OCR stipulating that it would immediately enroll all minority students on its waiting list and engage in more extensive recruitment of minority students and teachers. Riverview also altered its admissions policy for 2010–11 to give preference to applicants who lived in zip codes with a higher percentage of minority residents.[24]

PATTERNS OF CHARTER SCHOOL ACCESS AND SEGREGATION

Expansion without Civil Rights Safeguards

Despite the lack of strong guidance on—or evidence of interest in—protecting the civil rights of its students, the charter school sector continues to expand. From 2000–1 to 2007–8, the total enrollment in charter schools nearly tripled, to more than 1.2 million students, and federal incentives have undoubtedly spurred increases beyond that. The number of charter schools doubled during this period, while the number of traditional public schools declined. In 2000–1, there were eight states with no charter schools, yet in 2007–8 four of them each had at least five thousand students enrolled in charters.

The growth of charter programs is not evenly spread across the country. The majority of charter school enrollment was concentrated in five states: California, Michigan, Arizona, Florida, and Ohio. In twenty-two other states, less than 1% of public school students were in charter schools. Outside of Washington DC, where nearly one in four students were in charter schools, the highest concentrations of charter school students were in Southwestern and Midwestern states, the latter of which may be seeing the growth of charters as an alternative to declining central city districts.

Racial Composition and Segregation

Nationally, charter schools enroll a disproportionately nonwhite group of students. In particular, the share of black students in charter schools (32%) is twice that of traditional public schools (16%). Latino students are also slightly overenrolled in charters (24% of enrollment, compared to 21% in traditional schools). However, in many of the states where Latino students constitute the highest share of public school enrollment, they are underenrolled in charter schools. Whites are a much lower percentage of students in charter schools (39%) than in public schools (56%), but this is not the case everywhere in the country. In one-quarter of all states with charter schools, these schools have a disproportionately high percentage of white students compared to other public schools, and all but one of these states (North Carolina) are in the West. Charter schools in the aggregate may be serving a larger proportion of minority students than traditional public schools, but this pattern differs by region. In particular, regional trends suggest that charter schools in the West—one of the most racially diverse areas of the country—may offer students less-diverse (i.e., more disproportionately white) educational settings.

While these aggregate trends give us a general sense of who charter schools are serving—and of the segregation between sectors—they tell us little about students' school-level experiences. To better understand this issue, we examined the racial concentration of students in individual charter schools. Whether on the national, state, or metropolitan level, we reach the same conclusion: even as minority segregation in public schools is the highest it has been in two decades, the percentage of students of every racial/ethnic background in racially isolated minority charter schools is substantially higher.[25] This finding is consistent with other research on charter school segregation, though few nationwide studies exist.[26]

Nearly 60% of charter students are in predominantly minority schools, and 36% are in schools where 90%–100% of the students are from minority backgrounds. Comparatively, just 15% of traditional public school students are in 90%–100% minority schools. The pattern is even more extreme for some racial groups (see table 6.1). Twenty-two states—or more than half of those that authorize charter schools—have majorities of black students in 90%–100% minority charter schools. Charter schools have a higher concentration of black students in 90%–100% minority schools than traditional public schools in every state, even those where charters enroll a disproportionately high share of white students. For example, in California the percentage of white students in charter schools is nine points higher than that of white students in regular public schools. Even

TABLE 6.1 Percentage of charter and public school students
in segregated minority schools, by race/ethnicity, 2007–8

	Charter			Public		
	50%–100% minority	*90%–100% minority*	*99%–100% minority*	*50%–100% minority*	*90%–100% minority*	*99%–100% minority*
White	19	2	0	13	1	0
Black	89	70	43	72	36	15
Latino	83	50	20	77	38	9
Asian	60	23	9	55	15	1
American Indian	61	31	11	49	20	9
All students	58	36	19	38	15	4

SOURCE: National Center for Education Statistics, Common Core of Data, "Public Elementary/Secondary School Universe Survey Data, 2007–08" data file.

so, 52% of California's black charter students are in intensely segregated minority schools, compared to 41% of black traditional public school students. In other words, the state's charter school racial composition cannot explain away the pattern of high minority concentration in its charter schools.

Although white segregation differs from minority segregation, it is also important to study because students in white isolated settings do not receive the educational benefits of students in diverse schools. In contrast to minority segregation, the concentration of white students in charter schools is less extensive than in traditional public schools. Just 7% of charter school students of all races are in 90%–100% white schools—considerably less than the rate for traditional public school students. Among white charter school students, however, the rate is 16%. Given that that fewer than 40% of charter school students are white, that figure is surprisingly high (although still lower than the percentage of white students in segregated white traditional public schools). And the higher share of white students in Western charters also results in higher percentages of students in 90%–100% white schools than in regular schools in that region.

Other Equity Issues: Class and Language Status

There are many ways in which charter schools—or any schools of choice—can be a nonviable option for some families. For example, not offering appropriate special education services can limit access for students who need such instruction.[27] Likewise, some families will be understandably hesitant to enroll their students in charter schools that do not have teachers who can educate non–native English speakers. Another fundamental civil rights concern is the availability of subsidized lunch programs at schools of choice.

Low-income students.   The U.S. Department of Agriculture (USDA) administers the National School Lunch Program (NSLP), which provides free or reduced-
price lunch (FRL) to students whose family income is up to 185% of the federal poverty threshold. The USDA provides two means of participation: schools
can either (1) have students fill out forms to determine individual eligibility, for
which the USDA reimburses the school, and charge non-FRL-eligible students
for school lunches, or (2) serve free lunch to all students for a period of four years
while only submitting paperwork in the first year to establish the number of low-
income students for reimbursement. While some in the charter school community have expressed concern about the administrative burden of the NSLP, the
second option allows schools a lot of flexibility.

Yet despite the importance of understanding the extent to which charter
schools enroll and concentrate low-income students, this is extremely difficult
thanks to serious gaps in federal data sets. In the aggregate, 38% of charter school
students and 41% of traditional public school students qualified for FRL in 2007–8.
However, nearly one-quarter of all charter schools, as shown in the National
Center for Education Statistics's (NCES) Common Core of Data, reported a missing value for this measure (only 5.5% of traditional public schools had a similar
missing value). There was also a higher share of charter schools than public
schools reporting no FRL-eligible students, which could either legitimately be the
case or represent the lack of a subsidized lunch program.[28] In a nationally representative sample of schools surveyed in 2007–8, nearly 21% of charter schools
and only 1.5% of traditional public schools reported that they did not participate
in the NSLP. Among charter schools that did offer subsidized lunches, a higher
share of students were FRL (58%) than among public schools (39%).[29]

The percentage of low-income students in charter schools with at least one
FRL-eligible student is higher than in traditional public schools with at least one
FRL-eligible student, 52% and 44%, respectively. A higher percentage of charter
school students attend majority low-income schools than do their traditional
public school peers.

More concerning, however, is that in the aggregate, charter schools without
evidence of participation in the NSLP enrolled student populations that were
just 8% black, while charter schools that offered subsidized lunches reported 34%
black enrollment on average. Furthermore, nearly 70% of students in the first
group of schools were white. These patterns suggest that some charters may be
disproportionately serving both white and economically advantaged students.
They also hold when looking at school-level relationships between FRL-eligible
students and racial concentration. In seven states at least a thousand students
per state attended charter schools without any FRL-eligible students and where
90% or more of the students were white. For example, nearly 60% of Michigan
students in charter schools without any evidence of a school lunch program were

in charter schools that were 90%–100% white. In some of these states, the only intensely white charter schools were those without any FRL-eligible students. Complementary overlaps exist in many states, with charter schools with heavy concentrations of nonwhite students reporting FRL data.

Linguistic minority students.   The extent to which charter schools serve English-learner (EL) students is also unclear. Part of the challenge in assessing this is due to the way in which data about EL students is reported. In the data set that contains the entire universe of public (including charter) school students, EL students are reported only by local educational agency (LEA; i.e., school district), not by school. There are major concerns about this data's validity. In 2007–8, NCES Common Core reported only seven EL students in California, a state that had more than a million students who grew up in non-English-speaking households.[30]

Among charter schools that are separate LEAs, 4.6% of students are classified as EL, similar to the 4.8% in LEAs without any charter schools. Of the 1,500 LEAs containing only one charter school, only one-quarter had 1% or more students who were EL. However, nearly 800,000 EL students are educated in LEAs that contain both charter and noncharter schools, making it impossible to know which sector of schools they are enrolled in.

We examined other federal data sets in an effort to get clearer answers about EL access to charter schools and what types of schools these students were in. In both data sets—which only contain samples of public schools—charter schools appear to be serving fewer EL students.[31] In one, 68% of traditional public schools and 52% of charter schools enrolled at least one EL student, but the percentage of EL students in charter schools (14% of all students) was higher than that in public schools (8%).[32] Among a separate sample of schools in 2005–6, public schools enrolled a somewhat higher share of EL students (9.9%) than charter schools (8.7%).[33]

Thus, even after examining multiple federal data sets, we find it impossible to draw strong conclusions about EL students in charter schools, due to the lack of comprehensive data. This is an area in need of research. Further, federal oversight is essential to ensure the collection of basic data necessary to answer simple yet significant questions about access and equity for a burgeoning group of K–12 students.

How Does Geography Affect These Patterns?

In many states, charter schools are created as separate LEAs, but without the regular LEAs' geographic basis.[34] Therefore, unlike regular public schools, they should be able to attract students across school district boundaries. Given the high levels of between-district segregation, this should theoretically give charter schools an advantage in achieving a diverse student enrollment.[35] Because charter schools in many places, regardless of whether they are separate LEAs or not, are able to attract students across traditional boundaries, comparisons to the districts in which they are located are misleading. While charter schools are disproportionately located in cities (56% in 2007–8, compared to 30% of traditional public schools), fewer geographic disparities exist between charter and noncharter schools when considering their distribution across metropolitan areas (e.g., city and suburban schools). Some argue that charters' urbanicity accounts for the differences in enrollment and segregation between the charter and public school sectors. However, our analysis challenges this as the explanation for charter school segregation.

The share of white students in city charter school enrollment was just seven percentage points less than that in traditional urban public schools. Similarly not-large gaps in white student enrollment also appeared between charters and noncharters in both the suburbs and town/rural areas, and there were likewise small differences in the percentages of low-income students in charters and in regular public schools in the same locale. Thus, it is likely that charters' student body composition is connected to their geographic skew. But differences in segregation patterns tell another story. In cities, 52% of charter students attended 90%–100% minority schools, while 34% of traditional public school students attended schools with similarly high levels of minority concentration. The difference was similar to the overall gap of twenty percentage points between students in segregated charter and noncharter minority schools across all locations. Further, although low, the percentage of students in segregated white schools in cities was higher for charters than for traditional public schools. It is therefore unlikely that the location of charter schools alone explains their higher segregation. Instead, these patterns suggest that the cross-district potential of charter schools to alleviate school segregation has not been fulfilled in urban areas.

CONCLUSION

It is perhaps not surprising that we see trends of increased segregation in charter schools and between traditional public and charter schools, given both the legal and policy contexts described above and the financial context in which charter schools operate. Janelle Scott has described the perverse funding incentives that might benefit segregated charter schools.[36] Private foundations—which, like the federal government, have helped to underwrite the expansion of charter schools—prefer donating money to programs (e.g., the Knowledge Is Power Program, or KIPP) and management organizations that can demonstrate improved educational opportunities and outcomes for extremely disadvantaged populations. More broadly, in many respects there is little incentive or oversight to motivate charter schools to deliberately seek out a diverse enrollment, particularly when this might mean extra outreach efforts, coordinating transportation beyond district boundaries, recruiting a more diverse faculty, and other such policies. These efforts would add to the workload of charter school staff, who already lack the kind of support that districts' central offices provide. Thus, as we consider how charter schools could truly become integrative schools of choice, we must think holistically about the policies governing them, the measures they are held accountable for, and the financial incentives to which their operators are responding. State charter school legislation should be amended with specific stipulations pertaining to enrolling a diverse student body and regulating charters' effects on any integration efforts of surrounding public school districts. State lawmakers should also review other charter policies—such as transportation and funding structures—to make sure they support efforts to create diverse schools.

When examining the trends in charter school segregation, it is worth remembering that they would have been viewed very differently under earlier legal standards. Policies allowing open enrollment in many northern districts (e.g., Boston and Cleveland), which resulted in patterns of segregation similar to the ones described here, were ruled to be discriminatory and therefore illegal.[37] Likewise, the 1972 Supreme Court *Emporia* decision prohibited the formation of a new school district seeking to break away from one that was implementing a desegregation order, simply because this would have impeded efforts to remedy segregation. The courts of an earlier era likely would have viewed skeptically the formation of charter schools as LEAs and their contribution to segregation as described above. While there are some examples of courts carefully evaluating how the establishment of charter schools will affect desegregation efforts, these contemporary rulings are more the exception than the rule.[38] Moving forward, courts should carefully investigate not simply the intent of parties interested in establishing a new charter school but also the likely effects such a school would have, as part of a holistic examination that considers the charter school's enrollment and outreach policies and, if a charter management organization is involved, the composition of other charter schools it operates.

At a time when Secretary of Education Arne Duncan has stressed reviving OCR, federal agencies should lead the renewed focus on charter schools by issuing new guidance about protecting the civil rights of all students who might be interested in school choice options and including charter schools and the surrounding school districts as a priority of technical assistance efforts, particularly following the December 2011 guidance about voluntary integration. OCR can also begin more visible enforcement efforts with charter schools. The federal government can make sure that charter school financing is not going to exacerbate racial isolation, which the Supreme Court has recognized is a compelling interest. Federal courts should renew their scrutiny of the effects of creating new educational agencies, like charter schools, as school districts continue to try to combat racial segregation. Finally, the federal government should require better reporting of basic information about whom charter schools serve so that simple questions about access and equity can be fully addressed. Without such information, taxpayers who finance charter schools are being shortchanged, unable to ascertain whether their money is supporting schools with limited access for certain subgroups of our population.

Although not an explicit focus of this chapter, public schools are, of course, affected by the rapid growth of charter schools. One of the earlier concerns about magnet schools was that they would cream the best students, leaving other schools with fewer academically talented, engaged students. As we consider charter schools, it is important to think about how students' choosing them affects public schools, which still enroll far more students. In some respects, charter schools, which may operate as independent agencies and therefore have little reason to care about the impact of their recruitment and enrollment (and attrition) on surrounding schools, may be more analogous to institutions of higher education, which are largely autonomous. Studying how colleges and universities have expanded access and created diversity might provide helpful lessons for charter schools.

It is up to researchers, educators, policy makers, and private foundations to refocus the discussion about charter schools. The dialogue must move away from debating outcomes or whether to alter policy so creating charter schools is easier, and toward figuring out how to make schools of choice available to all and, subsequently, how to make these choices high-quality, integrative experiences for all. Without such coordinated effort, we may end up inadvertently funding a dual sector of public schooling whose existence to date has shown uneven performance and extensive segregation.

NOTES

This chapter is drawn in part from Frankenberg, Siegel-Hawley, and Wang, "Choice without Equity: Charter School Segregation," and Siegel-Hawley and Frankenberg, "Does Law Influence Charter School Diversity? An Analysis of Federal and State Legislation."

1. For example, in the aftermath of Hurricane Katrina, the U.S. Department of Education provided substantial funding for establishing charter schools in areas affected by the storm, with most of the money going to New Orleans. Charter schools now educate the majority of public school students in the city and are seen as a model of how school choice can improve urban education. See chapter 8.

2. eSchool News, "Race to the Top Program Spurs School-Reform Debate."

3. See, e.g., Center for Research on Educational Outcomes, *Multiple Choice: Charter School Performance in Sixteen States*; Booker, Gilpatric, and Gronberg, "The Effect of Charter Schools on Traditional Public School Students in Texas: Are Children Who Stay Behind Left Behind?"; Carr and Ritter, *Measuring the Competitive Effect of Charter Schools on Student Achievement in Ohio's*

Traditional Public Schools; Hoxby, "Achievement in Charter Schools and Regular Public Schools in the United States: Understanding the Differences"; Zimmer et al., "Charter Schools in Eight States: Effects on Achievement, Attainment, Integration, and Competition."

4. Vaznis, "Charter Schools See More Attrition: Fewer Students Are Graduating, Union Study Finds"; Booker, Gilpatric, and Gronberg, "The Effect of Charter Schools on Traditional Public School Students in Texas."

5. Karp, "One in 10 Charter School Students Transfers Out."

6. Weiher, *The Fractured Metropolis: Political Fragmentation and Metropolitan Segregation.*

7. Orfield, "Schools More Separate: Consequences of a Decade of Resegregation."

8. Linn and Welner, eds., *Race-Conscious Policies for Assigning Students to Schools: Social Science Research and the Supreme Court Cases.*

9. Ibid.; Ni, *Are Charter Schools More Racially Segregated than Traditional Public Schools?;* Renzulli and Evans, "School Choice, Charter Schools, and White Flight."

10. Frankenberg, Siegel-Hawley, and Wang, "Choice without Equity," 6–8.

11. Orfield, *The Reconstruction of Southern Education: The Schools and the 1964 Civil Rights Act.*

12. Federal guidance issued in December 2011 on race-conscious policies in K–12 schools presumably applies to charter schools, although they were not specifically mentioned.

13. Frankenberg and Siegel-Hawley, "Overlooking Equity: Charter Schools and Civil Rights Policy."

14. For the specific categorization for each state, see Siegel-Hawley and Frankenberg, "Does Law Influence Charter School Diversity?"

15. In their article "Charter Schools: Racial Balancing Provisions and *Parents Involved,*" Oluwole and Green labeled these provisions "racial balancing" and found that fourteen states were in this category. Our count includes Massachusetts and Colorado, which amended their charter school legislation in 2008, the year of publication for Oluwole and Green.

16. The 2001 *Alexander v. Sandoval* decision in particular would make it difficult to enforce nondiscrimination in charter (and other) schools.

17. Further, Wendy Parker has argued that the guidance in this type of legislation is somewhat vague. See "The Color of Choice: Race and Charter Schools."

18. Oluwole and Green, "Charter Schools."

19. See ibid., 50–52, for suggestions of how charter schools in states with racial balancing provisions may comply with *Parents Involved.*

20. The disparate types of legislation regarding the importance of avoiding racial isolation in charters contrast starkly with the original goals of many magnet programs.

21. Reardon and Yun, "Integrating Neighborhoods, Segregating Schools."

22. See, e.g., Green and Mead, *Charter Schools and the Law: Establishing New Legal Relationships,* 114–17.

23. *Davis v. East Baton Rouge Parish School Board et al.; Berry v. School District of Benton Harbor.* In the latter case, the court denied the establishment of a charter school because of a lack of information about its potential student body composition.

24. Cerve, "Riverview Charter School Approves New Lottery Enrollment Plan."

25. Orfield, "Reviving the Goal of an Integrated Society: A 21st Century Challenge." We draw similar conclusions from our analysis of racial exposure/isolation of students, another measure of segregation. See Frankenberg, Siegel-Hawley, and Wang, "Choice without Equity."

26. See Miron et al., "Schools without Diversity: Education Management Organizations, Charter Schools, and the Demographic Stratification of the American School System"; Finnegan et al., "Evaluation of Charter Schools Program: 2004 Final Report."

27. Welner and Howe, "Steering Toward Separation: The Evidence and Implications of Special Education Students' Exclusion from Choice Schools"; see also chapter 7.

28. National Center for Education Statistics, Common Core of Data, "Public Elementary/Secondary School Universe Survey Data, 2007–08" data file.

29. National Center for Education Statistics, Schools and Staffing Survey, 2007–8 data file.

30. National Center for Education Statistics, Common Core of Data, "Public Elementary/Secondary School Universe Survey Data, 2007–08" data file.

31. U.S. Department of Education, Office for Civil Rights, Civil Rights Data Collection, 2005–6; National Center for Education Statistics, Schools and Staffing Survey, 2007–8 data file.

32. National Center for Education Statistics, Schools and Staffing Survey, 2007–8 data file.

33. U.S. Department of Education, Office for Civil Rights, Civil Rights Data Collection, 2005–6.

34. In fifteen states all charter schools are separate LEAs, in six others the vast majority are separate LEAs, and in another six only some are separate LEAs.

35. Reardon and Yun, "Integrating Neighborhoods, Segregating Schools"; Clotfelter, "Private Schools, Segregation, and the Southern States."

36. Scott, "The Politics of Venture Philanthropy in Charter School Policy and Advocacy."

37. *Morgan v. Hennigan; Reed v. Rhodes.*

38. Siegel-Hawley and Frankenberg, "Does Law Influence Charter School Diversity?"

7

Failed Promises

Assessing Charter Schools in the Twin Cities

Myron Orfield, Baris Gumus-Dawes, and Thomas Luce

Minnesota passed the nation's first charter school law and has been at the center of a debate over the possible contribution of the surging charter school movement to equalizing opportunity for students of color, who are increasingly isolated in low-performing schools that are segregated by ethnicity and poverty. Unfortunately, data from the Twin Cities, two decades after charters began, shows that these schools are more segregated and unequal than public schools. Policies that produce true access to higher-achieving and more integrated schools, this study concludes, might well rely on more successful Minnesota experiments with regional approaches designed to voluntarily integrate schools across district lines through parental choice.

Minnesota pioneered the charter school concept in 1991.[1] Charter schools have been promoted as a means to improve the performance of students who have no alternative to low-performing traditional public schools. Proponents also claim that charter schools will extend school choice to low-income families and families of color, who do not have the choices that many families of means offer to their children, and that, by severing the link between neighborhoods and schools, charter schools will allow students of color to escape the racially segregated schools they attend.

However, an analysis of current and historical data for all charter schools in the Twin Cities metropolitan area shows that charter schools have failed to deliver on these promises. They are far more segregated than traditional public schools, even in school districts where traditional public schools are already racially segregated. The data also show that after almost two decades of experience, most charter schools still perform worse than comparable traditional public schools.

These findings make it clear that most charter schools offer a poor choice to low-income students and students of color—one between low-performing public schools and charters that do even worse. Other public school choice programs in the region offer much better choice schools to low-income students and students of color. Finally, the means that charter schools in the metro use to compete with their traditional counterparts have hurt public education by encouraging racial segregation in the traditional public school system.

CHARTER SCHOOLS AND SEGREGATION IN TWIN CITIES SCHOOLS

Charter school enrollments in Minnesota grew rapidly from the early 1990s to around twenty-four thousand students in the 2006–7 school year. This represents about 3 percent of the state's K–12 student population.[2] The most rapid growth happened late in the period—between the 2000–1 and 2005–6 academic years, Minnesota's charter school enrollments increased by nearly 120 percent, while traditional public school enrollments fell by 2 percent.[3] Much of the increase has been from the growth in enrollment of students of color, especially in the Twin Cities metropolitan area. In 2007, more than half of charter school students were students of color, compared to about one-fifth of traditional public school students.[4]

Similarly, poverty concentrations are even higher in charter schools than in traditional public schools. In 2007, more than half of charter school students were eligible for free or reduced-price lunches, compared to 30 percent of traditional public school students.[5]

Charter schools are highly concentrated in the core of the Twin Cities metropolitan area. About a quarter of the state's charters are in Minneapolis, while St. Paul hosts another 20 percent. The suburbs of the Twin Cities metro had more than a fifth of the state's charter schools, while a third were outside the metro area.[6] This uneven distribution contributes to the heavy concentration of low-income students and student of color.

Metro area charter schools are highly segregated. By 2008, more than half (53 percent) of these schools were nonwhite segregated, compared to less than a fifth (18 percent) of traditional public schools.[7] Segregation in charter schools has also increased over time—in 1995, less than a third (29 percent) were nonwhite segregated.

Charter schools are also much less likely than traditional schools to be integrated. The share of integrated schools among charters hovered around 20 percent from 1995 to 2008. In contrast, the trend was clearly upward in traditional public schools, 39 percent of which were integrated in 2008, up from 25 percent in 1995 and almost twice the percentage for charters.

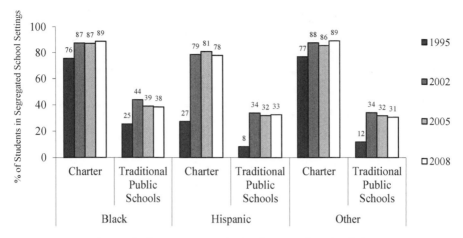

FIGURE 7.1. Students of color in segregated school settings by school type, Twin Cities.

As a result of these differences, an overwhelming majority of students of color attending charter schools are in segregated settings. In fact, students of color who attended charter schools in 2008 were more than twice as likely as their counterparts in the traditional public schools to be in a segregated setting (see figure 7.1).[8]

Racial segregation of this degree is inevitably accompanied by concentrations of poverty because virtually all nonwhite segregated schools have high concentrations of poverty.[9] High-poverty schools, of course, are associated with a wide range of negative educational and life outcomes for students, including low test scores, high dropout rates, low college attendance rates, low earnings later in life, and greater risk of being poor as adults.[10]

In the Twin Cities in 2008 the poverty rate in nonwhite segregated schools of all types was almost six times the poverty rate in predominantly white schools and more than two and a half times the poverty rate in integrated schools.[11] The relative poverty rates of charter and traditional schools reflect this pattern. Student poverty rates in charter schools are much higher than in traditional public schools in the Twin Cities region.[12] Moreover, the gap has increased over time. In 2008 half of the students in charter schools were free lunch eligible, compared to only slightly more than a fifth of the students in traditional public schools, a difference of twenty-eight percentage points. In 1995 the difference was only eighteen points—36 percent poverty in charters compared to 18 percent in traditional schools.

The claim that charter schools would liberate students of color from racially segregated school districts by severing the link between the racial composition of schools and of neighborhoods does not hold up in the Twin Cities metro. On the contrary, the racial makeup of charter schools and their neighborhoods strongly resemble each other. Most nonwhite segregated charters are in either racially segregated urban school districts or inner suburbs experiencing racial transitions. Predominantly white charters, in contrast, are mostly in white suburban school districts, with a few in white urban neighborhoods with racially diverse district schools.[13]

The differences between charters and traditional schools in figure 7.1 are not simply the result of where charters locate. In the central cities—where the concentrations of charters are greatest—they also compare unfavorably with traditional schools in many ways.

In St. Paul, nearly 90 percent of all students of color who attended charter schools did so in segregated settings, compared to about three-quarters of those in traditional public schools. Moreover, there are a few predominantly white charter schools in St. Paul, a school district with no predominantly white traditional schools, suggesting that charter schools create an avenue for white flight for the students who live in this racially diverse school district. Fully one-half of white students in charters in St. Paul were in predominantly white schools in 2008.

In Minneapolis, segregation among charter school students was even more intense. Roughly 96 percent of the nonwhite students in Minneapolis charter schools attended school in segregated settings, compared to 80 percent of the nonwhite students in traditional public schools.

Charter schools have also contributed to increasing segregation by income in the two central city districts. In 1995, rates of student poverty in charters and traditional schools in Minneapolis were similar—just over half of the students in both systems were free lunch eligible. By 2008, 73 percent of charter students qualified for free lunches, compared to 57 of traditional public school students.[14]

Student poverty rates in the St. Paul Public School District showed a more complicated pattern. In 1995, average student poverty rates in St. Paul were higher in charter schools than in traditional public schools—77 and 49 percent of students were free lunch eligible, respectively. By 2008, the pattern was reversed—50 percent in charters versus 73 percent in traditionals. However, this change was due entirely to the growing number of white segregated charter schools in the district. In 1995, it had only one white segregated charter school. By 2008, there were seven, with poverty rates well below average. This led to a decline in overall student poverty rates among the district's charters. The average student poverty rate in the district's white segregated charter schools in 2008 was 18 percent. In contrast, the average student poverty rate in the district's nonwhite segregated charter schools in the same year was 84 percent—much higher than the 71 percent average poverty rate in the district's traditional public schools.[15]

In sum, virtually any way that you cut the data, charter schools have clearly increased the degree of segregation by race and income in schools in the Twin Cities metropolitan area and in the region's central cities.

CHARTER SCHOOLS AND STUDENT PERFORMANCE
IN THE TWIN CITIES

Some proponents of charter schools have argued that they are still a worthy educational innovation if they can educate students better than traditional public schools, even in segregated school settings.[16] This argument, which is essentially a "separate but equal" justification for school segregation, relies on claims of quality educational performance in charter schools. To assess the validity of this argument, we performed a statistical analysis of charter school performance in the Twin Cities.

The statistical analysis compared the performance of different types of elementary schools in the region in two dimensions—student performance in math and reading proficiency.[17] Separate statistical models for reading and math proficiency in the 2007–8 academic year for all elementary schools in the Twin Cities metropolitan area show that traditional schools outperformed charter schools after controlling for school size and student poverty, race, special education needs, limited language abilities, and mobility rates.

The percentages of students proficient in reading or math were the dependent variables—the measures to be explained by the statistical model—in the multiple-regression analysis used to test the hypothesis of performance differences in the different types of schools.[18] Both of the models controlled simultaneously for school size and racial mix and student poverty, special education needs, limited-language abilities, and mobility rates. Finally, two variables were included to determine whether test scores were systematically lower in charter schools or suburban schools participating in the Choice Is Yours Program. This is another education program in the metropolitan area designed to provide students in high-poverty environments an alternative to their traditional neighborhood school.[19] It enables poor students in the Minneapolis School District to attend lower-poverty, less-segregated schools in nine participating suburban districts.

Two multiple-regression models were run—one for reading test scores and one for math scores. Consistent with the extensive literature that emphasizes the importance of student poverty rates on academic performance, the results implied that the percentage of poor students is the most significant determinant of pass rates in elementary schools in the Twin Cities region. Poverty rate showed the strongest correlation with test scores of all of the included variables in both models.[20]

In both models, the coefficient for the charter school variable was significant at the 99 percent confidence level and negative.[21] This means that in both reading and math, a lower percentage of charter school students reached proficiency

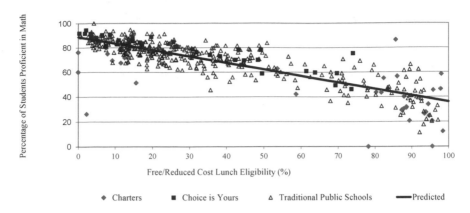

FIGURE 7.2. Poverty and math proficiency rates in Twin Cities elementary schools, 2007–8 (simple correlation: -0.84).

compared to students who attended traditional elementary schools with identical characteristics across all of the variables included in the model. The average difference was 8.77 percentage points for reading proficiency and 9.59 for math. Other variables that showed statistically significant effects on both proficiency rates included some of the race measures and the percentage of students in special education programs.

As noted above, the percentage of students in poverty was found to be the strongest factor in school pass rates. The poverty effect is so strong that a simpler, more intuitive comparison of the bivariate relationship between poverty and performance can be used to assess performance across school types. Figure 7.2 plots this relationship and shows that charter schools are far from providing superior educational opportunities to students. In 2008, the math performance of students in 79 percent of charter schools was lower than expected given the poverty levels of these schools. In striking contrast, 88 percent of the schools that participated in the Choice Is Yours Program performed better than expected in math. The Choice Is Yours Program clearly offers students a much better selection of schools than charter schools. Traditional schools also outperform charters—53 percent of traditionals performed better than expected.[22]

CHARTER SCHOOL COMPETITION AND
SEGREGATION IN TRADITIONAL PUBLIC SCHOOLS

Charter schools intensify segregation in the public education system by encouraging ethnicity-based niche competition from the traditional school system. This deepens racial and economic segregation in traditional public schools. School districts in the Twin Cities metro have responded to charter competition in two ways that intensify racial and economic segregation.

First, they have sponsored targeted ethnic charter schools of their own in an attempt to recapture the district students who left for charters. Like the vast majority of the charters in the Twin Cities metro, district-sponsored charters were mostly nonwhite segregated schools with high concentrations of poverty. In St. Paul in 2008, five of the eight charter schools sponsored by the district were nonwhite segregated schools with very high poverty rates. One of the remaining three also had a very high poverty rate. District-sponsored charters intensified racial and economic segregation in Minneapolis as well. Four of the five district-sponsored charters there were nonwhite segregated schools with high poverty rates, while the other one was a predominantly white charter school with a low poverty rate.[23]

Second, school districts responded to ethnic-niche-based competition from charter schools by initiating ethnocentric programs and magnet schools. In both Minneapolis and St. Paul for instance, as the school districts lost students to Hmong-focused charter schools, they started their own Hmong-focused programs or magnet schools. In Minneapolis, the district responded to charter competition by initiating the Hmong International Academy—a Hmong-focused program within the Lucy Laney Elementary School. Located in north Minneapolis, this school originally had a relatively small group of Hmong students along with the African American students who made up the majority of the student body. As participation in the program grew, the district moved it to a separate building, also in north Minneapolis. Initially, the Hmong International Academy operated as a school within a school that separated Hmong students from African American students. When the program moved to a different physical site, it resulted in the creation of two separate school facilities—each serving a specific racial/ethnic group.

In St. Paul, the district responded to losses of students to Hmong-focused charters by creating a Hmong-focused magnet school in the heavily Hmong-populated Phalen Lake area.[24] This decision transformed a neighborhood school that was already 63 percent Asian and 93 percent poor into a magnet school with an even greater concentration of Hmong students. The change was needed so the district could provide the same transportation options to Hmong students in other parts of the city as Hmong-focused charters do. Since these changes have not reduced the school's extremely high poverty rate, the overall opportunities available to Hmong students in the district have not been enhanced.

To the extent that charter schools deepen existing concentrations of poverty in the school system as a whole, they undermine opportunities for educational equity for students of color.

CONCLUSIONS AND POLICY RECOMMENDATIONS

The national spotlight on Minnesota's experience with choice has focused on its key role in launching the charter school movement but has given far less attention to the deeply disappointing results. Charter school advocates said that their movement would provide access to better schools than the segregated and impoverished city districts could provide, but the opposite has occurred. Minnesota has, however, been gradually developing other regional integration approaches that show better social and educational outcomes.

Charter schools have not served the students of the Twin Cities metro well. They perform worse than similar traditional public schools academically (measured by test scores) and socially (measured by segregation rates). Other choice programs—Choice Is Yours in particular—offer students of color and low-income students access to better-performing, less-segregated schools. In some areas, charter schools segregate white students as well, in predominantly white charter schools, acting as an avenue for white flight. Finally, charter schools hurt the public school system because they have led to competition to create segregated schools. Districts in the Twin Cities metro area have responded to charter competition by creating ethnocentric charter schools, programs, and magnet schools. Overall, charter school competition in ethnic niches has been particularly detrimental for students of color and low-income students because it deepens the level of racial and economic segregation in the traditional public school system.

Many of the problems associated with charter schools result from the fact that there is no legal mandate in Minnesota to socially and economically integrate them. Charter schools do not have to be segregated; on the contrary, they should more proactively integrate the region's students across social and economic fault lines. However, charter schools in Minnesota are exempt from the state's desegregation rule, which applies to other public schools. As a result, they do not participate in the state's School District Integration Revenue Program, which distributed about seventy-nine million dollars in integration revenue funds to eighty school districts in 2005. At a bare minimum, charter schools, which are much more segregated than the region's traditional public schools, should be subject to the same desegregation and integration standards as traditional public schools. They are, after all, public schools and receive taxpayer funding, so should be equally subject to civil rights law and policy.

However, simply subjecting charter schools to Minnesota's desegregation rule is unlikely to reduce their social and economic segregation because, in its current form, the rule does not even effectively promote integration in the traditional public school system. The main problem is that it is intended simply to increase "racial contact" among students of different backgrounds rather than decrease racial segregation in schools.[25]

In the name of promoting racial contact, school districts have used integration revenue funds for a wide array of projects, ranging from one-day multicultural events to interdistrict magnet schools and cross-district transportation. The majority of these activities have done little to encourage physical or educational integration. The rule should be changed to unambiguously and proactively support the integration of school districts, schools, and classrooms.

The existing rule also creates perverse financial incentives. Under the School District Integration Revenue Program's current formula, a district would cease to receive integration aid once it became desegregated. Right now the program simply distributes resources to segregated districts and schools. It has a substantial pool of money and should be restructured to reward the school districts, schools, and programs that actually integrate schools and classrooms. Those that fail to reduce segregation should lose integration revenue funding.

Substantially increasing the financial incentives of the Integration Revenue Program could have a significant impact at times, like now, when school districts are facing severe budget pressures. One efficient way to do this would be to use the funding formula to reward school districts on a per-student basis for documented pro-integrative movements. This would focus efforts on outcomes.

It is important to create incentives for schools and school districts to implement pro-integrative measures because they face numerous disincentives, including parent resistance and transportation costs. These disincentives frequently lead to segregated schools, even in districts that understand the academic and citizenship values of integration.

Another important feature of an incentives-based strategy is the treatment of districts that lose students as a result of pro-integrative strategies. The majority of school segregation in the Twin Cities is the result of segregation between school districts rather than between schools within individual districts. Until housing patterns become truly integrated on a regional scale, integrating schools will require that some students cross district boundaries. Integrative programs, such as the Choice Is Yours Program, have shown that when incentives are attached to integrative moves, school districts are very willing to accept students. However, sending districts—Minneapolis, in the case of Choice Is Yours—that participate in interdistrict programs now face a financial penalty when students leave them, because state funding follows the student to his or her new district. (Although the associated enrollment decline also reduces costs, the cost reduction for the sending district will almost inevitably be less than the loss of revenue, because of fixed costs, hiring-firing rules, and other factors.)

A revised formula could avoid this problem by compensating both receiving and sending districts for pro-integrative interdistrict moves. For instance, both participating districts could get extra revenue when a white student from a predominantly white-assigned school moved to an integrated or predominantly nonwhite school in another district, or when a student of color from a predominantly nonwhite-assigned school moved to an integrated or predominantly white school in another district.

Finally, an incentives-based program could encourage the creation of pro-integrative attendance areas by providing extra money to districts with students in schools meeting a predetermined definition of racial integration.[26]

The Twin Cites already have three large-scale multidistrict collaboratives—the West Metro Education Partnership (WMEP), the East Metro Education District (EMID), and the North West Suburban Integration School District (NWSISD). By many measures, these districts have impressive programs. WMEP and EMID both run several integrated, high-performing schools that are available to students across their member districts. NWSISD provides transportation to magnet programs across its district. All three organizations run programs geared to promoting integration in classrooms and educating teachers.

These collaboratives, however, have not been entirely successful. They have not prevented the segregation and resegregation of schools in their member districts. All three include districts that have made segregative boundary decisions, which the integration districts do not have the power to greatly influence. This inability is a serious shortcoming.

While intradistrict decision making is important, interdistrict segregation explains the bulk of segregation in the Twin Cities metropolitan area. The collaboratives' interdistrict desegregation plans are therefore potentially very important. However, these programs are relatively limited in scope. The scale of segregation in the Twin Cities is large—there are currently more than one hundred nonwhite segregated schools in the region, for instance—and the three integration districts presently provide integrated education to only a limited number of students. For example, the two magnet schools administered by WMEP only enroll about one thousand students in total. Further, underparticipation, often by the wealthiest and whitest districts, also undercuts the integrative potential of the districts.

For integration districts to serve a significant role in integrating schools within their boundaries—both within and between member districts—the state legislature will have to expand their powers and programs.

While the three interdistrict collaboratives have had some successes in increasing the amount of school integration across the metro area, they cannot remedy segregation. School and residential segregation occur on the metro, not the district, level. Attempting to remedy school segregation in just one sector of the metro region is likely to create conditions for school resegregation in the rest. Further, even school districts within interdistrict collaborations have been continually expanding their magnet school programs, often at great expense, to keep students in their district or attract students from other districts. This competition is costly and can be counterproductive.

A region-wide integration district—or a system of four or five districts—would not have a magic bullet policy to solve all problems. This district could, however, engage in several activities with the possibility of lessening segregation. Two areas with significant potential are creating magnet schools and making school boundary decisions.

Integration district magnet programs could include metro magnets, designed to draw students across district boundaries, and district magnets designed to reduce within-district segregation. High-quality magnets provide one avenue for metro-wide integration. The metro integration district could create new magnets designed to both maximize integration and offer students different curricula than they would have access to in individual districts. One strategy could be to offer specialized magnet schools at large, high-density job centers, like Minneapolis's central business district or suburban job centers on parts of the interstate ring-road system.

Magnet schools at job centers have tremendous integrative potential and can be an attractive alternative for commuters. Job center magnets allow working parents to more easily attend parent-teacher conferences and after-school events and pick their children up after work. In other metros, parents who send their children to job center magnets are able to lunch with their children. Since parents often commute across significant distances, it makes sense for these job center magnets to be available to students on a metro-wide basis and run by a metro integration district. Job center magnets can also maintain integrated student bodies by enrolling students whose parents work in the job center while guaranteeing a certain number of seats to students who live in a nearby designated attendance zone.

Regional integration districts could also be effective in coordinating district-run magnet schools. School districts face conflicting incentives in sending students to interdistrict magnet schools. While districts are presumably happy to offer more choices to their students, losing students means lost funding and, potentially, public criticism for being unable to maintain enrollments. While these disincentives can be eased by reforming the Integration Revenue Program, it will still often make sense for districts, especially large ones, to operate their own magnets aimed primarily at their own students.

Finally, segregation in schools and housing are inextricably linked. Segregated neighborhoods lead to segregated neighborhood schools. Segregated schools in turn contribute to the process that creates and maintains segregated neighborhoods. Potential residents, especially families with children, evaluate local schools when deciding where to live. As a result, segregated schools or schools in the midst of racial or economic transition accelerate neighborhood transition. Any strategy to create a more integrated region must therefore deal with housing and school segregation simultaneously.

An important implication of this is that the placement of affordable housing and the public programs supporting affordable housing are critical parts of any regional strategy to integrate schools and neighborhoods. Concentrating affordable housing in racially segregated or poor neighborhoods deepens segregation. By encouraging the construction of affordable housing units in such neighborhoods, many government programs contribute to residential segregation. This in turn worsens school segregation.

More effective regional management of the two largest federal affordable housing programs—the Low Income Housing Tax Credit (LIHTC) and Department of Housing and Urban Development Section 8 programs—would provide significant integrative potential. For instance, since the inception of the LIHTC program, approximately five thousand LIHTC units have been built in Twin Cities suburbs and an equal number in the central cities.[27] Although this fifty-fifty split seems fair, it does not reflect the fact that Minneapolis and St. Paul represent just 23 percent of the region's total population. Given the much greater minority shares and poverty rates in central city schools and neighborhoods, a subsidized housing distribution that more closely matched population shares would be much more likely to promote integrated neighborhoods and schools than the current distribution. Instead, the current pattern concentrates low-income households in racially segregated or transitioning neighborhoods and intensifies school segregation by creating more racially identifiable schools with very-high-poverty enrollments.[28]

The distribution of low-income housing under Section 8 programs also contributes to residential segregation in the region. Like LIHTC units, low-income housing units and people who use vouchers provided by the Section 8 program are disproportionately in the central cities and stressed inner suburbs, where the shares of minority and low-income residents are already high. The distribution of households of color who have access to housing through Section 8 programs is also heavily skewed toward the central cities and stressed inner suburbs.

The skewed distribution of Section 8 units and Section 8 voucher use leads to not only further concentrations of race and poverty in neighborhoods but also more racially identifiable schools with high-poverty enrollments. By locating low-income residents of color and their children in highly segregated elementary school attendance zones, Section 8 programs intensify school segregation in the region.

The Institute on Race and Poverty has estimated the potential effects on school integration of different types of housing policy reforms.[29] These simulations show that the impact of two straightforward, integrative changes in the LIHTC and Section 8 programs could be very significant. If LIHTC and Section 8 units were assigned randomly by race and located across the region in proportion to population, then the resulting increases in nonwhite households (and therefore students) in districts that are now largely white could reduce school segregation in the region by a third. If Section 8 vouchers were also distributed this way, the result would be another 15 to 20 percent reduction in segregation rates. Thus, a simple strategy to use federal affordable housing programs in race- and location-neutral ways could have a significant effect on region-wide school segregation.

Clearly, these kinds of simulations represent fairly rough estimates. However, the fundamental message is equally clear. Given the distributions of both affordable housing under these programs and of students in Twin Cities schools, relatively modest housing policy changes have the potential to make a serious dent in school segregation. Further, many of these very worthy school integration programs currently have long waiting lists for participation. If they were expanded to levels commensurate with demand, they might create something very special in America—a stably integrated regional school system.

NOTES

This chapter is a short version of Institute on Race and Poverty, "Failed Promises: Assessing Charter Schools in the Twin Cities."

1. U.S. Department of Education, *Evaluation of the Public Charter Schools Program: Final Report.*

2. State of Minnesota Office of the Legislative Auditor, "Evaluation Report: Charter Schools."

3. McMurry, "Minnesota Education Trends, 2000 to 2005."

4. State of Minnesota Office of the Legislative Auditor, "Evaluation Report."

5. Ibid.

6. Ibid.

7. Nonwhite segregated schools are defined as those where the share of black, Hispanic, or Asian students exceeds 50 percent, or where the relative share of white students does not exceed 30 percent. Predominantly white schools are those where the black, Hispanic, and other nonwhite shares are each less than 10 percent. All remaining schools are classified as integrated. The methods used to classify schools are described in Orfield and Luce, eds., *Region: Planning the Future of the Twin Cities,* appendix A, 293–94.

8. For students of color, a segregated setting was defined as a school that was nonwhite segregated.

9. G. Orfield and Lee, *Brown at 50: King's Dream or Plessy's Nightmare;* ibid., *Racial Transformation and the Changing Nature of Segregation;* ibid., *Why Segregation Matters: Poverty and Educational Inequality;* Wirt et al., *The Condition of Education 2005.*

10. G. Orfield and Lee, *Brown at 50;* ibid., *Why Segregation Matters;* Balfanz and Legters, "Locating the Dropout Crisis: Which High Schools Produce the Nation's Dropouts"; Swanson, "Sketching a Portrait of Public High School Graduation: Who Graduates? Who Doesn't?"; Kahlenberg, *All Together Now: Creating Middle-Class Schools through Public School Choice.*

11. The average poverty rate (measured by the percentage of free and reduced-price lunch eligible students) in nonwhite segregated schools was 81 percent, compared to 14 percent in predominantly white schools and 31 percent in integrated schools. M. Orfield and Luce, *Region.*

12. Student poverty rates for charters were measured by free lunch eligibility rather than free and reduced-price lunch eligibility because reduced-price lunch statistics for 1995 were not available. Adding reduced-price lunch eligibility for later years did not change the results.

13. Institute on Race and Poverty, "Failed Promises: Assessing Charter Schools in the Twin Cities," has a map showing the distribution of charters in the region.

14. Ibid.

15. Ibid.

16. Manno, Vanourek, and Finn, "Charter Schools: Serving Disadvantaged Youth."

17. Full results for the multiple-regression models discussed in this section are in Institute on Race and Poverty, "Failed Promises."

18. The multiple-regression analysis was for elementary schools only. There are many reasons for this choice. First, performance rates differ by type of school—pass rates are lower for middle and high school students than for elementary students. An analysis of all schools would have to account for these differences carefully, complicating it significantly. Average math pass rates were 69 percent for elementary schools, 61 percent for middle schools, and 32 percent for high schools. In reading, they were 70, 66, and 64 percent respectively. Second, there are reasons to believe that school poverty data is more reliable at the elementary school level than it is at the middle and high school levels. Low-income students at the middle and high school level frequently avoid declaring free and reduced-price lunch eligibility, to avoid the stigma of poverty. Elementary school students are likely to be less prone to this behavior, and as a result the discrepancy between reported and actual eligibility rates is likely to be smaller for this age group. Third, middle and high schools are limited in number, making the multiple-regression analysis less reliable because of the smaller sample size. There were more than 400 elementary schools but only 128 middle schools and 115 high schools with data for all of the relevant variables. The regression model was run for middle and high schools separately, and the results were similar to those reported for elementary schools. In particular, the measured charter school effects were negative.

19. See Institute on Race and Poverty, "The Choice Is Ours: Expanding Educational Opportunity for All Twin Cities Children," for a full description of the program.

20. This can be seen by comparing the t statistics: the higher the t statistic, the stronger the correlation after controlling for all of the other variables in the analysis. Poverty had the largest relative impact in each regression—the standardized coefficients are larger for poverty than for any of the other included variables. The charter school variable shows the second-largest effect in both models.

21. "Significant at the 99 percent confidence level" means that the probability that the relationship found in the regression analysis is simply the result of chance or sampling error is less than 1 percent.

22. The results are similar for reading scores (not shown in figure 7.2). Only 24 percent of charters performed better than expected in reading, compared to 79 percent of Choice Is Yours Schools and 54 percent of traditional schools.

23. Institute on Race and Poverty, "Failed Promises."

24. Moua, "Are Hmong Students Making the Grades?"

25. Hobday, Finn, and Orfield, "A Missed Opportunity: Minnesota's Failed Experiment with Choice-Based Integration."

26. See Institute on Race and Poverty, "A Comprehensive Strategy to Integrate Twin Cities Schools and Neighborhoods," for a full description and a simulation of the impact of these proposals.

27. Khadduri, Buron, and Climaco, "Are States Using the Low Income Housing Tax Credit to Enable Families with Children to Live in Low Poverty and Racially Integrated Neighborhoods?"

28. Institute on Race and Poverty, "A Comprehensive Strategy to Integrate Twin Cities Schools and Neighborhoods," 28.

29. See Institute on Race and Poverty, "The Choice Is Ours," for a complete description of these simulations and the distribution of Section 8 housing and voucher use with a full set of maps. See also ibid., "A Comprehensive Strategy to Integrate Twin Cities Schools and Neighborhoods." Both studies are available at www.irpumn.org.

8

The State of Public Schools
in Post-Katrina New Orleans

The Challenge of Creating Equal Opportunity

Baris Gumus-Dawes, Thomas Luce, and Myron Orfield

Charter schools in New Orleans have been hailed as the silver lining from Hurricane Katrina. The state of Louisiana used the hurricane as an opportunity to rebuild the entire New Orleans public school system, considered among the worst in the country, and launched the nation's most extensive charter school experiment. These rebuilding efforts focused on charter schools not only as the primary means of expanding school choice in the public school system but also as a way of holding failing traditional public schools accountable at the district level. This chapter evaluates how this experiment has fared in providing quality education to all students of the New Orleans public school system.

The new system steered a minority of students, including virtually all of the city's white students, into a set of selective, higher-performing schools and another group, including most of the city's students of color, into a group of lower-performing schools. Segregation of students is a cause for concern. Racial and economic segregation undermine the life chances and educational opportunities of low-income students and students of color. School choice does not by itself empower students of color to escape this, especially when it leads them to racially segregated, high-poverty schools.

All of the major components of the city school system serve large majorities of black and poor students. The few schools with significant numbers of white students represent the only integrated schools in the system. These few sites serve essentially all of the city's white students. To guarantee equal educational opportunities to all of the city's students, the school system must both look inward—

limiting the selectivity system, which favors a few schools over the majority of the system, and renewing its commitment to the city's traditional public schools— and outward, taking a more balanced, regional approach to school choice in the form of regional magnet schools and new interdistrict programs, which do not yet exist.

RACE AND POVERTY IN NEW ORLEANS METROPOLITAN AREA SCHOOLS

The schools of New Orleans were overwhelmingly black and poor before Hurricane Katrina, and they remain so today. Students of color represent 95 percent of the student body in city schools and 50 percent in the suburbs. Nearly all of the small number of white students in city schools are concentrated in just a few schools, and nearly half of suburban schools are integrated. Three-quarters of students of color in the region attend highly segregated schools, compared to only 22 percent of white students. (Segregated schools have 0–30 percent white students.)

Race and income are closely correlated. As a result, racial segregation concentrates students of color in very-high-poverty schools. In 2009, 65 percent of New Orleans students of color attended schools with free and reduced-price lunch eligibility rates in excess of 75 percent, compared to 19 percent of white students.

Despite the massive displacement that Hurricane Katrina caused in 2005, the racial demographics of the New Orleans metropolitan area in 2009 (2008–9 school year) looked only slightly different from those of 2004 (2003–4 school year). The nonwhite share of students in the region was 65 percent in 2004 and 61 percent in 2009. Most schools in the city had shares of students of color greater than 90 percent in both years. Many suburban schools also had substantial shares of students of color, especially in areas close to New Orleans, but black students especially were concentrated in the city both before and after Katrina. City schools were more than 90 percent black in both 2004 and 2009. Hispanic and other students of color, on the other hand, were largely in suburban schools. In 2009, 43 percent of the black students in the region attended school in the city of New Orleans, compared to only 9 percent of Hispanic students and 17 percent of other students of color.

Student poverty rates increased between 2004 and 2009 in both the city and the suburbs—from 75 to 85 percent in the city and from 58 to 62 percent in the suburbs. Although poverty rates are clearly higher in the city, poverty was prevalent across the region. Poor students in suburban school districts actually outnumbered those in city schools in both years. In 2009, 69 percent of the region's poor students attended school in suburban school districts—compared to 57 percent who did so in 2004.

The pattern of racial segregation in schools did not change much between 2004 and 2009. City schools remained mostly nonwhite segregated, while predominantly white and integrated schools were dispersed across the suburbs.[1] Region-wide, three out of every five schools were nonwhite segregated and about a third of schools were integrated in both years. The share of predominantly white schools hovered around 10 percent during this period. However, suburban schools were far more integrated than city schools. Nearly half of the former were integrated during this period, while more than 90 percent of the latter were nonwhite segregated.

High racial segregation in city schools and modest but increasing levels of racial segregation in suburban schools meant that most of the region's students of color attended school in a segregated setting.[2] In 2009, 73 percent of all students of color in the region attended a segregated school—down from 80 percent in 2004. In contrast, only 22 percent of white students in the region attended a segregated school in 2009. Representing the overwhelming majority of students of color in the region, blacks faced the highest levels of segregation in both the city and the suburbs. Although the percentage improved slightly post-Katrina, 78 percent of black students in the region were still in segregated settings in 2009 (down from 84 percent in 2004). Hispanic students did not experience as much segregation as black students. Nevertheless, segregation rates increased for Hispanics—48 percent were in segregated schools in 2009, up from 43 percent in 2004.

Racial segregation was less extreme in suburban schools than in the city. However, many students of color (including most black students) in the suburbs still attended segregated schools. Overall, nearly 60 percent of suburban students of color attended segregated schools in both 2004 and 2009. Black students experienced the highest rates of segregation (64 percent in 2009), followed by Hispanics (44 percent), other students of color (40 percent), and white students (23 percent). The largest change pre- and post-Katrina was for Hispanic students, who experienced a seven-point increase in segregation.

Racial segregation particularly harms students of color. Virtually all nonwhite segregated schools have high concentrations of poverty, while white segregated schools tend to have low rates of poverty.[3] Students face vastly different levels of poverty depending on the racial composition of the schools they attend. In 2009, the average poverty rate in nonwhite segregated schools (68 percent) was twice that (34 percent) of predominantly white schools, with the rate of integrated schools falling in the middle.

Almost all of the nonwhite segregated schools in the region in 2009 had very high poverty rates. In fact, 99 percent of them met the standard definition for high poverty (40 percent of the student body eligible for free or reduced-price lunch), and 84 percent were very high poverty (free and reduced-price lunch eligibility rates above 75 percent). In 2009, a student of color was 1.5 times more likely than a white student in the region to attend a high-poverty school. Black and Hispanic students were most likely to attend high-poverty schools, with Asians and American Indians only slightly less so.

The discrepancy between white and nonwhite students is even greater for very-high-poverty schools. In 2009, students of color in the New Orleans region were nearly 3.5 times more likely to attend very-high-poverty schools—65 percent of nonwhite students were in very-high-poverty schools, compared to just 19 percent of white students. Black students were most likely to be in very-high-poverty schools, at nearly 70 percent. The corresponding shares for Hispanics, Asians, and American Indians were 46, 41, and 43 percent respectively. Students from all races experienced an increase in impoverished classrooms from 2004 to 2009.

A substantial research literature documents that high- and very-high-poverty schools are not environments conducive to quality education. They tend to have high teacher turnover, resulting in less-qualified and less-experienced staff. They offer limited curricula, taught at less-challenging levels. They lower the educational expectations of students and fail to provide positive peer competition and influence.[4] High-poverty schools are associated with a wide range of negative educational and life outcomes for students, including low test scores, high dropout rates, low college attendance rates, low earnings later in life, and greater risk of being poor as adults.[5]

A NEW GOVERNANCE STRUCTURE:
THE EMERGENCE OF CHARTER SCHOOLS

The New Orleans region experienced a major transition in school governance. The hurricane virtually wiped out the city's schools, creating a policy vacuum that the state government and the George W. Bush administration used to launch a citywide charter experiment.

The role of charter schools has increased dramatically. In 2004 the region had 6 charter schools, educating 2,307 students, just 1 percent of those in the area. By 2009 it had 49 charter schools, educating 21,294 students, or 15 percent. All but two of these were in New Orleans, where the share of students attending charter schools increased from just 2 percent in 2004 to 57 percent in 2009, making this the city with the highest percentage of charter school students in the nation.[6]

This rapid growth has occurred within a complicated governance structure with five distinct governance structures. The five categories are: (1) Orleans Parish School Board (OPSB) traditional schools, (2) OPSB charter schools, (3) Recovery School District (RSD) traditional schools, (4) RSD charter schools, and (5) Board of Elementary and Secondary Education (BESE) charter schools.

Historically, the OPSB oversaw all public schools in the city of New Orleans. Just before Katrina, the state of Louisiana declared many of the public schools in the city to be failing and created the RSD to manage these schools. BESE directly authorized two charter schools. Hurricane Katrina accelerated the expansions of the RSD and the charter system, as it led to the passage of Act No. 35 in November 2005. Act No. 35 expanded the power of the state to interfere in failing school districts and authorized it to transfer the majority of district schools to the state-operated RSD for a period of five years.[7]

Initially, the OPSB district retained control over only five high-performing traditional public schools, but it quickly expanded in the wake of Katrina. Significant resources from the federal government and the philanthropic community earmarked for charter schools became available immediately after Katrina. At the same time, the Federal Emergency Management Agency (FEMA) was slow in releasing aid to traditional public schools. As a result, charter schools became the main instrument of recovery efforts.[8]

CONSEQUENCES OF THE RAPID EXPANSION OF THE CHARTER SYSTEM

Important consequences of the extremely rapid emergence of the charter sector in New Orleans can be seen in several dimensions, including how different parts of the school system compete for students and resources, the potential for future growth of the charter and traditional systems, and the accountability of the entire school system. The most important competitive consequence is that the playing field is not level for the different sectors of the system. This is primarily because of the formal and informal tools available to some sectors, which enable selective admissions. There are good reasons to believe that in the long run, a fully charterized system is not sustainable. Finally, the underlying characteristics of the charter system and experiences in other parts of the country imply that the accountability usually demanded of programs using tax money will eventually become a problem, in the form of either increasing costs or financial irregularities.

Unequal Competition

New Orleans's five school sectors are governed by different rules and do not compete for students on a level playing field, which directly affects the ability of schools to shape the characteristics of their student populations. Louisiana is the only state in the nation that allows selective admission standards for charter schools.[9] Many of its charter schools therefore have explicit academic standards for incoming students.[10] This gives them the ability to skim the most-able, least-costly-to-educate students from the city's traditional public schools.

Even charters without admissions requirements have more control than their traditional counterparts over student body characteristics. They exercise this control through a variety of means, including enrollment processes, discipline and expulsion practices, transportation policies, location decisions, and marketing or recruitment efforts.[11]

The enrollment processes for charter schools—which include recruiting efforts, information and publicity dissemination, and setting admission requirements—give them many opportunities to control the characteristics of their students.[12] The admission process usually requires parent meetings with school officials, where the fit between the school and the family is informally scoped out.[13] During these meetings, officials may steer students to apply or not apply. Charter schools may also ask parents to sign a parental involvement contract requiring them to volunteer a number of hours at the school.[14] These schools can deny admission to, for example, low-income students whose parents cannot commit to these contracts.[15]

Charter schools also have the liberty of weeding out hard-to-educate students after admission through their discipline and expulsion practices. Unlike traditional public schools, charter schools can state in their contracts and enforce strict expectations regarding student performance, effort, and behavior.[16] As a result, it is much easier for charter schools than public schools to expel students.[17] Traditional public schools have to take in all kinds of students, including those with discipline problems. They must therefore dedicate a significant portion of their already scarce resources to hiring security officers. In 2007, RSD spent $465 per student on security—"a rate 10 times higher than it was for NOPS [New Orleans Public Schools system] schools before Hurricane Katrina."[18] Some RSD schools had more security guards than teachers per pupil.[19] In 2008, there was one security guard for every 49 students in RSD-run high schools, compared to one for every 167 students in OPSB-run high schools.[20]

Charter schools can also influence the characteristics of their student body through their transportation policies. Traditional public schools must provide free transportation to their students. In contrast, charter schools can effectively restrict the access of low-income students by not providing free transportation. In 2009, all six of the public schools in the city of New Orleans that did not provide free transportation were charter schools. Both of the public schools that provided only limited transportation were also charters. A number of charter schools provide free Regional Transit Authority (RTA) tokens either in lieu of or to supplement their limited yellow bus services.[21] But as of May 2009, only 30 percent of the city's pre-Katrina bus fleet was operational and only half of the former bus routes were open.[22] Informal surveys show further limitations on free transportation by charter schools, including free transportation only to addresses within a mile of the campus and transportation on a first-come, first-served basis.[23] Given that a majority of students in the district now attend schools of choice, most of which are not neighborhood schools, transportation is a crucial component of access. Louisiana state law requires local public school districts to provide free transportation even to private schools but not to charters.[24]

The location decisions of charter schools are an additional instrument for shaping their student body composition.[25] Charter schools have great flexibility in choosing the neighborhoods they will serve. Geographical proximity and convenience play an important role in determining which schools parents choose for their children.[26] There is evidence from New Orleans that charter schools are indirectly shaping their enrollments through their location strategies. Recent research found that while many charters were in low-need locations, district schools were mostly in more challenging, high-need areas. Charter schools were in zip codes with lower crime rates than those of public school zip codes.[27]

The city of New Orleans presents a substantial opportunity for charter school operators to expand because of its exceptionally large private school sector. Private schools enroll an average 10 percent of the students in most southern regions, and this percentage has tended to stay fairly stable.[28] In striking contrast, private schools in New Orleans enroll nearly a third of all students in the city.[29] Charter schools could potentially lure students from private schools by locating close to them. In fact, a spatial analysis of all schools in New Orleans shows that most charter schools, including the RSD charters, are within a stone's throw of private schools.[30]

Charter schools also shape their student enrollments through marketing and recruitment efforts.[31] Since charter school revenues come from per-pupil funding by the state, they often need a certain number of students to break even. To reach this critical number, they tend to advertise broadly, especially during their initial years. Many neighborhoods in New Orleans are plastered with charter school posters tacked to telephone poles, the city's streetcars are often full of charter school advertisements, and placards touting open enrollment to charter schools are often placed in the grassy areas between traffic lanes.[32]

In sum, enrollment processes, discipline and expulsion practices, transportation policies, location decisions, and marketing strategies give RSD charter schools many opportunities to select their students. Moreover, RSD charters also have the ability to cap their enrollment to maintain a student-to-teacher ratio of twenty to one.[33] In contrast, RSD traditional schools have to take all students, even if they arrive midsemester. All of these factors leave RSD charters in a good position to maintain lower student-to-teacher ratios and to skim the most-motivated students.

RSD traditional schools, in contrast, continue to act as schools of last resort, with not much control over their enrollment. As such, they do not have selective admissions and must often operate on double shifts, expand capacity by adding mobile classrooms, raise class sizes, and enroll students who do not find spaces in charter schools, including special needs students who may be turned down by charter or other selective-admissions schools.[34]

As a result of these rules, which effectively put RSD traditional schools at a competitive disadvantage, many in the community derogatorily refer to the RSD traditional school sector as "the Rest of the School District."[35] Similarly, during its extensive interviews with school principals, superintendents, parents, students, and community groups, the Boston Consulting Group found that "RSD-operated schools are viewed as an unofficial 'dumping ground' for students with behavioral or academic challenges."[36]

Similar inequities apply to teacher recruitment. The most successful school sectors in the city of New Orleans have strikingly high percentages of experienced teachers. Fewer than 5 percent of teachers in OPSB-run traditional schools have less than a year's experience in teaching, in striking contrast to the 60 percent in RSD-run traditional schools.[37] Similarly, in BESE charter schools, only 10 percent of teachers have less than a year's experience. In the OPSB charter sector, half of the teachers have more than ten years' experience. In RSD-run traditional schools, only 15 percent have more than ten years' experience.[38]

Meanwhile, the RSD's heavy recruitment of teachers certified through nontraditional programs like Teach for America (TFA) recently created a surplus and allowed RSD to lay off a number of its teachers, among them many veterans, leading critics to accuse the district of favoring inexperienced outside teachers over experienced locals.[39]

The Potential for Future Growth

The Barack Obama administration's boost to the charter sector came at a time when the charter school system had almost reached capacity in New Orleans, where the number of post-Katrina returning students has slowly started to plateau. Prior to Katrina, NOPS enrolled around 63,000 students and was capable of educating up to 107,000. In contrast, today "the district runs only slightly under capacity with the number of students in the district nearly maxing out at an available 35,000 seats." And as the executive director of the Louisiana Association of Public Charter Schools put it, the charter sector in New Orleans is "pretty much at saturation point."[40]

Despite this saturation, charter school operators are still making plans to increase the number of charter schools.[41] In fact, a growing trend in the city of New Orleans is the proliferation of charter schools through charter clusters.[42] The city has a number of well-established charter networks, including the Knowledge Is Power Program (KIPP), the five-school University of New Orleans (UNO)–Capital One charter network, and the nine-school Algiers Charter School Association.[43] Nonprofit charter management organizations (CMOs) usually manage the administrative affairs of these clusters, to achieve economies unavailable to stand-alone charters and to enable schools to focus on educating their students. CMOs facilitate the proliferation of charter schools.

Numerous CMOs have announced their plans to expand in the city of New Orleans. Some new charter clusters are emerging with the sole purpose of taking over failing schools. For instance, No Excuses began operating two charter schools in the 2010–11 school year and is expected to take over as many as fifteen traditional public schools in the coming years.[44]

A number of issues jeopardize the viability of a district-wide system that nearly or fully comprises charter schools. The RSD model replaces failing traditional public schools with charter schools that focus on improving the educational outcomes of at-risk students within high-poverty schools. But such charter schools face several challenges to long-run sustainability. Models like the KIPP schools have been successful, but on limited scales, and recent evidence questions how replicable this model can be at the system level.[45]

For instance, one study warns that the expansion of this charter school model could negatively affect quality, citing the fact that KIPP closed some of its schools and removed its brand from others.[46] Another study raises similar questions, "especially in relation to the difficulty of sustaining gains dependent upon KIPP's heavy demands on teachers and school leaders."[47] Other studies argue that it is not realistic to think of the KIPP model as a panacea for distressed systems and that it should instead be viewed as a potential tool that may contribute to but not substitute for systemic improvement.[48]

KIPP-like models have also been shown to suffer from high student attrition rates, prompting some to argue that their success is due not necessarily to their long hours and intense teaching but to informal selection processes that weed out low-achieving students.[49] The achievement gains that KIPP schools report would likely decline without this attrition. Given this, the KIPP strategy of extending the school day or year, whose greater costs are probably not sustainable at the district level, might not even have the expected performance benefits. Additionally, on a global level, shifting low achievers out of KIPP does not raise achievement.

Finally, a recent report from Education Sector raised serious questions about the ability of charter schools and CMOs to scale up as dramatically as their supporters might hope. It found that "the extraordinary demands of educating disadvantaged students to higher standards, the challenges of attracting the talent required to do that work, the burden of finding and financing facilities, and often-aggressive opposition from the traditional public education system have made the trifecta of scale, quality, and financial sustainability hard to hit."[50]

Charter schools face other challenges in scaling up their operations. Their small size and commitment to low pupil-teacher ratios add to their costs; high student attrition rates at some schools raise per-pupil costs, as do high rates of teacher turnover, which force schools to spend to recruit new teachers. Many

CMOs also struggle to reduce their central administration costs as they confront the administrative challenges that face all large education bureaucracies. Most charter networks rely heavily on private philanthropy, which has provided a total of $600 million in the past ten years to support the movement. Some charter networks, such as the KIPP schools, are quite open about the fact that they are likely to require permanent subsidies from philanthropists for some of their schools. As Ben Lindquist, an executive of the Charter School Growth Fund, sums up the situation, "The risk right now is that we will drastically overestimate the capacity of the national charter sector to deliver new, high-quality seats for underserved families at sustainable cost to the taxpayer. . . . If we're not careful, we will get a large market segment that is littered with mediocrity."[51]

Accountability

As for-profit and nonprofit CMOs displace traditional public school bureaucracies, public accountability often becomes an issue. Legally, it is much harder to monitor the books of for-profit or nonprofit charter schools than those of school districts. The monitoring of charter schools is diffused between charter authorizers, charter board members, and state departments of education. As a result, charter schools are typically only loosely supervised, often leading to financial irregularities.[52]

Educational bureaucracies are created to ensure public accountability, foster public scrutiny, and enable the more effective exposure of corruption. Charter schools, however, tend to view such scrutiny as an attack on their autonomy and frequently resist public attempts to better monitor them.[53]

RACE AND POVERTY BY SCHOOL SECTOR IN THE CITY OF NEW ORLEANS

The city's remarkably complicated school governance and enrollment policies clearly shape the distribution of different types of students across the system. For instance, one outcome is that the OPSB sectors have proportionately more students classified as talented or gifted and lower percentages of students with disabilities compared to the other parts of the system.[54] Even more striking are the resulting racial patterns. In 2009, black students were 90 percent of the city's total, other students of color represented another 5 percent, and 83 percent of students were eligible for free or reduced-price lunch. As a result, the majority of students in each of the five sectors were low income or students of color, but the OPSB and BESE charter sectors had relatively high percentages of white students, low percentages of black students, and low rates of poor students (see table 8.1).

Although the racial shares within sectors in table 8.1 are not overwhelmingly different from one another, they translate into dramatically different distribu-

TABLE 8.1 Percentage composition of schools by sector, city of New Orleans

	Black		Hispanic		White		Other		Low income	
	2007	2009	2007	2009	2007	2009	2007	2009	2007	2009
OPSB traditional	94	93	1	1	0	1	4	5	71	89
OPSB charter	68	70	3	3	22	21	7	6	71	66
RSD traditional	97	98	1	1	1	1	1	1	68	87
RSD charter	97	96	1	2	1	1	1	1	69	94
BESE charter	74	67	9	15	15	16	1	1	67	70

NOTE: Percentages may sum to more or less than 100 due to rounding.
SOURCES: National Center for Education Statistics; Louisiana Department of Education.

TABLE 8.2 Percentage of students per school sector,
city of New Orleans

	2007	2009
OPSB traditional	11	7
OPSB charter	24	20
RSD traditional	34	36
RSD charter	28	34
BESE charter	3	2

NOTE: Percentages may sum to less than 100 due to rounding.

tions by race across the sectors. The system sorts most white students into just a few OPSB and BESE schools, with the vast majority of students of color going to schools in the poorer, more segregated, and lower-performing RSD sector. Three-quarters of all black students in the city attended an RSD school in 2009, compared to only 11 percent of white students. Eighty-seven percent of all white students in the city attended OPSB or BESE charters, while just 1 percent attended OPSB traditional schools. Asian students were over three times and Hispanic students two and a half times more likely than black students to attend an OPSB or BESE charter school.

These imbalances increased as enrollments rebounded in the wake of Katrina. Student enrollment increased more than 40 percent in just two years, from 25,551 students in 2007 to 35,887 in 2009. Much of this growth was poor students. Student poverty jumped dramatically, from 69 percent in 2007 to 85 percent in 2009. Most of these new low-income students enrolled in RSD schools, where poverty also jumped dramatically (see table 8.2).

At the same time, the likelihood that nonwhite students were in OPSB schools declined. Overall, the share of nonwhite students attending OPSB schools declined from 32 percent in 2007 to 25 percent in 2009. Both black and Hispanic students were significantly less likely to be in OPSB schools in 2009 than in 2007, a pattern that reflects the way that newly added students were sorted across schools during this time.

TOWARD A REGIONAL APPROACH

It is clear that the demographic makeup of the students in the New Orleans public school system makes the task of integrating the city's schools difficult. Given that the overwhelming majority of students are students of color (95 percent) or poor (83 percent), the city must look outward if it wishes to truly integrate its schools. There are three obvious directions to pursue.

First, more than a third of city students currently attend private schools. This represents an opportunity for traditional schools in the city as well as charters. The mix of students in these private schools means that bringing a good portion of them into the public schools could make the public system significantly more integrated. In 2009, public schools in the city of New Orleans enrolled about 36,000 students. Private schools enrolled 18,500 students, 10,500 of whom were white and 6,700 of whom were black.[55] Switching to reputable public schools, whether traditional or charter, might be an enticing option for many parents, white or black, now spending money on private schooling.

Second, region-wide data show that cooperative programs with suburban school districts also provide the potential for a much more integrated system. In 2009 there were three times as many students in suburban public schools as in the city system (110,000 compared to 36,000) and suburban schools were much more racially balanced—the white-nonwhite split was 50–50, compared to 5–95 percent in the city. Poverty rates are also much lower in suburban schools than in the city—62 percent compared to 85 percent in 2009.[56] This means that the full regional school system has much more potential for integration efforts than the city alone. An effective regional system would also almost certainly fare better than the city alone in competition with the private system.

Third, special programs or schools in the city—such as magnets—could be used to draw students from the suburbs or the private system. Locating high-quality programs near job centers could further enhance their viability as alternatives for suburban parents who work in the city.

None of these ideas would necessarily be easy to implement, but the important point is that there are realistic options available to integrate more public schools in the city. It is also clear that a charter strategy cannot do the job alone.

SCHOOL PERFORMANCE BY SECTOR

Compared to charter schools in many other parts of the country, those in the New Orleans region have positive performance data. However, these data and several recent studies show improving performance across the entire New Orleans region, in all types of schools—not just charters in the city. In addition, the performance advantages observed for some parts of the charter community are modest and may previously have been the result of student selection. Comparing charters to traditional public schools in New Orleans does not generate the largest differences in performance rates. Instead, performance differs widely across sectors—OPSB schools versus RSD schools versus suburban schools.

Recent analyses by the Southern Education Foundation (SEF), the Scott S. Cowen Institute, and the Boston Consulting Group document these patterns. In each, the performance difference between OSPB schools and RSD schools in 2008 or 2009 was roughly forty-five percentage points, while differences between charters and traditional schools were between ten and twenty-five points, depending on the year, the test subject, and the grade tested.[57] The most significant differences between charters and traditional schools were in RSD schools. However, each report noted that the measured disparities are at least partially explained by differences between traditional and charter schools that were not included in the analyses, such as student mobility rates (higher in traditional schools), special education rates (higher in traditional schools), and selective admission policies (formal and informal) in many charters.[58]

Our analysis examined the pass rates of students in seven groups of schools (OPSB Traditional, OPSB Charter, RSD Traditional, RSD Charter, BESE Charter, Suburban Traditional, and Suburban Charter), four subjects (English, math, science, and social studies), and two grade levels (fourth and eighth grade).[59] The differences in 2009 were generally much greater across sectors (OPSB versus RSD versus suburban) than between charters and traditional schools (see figures 8.1 and 8.2). On average, OPSB schools had pass rates forty-three percentage points higher than RSD schools for both grade levels. The average differences between suburban and RSD schools were thirty-one and thirty-four points for fourth and eighth grade respectively.

In contrast, the charter and traditional school differences were less consistent and much narrower. In the fourth grade tests, traditional OPSB schools actually outperformed charters, and the differences were relatively narrow for RSD and suburban schools—sixteen and eight points on average respectively. Charters in the city of New Orleans compare better in the eighth grade results, with twenty-three-point average differences in OPSB and RSD schools, but this is still only about half of the average overall difference between OPSB schools and RSD schools.

Pass rates have been changing in recent years (see figures 8.3 and 8.4). The fourth grade test results show two striking patterns for city schools. First, traditional schools in both the OPSB and RSD sectors outperformed charters, with improvements on average nine points greater in RSD traditional schools than in RSD charters and two points greater in OPSB traditional schools than in OPSB

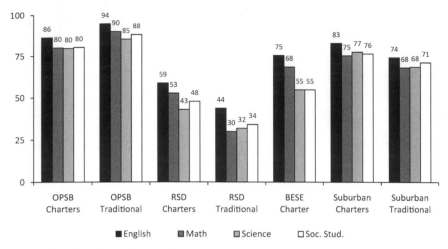

FIGURE 8.1. Fourth grade pass rates, 2009.

charters. Second, RSD schools in general were closing the student achievement gap with OPSB schools—pass rates increased by an average of six points more in RSD schools than in OPSB schools. The eighth grade data also show pass rate changes in traditional schools matching or outpacing those in charters. However, at this grade level the gap between RSD and OPSB schools widened rather than narrowed.

Overall, the performance data show that factors other than the innate differences between charters and traditional schools are driving pass rate differences. The gaps between OPSB or suburban schools and city schools are much wider than those between charters and traditional schools. Further, for the most part, traditional schools have been closing the student achievement gap with charters, suggesting that any advantages that charters have shown are not sustainable, especially as the charter system grows to include a more and more representative sample of the region's students.

The weakness of these simple comparisons is that they cannot account for differences across schools and sectors in other factors affecting test scores—such as school poverty, student mobility, and special education rates. Some portion of the difference between pass rates in RSD and OPSB schools is due to higher poverty, mobility, or special education rates in RSD schools. The empirical literature on this subject clearly shows that these factors affect test results.[60] Eight statistical analyses were performed on data about New Orleans metropolitan area schools in the 2008–9 academic year—one for each of the four testing subjects in the fourth and eighth grades. All of the models controlled simultaneously for school

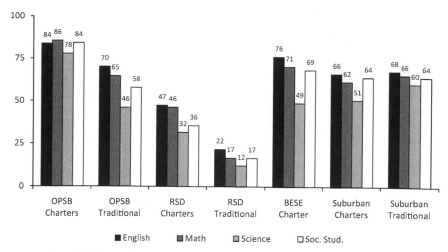

FIGURE 8.2. Eighth grade pass rates, 2009.

size and student poverty, racial mix, limited-language abilities, mobility, and special education rates. They also included six variables to determine whether test scores were systematically different across the school sectors (OPSB, RSD, suburban) or between charter and traditional schools within each sector. While this method is not ideal—it cannot, for instance, track individual students over time—it provides significant results.[61]

The results largely confirm that pass rates differ much more between sectors than between charters and noncharters. For instance, the expected difference between OPSB traditional schools and RSD traditional schools in fourth grade English pass rates, after controlling for all of the other included characteristics, was 51.8 percentage points. If the OPSB school were a charter, the expected difference would be 22.9 points less, or 28.9 points. Similarly, the difference between suburban traditional schools and RSD traditionals was 17.7 percentage points, with expected charter scores just 1.9 points higher.

The measured fourth grade effects for OPSB charters were all negative, implying that other things being equal, OPSB charters have lower pass rates than OPSB traditional schools. The measured effects for suburban charters were all positive, but they were not statistically significant—which means that they are indistinguishable from zero.

The only statistically significant positive effects for charter schools in the fourth grade analysis are for RSD charters. However, as with the simple comparisons in figure 8.1, these effects, which ranged from 8.5 to 21.5 percentage points, were much less than the differences across sectors.

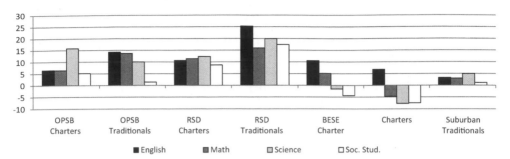

FIGURE 8.3. Percentage point change in fourth grade pass rates, 2007–9.

The eighth grade results showed differences between the OPSB and suburban sectors and RSD traditional schools that were positive and statistically significant, while the charter effects in the first two sectors were positive but not statistically significant. The analysis shows that eighth graders in RSD charters outperform their counterparts in RSD traditional schools slightly more than RSD charter fourth graders outperform their RSD traditional school counterparts but by amounts substantially less than the differences across sectors.

The effects of the other included variables were consistent with the findings of the empirical literature on this subject. Higher student poverty rates, special education shares, limited English shares, non-Asian minority shares, and mobility rates were negatively associated with pass rates in general, although they were not always statistically significant.

Overall, the school performance data clearly show that the differences between sectors—OPSB, RSD, and suburban schools—are much more substantial than those between charters and traditional schools. In fact, OPSB and suburban charters do not outperform their traditional counterparts at all. Although RSD charter schools outperform RSD traditional schools, the margins are modest compared to the between-sector differences and are narrowing for fourth graders. These results remain after controlling for differences in school demographics.

The data available for this analysis do not allow us to control for the effects of selection bias, a critical potential bias.[62] The discussion in previous sections of how charters can use admission requirements, enrollment processes, discipline and expulsion practices, transportation policies, location decisions, and marketing or recruitment efforts to shape their student bodies clearly implies that selection bias is almost certainly working to make pass rates in charters, all else being equal, greater than those of traditional schools.

This means that the relatively modest performance advantages of RSD charters seen in the 2009 data are likely to erode if the charter system continues to expand. As the charter school share of enrollments grows, charters will no longer

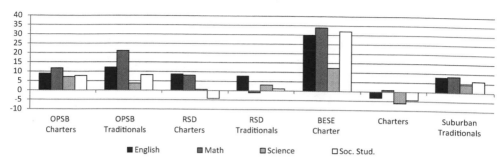

FIGURE 8.4. Percentage point change in eighth grade pass rates, 2007–9.

be able to use selection practices to limit enrollments. What will be left are the more substantial differences between RSD schools and their OPSB and suburban counterparts. In the long term, finding ways to effectively merge these systems offers the greatest opportunities for creating higher-performance learning environments for city students presently in low-performing schools.

CONCLUSIONS AND POLICY RECOMMENDATIONS

Racial and economic segregation undermine the life chances and educational opportunities of low-income students and students of color in New Orleans schools. School choice in a system like New Orleans's does not by itself empower students to escape this. Each of the components of the city's school system teaches mostly poor and overwhelmingly students of color. The choice system exacerbates the segregation by steering a minority of students, including most white students, into a few higher-performing schools and another, larger group, including most of the city's students of color, into a set of lower-performing schools. To guarantee equal educational opportunities to all of the region's students, the city school system should look both inward, moderating its rush to charters and renewing its commitment to traditional public schools, and outward, enhancing choices for students in the form of regional magnet schools and new interdistrict programs.

Halt the Haphazard Charge Toward a Fully Charterized System

The charter school sector in the city of New Orleans has been growing in a haphazard way in response to strong financial and policy incentives and not because of these schools' superior educational performance. The system has seriously undermined equality of opportunity among public school students, sorting white students and a small minority of students of color into better-performing OPSB and BESE schools while confining the majority of low-income students of color to the lower-performing RSD sector.

Moreover, there are good reasons to believe that in the long run, a fully charterized system is not sustainable. Recent studies raise serious questions about the ability of charter schools and CMOs to scale up as dramatically as their supporters might hope they can. In addition, the underlying characteristics of the charter system and experiences in other parts of the country imply that charter systems must either increase accountability (and administrative costs) to levels usually demanded of programs using tax money or deal with the financial irregularities common to unregulated systems.

Despite these issues, the charter system in New Orleans is gearing up to grow even further. With the help of new legislation that facilitates the expansion of the charter sector, publicly funded charter schools are expected to outnumber traditional public schools three to one by 2012. At this point, the continuing expansion of the charter sector is jeopardizing the very existence of the city's traditional public school sector. This type of predatory expansion—especially if it leads to charter schools being the only option rather than one among many— runs counter to the promise of expanding school choice for New Orleans parents and students.

In light of all these arguments, it is time to reevaluate the decision to rely exclusively on charter schools in providing education to public students in New Orleans and to expand the portfolio of strategies used for restructuring the city's school system in the aftermath of Hurricane Katrina. This is an opportune moment to slow down the planned expansion of the charter sector, take stock of where the traditional public school system is, and reevaluate where the entire school system needs to be.

Renew the System's Commitment
to the RSD Traditional Public Sector

An improving traditional public school sector should remain part of an expanded portfolio of choices available to the city's students. The playing field is clearly not level. This chapter has documented the rules and practices that put RSD traditional schools, which educate 36 percent of the city's students (the majority low-income students of color), at a competitive disadvantage. OPSB and BESE schools and RSD charters have the power to tailor their student populations in ways that RSD traditional schools cannot. Despite this, performance in RSD traditional schools is improving. But RSD traditional schools cannot continue to improve if they remain schools of last resort. The district must be as committed to improving these schools as it is to the rapidly expanding charter sector. Traditional schools must be provided with the resources they need to continue their improvement. For instance, making sure that RSD traditional schools have access to a sufficiently experienced teacher pool would be an important step.

Reinvest in Magnet Schools
as an Alternative School Choice Strategy

School choice does not have to undermine equality of opportunity in urban school districts. It can in fact reduce existing inequities in access to high-quality education if it is guided by strategies that promote racial and economic integration. Such strategies have also proved effective in reducing gaps between the performances of white students and students of color. It is not a coincidence that the most successful school sectors in the New Orleans metro area are also the most integrated ones.

The expansion of school choice through magnet schools is one such strategy. Originally, magnet schools were designed to use incentives rather than coercion to desegregate the public school system. Early magnet schools had strong civil rights protections, such as good parent outreach and information, explicit desegregation goals, free transportation, and in most cases, open admission processes. Many were extremely popular and successful and served as effective tools for voluntary integration. In fact, many of the most successful schools in the city of New Orleans, which are currently in the OPSB sector, started as magnet schools and are still magnets. Over time, however, many magnets lost their original desegregation mechanisms, for a number of reasons. If these are restored, magnet schools can resume their role in providing successful educational outcomes, parental choice, and integration simultaneously.

The presence of a large private school sector—with nearly 18,500 students, more than 10,000 white—in the city of New Orleans represents an opportunity for magnet schools as much as it does for charter or traditional schools. High-quality, reputable magnet schools have worked to attract white students to urban settings in many parts of the country. They have also succeeded in New Orleans in the past and could certainly be an enticing option for many parents, white or black, who are now spending money on private schooling. The traditional public school system could also make magnet schools an enticing option for many suburban parents who work in the city by locating the schools near urban job centers. Placing magnet schools in locations that are convenient to both urban and suburban parents could further enhance their viability, making them an additional instrument of school choice in the city of New Orleans.

Make Region-Wide Efforts to Expand
the Choices Available to Students and Parents

It is unrealistic to expect magnet, charter, or traditional schools in the city to fully integrate the public school system. Students of color make up 95 percent and free and reduced-price lunch eligible students constitute 83 percent of the students in the New Orleans public school system. These demographics make it impossible to racially and economically integrate the city schools in isolation. However, more than 10,000 white students in New Orleans attend private schools, and many of the city's 18,500 private school students are likely to be middle class—presenting an opportunity for further integration.

The city must also look outward, toward the rest of the metropolitan area, if it wishes to integrate its schools. The regional data show that cooperative efforts between the city and its suburbs have the potential to create a much more integrated system. In 2009 there were three times as many students in suburban public schools as in the city system. The racial and income mix of the full regional school system clearly provides much more potential for integration efforts than the city alone. An effective regional system would also likely fare better in competition with the private system than the city alone. The important point is that even as daunting as the raw numbers appear, there are realistic options available to integrate public schools in the city.

One approach is to combine operations with suburban areas. Large-scale, nearly region-wide school systems in Louisville, Kentucky, and Raleigh, North Carolina, are good examples of this. In these areas, the city school districts consolidated with the surrounding districts into a single county-wide district.

Voluntary interdistrict transfer programs that enable low-income students to transfer to low-poverty schools in suburban school districts can also be an important part of a metropolitan portfolio of school choice. Suburban schools in the New Orleans metropolitan area, which tend to be less racially segregated and have lower poverty rates than their city counterparts, offer good educational outcomes and life opportunities to low-income students and students of color.[63] Such a program is already in place in the Twin Cities metropolitan area (see chapter 7).

Voluntary interdistrict transfer programs involving high-quality suburban schools can be a great complement to magnet schools in urban areas. The two choice options can work together to reduce racial and economic segregation in a region's public schools. An example comes from St. Louis Public Schools in Missouri—a public school district with a student body very similar to New Orleans's. In St. Louis, the district established a successful voluntary interdistrict program in response to a court order to desegregate its schools. It provides for the voluntary transfer of city students into suburban districts and suburban students into magnet schools in the city. Around a quarter of the district's student body takes advantage of the program.

The program has been very successful in boosting graduation and college attendance rates among its students. Program participants graduated at rates double those of students in the city schools where they would have otherwise enrolled, and 77 percent attended two- or four-year colleges—significantly above the statewide average of 47 percent for students of color. When combined with magnet schools, voluntary interdistrict programs could not only reduce the racial and economic segregation of public school students at the regional level but also decrease the unacceptable opportunity gap between white students and students of color in the New Orleans metropolitan area.

NOTES

1. This racial typology is based on a more detailed one that divides schools into twelve categories depending on their racial composition. For details, see appendix I in M. Orfield et al., "Neighborhood and School Segregation." Each of these twelve categories was then assigned to one of the three categories discussed in this report. In this study, nonwhite segregated schools are defined as those where either the share of blacks, Hispanics, or other students of color exceeds 50 percent or where the relative share of white students does not exceed 30 percent. In predominantly white schools, the share of each nonwhite group is smaller than 10 percent. Any school that is neither nonwhite segregated nor predominantly white is considered integrated.

2. For students of color, a segregated setting was defined as a school that was nonwhite segregated, while for white students it was defined as a school that was predominantly white (or white segregated).

3. Studies document the close link between school racial composition and poverty rates. See, for instance, G. Orfield and Lee, Brown at 50: King's Dream or Plessy's Nightmare; ibid., Why Segregation Matters: Poverty and Educational Inequality. In 2002–3, 88 percent of high-minority schools—defined as at least 90 percent minority—were high-poverty schools, with more than 50 percent of students receiving free or reduced-price lunches. In contrast, only 15 percent of low-minority schools—defined as less than 10 percent minority—were also high poverty. See Orfield and Lee, Brown at 50. According to the National Center for Education Statistics, larger percentages of black, Hispanic, and American Indian students than of white students attend high-poverty schools. See Wirt et al., The Condition of Education 2005.

4. G. Orfield and Lee, Brown at 50.

5. G. Orfield and Lee, Racial Transformation and the Changing Nature of Segregation; Balfanz and Legters, "Locating the Dropout Crisis: Which High Schools Produce the Nation's Dropouts"; Swanson, "Sketching a Portrait of Public High School Graduation: Who Graduates? Who Doesn't?"; Kahlenberg, All Together Now: Creating Middle Class Schools through Public School Choice.

6. National Alliance for Public Charter Schools, Top Ten Charter Communities by Market Share—Fourth Annual Edition.

7. Boston Consulting Group, The State of Public Education in New Orleans; Act No. 35 is now Louisiana Revised Statute §17:10.7, "School and District Accountability; Schools in Districts in Academic Crisis; Transfer to Recovery School District."

8. Ibid.; Torregano and Shannon, "Educational Greenfield: A Critical Policy Analysis of Plans to Transform New Orleans Public Schools"; Dingerson, "Narrow and Unlovely"; Saltman, "The Rise of Venture Philanthropy and the Ongoing Neoliberal Assault on Public Education"; United Teachers of New Orleans (UTNO), Louisiana Federation of Teachers (LFT), and the American Federation of Teachers (AFT), "'National Model' or Flawed Approach? The Post-Katrina New Orleans Public Schools."

9. "Admission requirements, if any, that are consistent with the school's role, scope, and mission may be established. Such admission requirements shall be specific and shall include a system for admission decisions which precludes exclusion of pupils based on race, religion, gender, ethnicity, national origin, intelligence level as ascertained by an intelligence quotient examination, or

identification as a child with an exceptionality as defined in R.S. 17:1943(4). Such admission require-ments may include, however, specific requirements related to a school's mission such as auditions for schools with a performing arts mission or achievement of a certain academic record for schools with a college preparatory mission. No local board shall assign any pupil to attend a charter school" (Louisiana Revised Statute Annotated §17:3991(B)(3) [2009]).

10. Authors' review of all OPSB schools (charter and traditional) and BESE charter schools in the New Orleans Parents Organizing Network in 2009; Lubienski, Gulosino, and Weitzel, "School Choice and Competitive Incentives: Mapping the Distribution of Educational Opportunities across Local Education Markets," 615. According to the Center for Action Research on New Orleans School Reforms, this was the result of the inappropriate conversion of magnet schools into charter schools: "Then, in its haste to take over all New Orleans schools and to turn all of the schools into charter schools, the State Department of Education failed to consider that some of the schools were magnet schools and not suitable for conversion. However, many magnet schools were converted to charter schools, and the charter school funds, which are for open admission schools, wrongfully went to those magnet schools" (Ferguson and Royal, "Admission Requirements and Charter Schools," 2).

11. Wells, "Beyond the Rhetoric of Charter School Reform: A Study of Ten California School Districts"; Cobb and Glass, "Ethnic Segregation in Arizona Charter Schools"; Walford, "Diversity, Choice, and Selection in England and Wales"; Becker, Nakagawa, and Corwin, "Parent Involve-ment Contracts in California's Charter Schools: Strategy for Educational Improvement of Method of Exclusion?"; Institute on Race and Poverty, "Failed Promises: Assessing Charter Schools in the Twin Cities."

12. The Boston Consulting Group notes that "six OPSB charters and all 17 RSD charters have open-enrollment policies although most require potential students to fill out applications—which may include essays, parental involvement clauses, or specific behavioral contracts. These kinds of requirements can serve as a subtle form of selection that can provide charter schools more flexibility managing their incoming classes, rather than having to accept every student who applies" (*The State of Public Education in New Orleans,* 14).

13. For instance, as part of its enrollment process, the Knowledge Is Power Program (KIPP) Believe College Prep Charter School makes arrangements for a teacher to "come to the family home to share more information about the school, discuss what it takes to make a school work, and officially register the student" ("How to Enroll," www.kippbelieve.org/o6/5enrol.cfm, accessed December 3, 2009).

14. For instance, 75 percent of the ninety-eight California charter schools in a 1997 survey required parental contracts. Powell et al., *Evaluation of Charter School Effectiveness: A Report Pre-pared for the State of California Office of Legislative Analyst.* On parental contracts, see Becker, Nakagawa, and Corwin, "Parent Involvement Contracts in California's Charter Schools"; Wells, "Beyond the Rhetoric of Charter School Reform," 46.

15. Dingerson, "Narrow and Unlovely," 6. In a study of charter schools in California, "44 percent of the 98 charter schools surveyed cited student's and/or parent's lack of commitment to the school's philosophy as a factor for being denied admission" (Wells, "Beyond the Rhetoric of Charter School Reform," 44). Many New Orleans charter schools, such as the new Benjamin E. Mays Preparatory School, use parental contracts. See Fenwick, "The Door-to-Door Salesman." Similarly, KIPP schools in New Orleans require all parents to sign a Commitment to Excellence Form, which is described as "an agreement between home, student, and school to do whatever it takes to help each child succeed" ("Five Pillars of KIPP Schools," www.kippneworleans.org/about/five-pillars.php, accessed Decem-ber 3, 2009). Among other things, it "promises that parents will comply with the extended school hours, school dress code, and the homework requirements" (Holley-Walker, "The Accountability Cycle: The Recovery School District Act and New Orleans' Charter Schools," 160).

16. For instance, OPSB traditional schools, the Algiers Charter School Association (a network of schools within the RSD charter system), and a number of schools chartered by the OPSB have adopted zero-tolerance discipline policies. See Tuzzolo and Hewitt, "Rebuilding Inequity: The Re-emergence of the School-to-Prison Pipeline in New Orleans," 64. Similarly, KIPP charters have exceptionally high student attrition rates. See Macey, Decker, and Eckes, "The Knowledge Is Power Program (KIPP): An Analysis of One Model's Efforts to Promote Achievement in Underserved Communities," 223; Payne and Knowles, "Promise and Peril: Charter Schools, Urban School Reform, and the Obama Administration," 231; Henig and MacDonald, "Locational Decisions of Charter Schools: Probing the Market Metaphor."

17. Dingerson provides evidence of this among RSD charters: "Pushing out students who don't fit the behavioral or academic norms of the school is also easier for charters. In March 2007, the first anecdotes of this practice began to emerge from New Orleans. At one Recovery District school, the principal complained that a number of students had arrived mid-year with strikingly similar stories. Each had been at a charter school. Each was having learning or behavioral difficulties. In each case, the parent had been called in and told that their child would be expelled from the charter, and consequently would be unable to enroll in any New Orleans school until fall. However, the parent was told, if you 'voluntarily withdraw' your child, a Recovery District will be obligated to accept them this school year. Not coincidentally, the principal speculated, the students arrived just one week before the state's standardized assessment was to be given" ("Narrow and Unlovely," 5–6). Reportedly, parents have been called into charter schools to discuss their child's behavior and upon arriving have been presented with a precompleted withdrawal form, then asked to sign and find a "more suitable school for their children" (Tuzzolo and Hewitt, "Rebuilding Inequity," 64).

18. Boston Consulting Group, *The State of Public Education in New Orleans,* 19.

19. For instance, John McDonough Senior High School, an RSD-run traditional public school, had "anywhere between 31–40 security guards, 2–4 NOPD [New Orleans Police Department] officers, and only 21–30 teachers present at any given time" (Tuzzolo and Hewitt, "Rebuilding Inequity," 66). These conditions were part of the impetus for the formation of a student group called the Fyre Youth Squad (FYS), which protested these conditions. Ibid., 65–66.

20. Scott S. Cowen Institute for Public Education Initiatives at Tulane University, *Public School Performance in New Orleans: A Supplement to the 2008 State of Public Education in New Orleans Report.*

21. Many RSD charters, such as the KIPP McDonogh 15 School for Creative Arts, KIPP Central City Primary, and KIPP Central City Academy, used either RTA tokens or a combination of yellow bus services and RTA tokens. OPSB charters such as the Audubon Charter relied exclusively on RTA tokens, while selective OPSB-run schools such as Benjamin Franklin High School offered limited yellow bus services or RTA tokens, depending on residential location. Author's review of all the schools listed in New Orleans Parents Organizing Network, *The New Orleans Parents' Guide to Public Schools,* 3rd ed.

22. Liu and Plyer, *The New Orleans Index Anniversary Edition: Four Years after Katrina.*

23. For instance, "an employee at one charter school said the school provided transportation, but that service in the east side of New Orleans [which is predominantly black] was 'not as good'" (United Teachers of New Orleans [UTNO], Louisiana Federation of Teachers [LFT], and the American Federation of Teachers [AFT], "'National Model' or Flawed Approach?," 22–23).

24. Louisiana Revised Statute Annotated §17:158(A)(1);(C);(F) (2009).

25. Frankenberg and Lee, "Charter Schools and Race: A Lost Opportunity for Integrated Education"; Henig and MacDonald, "Locational Decisions of Charter Schools"; Renzulli and Evans, "School Choice, Charter Schools, and White Flight"; Lacireno-Paquet, "Do EMO-Operated Charter

Schools Serve Disadvantaged Students? The Influence of State Policies"; Andre-Bechely, "Finding Space and Managing Distance: Public School Choice in an Urban California District."

26. Bell, "Space and Place: Urban Parents' Geographical Preferences for Schools"; Harvey and Hill, "Doing School Choice Right: Preliminary Findings"; Kleitz et al., "Choice, Charter Schools, and Household Preferences"; Henig and MacDonald, "Locational Decisions of Charter Schools"; Lubienski, Gulosino, and Weitzel, "School Choice and Competitive Incentives."

27. Lubienski, Gulosino, and Weitzel, "School Choice and Competitive Incentives."

28. Southern Education Foundation, *A New Diverse Majority: Students of Color in the South's Public Schools.*

29. Liu and Plyer, *The New Orleans Index Anniversary Edition.*

30. Some charter operators in New Orleans are fairly explicit about their desire to attract private school students. The principal of the new Benjamin E. Mays Preparatory School conceded that "adding 'Preparatory' to the name is intended to make it sound like a private school" (Carter and Fenwick, "Charter X: What's in a Name?"). See also Lubienski, Gulosino, and Weitzel, "School Choice and Competitive Incentives," 614; Miron and Nelson, *What's Public about Charter Schools? Lessons Learned about Choice and Accountability;* Cech, "Catholic Closures Linked to Growth of City Charters."

31. Wells, "Beyond the Rhetoric of Charter School Reform"; Lubienski, "Marketing Schools: Consumer Goods and Competitive Incentives for Consumer Information,"; ibid., "School Competition and the Emergence of Symbolism in a Market Environment"; Fenwick, "Finding Zion."

32. Fenwick, "The Wisdom of the Marketplace."

33. Dingerson, "Narrow and Unlovely"; Boston Consulting Group, *The State of Public Education in New Orleans.*

34. United Teachers of New Orleans (UTNO), Louisiana Federation of Teachers (LFT), and the American Federation of Teachers (AFT), "'National Model' or Flawed Approach?," 17.

35. Quigley, "Part 1: New Orleans' Children Fighting for the Right to Learn, Part 1," 10.

36. Boston Consulting Group, *The State of Public Education in New Orleans,* 13.

37. Scott S. Cowen Institute, *Public School Performance in New Orleans,* 27.

38. Some community advocates accused charter schools of skimming the best teachers post-Katrina. They argued that TeachNOLA steered most of the experienced or certified teachers it recruited from across the nation to charters while directing most of the inexperienced and uncertified teachers to the RSD sector. Quigley, "New Orleans' Children Fighting for the Right to Learn, Part 1," 17. Whether or not this claim has merit, the striking experience differences among the teaching force of each sector remain.

39. Carr, "Recovery School District to Lay Off Dozens of Teachers Today," notes that "New Orleans public schools now feature completely decentralized hiring: Seniority guarantees nothing, collective bargaining does not exist, and teachers keep their jobs only at the discretion of their principals."

40. Fenwick, "The Wisdom of the Marketplace," 2.

41. Thevenot, "New Orleans Charter School Operator Plans Expansion"; Carr, "Charter Numbers Expected to Grow; 19 Groups Apply to Operate 24 Schools."

42. This trend is not unique to New Orleans. Citing literature showing the growing number of educational management organizations (EMOs) and charter management organizations (CMOs), Janelle Scott and Catherine DiMartino note that "as the charter school movement has matured, autonomous, locally grown schools are less common. More prevalent now are charter school networks and management organizations that manage franchises of schools across different districts and states. Philanthropists have dedicated millions of dollars to encourage the growth of such management organizations that boast high student achievement in their school in urban districts"

("Public Education under New Management: A Typology of Educational Privatization Applied to New York City's Restructuring," 440).

43. Thevenot, "New Orleans Charter School Operator Plans Expansion."

44. Ibid.

45. Henig, "What Do We Know about the Outcomes of KIPP Schools?"; Education Sector, "Growing Pains: Scaling Up the Nation's Best Charter Schools."

46. Bennett, "Brand-Name Charters."

47. Henig, "What Do We Know about the Outcomes of KIPP Schools?"

48. Payne and Knowles, "Promise and Peril"; Higgins and Hess, "Learning to Succeed at Scale."

49. Robelen, "KIPP Student-Attrition Patterns Eyed"; Mathews, "Inside the Bay Area KIPP Schools."

50. Education Sector, "Growing Pains," 2.

51. Viadero, "Study Casts Doubt on Strength of Charter Managers: Author Says Final Text Eased Negative Findings on CMOs." The Lindquist quote is on p. 13.

52. For instance, a recent study in Minnesota revealed major accountability problems in the state's growing charter school sector. The report drew attention to persistent and widespread financial irregularities in charter schools that have not been properly addressed for years. Fitzgerald, "Checking In on Charter Schools: An Examination of Charter School Finances."

53. Louisiana Charter School Association, "2009 Louisiana Legislative Session: Bills to Watch."

54. As of February 2008, only 4 percent of the students in OPSB charters and only 6 percent of the students in OPSB-run traditional public schools had disabilities, compared to 11 percent of all the students in the state of Louisiana. By comparison, 6 percent of the students in RSD charters and 10 percent of the students in RSD-run traditional public schools had disabilities. Ibid.

55. Liu and Plyer, *The New Orleans Index Anniversary Edition*, table 5; Southern Education Foundation, *New Orleans Schools Four Years after Katrina: A Lingering Federal Responsibility*, 10.

56. Institute on Race and Poverty, "The State of Public Schools in Post-Katrina New Orleans: The Challenge of Creating Equal Opportunity," 14–24; National Center for Education Statistics, http://nces.ed.gov.

57. Scott S. Cowen Institute, *Public School Performance in New Orleans*, 16; Southern Education Foundation, *New Orleans Schools Four Years after Katrina*, 15; Boston Consulting Group, *The State of Public Education in New Orleans*, 23.

58. A recent national analysis—CREDO, 2009—that includes New Orleans area schools finds positive outcomes for Louisiana charters compared to traditional schools. However, the methodology for this work, which matches charter school students with "virtual demographic twins" in traditional schools, results in many students being excluded from the analysis because no match could be found. In Louisiana, the unmatched students were disproportionately low-income students of color. The student sample included in the analysis for Louisiana was 77 percent black and 65 percent free or reduced-price lunch eligible. Center for Research on Educational Outcomes, *Multiple Choice: Charter School Performance in Sixteen States*, table 2, p. 19. The corresponding statewide percentages in Louisiana in 2007 were 82 and 67 percent respectively. Although the aggregate differences are small, they imply that the students left out of the analysis were 75 percent free or reduced-price lunch eligible—an eight percentage point difference from the population rate—and virtually all children of color, an 18 point difference. In addition, the methodology does not eliminate selection bias issues.

59. *Pass rate* is defined as the percentage of students scoring at a "basic," "proficient," or "advanced" level in Louisiana Educational Assessment Program (LEAP) testing.

60. See Institute on Race and Poverty, "Failed Promises: Assessing Charter Schools in the Twin Cities," 20–22, for a summary of school studies in the Twin Cities that document these relationships.

61. See Institute on Race and Poverty, "The State of Public Schools in Post-Katrina New Orleans" for the full results of the multiple-regression models.

62. Selection bias occurs when an analysis cannot fully control for variations in unobservable characteristics, such as student motivation. In this case, any observed performance differences between charter and traditional public school students could simply result from unobserved differences in the characteristics of students who self-select into charter schools (self-selection bias) rather than from differences in the quality of the schools.

63. Institute on Race and Poverty, "The State of Public Schools in Post-Katrina New Orleans," 18, chart 1.

PART FOUR

Lessons about Conditions under Which Choice Furthers Integration

9

The Story of Meaningful
School Choice

Lessons from Interdistrict Transfer Plans

Amy Stuart Wells, Miya Warner, and Courtney Grzesikowski

For the past twenty years, enthusiastic calls for more school choice—from both the political right and left—have eclipsed most other educational reform proposals. Wealthy philanthropists have eagerly poured money into charter schools in urban neighborhoods where regular public schools are struggling to overcome the impact of poverty on too many families' lives. The popular film *Waiting for "Superman"* captured the hope these school choice supporters have placed in charter schools to save poor children from the cruel circumstances of separate and unequal neighborhoods and public schools.

Lost amid the hype about charter schools and supermen are the increasing number of arrests of African American mothers in urban school districts—similar to many of those in the film—who try to exercise school choice by enrolling their children in nearby predominantly white suburban school districts. Rather than being celebrated and profiled by school choice advocates and filmmakers, these women have gone to jail. Stories from Akron, Ohio; Baltimore, Maryland; and Bridgeport, Connecticut, emerged in early 2011 as district officials and local prosecutors decided to get tough on black parents who managed to get their children into predominantly white suburban schools.[1]

Framed as responsible economic decisions in the midst of difficult education budget cuts, the suburban school districts' severe responses to these mothers were designed to keep them and others like them from making the educational choices they think are best for their children. But in fact, there was much legal ambiguity regarding their choices. For instance, the Akron mother did not find the suburban district she chose for her daughters by chance; her father lives there and was both a legal guardian and after-school caregiver for her children. The Bridgeport mother was homeless, living in a van with her son in the suburban district where he attended school. And the Baltimore mother was renting a space where the family sometimes slept in the suburb where her children went to school.

Despite the circumstantial evidence that these mothers had a legal leg to stand on in making the school choices they did and the support they garnered from civil rights groups as a result, there was no public outrage from the proponents of charter schools or tuition voucher programs when they were hauled off to jail.

This silence is puzzling to researchers who have studied different types of school choice programs and see the differential outcomes they have produced in terms of closing black-white (or Hispanic-white) achievement gaps and improving the graduation rates and long-term mobility of low-income students of color. In fact, the evidence points to the efficacy of the urban-to-suburban school choices that these three mothers were trying to exercise for their children over the more recently established competitive, free-market-based school choice programs, including most charter school and voucher options, that keep poor students in poor schools and neighborhoods.

This research helps explain why these and other low-income African American and Latino mothers would bypass urban charter schools in cities such as Akron, Bridgeport, and Baltimore and risk going to jail to get their children into suburban, more affluent, and predominantly white schools. These mothers are driven to remove their children from poor urban public schools—but not, as charter school and voucher advocates may lead us to believe, because those schools are *publicly* run as opposed to *privately* operated. In fact, they are choosing schools based not on an ideology of a market but rather on their knowledge that few institutions—be they public *or* private, government run *or* market driven—operate effectively when most of their constituents are poor people of color.[2] Thus, despite many closer-to-home options—regular public and charter schools—these mothers (and others) wanted their children educated in less-poor contexts, in places where schools respond to the needs of their students because the local community has voice, power, and the authority to demand accountability.[3]

Thousands of black and Latino mothers in poor neighborhoods have sent their children on long bus rides every school day to more affluent and predominantly white suburban schools through eight interdistrict desegregation or transfer programs that have been completely overlooked in the policy debates of the past twenty years. These successful programs have allowed thousands of students to cross school district boundaries. These interdistrict transfer plans—started through court orders and state laws in places like Rochester, New York; Boston; and St. Louis—were designed to be the ultimate school choice programs as far as poor parents and students of color were concerned. They were created to provide families that have historically had the fewest school choices with high-quality educational options. This chapter tells the story of these eight existing—some barely so now—interdistrict school desegregation plans.

If the goal of school choice policy is to equalize the educational playing field, then policy makers should pay attention to the evidence on which types of plans best do this. Charter schools and voucher plans offer low-income students of color very different choices than do interdistrict desegregation plans. The former provide parents and students the choice to remain in the same context but to attend a school that is privately instead of publicly run—a choice of school management. Because charter and private voucher schools generally offer new management systems within the same impoverished context, they are often even more racially and socioeconomically segregated than regular public schools.

Interdistrict transfer or desegregation policies offer, by contrast, the choice of a different context, in which the public management of schools generally works better than in urban contexts because of the affluence and political power of the suburban constituents. Our recent research on school segregation in the New York metropolitan area supports such interdistrict choices because it illustrates the ways in which public school officials are more likely to respond to the needs of affluent versus low-income constituents.[4] Poor students, therefore, benefit from greater association with school constituents in affluent communities, where public institutions are generally more attentive to students' needs.

Given this deeper understanding of the importance of school "context" in the lives of students, the experiences of the thousands of children who have participated in these innovative interdistrict programs should be a part of the public debate on what types of school choice policies are most effective for low-income children.

WHY SCHOOL CONTEXT AND DISTRICT BOUNDARIES MATTER: THE MISSING TOPIC IN SCHOOL CHOICE DEBATES

Despite the intense policy focus on providing poor urban children access to charter schools and private schools via educational vouchers, there is a great deal of evidence that such strategies are not effective solutions for closing achievement gaps. More often than not, when they are located in poor urban school districts and serve a mostly poor population, schools of choice—charter schools or private schools that accept vouchers—are not different enough from (and are sometimes worse than) the nearby regular public schools down the street in the rigor of their curriculum; their teachers' preparation, experiences, and expectations; and a wealth of other factors that influence learning on a daily basis and are strongly correlated with race and class segregation.[5] Research suggests that these schools' contextual factors—their location in poor communities and the high percentage of poor students in their classrooms—limit their effectiveness as educational interventions.

Furthermore, when we think about the context of schools, we need to consider not just local neighborhoods but also local school districts and their boundary lines. These boundaries circumscribe so many important tangibles (namely, resources) and intangibles (curriculum, expectations, etc.) that define a school and the opportunities it provides. Meanwhile, school district boundaries also define access and who "belongs"—distinctions that are shaped by age-old discriminatory housing policies and the current real estate market.[6]

In the United States, school segregation along racial/ethnic and social class lines is increasingly defined by school district boundaries.[7] According to Charles Clotfelter, a full 84 percent of racial/ethnic segregation in U.S. public schools occurs between and not within school districts.[8] At the same time that school district boundaries have come to play a larger role in dividing children and their educational opportunities, thereby making segregation more problematic and more intractable, policy makers have turned their backs on any efforts to solve segregation and the resulting inequality. In fact, charter school policies, the school choice policies now receiving the most support from policy makers on both sides of the political aisle, have exacerbated rather than alleviated racial segregation. Indeed, the evidence is strong that charter schools are more racially and socioeconomically segregated than regular public schools, especially for black students.[9]

Meanwhile, the federal courts have largely dismantled legal avenues for achieving school desegregation, especially across school district boundary lines. In the landmark 1974 case *Milliken v. Bradley,* the Supreme Court solidified the segregative impact of district boundaries, ruling that federal judges could not order school desegregation remedies that send students across urban-suburban district boundaries absent substantial, hard-to-document evidence that the suburban districts intentionally created the between-district racial segregation. This ruling made school district boundaries virtually impenetrable to desegregation remedies, assuring that poor students of color remained in separate and unequal schools and districts.[10] Subsequent Supreme Court decisions, culminating in the 2007 ruling in the *Parents Involved* case, have made desegregation efforts all but impossible. [11]

As policy makers have ignored issues of segregation and inequality, their focus has been on market-based school choice programs and closing the achievement gap. And yet, it is clear that standards, tests, and charter schools alone will not improve schools or create adequate educational opportunities.[12] In fact, the social science evidence suggests that unless we address the separate and unequal contexts in which students are being educated, we will never significantly narrow achievement gaps across race or social class lines.[13] As a result, breaking down some of these district-level barriers—or at least allowing disadvantaged students to cross them—should be a high priority for policy makers, particularly as our society becomes increasingly diverse.

In the next section of this chapter, we highlight the evidence to date on eight interdistrict transfer programs in which poor urban students of color can make meaningful school choices across school district boundary lines, guaranteeing them the maximum amount of choice possible and allowing them to escape poor urban schools and the high concentration of poor students within them. In the second half of this chapter we describe the policies behind these programs and their relationship to the opportunities provided to students.

These eight programs—spread across the country from Boston to East Palo Alto—illustrate the educational and social benefits of enabling disadvantaged, black, and Latino students to choose to attend more affluent, predominantly white and privileged suburban public schools. It is no accident, therefore, that all but one of these eight programs grew out of the civil rights movement.

Despite the fact that these interdistrict desegregation programs are out of sync with the current political framing of problems and solutions in the field of education, the research on their outcomes suggests that they are far more successful than recent choice and accountability policies at both closing achievement gaps and offering meaningful school choices. The evidence is clear that good management alone will not overcome the harms of concentrated poverty and lack of political clout that accumulate in poor communities and make these contexts less responsive to the needs of children.

THE RESEARCH ON INTERDISTRICT DESEGREGATION: EVIDENCE THAT CONTEXT MATTERS

Our research team pulled together the first-ever extensive review of the emerging body of research on these eight unique interdistrict transfer programs and present below an original summary of the mounting evidence that policies allowing disadvantaged students to attend school in more privileged contexts have numerous positive outcomes.

What we learned is that this research explains why simply fixing up segregated and poor urban schools will never solve the deep and structural inequalities across spaces and institutions in our society—physical divides that can only be challenged when disadvantaged students are allowed to cross the barriers and choose between separate and unequal educational contexts that distinguish the rich from the poor, the black or Latino from the white, and so forth. The evidence from these interdistrict school desegregation plans also helps us see why racial and social integration is important to the democratic development of children and adults who live in predominantly white and privileged spaces—and why it is so difficult to do in a manner that is respectful to all. In other words, these programs are not solely about providing low-income students of color with better educational opportunities but also about enabling a vast array of people across each of these eight metropolitan areas to learn to live and get along in an increasingly diverse and complex society.

Here we provide a brief overview of our research and other published information on these eight interdistrict desegregation programs to illustrate these points about educational opportunities and school contexts. We have divided this review into four subsections—academic achievement and outcomes, racial attitudes, the long-term effects on the students who transferred, and the popularity of these programs.

Student Achievement Data:
When Access to High-Achieving Schools Matters

Although there is not a large body of research on the impact of these interdistrict voluntary desegregation programs on student achievement, what exists strongly suggests that poor urban students who transfer into affluent suburban schools have higher achievement than their peers left behind in poor neighborhoods. Furthermore, we can see the connection between the context in which students attend school and their academic outcomes—a relationship that most parents understand intuitively but most policy makers ignore when thinking about poor people's children. While most of this short-term "achievement" data—evidence of what students accomplish while still in K–12 schools—is in the form of standardized test scores, we believe that a broader conception of achievement should be the yardstick for measuring progress for these and other educational programs. Thus, when possible, we have other important measures, including dropout and graduation rates. In the section below on the long-term effects of these programs on their student graduates, we discuss several more criteria of school success.

The best analysis of interdistrict transfer students' achievement comes from the old Hartford, Connecticut, Project Concern (now Project Choice) plan, which allows for urban-to-suburban school transfers. Project Concern's random selection and recruitment process created a desegregation program with a close to perfect experimental design, with control and treatment groups. A 1970 report on student achievement among Project Concern students found that in reading, the randomly selected African American students who transferred to suburban schools had significantly higher test scores than students from similar backgrounds remaining in urban schools. Furthermore, the longer these students attended school in these more affluent suburban contexts and the younger they were when they started, the better they did.[14]

The findings on increased graduation rates and decreased dropout rates for

Project Concern students were also impressive. Evidence on dropping out of high school was particularly strong for male Project Concern participants, whose dropout rate was 0 percent, while the dropout rate for male control group students in the city was 36 percent.[15]

These important findings are the most significant available because of the controlled, experimental nature of the program. The subsequent research on achievement and interdistrict transfers is less methodologically sound because of issues of self-selection. In other words, the students whose parents choose to place them in an interdistrict transfer program may be distinct from other students of color in urban contexts in ways that will affect their academic outcomes regardless of whether they transfer to suburban schools. Still, the evidence strongly suggests that interdistrict programs do matter, in large part because the students who transfer to the suburbs are transcending rigid boundaries that separate more-privileged contexts from far-less-privileged ones.

For instance, more recent evidence from the newer version of Project Concern, the Project Choice program, which does not randomly select students, demonstrates that participating Hartford students perform better on standardized achievement tests. More than half of Project Choice students are performing at or above proficiency on state standardized tests in both math and reading, rates higher than those of their Hartford Public School peers and black and Latino students statewide.[16]

These findings from Hartford echo some of the most important research on student achievement to come out of the St. Louis interdistrict transfer program. African American students from St. Louis city who transfer to suburban schools do not show significant gains on academic tests in the elementary grades, but the achievement of those who remain in the program improves over time to far surpass that of their peers in the city's magnet or neighborhood schools when they reach the tenth grade.[17] In fact, it appears that the longer the black transfer students remain in suburban schools, the more pronounced their academic growth by high school. Other studies of the academic outcomes of the St. Louis urban-suburban desegregation program found the same thing.[18]

For instance, William Freivogel noted that the positive academic outcomes of black students who transferred through the desegregation plan to suburban St. Louis schools must be related to the institutional effects of attending high-status, more-affluent schools in which college-going rates for graduating classes are as high as 95 percent. For instance, he found that the segregated city schools teach fewer foreign languages, have fewer counselors, and offer fewer advanced courses in math and science. They also lack music programs and up-to-date science labs and libraries.[19] Amy Stuart Wells and Robert L. Crain's qualitative data provides the contextual explanations for Freivogel's statistical findings. For their book on the St. Louis interdistrict program, *Stepping Over the Color Line,* Wells and Crain interviewed three different categories of African American students from the city of St. Louis: those who had successfully transferred to suburban schools and were still enrolled there, those who had remained in the city schools, and those who had transferred to the suburbs and then returned to city schools or were dropouts. The interviews with successful urban-to-suburban transfer students stood out in terms of the importance of the more affluent and privileged contexts of their suburban schools and how attending these schools had exposed them to new knowledge and experiences about college entrance exams and test prep courses, scholarship programs, internships, and jobs they said they never would have heard of in their urban schools.[20]

Recent evidence from the Boston METCO program, named after the entity that started it, the Metropolitan Council for Educational Opportunity, shows similar positive outcomes for students who transfer to the suburbs. In fact, the African American and Latino students who attended suburban schools through METCO dramatically outperformed the students in the Boston Public Schools on state achievement tests. [21]

The most striking evidence from METCO, however, is the improved graduation and college-going rates for transfer students. According to Susan Eaton and Gina Chirichigno, in 2009, 93 percent of METCO students graduated high school on time, compared with 81.5 percent of students statewide and 61 percent in the Boston Public Schools. Similarly, the dropout rate for METCO students—2.8 percent in 2009—is far lower than the state average of 9.3 percent, and the college-going rate is much higher.[22]

While the research on academic outcomes from the other five interdistrict programs is far less comprehensive than that from Hartford, St. Louis, and Boston, it does, with the one exception of the still-evolving, income- and not race-based transfer program in Minneapolis, demonstrate that such programs have a positive impact on the achievement levels and graduation rates of the students who are able to transfer out of low-income schools and communities to attend schools in more privileged contexts.[23]

The evidence in favor of interdistrict school desegregation programs as mechanisms to boost the academic achievement and graduation rates of low-income students of color is strong and consistent. It implies that future school choice programs designed to serve the lowest-income students of color should focus on removing them from highly concentrated poverty contexts, where outcome data is consistently and almost universally bad.

Changing Racial Attitudes
and Growing Acceptance of Diverse Schools

Another extremely important theme that emerges from the research on these interdistrict school desegregation programs is that they help to foster better understanding and acceptance across the racial divides. For instance, there is ample evidence that suburban residents, educators, school officials, and students grow to appreciate these programs more the longer they continue.[24] In many of the eight metropolitan areas, opposition to the interdistrict transfer plans on the suburban side of the racial divide was initially fierce. More often than not, court orders and state laws were the only mechanisms that could force the suburban school districts to participate. Yet despite the initial opposition to these programs in the 1960s, 1970s, and 1980s, when most began, there is evidence of growing acceptance of and even strong political support for them in the suburbs.

In several cases, protests against efforts to end these programs were organized in the suburbs. For instance, in 1999, the superintendent and school board of the Lynnfield School District in suburban Boston threatened to withdraw from the METCO program. In response, hundreds of people showed up to protest, including many white Lynnfield residents. During these protests, according to Eaton and Chirichigno, a racially diverse coalition of educational leaders from suburban school districts spoke publicly about the benefits of the program for both the transfer students from the city and the "otherwise isolated white students who are living in an increasingly diverse country."[25]

More recently, in the affluent suburb of Clayton, which borders St. Louis City, hundreds of white and black high school students walked out of class to protest efforts on the part of their local school board to end the voluntary interdistrict desegregation plan. According to one report of this incident, the students organized the walkout to "show support for diversity in this top-ranked school district. . . . Organizers asked students to sign petitions to maintain the school's diverse student population."[26]

This youth activism in the suburban school districts participating in these interdistrict programs is symbolic of another theme we see across these eight sites, namely that the younger white suburban residents—both the current students and recent graduates of the desegregated schools—are the strongest supporters of desegregation. For instance, a poll taken in 1988, five years after the St. Louis interdistrict plan started, showed that white suburban students were more supportive than white suburban teachers and parents of the plan. In fact, 71 percent of the white high school students said that it was a good idea to mix black city students with white county students, while only 54 percent of white parents agreed. In 1998, after fifteen years of urban-suburban desegregation in the St. Louis metro area, an opinion poll found even more support for the program among whites of all ages.[27]

Meanwhile, a 1994 survey by the Indiana Youth Institute found that both students who graduated from desegregated schools and their parents backed the Indianapolis interdistrict school desegregation plan. The study noted that "large majorities of both races said students who attend interracial schools gain a positive advantage. Blacks from integrated schools received little serious racial bias. And data from suburbs found a 'remarkable level of friendship' among blacks bused from segregated city neighborhoods and white students from mostly white suburbs."[28] In the Milwaukee metropolitan area, another place where suburban support for racial integration was not initially forthcoming, the students who lived through the Chapter 220 program—both white and black—were highly optimistic about its impact on their lives.[29]

Still, what is perhaps most significant about the growing support for these programs among suburban whites is how hard the once-upon-a-time resisters of desegregation come to fight to keep the plans alive when they are threatened politically or legally. For instance, in St. Louis, it had taken a federal court lawsuit to force the suburban school districts to enroll urban transfer students, but when the federal judge in the case ended the consent decree and the obligation of the state to pay costs of this program, sixteen of the districts voted unanimously to extend it for five years. Furthermore, mostly white voters in thirteen of these sixteen school districts voted to accept new African American transfer students during the extension, even though the state funding for each transfer student was reduced from whatever the receiving district's average per-pupil expenditure was—an amount that varied significantly across districts and was much higher in more affluent districts—to a flat rate of eight thousand dollars per transfer student per year.[30]

Similarly, in Indianapolis, Rochester, and Boston, when the interdistrict school desegregation programs were threatened in either the courts or the state legislatures, suburban school district officials and residents stood up and tried to preserve them. Often the very people who had resisted these programs when they began had become their most vocal supporters. When a Federal District Court judge ordered the establishment of an interdistrict transfer program in Indianapolis in 1981, the suburban townships slated to receive the black urban transfer students vigorously opposed it. But their stance changed over time, and eventually they fought the city's efforts to reclaim the students.[31]

In March 2003, the Boston suburb of Lincoln held a nonbinding referendum on whether to increase, decrease, or hold constant the number of METCO students in its school district. In the end, 64 percent of voters supported maintaining the district's participation at its current level, a decision the school committee decided to honor. According to one report, at a Lincoln Town Meeting, "parents of young children spoke passionately about METCO's critical role in exposing suburban students to a world that is increasingly diverse. Senior residents spoke elatedly of METCO's inception and strides made during the civil rights era. And METCO's president delivered an emotional speech, quoting Martin Luther King Jr. and bringing many townspeople to their feet."[32]

Yet another sign of growing suburban acceptance of urban-suburban voluntary desegregation plans is that in several of these eight sites, over the years more suburban districts have signed on to accept students from the cities. For instance, in 2005 a ninth suburban school district agreed to participate in the Minneapolis Choice Is Yours program and began accepting urban transfer students. And in 2008 in Rochester, a suburban school district that had not historically participated in the forty-three-year-old urban-suburban transfer program signed on to the plan and began accepting minority students from the city.

Indeed, the evidence is quite strong that suburbanites and graduates of the urban-suburban transfer programs came to accept—and then embrace—the eight programs over time, as racial and social class barriers broke down. Indeed, this research suggests that a growing number of Americans realize it is important for schools to help prepare students for our increasingly diverse society—something that few, if any, of the backers of charter schools and voucher plans acknowledge.

Long-Term Outcomes for Mobility and Opportunity

An understudied but critical aspect of school desegregation is the longer term effects of these programs on the lives and opportunities of students of color—as they matriculate through suburban schools and well beyond. Where research on long-term effects has been done, it shows that they are promising. Furthermore, this limited body of research on the long-term impact of these eight interdistrict plans comes to similar conclusions as a larger body of research on the long-term outcomes of school desegregation in general, which are very positive in terms of mobility factors for students of color and improved racial attitudes across different racial groups.[33]

For instance, the landmark study by Robert L. Crain and his colleagues of African American former students who had participated in the Project Concern program to attend suburban Hartford schools found very positive results years after they graduated from high school. The sample of former students involved in this study was drawn from the Project Concern "lottery winners"—those chosen to attend a suburban school—and was then divided between graduates of the Project Concern program and a second control group of young adults who had been chosen to participate via a lottery but who decided not to transfer to the suburbs. The authors of this report concluded that black students who attended suburban schools through Project Concern were more likely to graduate from high school and complete more years of college than members of the control group, who remained in the Hartford Public School System. The dropout rate findings were particularly strong: 0 percent of male Project Concern participants dropped out of high school, compared with 36 percent of male control group students who attended city schools.[34]

In addition, Crain and his colleagues found that the Project Concern graduates had a greater sense of interracial comfort in predominantly white settings.

Male Project Concern graduates also were less likely to have sensed discrimination during and after college and had far fewer encounters with the police than the control group of black males who attended city schools. Furthermore, both male and female Project Concern graduates were more likely than city school graduates to have closer contact with whites as adults, such as living in integrated neighborhoods or having more white friends.[35]

A second study of Project Concern adult graduates, by Robert Crain and Jack Strauss, found that the black Project Concern graduates of predominantly white suburban schools are far more likely to work in white-collar jobs, mostly in the private sector, while those in the control group who attended schools in the city of Hartford were more likely to have government or blue-collar jobs.[36] Furthermore, Project Concern graduates were more likely to have career plans that were consistent with their occupational aspirations, work history, and post-graduation activities.[37]

Similarly, Susan Eaton found in her research on adult African American graduates of the METCO plan that the vast majority said they would participate in the program again if they had it to do over again. METCO graduates also said they were more likely than other African Americans they knew who had grown up in more segregated environments to enter racially mixed settings and feel more comfortable around whites. They reported that, as a result, they had greater access to more prestigious educational institutions and job opportunities. This finding regarding METCO graduates is a strong indicator of the significance of educational contexts. METCO graduates perceived that their ability to associate themselves with well-regarded learning institutions allowed authority figures (many of whom were white) "to see them as capable of success in an academically or professionally competitive environment."[38]

While an argument could be made that "well-regarded learning institutions" exist in less affluent contexts, it is also true that, given how stratification and inequality work, they are more likely to exist in contexts of concentrated privilege and that these are the reputable learning institutions that authority figures are most likely to recognize or know most intimately. This institutional recognition is corroborated in other studies that found white-owned businesses more likely to hire African American graduates of white suburban high schools than similarly successful graduates of all-black inner-city schools.[39]

Another recent study compared the experiences of thirty-eight students enrolled in METCO and twenty-six students who had applied for METCO but remained on a wait list and thus were never able to transfer to a suburban school. Thus, all sixty-four of these black students had parents who tried to get them into the METCO program, which meant they all had similar levels of parental involvement—one of the main factors in selection bias with school choice studies because parents who make school choices tend to be more involved. The author concluded that the METCO students benefitted from what was described as the "entitlement culture" that permeates affluent suburban schools.[40] Exposure to this culture has several potential long-term benefits related to the efficacy of the more privileged class, most notably that the students "learned that they could negotiate with authority figures to further their academic interests."[41]

Much of this research speaks to the contextual or institutional effects of desegregation discussed above and underscores why proactive policies such as these are needed: to both overcome the harms of racial and socioeconomic segregation in our society and tear down the spatial and physical barriers that divide us.

High Demand: When Popularity Is Not about Markets but about Addressing Inequality

Evidence that parents of low-income students of color understand the significance of educational context is apparent in the strong demand for these programs and the ends to which parents will go to get their children into more affluent suburban schools. Despite the fact that not all of these programs maintain wait lists of urban students who have applied for seats in suburban schools, we do know that every year there are more applicants than spaces available across these eight programs. While the exact number of students who apply each year varies and may be less in those programs that lack the resources to conduct outreach, all indicators suggest that interest and demand remain quite high.

The largest wait list is the one for Boston's METCO program, estimates about which run as high as thirteen thousand minority students from the city waiting to attend a suburban school. In fact, the demand runs so high among Boston parents who want to enroll their children in suburban schools that about 25 percent of the children on the METCO wait list were signed up before turning one year old.

From Boston to East Palo Alto, there is no shortage of poor students of color who want to transfer from their mostly poor communities to attend school in contexts where public institutions are more responsive to students' needs. Clearly, there is no lack of demand for interdistrict desegregation programs that are grounded not in free-market rhetoric but in meaningful choices for the students who have been most disadvantaged by the status quo in public education in the United States.

This evidence leads us to wonder why policy makers do not pay more attention to programs that have demonstrated student academic success, societal benefits, and popularity. In the following section, we describe the design of the eight interdistrict school desegregation programs that are the origins of the positive academic and social outcomes described above. We focus in particular on how these programs differ from charter school and tuition voucher policies to help guide policy makers, advocates, and others who care about low-income students

of color and their educational opportunities toward the creation of more meaningful school choice programs.

THE DETAILS OF INTERDISTRICT SCHOOL DESEGREGATION PLANS: THE SPECIFICS THAT LEAD TO THE OUTCOMES

There are several key components of these eight interdistrict transfer programs
(see table 9.1) that distinguish them from more recent and widely known free
market school choice programs, such as charter schools and voucher plans. These
characteristics are symbolic of the distinct political origins, designs, and ongoing
support of desegregation plans, which were created to achieve greater equality,
versus more free-market-based school choice plans, which are predicated on the
need for greater competition among educational institutions.

In this second half of this chapter, we describe the disparate origins and purposes of these two types of school choice policies—the more recent, free market
choice-oriented programs versus the older voluntary school desegregation plans.
Related to these distinct origins and purposes are meaningful programmatic
differences—namely, the choice options available, students' access to schools of
choice, and the support provided to students and schools—that translate into
profound differences in the day-to-day lives of children in each type of program.
We describe these differences as well in our effort to explain the relationship
between the details of school choice policies and the opportunities they provide
to low-income students of color.

We divided all of the above into three sections: (1) the different origins and
purposes of types of school choice polices and how they relate to the choices
provided, (2) the design of interdistrict desegregation school choice policies and
how their design shapes students' access to particular schools and opportunities,
and (3) support systems available through some of these interdistrict plans that
are missing in more recent free market choice programs.

Origins and Purposes: How Different School Choice Policies Enable Different Choices

What most clearly differentiates voluntary interdistrict school desegregation
programs from charter schools and voucher plans is the historic grounding of
the former in the social justice efforts of grassroots organizers and the civil
rights movement more broadly. Unlike charter school and voucher plans, which
became popular with state and federal policy makers in the 1990s as beliefs in
the free market's ability to solve all public problems took root, the interdistrict
programs were grounded in efforts to promote racial equality.

This civil rights movement origin translated into distinct program characteristics. For instance, interdistrict plans, because they are urban-to-suburban

desegregation plans, target students who are disadvantaged because of their race/ethnicity and/or social class and the fact that they live in segregated urban neighborhoods. The goal of these programs, therefore, is to ensure that these students have access to higher-achieving schools in more-privileged contexts as a remedy for past injustices and ongoing segregation.

The shared sense of mission and focus on equity across these eight voluntary interdistrict programs is noteworthy because they have disparate legal origins: three (Indianapolis, Milwaukee, and St. Louis) were codified in federal court actions, three (Hartford, Minneapolis, and East Palo Alto) were formalized via state court orders grounded in state constitutional guarantees of equal educational opportunities, and two (Boston and Rochester) were supported by state legislation and local policies that specifically sought to create more racially diverse public schools across city-suburban dividing lines. Still, the philosophy guiding the creation of each of these eight programs was an understanding that separate is inherently unequal.

Choice of Educational Contexts   Following their philosophical distinctions, interdistrict school choice policies and charter school and voucher programs offer fundamentally different types of choices to students. Geography first and foremost differentiates the parameters of those choices.

Supporters of interdistrict plans believe that educational opportunities correlate highly with the concentration of wealth in certain communities and work to get poor students into schools in those contexts.[42] Charter schools and voucher plans, on the other hand, generally provide low-income students of color with options to attend choice schools that are in low-income urban communities and that enroll mostly poor students of color. According to recent data from the National Center for Educational Statistics, only 22 percent of students enrolled in charter schools live in suburbs, and only about one-third are white (compared to more than half of the overall K–12 public school population).[43] We also know that charter schools and private schools are even more racially and socioeconomically segregated than regular public schools.[44]

Putting all these demographic pieces together, it is safe to say that charter schools and voucher plans generally do not remove poor students of color from educational contexts circumscribed by poverty. This makes sense given that the emphasis of these free-market-based school choice programs has been and continues to be on who manages and operates the schools—the regular public system versus private providers, including Educational Management Organizations (EMOs)—as opposed to the context of those schools as it relates to privilege in society and access to high-status educational institutions.[45]

Parents of low-income students of color who participate in interdistrict school choice plans, by contrast, choose between public schools in different contexts

TABLE 9.1 Key characteristics of charter school and voucher plans versus interdistrict desegregation plans

	Charter schools and voucher plans	Interdistrict desegregation plans
Origins and purposes of different choice policies	Market-based school choice programs grew out of a political ideology that placed great faith in competition and the private management of schools as solutions to what ailed public education in the late 1980s and early 1990s. The charter school and tuition voucher legislation that resulted provides choice mostly to those students who live within close proximity of participating schools—most of which (64 percent of charters and the vast majority of private schools that redeem publicly funded vouchers) are in poor urban neighborhoods and enroll poor students of color only.	Grounded in the civil rights era and social justice movements, these programs provide choice specifically to those students whose families have suffered most from the harms of segregation. Thus, they allow students enrolled in poor, failing school districts to access high-achieving schools of choice. The choices are thus generally to attend more-affluent, predominantly white suburban public schools with better outcomes and reputations than their urban counterparts. In this way, the choice is about educational context—poor versus nonpoor.
Policy design and student access to high-achieving schools	These plans provide access based on the physical locations of the schools, the word-of-mouth networks through which parents find out about them, and the school-level admissions process. In other words, recruitment, access, admissions, and expulsions are all determined at the school level with little or no oversight. Because most of these programs do not provide transportation to students, geography and whether or not the family can transport the student to school each day strongly limit access (see below).	Interdistrict plans, because they are dictated by federal or state court orders or state legislation, must, as noted above, target the students whose families have suffered most from the harms of segregation. They must also conduct extensive outreach to and recruitment of all eligible students in failing school districts that are part of the plan. Suburban schools either are required or have agreed to admit and serve these students, generally up to a certain percent of their total student bodies, with little or no screening of applicants. A central agency, not individual schools, handles admissions, and students receive free transportation (see below).

Support systems to help students succeed in schools of choice

Families usually must take or leave the charter and private schools as they are. For instance, special education students are regularly told that the charter for the school is their Individualized Educational Plan, or IEP. Unlike regular public schools that must adapt their curriculum and instruction to meet the needs of special education students under federal law, charter schools and private schools operate with great autonomy and can thus force students to fit their molds or go elsewhere. Indeed, both charter and private schools usually maintain the right to expel students who do not fit. In terms of funding, charter schools receive a portion of or the total per-pupil expenditure, depending on the state law, for general operating costs. They usually receive no capital funding and must raise private funds for their building costs or else take those costs out of their operating budgets. Voucher plans offer private schools a set amount of per-pupil funding per student, which is often well below the tuition cost of the most prestigious private schools. It is extremely rare for private schools participating in tuition voucher plans to provide transportation to their students.

In most cases, the suburban school districts participating in inter-district programs have little or no say in which urban transfer students attend their schools. The placement of transfer students is centrally decided and usually based on student preferences and the capacity of the suburban schools. Furthermore, once transfer students enroll, suburban schools must provide whatever special services they require, including special education services. Several of the interdistrict programs have counseling or support centers for students transferring across district lines. Some have coordinating councils that work with suburban educators, who are usually white, to make suburban schools more welcoming. Interdistrict school desegregation plans generally provide either a portion or the equivalent of the receiving districts' average per-pupil cost for educating resident students. Some plans provide the receiving district with the average amount of state funding (with or without compensatory funding) per student across the state. In most instances, students who participate in these programs get free transportation to and from school.

(poor urban versus more affluent suburban)—something that parents with greater means do all the time. In fact, the significance of context explains why affluent parents will spend an extra two hundred thousand dollars or more for a nearby and similar home across the school district boundary line in a predominantly white and affluent suburban school district.[46]

In our recent research on Long Island, we learned that local constituents in the poorer communities often lack the political power and information needed to hold school officials and educators accountable for the quality of the education they provide. Such lack of political clout—directly related to the concentration of families with limited economic and social capital—stunts the development of vibrant democratic institutions, which local school districts are intended to be.

In fact, the experiences of students and educators in the poorest school districts contrast sharply with those of students and educators in affluent districts, where public school officials are far more receptive to their economically and politically powerful constituents. Few, if any, of the educators who work in these wealthy districts can afford to live in them, and the economic gap between them and the people whose children they educate is wide. As a result, the educators—be they central district office administrators, principals, or teachers—work together to provide the most challenging curriculum and the most competitive education (in terms of preparing students for the college application process). They know that if they don't they will be held accountable by their highly educated, affluent, and empowered parents and voters. [47]

The contrast between how public educational systems serve the rich and the poor, the white and the black or Latino, and the empowered and the disenfranchised tells us a great deal about why many parents of color who reside in poor urban school districts want to remove their children from schools that are failing. These schools, more often than not, are caught between a politically bankrupt educational system and the extra poverty-related needs of their students. Some of the same power dynamics that make public schools unresponsive to high concentrations of poor students can and often do play out in a similar manner in the private and charter school sector. Indeed, there is no reason to believe that poor people have been (or will be) treated more fairly or respectfully by free-market institutions than by publicly controlled institutions. Historical evidence suggests otherwise.[48]

The thinking behind many school desegregation programs, especially those that allow students to cross school district boundaries, is that one of the best ways to assure more equal educational opportunities is to address the harms of segregation, including poor parents and students' complete lack of power as politically marginalized educational constituents. One strategy, then, is to let disadvantaged children cross school district boundaries into communities with politically empowered parents and their more responsive school systems. Programs such as the eight interdistrict desegregation or transfer programs do this. Charter and private-voucher-redeeming schools that keep poor kids in poor schools and communities do not.

Still, interdistrict school desegregation or transfer programs are not utopian—poor students of color and their parents can be treated unfairly within such high-functioning schools and districts. But the access to better educational opportunities, resources, and facilities over the boundary lines outweighs the costs, and the boundary crossing itself creates the context in which truly integrated and fair education settings can be created, with a lot of hard work.

Policy Design and Student Access to High-Performing Schools: Not All School Choice Plans Are Created Equal

Because interdistrict transfer and more free-market-based programs have different origins and purposes, they are designed differently. Careful study of these and other school choice plans shows that the design details of each program are critical in determining who has choice, what sort of choices they have, and whether or not the most disadvantaged students in any given context are gaining access to significantly better educational opportunities.

Too often school choice advocates assume that just because schools and policies that theoretically provide families choices are in place, all students have equal choice. This reflects a rather naïve understanding of how school choice policies and programs actually interact with the lives of low-income families in poor communities. In fact, not all school choice programs are created equal when it comes to giving children meaningful educational options. For instance, the research evidence and our understandings of how and why context matters leads us to believe that meaningful choices for poor children may require that they travel long distances and have access to schools outside their resident school districts and student assignment zones.

Based on our review of the research on voluntary interdistrict desegregation plans, we identified several aspects of these programs that make them far more accessible to those students who are most disadvantaged in terms of income, race/ethnicity, residence, parents' education, and degree of parental involvement in their day-to-day education. It is true that, like any type of school choice program, these interdistrict plans attract a self-selected group of students—far from the population of students who would be enrolled through a perfectly randomized lottery (although one of these programs used to operate that way). Even those interdistrict programs that use a lottery system to select students from a pool of applicants start out with a self-selected group of parents who opted to apply.

Still, there are several key details in most of these eight interdistrict programs that minimize the extent of self-selection bias and assure that more students have access to high-achieving schools. These components basically assist parents and students in making difficult decisions about schools that are often far from their homes, and provide an infrastructure that enables them to act on their choices. The details include outreach, recruitment, fair application procedures and guaranteed access, and transportation. In addition, many of these interdistrict programs offer support services for families and schools to help make the transfer students' experiences more positive and to help more suburban schools become the kinds of integrated educational settings that embrace diversity.

It is clear that these programs skew access, opportunities, and outreach and recruitment efforts toward the most disadvantaged students, preferably students of color from low-income communities. They also provide ongoing support and scaffolding to transfer students and their families. In other words, what we describe in this section are the kinds of services that assist the most disadvantaged students and enable them to make meaningful school choices—services that free-market programs such as charter schools and voucher programs rarely provide.

Admissions Processes: Outreach, Recruitment, Application Procedures, and Required Access   The eight interdistrict plans vary in their parameters and guidelines, leading to more openness and greater student access in some plans than others. Furthermore, all of them, with the exception of the soon to be defunct Indianapolis program, rely on voluntary student participation, just like any other school choice plan. And while they are first and foremost school choice plans, they are also, at their core, school desegregation plans. With the exception of the Minneapolis plan, which bases eligibility on student family income and not race, all of these plans have racially integrated what would otherwise be overwhelmingly white suburban schools.

Thus, while the eight interdistrict desegregation plans vary, they were all designed to guarantee access to suburban schools to children who would not otherwise have such access. They require—through court orders or other formal agreements—that more-affluent suburban schools enroll a minimum number of poor students, usually students of color. The specifics of these policies—particularly regarding the outreach and recruitment of students and the application and admissions process—are critical in both shaping and constraining student access.

Like all school choice plans, these interdistrict programs rely on students and parents to make choices. As a result, they all, to some degree, enroll a self-selected group of students.[49] Furthermore, a handful of these programs screen students for prior achievement or other factors, which limits the access of some students. But this selection bias is offset to some degree by formal outreach to and recruitment of a broad range of urban students and the coordination of the cross-district transfer process by bringing administrators from each of these districts together to assure a smooth transition for students.

When we examined all eight of these programs, the St. Louis voluntary inter-district desegregation plan stood out as being the most aggressive in outreach and recruitment and the most accessible to a large proportion of the African American students who live in the city and choose to attend school in the sub-urbs. A central coordinating body—originally called the Voluntary Interdistrict Coordinating Council but renamed the Voluntary Interdistrict Choice Corporation (VICC) as part of a 1999 settlement agreement—runs the program. This coordinating council recruits, places in suburban schools, and counsels African American transfer students from the city. Every year, VICC sends out information on the transfer program to all eligible families in the city of St. Louis. Potential urban-to-suburban transfer students in St. Louis are not screened based on prior achievement or test scores, but they can be denied access if they have a poor disciplinary record.[50]

VICC makes all placement decisions; suburban school districts are not allowed to pick the transfer students they would like to enroll. Following the 1999 settlement agreement, however, certain areas of the city were zoned or matched with designated suburban school districts to lessen students' commute times and transportation costs. Prior to this adjustment, any black student living anywhere in the city of St. Louis was eligible to apply to attend any of the sixteen participating suburban school districts.[51]

Boston's METCO program conducts little to no outreach or recruitment because it is already oversubscribed. This means that information on the existence of the programs travels mostly through word of mouth and social networks, limiting who learns about it and thus who applies.

In Rochester, parents also learn about the local interdistrict program via social networks and word of mouth. Furthermore, the application to transfer to a suburban school requires information on the student's prior achievement and disciplinary records, if applicable.[52] After the Board of Cooperative Educational Services (BOCES), which administers the Rochester Urban-to-Suburban Interdistrict Transfer Program, receives the applications, representatives from the suburban school districts review them and choose which students they want to interview for their open slots. Students and parents have no say in which district the transfer student is placed. We learned on a visit to Rochester that one mother with four children had a child enrolled in each of four different school districts at one time.

In Indianapolis, which is phasing out its interdistrict program after a federal court ended the plan, issues of outreach and access were less salient because the

African American students who opted to participate were zoned, based on their residence in designated areas of the city, and assigned to certain suburban schools as if they were their neighborhood schools. This novel system of assignment meant that families had no choice about which suburban school their children would attend. It also meant that relationships could form across the matched urban and suburban communities based on school assignments.

Perhaps the most impressive system of outreach to and recruitment of new students to these interdistrict choice plans that allow them to cross school district boundaries—as well as racial, socioeconomic, and cultural boundaries—is woven into the Minneapolis Choice Is Yours program and supported by both federal and state funds. Specifically, the outreach activities of the Minnesota Department of Education and Minneapolis Public Schools, coupled with a system of parent information centers in communities throughout the metro Minneapolis area, cast a much wider net for attracting and drawing in potential transfer students and their families than is available through most of these other programs. Examples of the outreach efforts led by the Minnesota Department of Education include newspaper, television, billboards, and radio advertisements; community outreach; partnership programs with Head Start centers; and on line school choice videos in multiple languages.

Meanwhile, state and local education officials in Minneapolis conduct numerous outreach activities, including annual school choice fairs and direct mailings on the choice program. In addition, state and federal funds support two parent information centers, which distribute information, hold parent meetings, and provide computer labs so parents can research their school choices. The support from the federal grant exemplifies the potential role that federal policy makers can play in assuring that the most disadvantaged families have real school choice.

Still, the data from the Minneapolis plan is somewhat disappointing. Because eligibility is based on poverty and family income and not race, the program has enrolled a disproportionate number of white students. For instance, while only 27 percent of students eligible for the Choice Is Yours program based on family income are white, 40 percent of the students who transfer out of the city to predominantly white suburban schools are white.[53] The fact that color-blind policies are leading to greater segregation speaks volumes about the ongoing salience of race in education and school choice programs. In other words, when race is not addressed directly through proactive policies designed to circumvent the norm, the norm is reproduced in the form of greater racial segregation.

In addition to the outreach and recruitment efforts described above, these eight interdistrict programs have something else that other programs, such as No Child Left Behind (NCLB) and open enrollment plans—or even charter schools and voucher programs—do not: a guarantee that many suburban, high-achieving schools have agreed to accept a particular number or percentage of students from low-income communities. Either because litigation required they participate or

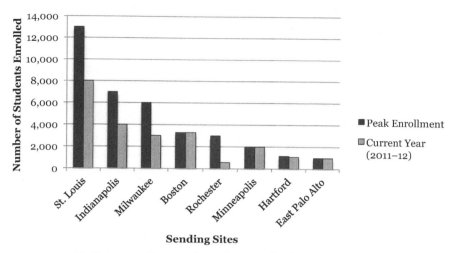

FIGURE 9.1. Declining enrollments of interdistrict school desegregation plans.

a state law coerces them to do so, or they volunteered to be a part of one of these programs, each of the receiving school districts in these interdistrict plans accepts and enrolls a certain number or percentage of students from low-income urban communities. These agreements or commitments on the part of high-achieving public schools are critical and yet so easily overlooked or brushed off by those who advocate that the market should dictate the terms of student choice.

In fact, the main factor limiting students' choices and access in these unique cross-district desegregation programs is their small scale. Despite the large demand for these programs among urban students of color across these metro areas, they have been compromised and cut over the years of charter school policy fascination and now enroll between five hundred and eight thousand transfer students each. Meanwhile, many of these programs have long wait lists of students who want to attend but cannot due to the shrinking pool of state funds to support them.

Figure 9.1 illustrates the dwindling enrollment in each of these programs. This shrinking enrollment does not reflect, therefore, waning demand for these programs, but rather shrinking political and legal support for interdistrict school desegregation, despite evidence that such plans provide more choice and mean-ingful educational opportunities to disadvantaged students than newer, more popular market-oriented choice plans.

Free Transportation: An Obvious Necessity to Guarantee Access   In contrast to state open enrollment plans, which allow students to transfer from one school district to another as long as the receiving district accepts them and they can pay for and often provide their own transportation, all eight of the interdistrict deseg-regation plans offer state-supported free transportation for transfer students. In most instances, the state is the direct provider of transportation services. In others, such as the Tinsley Plan in the Palo Alto area, the state of California reimburses the local districts for the cost of transporting students from East Palo Alto to several nearby districts. In either case, the states pay for all, or at the very least, a large portion of the cost of transporting urban transfer students many miles to and from suburban schools. This cost can be quite high—more than two thousand dollars per student per year, depending on the distance traveled.

Despite the expense, free transportation is particularly important for students from low-income urban families that too often do not have cars or work schedules that allow them to drive children to schools in suburban communities. Parents on both sides of the urban-suburban dividing line lack exposure to and familiarity with neighborhoods inhabited by people of different racial/ethnic backgrounds.[54] Thus, free transportation—the kind missing for students who attend most charter and voucher schools—is critical to assure meaningful choice for all students.

In fact, several of the studies on these interdistrict plans emphasize the importance of free transportation between urban and suburban neighborhoods in enabling the transferring students to participate. For instance, one report on school choice programs in Wisconsin concluded that the Milwaukee Chapter 220 program's free transportation for all participating students makes it a far more accessible program than the state interdistrict open enrollment plan, which requires participating families to provide their own transportation to schools in other districts. While low-income families can apply for reimbursement of their transportation costs through the open enrollment program, they have to first have the means—including the time and flexibility—to provide that transportation on a daily basis. These authors argue that while the Chapter 220 transportation costs are quite high—in the ten-to-eleven-million-dollar range in recent years—it is a critical component in guaranteeing greater access to schools of choice for poor students in particular. Students participating in a survey about Chapter 220 indicated that "the bus is very valuable" in enabling them to attend suburban schools and participate in extracurricular activities at their suburban choice schools.[55]

Similarly, the transportation of Minneapolis students to suburban schools under the Choice Is Yours (CIY) program is paid for by the state through Minnesota's desegregation transportation funding formula and provided by the Wide Area Transportation System (WATS).[56] Like many of these interdistrict desegregation programs, CIY assures that transfer students who participate in after-school activities have activity buses available to them. Similarly, the Western Metro Education Program suburban districts provide transportation to ensure that parents of CIY students can attend school conferences and other family events. Only one-third of the CIY parents whose children were attending suburban schools said they would "definitely" choose the same school for their child whether or not free transportation was available.[57]

While services such as free transportation and outreach that provide students with more meaningful school choices are not the most interesting or compelling aspects of the story of interdistrict school desegregation plans, they are fundamental nuts and bolts that ensure students of color in poor urban districts have access to schools in more privileged spaces—schools that embody that privilege and the sense of possibility it imbues in students. To succeed in their mission to redistribute this privilege more evenly across a highly unequal society, interdistrict programs must include these key components—including the recruitment and transportation services described above and the on-going support systems for enrolled students described in the next section—which distinguish them from the more laissez-faire and less equity-minded but far more popular school choice policies of recent years.

Support Systems in Place to Assure Success
in High-Achieving Schools

The history of school desegregation programs and other policies targeted toward the most disadvantaged children tell us that applying and enrolling is only the beginning of the process of ensuring that students stay and succeed in their schools of choice. Indeed, racially diverse schools are generally far from utopian, and too often poor students of color and their parents are treated unfairly *within* high-functioning schools. Because of their history as part of a larger struggle for greater equality (as opposed to emanating from a political effort to apply free-market ideology to public institutions), some of these interdistrict school desegregation programs were established with the kind of infrastructure needed to ensure ongoing support for students crossing racial, cultural, and socioeconomic boundaries. But not all interdistrict plans are created equally, and others, because of a lack of funding or perceived need, do not provide these supportive services. Research related to the effect of these services is minimal but would be helpful to educators and parents thinking about critical components for successful integration.

Still, despite the unevenness of these programs regarding these services, interdistrict desegregation programs on average do far more to support students and families who have had the least access to and the fewest choices of high-performing and high-achieving schools than schools and programs founded upon laissez-faire, free-market principles—be they charter schools, voucher-redeeming schools, or open enrollment plans.

Counseling, Advocacy, and Assistance: Critical Support Systems for Transfer Programs   A key component of making interdistrict school desegregation plans more successful is supporting both the transferring students in coping with their new educational environment and the receiving suburban schools in raising awareness and understanding of how to create academically and socially supportive schools for all students within a diverse student body. While specific support services for transfer students and schools vary across programs, we describe here a few of the programs available through several interdistrict plans.

In St. Louis, the Voluntary Interdistrict Choice Corporation (VICC) is both a formal, public coordinating policy-making body with representatives from each of the involved school districts and an outreach, recruitment, and support center for the urban transfer students. VICC also works with transfer students, their families, and suburban schools to help ease the students' transition from the city to county schools.[58]

In the Boston area, the nonprofit organization METCO Inc. employs two social workers, a guidance counselor, and a student services administrator. Its central role is to place Boston students in the participating suburban school districts. Yet once students of color from Boston are enrolled in suburban schools, they receive support from METCO directors, which most of the suburban school districts have and pay for out of their operating budgets. All of these directors are people of color, and their main responsibilities are to coordinate METCO-related activities, help place minority students in suburban districts, and serve as liaisons to the families—aiding both parents and students in bridging the gap between Boston and the unfamiliar suburban communities.[59]

In the Indianapolis plan, each of the six participating suburban school districts employed a Marion County coordinator of integrated education with specific responsibilities to supervise staff, students, and programs as African American students began enrolling in their predominantly white schools. These coordinators were also responsible for collecting data, which helped the federal court overseeing the transfer program and assured that the program was accessible to those who were supposed to benefit from it.[60]

In several of these eight metro areas, advocacy organizations to support the transfer students and their parents have formed. In the Milwaukee metro area, for example, an organization called Parents Concerned about Chapter 220 formed in the early 1990s to represent the educational interests of Milwaukee Public School transfer students. At the same time, according to the Wisconsin Advisory Committee, several suburban school districts took a variety of steps to address problems that transfer and suburban students faced in the course of the cross-district transfer process. For instance, one suburban school district hired its own Chapter 220 program administrator and human relations coordinator. Another district adopted a multicultural curriculum, and another created a new staff position to oversee the Chapter 220 program and provide counseling to the families when their students are involved in racial incidents at school. Some suburban school districts decided to employ a school-community liaison to work with MPS transfer students and parents; others hired human relations specialists. Finally, some suburban districts in the Milwaukee metro area started host family programs, to provide a place for transfer students to stay overnight if necessary and a home base for them when they are far from home. At the same time, these host family programs, also implemented in the St. Louis suburbs, provided an opportunity for greater interaction between city and suburban families.[61]

What this information from these interdistrict programs suggests—based on the information we gathered through the internet and personal communication with transfer plan officials—is that providing meaningful choice and access to the most disadvantaged students in the worst-performing public schools is not easy or inexpensive. Thus, public funding for all the activities described above is critical. While the past twenty-five-plus years of conservative thinking about racial inequality and school choice policy have not created a favorable context in which these types of programs can flourish, the fact that they have survived is noteworthy and gives us hope. But as we illustrate in the following section, more resources are greatly needed for each of these plans to fulfill its mission.

Resources to Support Transfer Students and Their Suburban Schools   Along with the extensive transportation costs described above, the other major expense of these interdistrict school desegregation programs is the incentive payments or funding for the receiving districts. These incentive payments are the per-pupil aid payment for the transfer students to attend suburban schools. They usually come from state education funds, although sometimes they are also drawn from local funds from the sending urban districts. And while they differ across these eight programs based on the specifics of the court orders or state laws that created them, there are four general forms of these payments.

1. *The equivalent of the receiving districts' average per-pupil cost.* This was the original model for the St. Louis voluntary interdistrict transfer plan, which was mandated by a federal court case that forced the State of Missouri to pay for the program. Each suburban school district received its per-pupil amount as an incentive payment for each transfer student. Meanwhile, the St. Louis public schools kept half of their per-pupil cost for each student who transferred to the suburbs. The city also accepted white suburban transfer students into its magnet schools and received the urban district's full per-pupil funding from the state for each of those transfer students plus several millions of dollars in state-funded school improvement monies.

Suburban districts' incentive payments in the Indianapolis–Suburban Township Plan were approximately equal to the total per-pupil funding level, although this plan is being phased out and only enrolls a handful of students. In fact, part of what led to the termination of this plan after the court order ended was the fact that the urban school districts—the Indianapolis Public Schools (IPS)—lost part of their state aid when students left to transfer to the suburbs. Furthermore, IPS could not accept suburban transfer students and did not receive school improve-ment money as the St. Louis Public Schools had. Thus, the Indianapolis program lacked the political support it needed from the city politicians who fought to end the program in the late 1990s and succeeded in getting a slow phase out of the program, resulting in thousands more black students remaining in one of the most racially segregated public school systems in the country.

2. *The equivalent of the sending urban districts' per-pupil funding, or a portion thereof.* A good example of this model of suburban district incentive payments is the Tinsley transfer plan in the mid-Peninsula section of the San Francisco Bay area. Through this plan, the suburban school districts receive 70 percent of the sending district's (the Ravenswood City School District in East Palo Alto) per-pupil funding for each transfer student. White students from the suburban districts that receive students from the plan are allowed to transfer into the Ravenswood district, but virtually none do so.

Through the Rochester interdistrict transfer plan, the suburban districts receive the Rochester City School District's per-pupil funding amount for each city student who transfers into one of their schools. This funding level is often close to—or greater than—the per-pupil spending in suburban districts.

3. *The average amount of state funding (with or without compensatory funding) per student across the state.* After modifications were made to the St. Louis inter-district transfer plan in 2008, the incentive payment formula for the participating suburban school district changed from the funding scheme described in #1 above to one in which the suburban districts will receive only state funds per transfer student (about eight thousand dollars in 2008), which is based on the average of their combined federal, state, and local funds. Similarly, the Minneapolis's Choice Is Yours program provides the suburban school districts the average per-pupil state aid for each transferring student. This plan does, however, also provide the sending districts with any state or federal compensatory funding earmarked for the transfer students they enroll.

4. *A set amount of money less than either the urban or suburban districts' or state average per-pupil funding.* Unfortunately, two of the programs—Hartford's Project Choice and Boston's METCO—provide far less funding and support for the participating suburban school districts. For instance, under each of these programs, regardless of their costs, the suburban districts receive a set amount of funding per pupil: about $2,500 in 2010 for Project Choice and only $4,960 in Bos-ton, far less than payments to charter schools in Connecticut and Massachusetts.

Of these four funding models, the first is the best from the receiving suburban school district's perspective. It is worth noting that the three programs that originally had that form of funding were all derived by strong federal court orders—the type of school choice policy for low-income students of color we are least likely to see in the near future. Our analysis demonstrates that to work, school choices—if they are to be meaningful—require a set of support systems and guaranteed access. If these programs can also fully compensate suburban school districts for the costs of educating transfer students and thereby provide them with greater financial incentives to participate, all the better.

Meaningful racial integration requires strong public policy and resources (see Table 9.1 for an overview of the distinctions between these and more recently developed choice plans such as charter schools and vouchers). It does not occur via the free market, as the history of our housing market has taught time and time again. Yet, as we illustrated in our review of research above, there is strong evidence that these complicated and costly programs are worth the extra resources—results that are not nearly so clear for charter schools or voucher programs. Our argument that the educational context matters in students' lives and academic success is not based on thin air. It is grounded in systematic research and analysis. The question is whether policy makers want to listen to these impressive results.

CONCLUSION

Shortly after the U.S. Supreme Court rulings in the 2007 school desegregation cases from Louisville and Seattle made creating racially diverse schools more difficult, Amy Stuart Wells and Erica Frankenberg reviewed the more than fifty amicus briefs submitted on behalf of the school districts and the choice-oriented school desegregation policies they had created.[62] Once they had read and coded the briefs and organized the information thematically, the authors saw six interrelated themes that help explain why separate is inherently unequal. These themes also illustrate the multidimensional way in which segregated school contexts translate into multiple disadvantages for poor students of color. The six themes, listed below, help to explain the self-fulfilling prophecy of segregated poor schools becoming and being bad.

Segregated public schools serving students of color tend to share the following characteristics:

· highly concentrated poverty;
· lack of qualified teachers and high teacher turnover;
· lack of college prep curriculum and other educational resources;
· low expectations and less-powerful social networks;
· low academic performance, graduation rates, and college-going rates; and
· lack of political support for public education, coupled with instability in the residential population and ongoing flight.

In other words, it is clear from the work of hundreds of researchers cited in these fifty briefs that once poor people of color are separated physically and materially from more-affluent white people, schools in their communities become worse because they lack the political power to make things right for their disempowered children or communities and they lose enrollment and political support. As a result, the schools in these communities are unable to attract a critical mass of highly qualified teachers who have the highest expectations and push students to learn the most challenging curriculum. All of this relates to low student achievement and poor outcomes, which only exacerbates the lack of political support and accountability in these districts.

But this more contextual way of understanding inequality and its solutions is not how most Americans make sense of inequality in the United States. We tend to think of it in individualistic terms, which leads us to believe it has individualistic solutions, such as simply changing the behavior of poor people. It does not. While programs such as interdistrict school desegregation do help individuals escape the brunt of the inequalities that they encounter, they also have the potential—if supported and sustained—to help dismantle the inequality. Policies such as these may be one part of that long-term solution by changing racial attitudes, helping low-income students of color succeed academically and go on to college, and by breaking down the barriers between separate and unequal urban-suburban contexts. The evidence to date suggests that they can help, while the types of school choice policies that policy makers currently embrace may just make things worse.

NOTES

This chapter is drawn from A. S. Wells et al., *Boundary Crossing for Diversity, Equity and Achievement: Inter-district School Segregation and Educational Opportunity.*

1. Applebome, "In a Mother's Case, Reminders of Educational Inequalities"; Franko, "Schools Boost Efforts to ID Fake Student Addresses."

2. Wells and Crain, *Stepping Over the Color Line: African-American Students in White Suburban Schools.*

3. Wells et al., "Why Boundaries Matter: A Study of Five Separate and Unequal Long Island School Districts."

4. Ibid.

5. See Wells and Frankenberg, "The Public Schools and the Challenge of the Supreme Court's Integration Decision" for a review of the research to date on these factors.

6. Wells and Roda, forthcoming.

7. Wells et al., "Why Boundaries Matter."

8. Clotfelter, *After Brown: The Rise and Retreat of School Desegregation.*

9. Mickelson, Bottia, and Southworth, *School Choice and Segregation by Race, Class, and Achievement;* Wells and Roda, "'Colorblindness' and Free-Market School Choice Policies: Political Rhetoric, Educational Research, and Racial Segregation."

10. Dreier, Mollenkopf, and Swanstrom, *Place Matters: Metropolitics for the Twenty-First Century;* Farley and Squires, *Fences and Neighbors: Segregation in 21st-Century America.*

11. *Parents Involved in Community Schools v. Seattle School District No. 1.*

12. Mickelson, Bottia, and Southworth, *School Choice and Segregation;* Darling-Hammond, *The Flat World and Education: How America's Commitment to Equity will Determine Our Future.*

13. Wells and Frankenberg, "The Public Schools and the Challenge of the Supreme Court's Integration Decision."

14. Frankenberg, *Improving and Expanding Project Choice,* 25.

15. Ibid.

16. Ibid., 2.

17. Wells and Crain, *Stepping Over the Color Line.*

18. Freivogel, "St. Louis: The Nation's Largest Voluntary School Choice Plan"; Trent, "The Continuing Effects of the Dual System of Education in St. Louis"; Wells and Crain, *Stepping Over the Color Line.*

19. Freivogel, "St. Louis," 20.

20. Wells and Crain, *Stepping Over the Color Line.*

21. Eaton and Chirichigno, *METCO Merits More: The History and Status of METCO.*

22. Ibid.

23. See, for example, Wisconsin Advisory Committee to the United States Commission on Civil Rights, *Impact of School Desegregation in Milwaukee Public Schools on Quality Education for Minorities—15 Years Later,* 15. On the Minneapolis program, see Aspen Associates Inc., *Minnesota Voluntary Public School Choice: 2005–2006.*

24. Wells et al., "Why Boundaries Matter."

25. Eaton and Chirichigno, *METCO Merits More;* Vigue, "Metco Students May Be Ousted from Lynnfield."

26. Wells et al., "Why Boundaries Matter"; see also Bower, "Clayton Students Walk Out to Back Transfer Program."

27. Freivogel, "St. Louis," 23, 24.

28. Ritter, "Across USA, Steps Forward and Steps Back / Indianapolis: A System That Seems to Be Working."

29. Rose and Pollard, *Perspectives on the Chapter 220 Interdistrict Student Transfer Program: What Have We Achieved? Phase One Report.*

30. Hampel, "Districts Vote to Extend Desegregation Program."

31. Hendrie, "In Indianapolis, Nashville, a New Era Dawns."

32. Wolcott, 2004, cited in Eaton and Chirichigno, *METCO Merits More.*

33. Wells and Crain, "Perpetuation Theory and the Long-Term Effects of School Desegregation."

34. Crain et al., "Finding Niches: Desegregated Students Sixteen Years Later—Final Report on the Educational Outcomes of Project Concern, Hartford, Connecticut."

35. Ibid.

36. Crain and Strauss, *School Desegregation and Black Educational Attainment: Results from a Long-Term Experiment.*

37. Frankenberg, *Improving and Expanding Project Choice.*

38. Eaton and Chirichigno, *METCO Merits More,* 23.

39. Cited in Wells and Crain, "Perpetuation Theory and the Long-Term Effects of School Desegregation"; Wells, "The 'Consequences' of School Desegregation: The Mismatch between the Research and the Rationale."

40. Ispa-Landa 2011, cited in Eaton and Chirichigno, *METCO Merits More.*

41. Eaton and Chirichigno, *METCO Merits More,* 20.

42. Lareau, *Home Advantage: Social Class and Parental Intervention in Elementary Education;* Anyon, "Social Class and School Knowledge"; Wells et. al., "Why Boundaries Matter."

43. Grady and Bielick, *Trends in the Use of School Choice: 1993 to 2007.*

44. Frankenberg and Lee, "Charter Schools and Race: A Lost Opportunity for Integrated Education"; Wells and Roda, "'Colorblindness' and Free-Market School Choice Policies."

45. Molnar, Miron, and Urschel, *Profiles of For-Profit Educational Management Organizations: 2008–09.*

46. Holme, "Buying Homes, Buying Schools: School Choice and the Social Construction of School Quality."

47. Wells et al., "Why Boundaries Matter."

48. See, for instance, Morland et al., "Neighborhood Characteristics Associated with the Location of Food Stores and Food Service Places."

49. Wells and Crain, *Stepping Over the Color Line.*

50. Ibid., and Freivogel, "St. Louis."

51. Ibid.

52. Monroe #1 Boards of Cooperative Educational Services, "The History of Project U-S, June 1963–June 2005."

53. Aspen Associates Inc., *Minnesota Voluntary Public School Choice.*

54. Wells and Crain, *Stepping Over the Color Line.*

55. Dickman, Kurhajetz, and Dunk, *Choosing Integration: Chapter 220 in the Shadow of Open Enrollment.*

56. Aspen Associates Inc., *Minnesota Voluntary Public School Choice.*

57. Palmer, *"The Choice Is Yours" after Two Years: An Evaluation.*

58. Heaney and Uchitelle, *Unending Struggle: The Long Road to an Equal Education in St. Louis.*

59. Frankenberg, *Boston's METCO Program: Lessons for Hartford,* 31.

60. Snorten, *An Analysis of the Effects of the Indianapolis Public Schools Desegregation Court Order, 1981–1982 through 1991–1992.*

61. Wisconsin Advisory Committee, *Impact of School Desegregation in Milwaukee Public Schools on Quality Education for Minorities,* 27.

62. *Parents Involved in Community Schools v. Seattle School District No. 1;* Wells and Frankenberg, "The Public Schools and the Challenge of the Supreme Court's Integration Decision."

10

School Information, Parental Decisions, and the Digital Divide

*The SmartChoices Project
in Hartford, Connecticut*

Jack Dougherty, Diane Zannoni, Maham Chowhan, Courteney Coyne,
Benjamin Dawson, Tehani Guruge, and Begaeta Nukic

Two rapidly expanding developments—public school choice and the World Wide Web—have dramatically altered U.S. elementary and secondary education during the past two decades. In many cities and states, traditional neighborhood school assignment patterns have given way to an increasing array of public sector options, such as magnet and charter schools. At the same time, we have witnessed a virtual explosion of school-level student achievement data across the internet. Many parents now go shopping for what they believe are the best public schools according to nationally popular websites hosted by GreatSchools, *Newsweek*, and *US News and World Report* and other digital search tools sponsored by state governments, local news media, and real estate agencies.[1]

Today many of us are swimming in a sea of school choice data, which can feel simultaneously empowering and overwhelming. How do parents, particularly in urban areas that have dramatically expanded school choice policies, navigate increasingly complex sets of options? What type of information influences their decision-making processes, and how do they interpret its meaning? We investigated these questions in the process of creating a public school choice search tool, collecting Web statistics on its use, and conducting workshops to guide parents and learn how they made sense of this new wave of information.

This chapter focuses on SmartChoices (at http://SmartChoices.trincoll.edu), a website launched in 2009 that offers a comprehensive, sortable list of all public school options, based on family residence and eligibility, in the metropolitan region of Hartford, Connecticut. When parents type in a child's home address and grade level, SmartChoices displays their specific list of district and interdistrict public school options on an interactive map, as well as a table for sorting and comparing distance from home, racial balance, and student achievement levels. Additional links point users directly to individual school websites, application forms, and transportation information. The site is available in both English and Spanish. Given the multiple (and competing) public school choice providers in the metropolitan Hartford region, SmartChoices fills the role of an independent consumer reports service that compiles information from more than two hundred schools across eighteen districts in one location. Yet by itself a website cannot bridge the digital divide, as urban parents who may have limited internet access, literacy skills, or computer experience need significant hands-on support to make sense of a mountain of school data.

Based on our overall user statistics and our study sample of urban parents in a computer workshop with one-on-one support, we found that providing more information influences decision making. Two-thirds of our sample either clarified or changed their top-ranked school after receiving hands-on guidance in their preferred language. Furthermore, our digital map and home-to-school distance calculator helped some parents find better schools (defined by increased test scores or racial balance) that were closer to their neighborhood than their initial top-rated choices. But making educational data more widely available is not a neutral act. We also observed some urban parents using our search tool to avoid schools with high concentrations of students from racial groups other than their own. Our study contributes to the literature in this volume (see chapters 3 and 11) and elsewhere that characterizes school choice as a double-edged sword, with potentially positive outcomes for some families and negative consequences for those left behind, by offering a closer look at one sample of parents who used our public school choice search tool as they attempted to cross over the digital divide.

CHOICE AND COMPETITION
IN METROPOLITAN HARTFORD

Hartford, Connecticut, is in a land of extremes. According to the 2000 census, the city of Hartford ranked as the nation's second poorest among those with a population of at least one hundred thousand (with 30.6 percent of families living in poverty), but it was surrounded by suburbs that had the fifth-highest median family income ($63,932) among U.S. metropolitan statistical areas.[2] Today's municipal boundaries were sketched out along colonial-era settlements, and during the past century of suburban growth, the state did not grant annexation power to the central city. In the Hartford region, school district boundaries generally follow city and suburban town lines. The Hartford public school district currently enrolls 94 percent minority students. In the United States, the size of the achievement gap between different racial and economic groups of students—as measured by the difference in eighth grade reading scores—is greatest in Connecticut.[3]

In an attempt to reduce these inequalities, nearly all education policy stakeholders in metropolitan Hartford support the idea of public school choice, but for very different reasons. One group, school integration advocates whom the 1996 *Sheff v. O'Neill* ruling in the Connecticut Supreme Court favored, support choice because voluntary desegregation is the only still politically viable remedy that they have been able to achieve to date. Although the court declared in its 4–3 decision that schooling racially segregated between Hartford and its suburbs violated the state constitution, the justices did not impose a remedy, goal, or deadline. Originally, some advocates envisioned a mandatory desegregation remedy that would dissolve city and suburban school district boundaries, but opposition by Democratic and Republican elected state leaders and judicial inaction forced several years of settlement negotiations. Under the terms of a court-approved *Sheff* settlement in 2003, the state legislature agreed to fund the expansion of voluntary desegregation programs such as interdistrict magnets and city-suburban transfers to reduce racial isolation. A subsequent settlement in 2007, known as *Sheff II,* expanded funding with more specific goals and timetables and began counting toward the broader racial balance goal any charter or technical schools that met its criteria.[4] By and large, *Sheff* advocates support choice primarily as the most viable political strategy toward achieving quality integrated education.

But a different group of reformers has embraced market-based public school choice as a means to increase accountability, empower urban parents to exit low-performing schools, and close the achievement gap. In 2008, Hartford superintendent Steven Adamowski, backed by the mayor-led school board, launched a district-wide public school choice initiative. The district replaced neighborhood school assignment with a citywide lottery mandatory for all students transitioning into elementary, middle, or high school but optional for any students who desired to change schools between those stages. Suddenly, Hartford parents who were accustomed to sending their children to the neighborhood school were surrounded with more choices, and when their child finished elementary or middle school, they were required to submit a choice application to advance him or her to the next grade level. Hartford's district-wide choice initiative complied with the federal No Child Left Behind policy by giving students in low-performing, high-poverty schools the option to transfer to another public school in the district. But the absence of racial balance goals and the lack of racial diversity within the city boundaries meant that Hartford's district-wide choice plan did not contribute to the state's court-mandated *Sheff* desegregation remedy. Whether or not these options improve public education for all, school choice policy discourse has been immensely popular in the Hartford region.

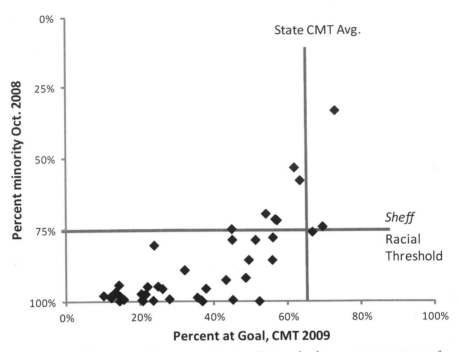

FIGURE 10.1. Minority and Connecticut Mastery Test goal-achievement percentages of public school options (limited to those with spring 2010 data in SmartChoices) available to Hartford K–8 families, 2010–11.

From a Hartford parent's perspective, the sheer volume of public school options has skyrocketed. In 1999 most Harford students attended a neighborhood public school, based on a residential attendance boundary system that the district had maintained for many decades. Only about five hundred Hartford students attended out-of-district public schools. But over the next ten years the number of interdistrict magnet schools in the Hartford region increased from five to twenty-six, and three interdistrict charter schools were created. Moreover, when Hartford Public Schools (HPS) implemented district-wide choice in 2008, it removed attendance boundaries for twenty-six elementary schools and six secondary schools. The number of choices for a typical Hartford sixth grade student grew from three to thirty-seven.

Although the new policy produced a greater quantity of choice, it did not necessarily mean a higher quality of options for urban families. During the spring 2010 application season, Hartford K–8 students were eligible to apply to forty-six public school options.[5] Of the forty-one for which we have data, as seen in figure 10.1, only eight met the *Sheff* definition for racially balanced schools (less than 75 percent minority), and only two of those rose above the state average (65 percent) of students scoring above the achievement goal on the Connecticut Mastery Test. Both of these were interdistrict school options: the Open Choice city-suburban transfer program and the University of Hartford Magnet School. While racially balanced schools are more likely to have higher test-goal levels, a handful of predominantly black or Hispanic schools earned relatively high scores compared to others with the same racial composition. The most prominent example was Jumoke Academy, a virtually all-black charter school where 52 percent of students met state test goals in 2009.

How many families participate in the choice process? We estimate that perhaps sixty-five hundred Hartford students (roughly 30 percent of the total district enrollment) submitted choice applications in spring 2010.[6] But Hartford parents who were savvy about school choice lotteries understood that the odds of admission were against them. Although Hartford residents submitted 42 percent of the applications to the main interdistrict school choice lottery in spring 2010, they received only 27 percent of the placements. (Hartford students are approximately 20 percent of the overall metropolitan enrollment.) This discrepancy is due to the relatively smaller share of suburban families that apply, combined with racial balance guidelines that favor applications from most suburbs to ensure that diversity goals are met.[7]

For parents, the choice process became even more complicated when competing school choice providers administered different application forms, deadlines, and lotteries. At present, the two largest choice providers are the Regional School Choice Office (RSCO), which manages most but not all interdistrict schools for *Sheff* compliance, and the HPS Choice Office, which handles district-wide applications. A handful of interdistrict magnets and charter schools operate their own, separate application processes. RSCO and HPS require different forms, with different deadlines. As a result, for each child, a typical Hartford family may submit one RSCO application (listing up to five choices), one HPS application (listing up to four choices), and separate applications for each of the other public schools. The process becomes more complex for parents of several school-age children.

Since choice providers compete against one another for students (and the public funds that accompany them), their informational campaigns promote their own brand rather than a comprehensive set of all public school options. Different catalogs show different lists of schools. Some Hartford parents have become confused or frustrated when attending events generically labeled as school choice information sessions that turned out to be organized by one provider and featured an incomplete list of schools.[8]

In general, Hartford families tended to view interdistrict magnet schools, which enrolled city and suburban children, as having higher status than most district schools. In a qualitative study we conducted in 2007, Hartford parents often stated their opinion that "magnet schools ... are better than the public schools."⁹ Many school choice providers marketed public magnet schools as comparable to exclusive private institutions. For example, a 2006 district magnet school video spot included the line "It's like a private school, except it's free."¹⁰ More recently, the nonmagnet district choice lottery was rescheduled to occur after the interdistrict magnet choice lottery, to reduce the number of parents who might initially accept admission to a district school, then withdraw after receiving an acceptance letter from a magnet.

SMARTCHOICES AND THE DIGITAL DIVIDE

Given this school choice policy context, we collaborated with Hartford community partners to create a digital tool that came to be known as SmartChoices. From our perspective as liberal arts college faculty, undergraduates, and academic computing staff, we had two goals. First, we wanted to make a confusing public school choice process more comprehensible to parents. Second, as researchers, we sought to learn from parents what factors influence their decision making. Our partner organizations included two nonprofit school reform advocacy groups: the Connecticut Coalition for Achievement Now (ConnCAN) and later, Achieve Hartford, the local public education foundation. The interests of the partner organizations differed from ours, yet we all agreed that to better understand the potential of choice and to make informed decisions, Hartford families needed access to reliable and coherent school information.¹¹

Together, we created a wish list of features for the ideal public school choice tool. The Hartford region needed an independent information source that comprehensively listed each family's entire set of eligible public school options. This source needed to stand apart from competitors' marketing materials and avoid favoring one brand over another. School listings had to allow parents to make comparisons across meaningful data categories (which we determined to be racial balance and student achievement), with a map to help them visualize each location and its distance from their home. Also, this information needed to appear in an easy-to-read format, in both English and Spanish, to serve a wide range of literacy skills. Additional links were required to point parents to the appropriate application procedures and transportation policies, which varied by school. Finally, we needed a regional approach that included all district and interdistrict public school choices for families living in the city of Hartford and its surrounding suburbs.

We believed the only way to deliver a truly comprehensive, timely, and dynamic set of eligible school choices was through a digital network. Although a printed booklet might initially appear to be better suited for urban families with limited computer access, a parent-friendly website with neighborhood outreach support had several advantages. First, the two major school choice providers already distributed catalogs displaying their own set of schools, which empha-sized glossy photos and slogans but virtually no racial or achievement data. By contrast, we designed our website to help parents sort schools by key data categories (including distance to their home) and linked to each school's website. Second, we frequently updated the SmartChoices website to reflect numerous last-minute changes made by school choice providers, which would not have been possible with a single print edition. Finally, we designed our website to personal-ize school eligibility information based on a student's address and grade level, to produce a more relevant, manageable set of choices. To encourage other regions to create and innovate with their own websites, we distribute SmartChoices code as free, open-source software upon request by email (SmartChoices@trincoll .edu).[12]

Parents were immediately attracted to our interactive online maps showing their eligible school choices, and the rise of freely accessible online geospatial tools made it much easier to create digital maps than paper ones. Our chal-lenge was to produce a precise set of public school choices for each family, based on their residence and child's grade level. These sets varied widely for several reasons. First, parents needed to see only those schools that offered their child's grade level, yet across the two hundred public schools in the metropolitan region, grade ranges were mixed and overlapping. Second, HPS divided the city into four zones and guaranteed bus transportation only for students attending school within their residential zone. Third, most district schools and some interdistrict programs limited eligibility to students from designated attendance zones or municipalities.

When we pilot-tested SmartChoices with Hartford parents, we were curious about how school information flows through their social networks and personal lives: the opinions of trusted relatives and neighbors, conversations with prin-cipals and teachers, and firsthand experiences or visits to different schools. In particular, we wanted to learn if and how parents incorporated selected data—such as distance from home, racial balance, or student achievement—into their conception of what made a good school for their children. Google, the ubiquitous search engine, reported that "school comparisons" was the leading type of public data search conducted on its website in November 2009.[13] This confirms that for better or worse, consumers are eagerly looking to the internet to help them make judgments about the relative quality of different educational options.

To be sure, access to school information and knowledge about how to search and interpret websites are not uniformly distributed. The digital divide was more commonly discussed a decade ago, but it remains one of the most challenging barriers to disbursing information about schools.[14] We were struck by the dif-ficulty of obtaining reliable, current data on the scope of the digital divide in the Hartford region. We derived our best estimate from the 2007 U.S. Census

"Current Population Survey," which posed this question to a national sample: "Do you (or anyone in this household) connect to the Internet from home?" After we subtracted omitted responses, the proportion who responded yes and resided in the city of Hartford was 34 percent, compared to 75 percent of those who said yes and lived in the three-county Hartford metropolitan statistical area.[15] Beyond this issue of internet access, we also lack comprehensive data on computer literacy among residents of the city of Hartford (as opposed to rates for residents of the metropolitan region or state).[16]

Despite these barriers, HPS eliminated paper forms and began accepting Web-only applications in January 2010, with some support provided through the city public library. Therefore, for families in our urban setting, knowing how to navigate the internet is now a requirement to advance from one public school to the next. While this policy switch saved money for the fiscally challenged city school district and provided efficient service to those familiar with the Web, the cost for other families is unknown. In December 2010 the Hartford Board of Education reversed this administrative decision by voting to allow parents the option of submitting a paper or online application. It also appointed a twelve-member Hartford Choice Advisory Committee to advise on choice issues that affect parents.

In response to the January 2010 policy switch, our partner organizations, ConnCAN and Achieve Hartford, expanded their outreach efforts with hands-on laptop sessions for parents across the city, including an innovative series of house parties to which women invited their friends to learn more about the choice process from a community organizer. A local public access cable channel broadcast a SmartChoices house party, and a local television network affiliate featured the site on its news hour show.

Familiarity with the internet has become a necessary ingredient in being an informed citizen-consumer of public education in Greater Hartford. Yet digital tools like SmartChoices are valuable only to people who have access to and knowledge of how to use and interpret them.

CHOICE, INFORMATION, AND THE INTERNET

A recent wave of psychological research on consumer behavior has puzzled over the paradox of what happens when shoppers are offered too many choices. In 2000, Sheena Iyengar and Mark Lepper published results from their grocery store experiments, which compared how two groups of consumers at a tasting booth reacted when asked to pick one flavor of a food product, such as jam or chocolate. They found that booths with larger assortments (such as twenty-four or thirty flavors) attracted larger crowds, but smaller assortments (six flavors) sold far more items. Furthermore, shoppers with fewer choices tended to be more satisfied with their decisions. National news media, political pundits, and corporate consultants leaped on this counterintuitive finding and its broader significance for American consumer culture.[17] Could too much choice be a bad thing?

While education choice policy and the internet have increased the quantity of school options for families, some educational researchers have sharply critiqued the quality of information available, particularly on school rating websites. Chris Lubienski has thoughtfully challenged the premise that school choice enhances parental empowerment by asking whether quality information about educational options is widely and equitably distributed. In his survey of forty school rating websites, he found that the majority offered simplistic inputs and outputs, with little insight on the educational processes inside schools. While most websites list test scores, Lubienski found very few that distinguish a school's effectiveness—with such measures as value-added assessments of individual students over time—from other demographic variables. Furthermore, school choice marketing often focuses on images and symbols associated with "exclusive schooling" rather than direct information about the productive processes of teaching and learning inside classrooms.[18]

In response to this critique, we designed the SmartChoices website to offer families meaningful data on school-level learning growth. In Connecticut, the state education department releases school-level test goal figures, which local news media heavily publicize. Yet the test goal figure reveals little about learning growth at a school, because higher levels may simply reflect the enrollment of students who already scored well on the test. In the Hartford region, families are already accustomed to seeing high test goals scores (80 to 90 percent) in wealthy suburbs, low scores in most of the impoverished city schools (10 to 40 percent), and others somewhere in the middle. To fill this information gap, we created a simple cohort analysis, called test gain, to show parents how the percentage of students meeting the goal had risen or fallen as they progressed through grade levels at a given school.[19] By viewing both test goal and test gain, respectively represented by a bar chart and a colored arrow on the SmartChoices website, parents can learn more about the quality of instruction at a school (as represented by standardized test data) than the state currently provides. Our test gain figure is not a perfect measure (it assumes zero student mobility), nor does it offer a sophisticated value-added analysis (since Connecticut does not make the necessary data readily available). But it reveals more about a school than test goal alone.

Some economists of school choice have delved further into how different types of school information may influence parental decisions. In Charlotte-Mecklenberg, North Carolina, Justine Hastings and Jeffrey Weinstein experimented with providing school data to parents in different paper formats. They found that low-to-medium-income parents who received direct information on test scores were more likely to choose higher-performing schools (especially those nearby) than parents who had no such direct information other than what they might have found on their own initiative, such as on a school rating website.[20]

Building on this finding, we designed the SmartChoices website to measure the influence of key categories of school information: distance from home, racial balance, test goal, and test gain. We created a sorting feature and tracked how frequently users sorted data by each column, after their initial results screen selected one column at random. We were particularly interested in how parents weighted distance compared to variables that represented school quality, such as achievement scores and demographics.

To better understand parental decisions on school choice, other researchers have created their own school rating choice websites and tracked users' mouse-click statistics. From 1999 to 2003, Jack Buckley and Mark Schneider followed how users interacted with a Washington DC website that compared traditional public and charter schools. They found that users displayed strong racial preferences in their behaviors, which differed from their race-neutral responses to survey questions. Although parents stated that the demographics of a school did not matter, when the website paired two schools with comparable achievement levels, they were more likely to eliminate the one with a higher percentage of black students.[21]

Given the original purpose of SmartChoices, we designed the website primarily as a public service to help parents access their comprehensive set of public school options. But we also consciously designed it to rank schools relative to an ideal population of 50 percent white and 50 percent minority students, reflecting the principle of the *Sheff* desegregation remedy. The website did not allow sorting by the percentage of students from any particular racial group, but a small pie chart represented each school's racial balance. Therefore, when organizing schools by this column, the most racially balanced, not necessarily the whitest, school appeared at the top of the list.

SmartChoices stands apart from the growing pack of school ratings websites produced by nonprofits, governmental organizations, and commercial providers. For example, nationally popular sites such as GreatSchools search for schools near a zip code, but the results are not the same as a particular family's set of eligible options. The true set of options is based on grade level and residence and includes several interdistrict choices that are more than five miles away (with free transportation) and thus would not appear through other search engines.

In regions with active choice programs, local governments and nonprofits have created customized school search engines, but most have serious limitations. In the District of Columbia, for instance, there were two competing public school search tools in spring 2010. District of Columbia Public Schools operates one site for district-run schools, while the Public Charter School Board operates the other. But neither offers a comprehensive list of the public school choices available to parents, because their providers are competing. Furthermore, both sites force users to drill down through individual pages to view student achievement and racial balance data, which makes side-by-side comparisons nearly impossible.[22] By contrast, California School Finder, operated by the state, provides a comprehensive search tool to sort and compare public schools by data categories and view their location on a map. However, this site does not automatically narrow schools to a student's eligible choice set, nor does it offer a Spanish-language interface.[23]

MEASURING SMARTCHOICES USAGE

Who used SmartChoices, and what areas did they search?[24] Based on website statistics collected during the five-month choice application period in 2009–10, more than 3,385 distinct searches were conducted using this digital tool.[25] More than three-quarters were conducted for addresses in the city of Hartford, while the remainder includes addresses in suburban towns and outside our immediate coverage area. The grade levels most commonly searched were kindergarten (16 percent) and ninth grade (14 percent), which matches the most common grade-level entry points in the system. The vast majority of SmartChoices users (98 percent) searched the site using the default English language setting. Based on our experience at parent workshops, we believe that many Spanish speakers might not have seen the language option at the top-right corner of the screen, or they may have accepted the English language default as the norm for interacting with the public school system, regardless of their level of proficiency or comfort with English.

How did people use SmartChoices, according to Web statistics? We created a sorting feature that allowed users to organize their search results in five different categories: school name, distance from home, racial balance, test goal, and test gain over the previous year. The website randomized the sorting of each user's initial results, to determine which categories were most frequently selected. Among users who sorted results, the most popular categories were distance (25 percent) and test goal (24 percent), with test gain (19 percent) and racial balance (17 percent) trailing behind. However, we observed that most users never sorted their results (70 percent of the 3,385 distinct searches), perhaps because they did not see the sort button or did not understand how it worked. Users in suburban towns were slightly more likely to sort results than city residents (35 versus 29 percent). Interestingly, patterns varied widely on frequency of sorting behavior, with more than 160 users sorting results five times or more. More than three-quarters of these "super sorters" conducted searches for addresses in the city of Hartford. Our Web statistics do not reveal whether these users were parents, school officials, or some other type.

SMARTCHOICES WORKSHOPS
AND PARENT DECISION MAKING

Our research team organized ten hands-on workshops in Hartford, conducted in both English and Spanish, during fall 2009. Undergraduate students were trained to follow a script that blended interview questions with personal guidance on the computer. After receiving informed consent, interviewers asked parents for their initial list of top-choice schools for one child in their family. Next they guided parents on entering a home address and grade level, interpreting the map and data labels, and sorting through their school options. Afterward they asked parents demographic questions and to name their final list of top-choice schools. Sessions lasted between fifteen and forty minutes, depending upon the level of parent interest. All were audio-recorded, transcribed, and matched to website statistics.[26]

Although our small, self-selected sample of ninety-three workshop participants was not designed to be statistically representative of the city, it did exemplify the range of urban families for whom we designed SmartChoices. More than 90 percent resided in the city of Hartford, and the vast majority identified their children as black or Hispanic. Nearly all were mothers, and one-third preferred Spanish. Parent education levels varied widely, with one-quarter having attained less than a high school diploma, one-half having completed a high school degree or some college, and one-quarter holding a college degree. We also observed a wide range of experience with the internet. One-quarter identified themselves as "new users," including many who had never before touched a computer. To focus our study, we limited interview participants to those who were parents of children entering elementary grade levels (pre-K to eight) in the next academic year. Nearly 40 percent identified as "mandatory choosers," meaning that their child was completing the final grade level of a school that did not automatically feed into another.

Workshop participants self-selected by voluntarily responding to a verbal invitation while walking by one of our workshops or to a flyer distributed at their school. About half of the interviews took place at large regional school choice fairs designed to attract parents who were shopping for schools, while the other half occurred in workshops held at neighborhood district schools. On average, parents at neighborhood events had much lower education levels and computer skills than those attending choice fairs. The most productive neighborhood events were organized with the assistance of family resource aides, whom district schools employed as parent liaisons. Those who cooperated with us did so after testing the website and recognizing its value as a powerful yet friendly information tool for parents.

Not all school officials welcomed SmartChoices workshops. Some district school leaders and their supporters perceived our choice workshops as a threat to their institution. One principal expressed concern, fearing that holding a workshop at the school might encourage parents to send their children elsewhere and reduce funding from the district's student-based budgeting system. Similarly, while the interdistrict program administrators cooperated with our outreach efforts, some school leaders denied or delayed permission to conduct parent workshops in their buildings. Most surprising, in our eyes, was a state official who turned us away from a choice fair sponsored by interdistrict schools, on the grounds that this public event was limited to "programming that supports *Sheff*." We understood this to mean that because SmartChoices gives parents a comprehensive list of all public options, including some relatively high-scoring predominantly black and Hispanic schools, it might distract them from applying to a narrower set of interdistrict schools designed to achieve court-mandated racial balance goals.[27] Our supposedly neutral parent information resource had been caught up in broader struggles over money, race, and power. Despite these restrictions on our study, we found sufficient cooperation to proceed with parent workshops in other settings.

How did the hands-on training with SmartChoices influence our ninety-three workshop participants' decision making about schools? In comparing responses to our pre- and postworkshop question about their top-choice schools, we found that our sample of parents divided into roughly equal thirds. About one-third (34 percent) changed their top choice, meaning the workshop experience led them to switch from one school to another. Roughly another third (29 percent) clarified their top choice, meaning they began with no response or one that was too vague for an application form ("the school near Walmart") and eventually selected a specific school. Finally, slightly more than a third (37 percent) did not change their top choice.

We compared the initial and final selections of the thirty-two workshop participants who changed their top choice, to measure the relative influence of the four key data categories in the SmartChoices search results. A postworkshop response was "similar" to a preworkshop response if it fell within one-third of a standard deviation from the mean difference, defined as follows: preworkshop test goal ± five percentage points, preworkshop test gain ± two percentage points, preworkshop racial balance ± six percentage points, and preworkshop distance ± half a mile. We marked responses that rose above the "similar" threshold as "higher" and those that fell below as "lower" (see table 10.1).

Based on this scale, the workshop participants who changed their top choice ultimately selected schools with higher test goal achievement level and test gain, followed by racial balance. Interestingly, distance was the least influential category in this phase of the analysis: roughly equal portions selected new schools that were farther from, closer to, or a similar distance from their home.

TABLE 10.1 Number of participants who changed their top-choice school postworkshop, by school characteristics

Difference in importance of characteristic	Test goal	Test gain	Racial balance	Distance
Lower	4 (14%)	5 (20%)	6 (20%)	9 (32%)
Similar	5 (17)	4 (16)	10 (33)	9 (32)
Higher	20 (69)	16 (64)	14 (47)	10 (36)
Total number of participants who changed per characteristic	29 (100)	25 (100)	30 (100)	28 (100)

NOTE: Thirty-two participants in all changed their top choice. All percentages are based on the number of valid responses.

Does this mean that school distance does not matter to parents? Absolutely not. When we compared how workshop participants sorted results, we found that test goal and distance were virtually tied (at 23 and 22 percent, respectively), followed by the other categories. Given that parents often make trade-offs between distance and the school quality factors they value, we infer that SmartChoices helped workshop participants to identify desirable schools that were closer to or not much farther from home than their initial top-ranked school. In other words, we suspect that the SmartChoices map and distance calculator helped workshop participants find good schools (based on their own definitions) that they were not previously aware of.

How did workshop participants use SmartChoices data in their understanding of what is a good school for their child? We thematically analyzed the interview transcripts (of the available twenty-five recordings) of the thirty-two participants who changed their top-choice school from the pre- to the postworkshop session, listening carefully to their views on why they had changed and what information in the website (if any) had influenced their decision. The most common theme expressed was "test scores matter" (64 percent), though people who said this were roughly split between those who mentioned test goal and those who mentioned test gain. The second most common theme was "racial balance matters" (32 percent), with participants roughly split between favoring more diversity and preferring that more students be the same race as their child. The third most common theme was "distance matters" (25 percent), with everyone who expressed this opinion preferring a school closer to home. (The total is more than 100 percent because multiple themes could be present in a single interview.)

How did workshop participants explain their SmartChoices searches in their own words? Using the same twenty-five interview transcripts, we found that parents' interpretations of the data are contextual, based on their past and present experiences of schooling their children. Some used SmartChoices in ways that matched the views of choice advocates for integration or accountability, but others were driven by very different motivations.

Many parents who concentrated on test scores also gravitated toward racially balanced schools, since the two were often (but not always) related. One typical parent was the mother of a Hispanic Hartford child entering fifth grade, who already had extensive knowledge of school choice programs, since she had applied the previous year, when her daughter had been placed on a wait list for a magnet school. She also identified herself as a regular computer user and had some college education. But when the website told her that she was eligible to apply to more than thirty schools, that number initially overwhelmed her. "Oh my God, that's a lot of options. Whoa!" she exclaimed upon viewing the results. As she scrolled through the list, she spent considerable time deciphering test goal and test gain. "That one's good. They're almost at the state average and improving," she commented about one school, comparing it to "this one [that] went down five points. . . . This is really cool." Test scores were important to her because, as she explained, her daughter "was one of the top students" in her Hartford district school. "The test goal and the gain . . . interest me more because I know she's gonna get her education. . . . I don't want to be bringing her to a school where she's going, 'Oh, I'm bored,' they're not doing nothing that's educational for her, 'cause I know her." She sorted her results three times, ranking them by test gain, test goal, and then racial balance. After exploring the website, she switched her top school from one interdistrict school program to another. Her postworkshop choice happened to have greater racial diversity and be farther away than her preworkshop choice, but the primary factor in her mind was a combination of test goal and test gain. Her words supported the views of school accountability supporters, but integration advocates also would have been pleased with the outcome.

Some parents focused on racial balance data, sometimes for reasons that diverged from the broader ideal of school integration. One typical parent was the mother of a black child in a Hartford district school who was preparing to enter fifth grade. This mother described herself as a new computer user with a high school diploma. She had arrived from a distant city less than a year ago and moved into a predominantly Hispanic South End neighborhood. When she scrolled through her search results, she spotted her child's current school and remarked on its relatively low test goal but then focused intently on racial balance for most of the workshop. "Let's go by [racial] balance first. Is this the one that I choose?" she asked her guide when sorting results. "I like this one; this has a [racial] balance, a nice balance, I would say," she explained when switching her top-ranked choice to an interdistrict magnet school that happened to be about a mile away. She complained that "the balance is unbelievable" in her daughter's current school because it was overwhelmingly Hispanic. A racially balanced school was important to her because "I think it helps kids learn better too. It would be any race, not just Spanish, three-quarters Spanish." While this black parent was attracted to a more integrated school, at the same time she was trying to move away from a predominantly Hispanic school, where her child was a racial minority. "I wish I had this [website] when I first got here, rather than shove them into the closest schools," she remarked. Other parents were more explicit in how they interpreted racial balance data. One Hispanic mother pointed to her computer screen and stated, "I like this [school] too," then paused to look at the colors on the racial pie chart. "But this is black, lots of black? Sometimes they like to fight with the Hispanic people, and I don't like that."

Still other parents cared only about keeping their children close to home and relied more on the SmartChoices map and distance calculator than either integration or accountability proponents would prefer. One Spanish-speaking mother, who had less than a high school education and did not feel comfortable around computers, explained that her daughter would be repeating fifth grade next year owing to language difficulties: *"Because she speaks English but still doesn't know how to read and write in English."* The following year, thanks to her daughter's current school's shift in grade levels, she would be required to submit a choice application. The map and distance information in SmartChoices pleasantly surprised this parent. *"Is this the mileage from my house to the school?"* she asked her interviewer. She had initially selected a relatively low-performing district school in her neighborhood, but the website helped her to see that a slightly better-performing interdistrict magnet school, which she had previously heard about, was also nearby. "La escuela es super-buenisimo. Le doy el número uno. *The [magnet] school is fabulous. I give it my number one choice,"* she decided, describing how its special curricular offerings would be a good match for her daughter's interests. This parent sorted her website results only once, focusing intently on the distance category, effectively eliminating all options that were not very close to her neighborhood. True, her daughter might attend a more integrated, better-performing school the next year, but one thing was certain in this mother's mind: her daughter would stay close to home.

CONCLUSION: INFORMATION IS NOT NEUTRAL

As we watched how workshop participants sorted and selected schools and listened to them describe what they saw on their computer screens, we gradually understood the dual outcomes of our data outreach project. On the one hand, as privileged members of a college community, we sought to aid less-privileged parents in our city in bridging the digital divide, to provide information tools that would help them make more thoughtful educational decisions amid the marketing campaigns of competing choice providers. Since merely building a website was insufficient, we also provided hands-on computer training to help less-skilled parents navigate complex sets of choices. Our research demonstrated how these workshops helped people understand school data and use it in decision making. Two-thirds of our workshop participants either clarified or changed their top-ranked school, and our digital map and home-to-school distance calculator helped some parents find better schools, however they defined them, closer to home than their initial top-rated choice.

But on the other hand, we also saw that our data led some parents to select schools for reasons that conflict with broader social goals. Our sample of urban parents was drawn more toward higher test scores than racial balance. While these two indicators tended to be associated, this was not always the case, which created tension between accountability and integration. Furthermore, we found that some parents who focused on racial balance data used it to avoid schools with certain racial groups or to identify those with more students from their own group. This is consistent with an earlier generation of research, such as *Who Chooses? Who Loses?*, in which Jeff Henig reveals a preference for schools with more same-race students in choice applications submitted by both white and minority families, and subsequent studies showing how privileged families use choice policies to opt out of public schools with greater concentrations of racially and economically disadvantaged students.[28]

As prior commentators have observed, public school choice is a powerful tool, with the potential for both positive and negative outcomes.[29] Our experience with SmartChoices underscores the importance of accessible school choice information, how different parents interpret it, and whose objectives it serves. We designed a website, but it was the one-on-one workshop support that made it possible for many urban parents to step across the digital divide, at least for this one online experience. Despite our original intent behind this public service project, disseminating school choice information is decidedly not a neutral act. While we were pleased to see many parents in our workshops discover higher-achieving or more-racially-balanced schools (sometimes closer to their homes), we were disheartened to discover others using the search results to avoid certain racial groups. Public school choice may be serving some urban families in the same way that suburban housing developments did their counterparts a generation ago: as a means to move across the educational dividing line and leave others behind. Without a doubt, school information websites are becoming more prevalent in today's digital age, and we need more research to better understand how different families access these tools, interpret their meaning, and incorporate them into the pursuit of their goals.

NOTES

This chapter represents a collaborative effort by faculty and student coauthors at Trinity College. Jack Dougherty, an associate professor of educational studies, coordinated the website design, research methods, and data collection and wrote the final draft. Diane Zannoni, a professor of economics, advised on the research design and supervised the quantitative analysis. Begaeta Nukic trained and organized student researchers; Courteney Coyne translated, transcribed, and coded parent interviews; and Maham Chowhan, Benjamin Dawson, and Tehani Guruge conducted the quantitative analysis. The authors thank Jean-Pierre Haeberly and David Tatem, who created the SmartChoices web application and provided GIS support; Jesse Wanzer and Nick Bacon, who digitized school attendance boundaries; Joel Caron, Chris Hunt, Rachael Barlow, and J. Hughes, who assisted with data analysis; all of the Trinity students who collected interview data; staff from ConnCAN, Achieve Hartford, Voices of Women of Color, Hartford Public Schools, and Regional School Choice Office; and most importantly, the parents and guardians who participated in our workshops. SmartChoices is a partnership between the Cities, Suburbs, and Schools Project at Trinity College, the Connecticut Coalition for Achievement Now (ConnCAN), and Achieve Hartford (which funded this study). The findings are the responsibility of the authors and do not necessarily represent the views of the partner organizations. An earlier version of this chapter was presented at the American Educational Research Association meeting in Denver in May 2010, where we received valuable feedback from commentator Jeff Henig.

1. See, e.g., GreatSchools, "Public and Private School Ratings, Reviews and Parent Community"; *Newsweek,* "America's Best High Schools 2010"; *US News and World Report,* "America's Best High Schools."

2. U.S. Census Bureau, "DP-3: Profile of Selected Economic Characteristics, Census 2000 Summary File 3."

3. According to the U.S. Department of Education, Connecticut had the largest gap in eighth grade reading scores in 2009 between white and black students (34 percentage points) and between students eligible or not eligible for free or reduced-price lunch (29 percentage points). National Assessment of Educational Progress, "NAEP State Comparisons" database.

4. Dougherty, Wanzer, and Ramsay, "*Sheff v. O'Neill:* Weak Desegregation Remedies and Strong Disincentives in Connecticut, 1996–2008," 123–26.

5. In addition to the forty-one school options for which data appeared in SmartChoices, there were five without data. Four of these enrolled only young children (state testing begins in third grade), and one was opening the next fall.

6. We cannot distinguish which students submitted applications to multiple choice programs. In June 2010, the Regional School Choice Office reported receiving 5,237 Hartford applications, and HPS reported 3,463, while nonaffiliated public choice schools received an additional unknown quantity. To get the percentage, we divided our estimate of sixty-five hundred by an approximate Hartford resident student enrollment of twenty-two thousand.

7. *Education Matters!,* "Highlights from the Regional School Choice Application Process."

8. Mozdzer, "Hartford's School 'Choice' Program Outlined; Some Parents Disappointed."

9. Wanzer, Moore, and Dougherty, "Race and Magnet School Choice: A Mixed-Methods Neighborhood Study in Urban Connecticut," 20.

10. Hartford Magnet Fair promotional video that appeared on television and the fair's website (see http://web.archive.org/web/20070102082935/http://www.hartfordschools.org/magnetschools/home.shtml) in December 2006. Video in possession of author.

11. We also decided that SmartChoices would not include private schools, primarily because of the lack of comparable data but also in recognition of the partner organizations' mission statements. See ConnCAN, "About Us"; Achieve Hartford, "Overview."

12. The design of SmartChoices was a team effort led by faculty, students, and staff at Trinity College. Undergraduate students in the Cities, Suburbs, and Schools Project digitized school attendance boundaries, compiled the school database from the Connecticut Department of Education and other public records, wrote Spanish translations, and designed the user interface based on data visualization principles. Academic computing staff developed the web application and its link to Google Map data. Drawing from Web 2.0 design guidelines, SmartChoices operates on a three-tier server architecture, which integrates the web server (for the search page and interactive map) with the application and database servers. Asynchronous requests allow users to initiate searches and view results without reloading the page as in a traditional form-based website. See SmartChoices, "About This Website"; Hughes, *Designing Effective Google Maps for Social Change: A Case Study of SmartChoices*.

13. Google defined "school comparisons" as any search on education from pre-K to higher ed, such as "douglas county schools" or "top law schools." Other categories might have ranked higher if Google had not broken out certain subgroups of searches, such as separating "cancer" from "health." Schwarzler, "Official Google Blog: Statistics for a Changing World: Google Public Data Explorer in Labs."

14. See, e.g., Zickuhr and Smith, "Digital Differences."

15. U.S. Census Bureau, "Current Population Survey," "Survey on Internet and Computer Use," question HENET3. The Hartford–West Hartford–East Hartford metropolitan statistical area (MSA) comprises three counties (Hartford, Tolland, Middlesex) and fifty-seven towns.

16. For the most recent county-level adult literacy data, see HartfordInfo, "National Assessment of Adult Literacy: State and County Estimates of Low Literacy."

17. Iyengar and Lepper, "When Choice Is Demotivating: Can One Desire Too Much of a Good Thing?"; Schwartz, *The Paradox of Choice: Why More Is Less*; Goldstein, "To Choose or Not to Choose: Sheena Iyengar Shakes Up Psychology."

18. Lubienski, "The Politics of Parental Choice: Theory and Evidence on Quality Information."

19. See sources and methods for calculating test goal and test gain in SmartChoices, "About This Website."

20. Hastings and Weinstein, "Information, School Choice, and Academic Achievement: Evidence from Two Experiments."

21. Buckley and Schneider, *Charter Schools: Hope or Hype?*

22. District of Columbia Public Schools, "Find a School"; District of Columbia Public Charter School Board, "Find a Charter School."

23. California School Finder, www.schoolfinder.ca.gov.

24. The figures in this section are from Dougherty et al., "How Does Information Influence Parental Choice? The SmartChoices Project in Hartford, Connecticut."

25. In compliance with Trinity's Institutional Review Board standards for ethical research, users must agree with an informed consent statement prior to entering the SmartChoices search engine.

26. See interview methodology and bilingual interview guide in Coyne, "Reputations and Realities: A Comparative Study of Parental Perceptions, School Quality, and the SmartChoices Website."

27. Emails sent to Jack Dougherty, October 27, 2009, and January 19, 2010.

28. Fuller, Elmore, and Orfield, eds., *Who Chooses? Who Loses?: Culture, Institutions, and the Unequal Effects of School Choice*; Henig, "The Local Dynamics of Choice: Ethnic Preferences and Institutional Responses"; Saporito and Sohoni, "Coloring outside the Lines: Racial Segregation in Public Schools and Their Attendance Boundaries"; Bifulco, Ladd, and Ross, "The Effects of Public School Choice on Those Left Behind: Evidence from Durham, North Carolina."

29. Nathan and Ysseldyke, "What Minnesota Has Learned about School Choice," 688; Wells, *Time to Choose: America at the Crossroads of School Choice Policy*, 5.

11

Experiencing Integration in Louisville

Attitudes on Choice and Diversity in a Changing Legal Environment

Gary Orfield and Erica Frankenberg

The Supreme Court has been drawn into the struggles over the use of choice in desegregation plans on several occasions. In 1968 it rejected most choice plans as inadequate to achieve real desegregation in *Green v. New Kent County*.[1] It approved limits on choice that were part of almost all desegregation plans, for example prohibiting transfers that would increase segregation. It forbade splitting up districts in ways that would foster segregation. In 2006, however, a group of parents from Louisville came into court claiming that their rights had been violated because the choice system was giving preference to the applications of parents whose children would increase integration in the school. A locally elected school board had adopted the plan in Louisville (Seattle had a similar plan), and surveys showed that a substantial majority of adults and students in the community supported it.

In June 2007, the Supreme Court handed down its judgment in *Parents Involved in Community Schools v. Seattle School District No. 1*, the first case relating to public school desegregation it had considered in more than a decade. Jefferson County (Louisville and most of its suburbs), Kentucky, was one of the two school districts whose student assignment plans the 5–4 decision ruled unconstitutional, overturning earlier precedents and giving individual choice a higher priority than desegregation or local control. The court held that while integration of the schools was in fact a compelling governmental interest, the districts were using impermissible policies to achieve their goals. In particular, it deemed unconstitutional the use of racial/ethnic classification to determine whether a student would receive his or her school choice. Justice Anthony Kennedy's controlling opinion authorized school districts to pursue integration but outlawed most of the existing voluntary plans. Kennedy suggested some other approaches, which had typically been ineffective in urban areas in the past.[2]

Prior to being declared unitary—meaning that the district's former dual system of segregated schools no longer existed—and formally released from court supervision of its desegregation efforts, Jefferson County had designed a desegregation plan that relied on parental preferences about where their child attended school but included integration guidelines that, along with capacity, determined whether parents' choices were granted. The district also had other choice options, such as magnet schools. After being released, it continued to implement the plan, largely without change, to voluntarily pursue racially diverse schools. Assuming space was available, parents' choices were granted unless that would result in the chosen school having a black percentage of less than 15 or more than 50 percent of the total enrollment.

Jefferson County Public Schools (JCPS) had vigorously defended its desegregation plan up to the Supreme Court. After it lost, local leaders were committed to finding a way to preserve diversity within the parameters of the *Parents Involved* decision. The district began an intensive planning process to determine how to continue many aspects of the plan that had been popular—such as parental choice and diverse schools—while also complying with the new legal restrictions. The basic plan was to divide the county into Area A and Area B, which were defined by their income levels, parental educational attainment, and racial composition. In fall 2009, JCPS began to implement its new student assignment plan.

This plan's geographic boundaries were fundamentally different and meant that many students were transferred to new schools. The changes caused considerable turmoil for the incoming first grade class during the first week of school in the first two years of implementation (fall 2009 and 2010), and grandfathering all students already in the system under the old plan created an extremely complex transportation system. The vast majority of parents who applied by the deadline received their first choice under the new system (more than 80 percent in 2010–11), but complaints of long bus rides were common, and the number of students requesting transfers to schools other than where they were initially assigned rose. There were 2,054 transfer requests for fall 2010. Despite the headlines, however, all of the incumbent school board members up for reelection won in November 2010.[3] Tension rose in the state legislature, where, in January 2011 and again in spring 2012, the House considered a bill that would require school districts to allow students to attend the school closest to their home. Although this bill did not pass, its sponsor is a former candidate for governor, suggesting that there will continue to be political challenges to making diversity a goal of choice. The Kentucky Supreme Court upheld JCPS's authority over student assignment in 2012.

Because school choice relies on parents viewing their options as attractive, and only a district supported by the public can sustain voluntary integration, since a school board can reverse it at any time, understanding how a community views integration choice policies is particularly important. As a result, this chapter examines parental attitudes toward the JCPS choice-based integration policy at a time of renewed legal and political scrutiny of both the policy's goals and its means of trying to attain integration. Since this is a community with a long history of support for integrated education but also one whose old plan was delegitimized by the Supreme Court and whose new plan produced many complaints and proposals by some local leaders to abandon the effort, it was particularly interesting to explore what its parents and students thought about these issues.

SURPRISING LONG-TERM TRENDS IN PUBLIC OPINION AND SCHOOL DESEGREGATION

People who criticize school desegregation plans often assert that busing has failed and the public has rejected it. In fact, busing—the term is used to describe the mandatory reassignment of students to distant schools—has not been a major policy in U.S. cities for many years, since desegregation plans began to embrace magnet and voluntary transfer policies in the mid-1970s. No major new mandatory plan has been adopted in the past three decades. Choice is now a central component of any integration plan.

Attitudes toward desegregation were most negative following the Supreme Court's 1971 *Swann v. Charlotte-Mecklenburg* decision, which led to the first implementation of major new mandatory busing plans in districts with a history of de jure segregation. The peak of the court-ordered changes came in 1971 and 1972, when scores of new plans quickly materialized, requiring rapid district-wide desegregation across the major cities of the southern and border states. The Supreme Court's 1973 decision in *Keyes v. Denver School District No. 1* brought desegregation to many northern cities over the next few years. During that period, almost all desegregation plans were designed by courts because local school boards refused to do so, were implemented suddenly, and involved the mandatory reassignment of teachers and students, with few educational options. Even African Americans, who supported integration and were supposed to benefit from these policies, were divided over them.

Attitudes about integration and busing are now quite different. Improving white attitudes toward integration in general have been apparent for many years, as shown in the responses to a Gallup question that asked white parents whether they would object to their child being in a school that had a few blacks, was half black, or had a black majority. Even at the height of the busing controversy, in the early to mid-1970s, 92 percent of whites said they would have no objection to their child being in a school with a few blacks, and 69 percent said they would accept a half-black school, but only 39 percent would not object if their child were in a majority black school.[4] The favorable trend in these attitudes over many years—in contrast to the extreme white opposition at the beginning of busing—indicate that urban desegregation has been framed not as an issue of integration but as some extraordinary governmental intervention via busing, even though more suburban and rural (and many private school) children than those in urban or other desegregating districts have gone to school by bus for many years. There have been few surveys about the kind of desegregation plan that has been dominant in the past three decades, with major emphasis on parental choice. Much of the survey data we have examines public attitudes about a form of desegregation—large scale, mandatory—that ended long ago in most regions.

There was a great deal of controversy when busing began, but it virtually disappeared as a major policy issue. The degree of public concern about desegregation and busing peaked about forty years ago. Every year between 1969 and 1973, between an eighth and a fifth of the public who participated in the Gallup Poll cited busing for desegregation as a top school problem. By the early 1980s the share of busing-concerned citizens was down to about 5 percent, which fell to 3 percent in the early 1990s.[5]

Black opposition to busing (or preference for neighborhood schools) was at its peak during the most intense period of the busing battle. One national poll showed 48 percent opposed, and another showed a very close division, with only 55 percent in favor. Black support of busing gradually increased in the 1980s and 1990s.[6] Black families, however, consistently showed overwhelming support for the idea of their children going to school with white students, including a large majority who were ready to have their children attend majority white schools. There is no poll evidence, except in some cities with plans that produced great conflict and little access to strong schools, for the claim of black abandonment of the integration ideal, though there has never been a consensus over the means to achieve integration.[7]

One of the most striking elements of research on desegregation and busing is that few surveys questioned those most affected—the students, their parents, and educators who worked in desegregated schools. One would presume that these stakeholders would have been the most concerned if busing for desegregation were a difficult and damaging policy. Newspaper accounts of desegregation attitudes were often written as if potentially affected parents most opposed the policy, but the surveys mostly questioned the general public. The Harris Survey questioned national samples of parents three times from 1978 to 1989. In 1978, not long after the busing issue peaked, 63 percent of black parents whose children were bused in integration plans said the experience had been "very satisfactory," and only one black parent in twelve and one white parent in six thought it was "unsatisfactory." By 1989, at the highest nationwide level of black-white desegregation ever recorded, opinions had become more positive: 64 percent of whites, 63 percent of blacks, and 70 percent of Asians whose children were bused for desegregation said that the experience was "very satisfactory," and only one black parent in twenty-five, one white in twenty, and one Asian in fifty reported that it was "unsatisfactory."[8] This could reflect the growing choice elements in desegregation plans. These figures are vastly more positive than those concerning parents' views of many other educational issues.

Initially there was overwhelming white opposition to desegregation in Louisville, even higher than the national average: more than nine-tenths of whites were opposed.[9] The federal district court ordered a plan with massive mandatory busing across the metro. This plan became more choice oriented, and over time and through their experience with desegregated schools, people changed their attitudes. When surveyed by the *Louisville Courier-Journal* in 1991, 81 percent of the black parents and 53 percent of the whites said that the experience was satisfactory.[10] Both when it was challenged in the 1990s and later, a number of surveys of the general public and of parents of schoolchildren showed strong support for continuing the plan, which still included race-conscious goals despite having become more driven by choice mechanisms.[11] By the time the case reached the Supreme Court, two generations of Louisville adults had grown up in diverse schools, which had become the norm in the community.

One of the important realities in surveys is that Americans strongly prefer contradictory things. For example, people usually say that they value high-quality public education but also want to cut the taxes that pay for it; they want to improve the environment but avoid regulation; they want greater food safety and smaller government. Throughout the surveys about desegregation there has been, for many years, a strong majority preferring integrated education but deep controversy over the means to achieve it. Most people would like integrated schools and the kind of educational choices they want, all right in their neighborhood. It would be ideal to have stably and well-integrated schools that children could walk to, or for everyone to get their first choice of school, which also has a diverse student body. In the real world, the art of government is doing as much as possible to realize both goals. For urban desegregation, this has increasingly meant using choice mechanisms to spur voluntary desegregation and giving as many people as possible their first choice. Parents now have fewer guarantees that their children can attend neighborhood schools but many more educational options that they willingly transfer their children to receive. They also have access to the diversity they prefer without the fear of resegregation, which would lose many of diversity's advantages.

This brief summary of public opinion surveys suggests that when policy makers hear claims that public opinion has turned sharply against desegregation plans, they should look more closely. It may be that people who have no direct experience of the plans are unfamiliar with the way they work and are repeating what they heard about the intense conflicts at the beginning of mandatory urban desegregation or something from the media or local politics. Systematic study of public opinion about school integration shows that opposition is much less dramatic than in the past and support has grown, especially among those most affected: students and their parents.

PARENTS' SUPPORT FOR INTEGRATION
AND CONCERNS ABOUT IMPLEMENTATION

IQS Research, based in Louisville, confidentially surveyed a random sample of parents of JCPS students in December 2010. It conducted a telephone interview with one adult at each home drawn from a list that was randomly sorted within each of the four target strata representing grade levels and regions of the city.

The research department of JCPS provided IQS Research with the file of home telephone numbers of households with children who were attending the district's schools. This list was deduplicated, so households with multiple children appeared only once and were questioned about only one child. The universe of possible households for this survey was approximately fifty thousand.

All interviews were conducted in English between the hours of 9:00 A.M. and 9:00 P.M. The average interview lasted thirteen minutes. The target groups were stratified to oversample parents of kindergarten and first grade students and those who lived in Area A (JCPS's plan defines A areas as those with lower educational attainment, lower household income, and higher shares of minority students; all other areas are B).[12] Eighty percent of respondents were female. Twenty-six percent had a high school degree or less, another third had some college education, and another 36 percent had a four-year college degree or more education. Thirty-eight percent of the sample lived in A areas and 62 percent in B. Finally, 36 percent of the sample was African American, 56 percent was white, and 8 percent was all other racial/ethnic groups.

Broad-Based Support for the Goals of Diversity and the Benefits of Integration

Parents of JCPS students strongly believe in the benefits of diverse schools. We asked a series of questions that probed different aspects of support for the goals of JCPS's current integration policy. District parents reported extremely high levels of support for the types of diversity that the student assignment plan reflects. Nearly nine out of ten (88 percent) agreed that schools should include students from different racial/ethnic groups. Since this is the goal that the district has pursued the longest, it is not surprising that its level of support was higher than those of the other school composition options. Nearly as high shares of parents believed that schools should have students from families with a range of incomes

(86 percent) and educational attainment (86 percent). While a large majority also approved of having diverse levels of student achievement in each school, this had the least-extensive support (78 percent), reflecting the response of JCPS parents to similarly worded questions in 2008.[13]

Integrationists have traditionally supported diverse schools because of the benefits to students who attend them and the longer-term benefits that the community receives.[14] This survey finds support for both of these rationales. More than 90 percent of JCPS parents agreed that attending racially diverse schools is important for their child's long-term personal and academic development. The last time this question was asked, in 1996, 86 percent agreed, suggesting that the longer the district has diverse schools, the more support it will get for them.[15] Black parents and those in A areas report the most agreement about the importance for diverse schools, but high levels of parents of all groups agree.

We also asked respondents to assess the effect of the decades of integrated schools on their community. Overall, 43 percent believed that JCPS's integration policies have improved the greater Louisville area, while 19 percent thought they had harmed it. Parents of first and second graders had the highest percentage of believers in improvement (46 percent), while those reporting transportation problems had the lowest (32 percent). Of course, people have differing ways of assessing integration's effects on the community, but these are promising findings.

In sum, parents of JCPS students remain in agreement with the district about the importance of diverse schools, the benefits of such schools for their children's academic and personal development, and the positive effect integration has had on the larger community for the past several decades. As we'll see next, however, these parents are less in agreement about how the district should design student assignment policy to achieve its goals.

Principles for Student Assignments— Parents' Contradictory Preferences

Our examination of parents' preferences finds generally high levels of support for a range of student assignment priorities, not all of which can be attained simultaneously. Large majorities of parents support school choice, yet schools of choice, by their nature, require extensive transportation to make schools available to students from across the district.

There is strong—even growing—support for student assignment guidelines that aim to create diverse schools. Nearly 90 percent of all JCPS parents think that the district's guidelines should "ensure that students learn with students from different races and economic backgrounds," including 62 percent who strongly agreed with this statement. Both percentages, particularly of those strongly agreeing, represent increases from the last survey about student assignment, in 2008. This seems to be due, at least in part, to increasing agreement with this priority from white parents, 86 percent of whom agreed this time.

It is one thing to generally support these priorities, but it is important to note that a majority of parents (55 percent) also said they would be willing to send their child to a school outside their neighborhood if this would help the district achieve diversity. Only 38 percent agreed with this in 1996. The increased support is seen in the responses of parents across all racial/ethnic backgrounds: 45 percent of whites, 69 percent of blacks, and 65 percent of other races/ethnicities.

JCPS's student assignment policy combines diversity guidelines with a variety of parental choice options. Parents are very supportive of options. Ninety percent wanted the opportunity to choose a school other than the one closest to where they lived, and all groups shared this preference. A lower percentage of parents—but still the vast majority (81 percent)—agreed that district policy should allow students to transfer, presuming space availability, even if that would increase segregation. A slightly different question about student transfers was asked in 2008, without reference to segregation, which had an even higher percentage of parent support.[16] Finally, virtually all parents said that they were willing to send their child outside their neighborhood for a specialized program that meets their child's needs. Taken together, these responses indicate a strong desire to have school choice options outside their neighborhood.

But parents also value the importance of proximity in student assignment. Seventy-nine percent agreed that their child should be allowed to attend the school closest to their home even when such an assignment would exacerbate segregation. White and B area parents were more likely to agree with this statement.

Almost all parents—90 percent—believed that "a student assignment plan should be designed to minimize the transportation time for students," including 70 percent who strongly agreed with this statement. These high percentages are not surprising. It's hard to imagine that anyone would prefer to have students spend more time than necessary on buses, though this clearly doesn't mean that parents think students should have to go to the nearest school. Parental attitudes on these student assignment issues have remained relatively constant.

Surprisingly, one of the student assignment principles that received the least support was feeder patterns, which ensure that elementary classmates attend middle school together, something that could produce more stability for children but would also mean less choice. Sixty-eight percent of parents surveyed agreed that this was at least somewhat important, similar to responses in 2008. This doesn't mean that parents don't value the familiarity that feeder patterns would provide, just that they rank it lower than other student assignment priorities, including broad educational choices.

Parents strongly value many student assignment principles embodied in JCPS's current policy: diversity, choice, and proximity. Because these values cannot always coexist, trade-offs are necessarily part of a student assignment policy, particularly in an expansive, residentially segregated district like theirs.

Policy Implementation: More Satisfaction with Individual
Experiences than with the Overall Student Assignment Plan

A major challenge of any educational policy that constrains parents' choices is how to maintain satisfaction with its goals and implementation when not all students are assigned to their first choice. This can be particularly difficult when demographically similar groups of parents perceive the same schools as desirable. Given this challenge, it is perhaps not surprising that parents' evaluation of the implementation of the student assignment policy was not as positive as their assessment of the value of the policy's goals. Notably, parents are more satisfied with the assignment for their child than with the overall assignment plan and its implementation. (Likewise, national surveys about both public schools and Congress often report that people believe the institutions are in grave trouble but their own school or representative is good.)[17]

High percentages of parents reported satisfaction (responses of 5, 6, or 7 on a seven-point scale) with the quality of education their child was receiving. This was particularly so with parents of younger students. Close to 90 percent of kindergarten parents were satisfied, and 45 percent were "completely satisfied" with the quality of their child's education. White and black parents shared similar levels of satisfaction (79 and 80 percent, respectively), while the level for the relatively smaller number of parents of other races/ethnicities (e.g., Latino, Asian) was even higher (87 percent).

Respondents indicated generally high levels of awareness of the district's student assignment policy, although this varied between groups. Seventy-one percent of all respondents reported being at least somewhat familiar with it. Given the extensive community education efforts that accompanied the new plan, it is somewhat surprising to see a substantial share of respondents who reported no familiarity with it (13 percent of all respondents and 15 percent of low-income parents). While someone in the household other than the person surveyed may have made decisions about schools for their child, these responses indicate a need to continue community education efforts to help parents understand the plan.

An encouraging finding is parents' generally high satisfaction with their experience of the student assignment process. Nearly 70 percent indicated that they were satisfied with how the district handled their child's student assignment process, including nearly one-third who were completely satisfied. There were few differences among parents of different demographic groups. The one noticeable difference was in the relatively small number of parents who indicated that transportation was unreliable (we discuss transportation more fully in the next section). Perhaps as a result of late or otherwise unreliable bus service, a consider-

TABLE 11.1 Satisfaction with school assignment for your child

	Overall	Bus on time	Bus not on time	Child doesn't ride bus
5–7	69%	72%	49%	68%
4	10%	10%	12%	11%
1–3	21%	18%	39%	21%
Total	1,852	1,146	193	519

NOTES: 1 = completely dissatisfied; 7 = completely satisfied. Of the 1,852 parents surveyed, six who said their child did not ride the bus nevertheless reported a response about whether it was on time.

ably lower share of those parents were satisfied with how the district dealt with school assignment for their child (see table 11.1). It appears that the transportation system did not always handle well the problems of starting up a complex new plan and that serious mistakes at the beginning of the 2009 school year harmed public opinion.

There was less agreement that the overall student assignment plan was working well, and assessments varied widely among groups of parents.[18] Forty-four percent of respondents gave a positive assessment of how well the plan was working (response of 5, 6, or 7). Those whose children did not ride the bus or rode for the longest time were the least likely to assess the plan positively (34 and 42 percent respectively), while more than half of those whose children rode the bus for forty minutes or less every day gave it a positive rating. Likewise, kindergarten parents gave generally positive ratings (52 percent said 5, 6, or 7). Majorities of A area, low-income, and minority parents rated the plan as working.

Finally, we asked parents about the district's implementation of the plan. A majority of respondents (54 percent) were satisfied (giving a response of 5, 6, or 7), with one-sixth indicating complete satisfaction. Substantial differences existed on this question as well. Parents in B areas and parents of white students and students who did not qualify for free or reduced-price lunch (FRL) were less satisfied with the plan's implementation. The gaps were smaller between A and B areas than between races/ethnicities or economic statuses. Parents of kindergarten students were the most supportive (58 percent). The minority of parents who rated transportation as unreliable were, unsurprisingly, less satisfied (42 percent) with the plan's implementation. There was also less satisfaction among parents whose children didn't ride the bus (47 percent), which might reflect dissatisfaction with their transportation options.

Although there is widespread support for the goals of the district's student assignment policy, there's less support for how it is working or has been implemented. A positive finding is that parents were more satisfied with their personal experiences with JCPS—its assignment of their children or the quality of their children's education. But considerable differences existed between groups of parents in assessing the policy and its implementation.

TRANSPORTATION CONCERNS

While school districts provide transportation for many reasons, it is an important element of a comprehensive effort to achieve integration. Unless they have requested a transfer, JCPS provides students with transportation if their school is more than one mile away from their residence or they have to cross a major barrier, such as an interstate or a major road, to get to school.

Given the headlines surrounding busing times during the first two years of implementing the 2010 JCPS student assignment policy, we interpret some of the responses below with caution. Even if the estimates of, for example, time spent on a bus or whether the transportation system has operated on time are not accurate, parents' perceptions are also important, particularly given the differences in their evaluations of the district's implementation of the student assignment policy, described above.

Seventy-two percent of respondents said their child rode the bus, with a median total daily ride time of forty minutes.[19] Median bus time was similar across demographic groups, but the percentage whose child did not ride the bus varied widely. In particular, higher shares of children from white, non-FRL-eligible, or B area households did not ride a school bus.

A substantial majority of parents—68 percent of all respondents—believed that the transportation system had always or almost always operated on time and as scheduled. More members of advantaged (73 percent of parents of non-FRL-eligible students) and nonblack households (69 percent of whites and 70 percent of other respondents) shared this favorable perception. Conversely, the groups that relied on transportation at a higher rate were less likely to believe that it operated on time, although 63 percent of A area respondents thought that it did.

While there is clear evidence of concern over the reliability of transportation, parents indicated that there were positive aspects of children's daily experiences on school buses. Here too we see somewhat contradictory messages. Fifty-five percent of parents agreed that the bus ride was "just another part of the school day." The next-highest response (46 percent) was more positive: that the bus had a child's friends or was enjoyable. Approximately one-quarter of respondents reported that their child complained about the bus ride (27 percent), and an almost equal share described it as tiring (28 percent). The question about the nature of their children's time on the bus allowed parents to select multiple responses and may reflect the variety of busing experiences that students will have over the course of a year.

Transportation has gotten many headlines while the district's new student assignment policy has been in place, and this survey of parents reveals mixed feelings about it. District-provided transportation is the way most American children get to school each day. At the same time, the associations we found between parental assessment of the student assignment policy and children's transportation experiences indicate that the district should improve the overall implementation, success, and equity of transportation to address parent concerns.

DISPARATE CHOICES:
UNEQUAL KNOWLEDGE AND PREFERENCES

Any choice-based student assignment policy relies on all parents having full information about the options available and being able to assess their relative merits. However, research has indicated that more-advantaged groups of parents have better access to school choice information.[20] Our survey data also reveal persisting patterns in knowledge gaps and access to information about schools and the choice-based assignment policy more generally among JCPS parents.

Those who answered that they knew they had the option to request a school other than the one their child was attending was relatively high (76 percent), but 81 percent had known this the last time the question was asked, in 1996. This decline could be due to the decrease in permanent parent assistance centers throughout the district. In particular, most of the decline stems from parents with FRL-eligible students, who went from 74 percent knowledgeable in 1996 to 68 percent in 2010. By contrast, more-advantaged groups—such as those not FRL eligible, B households (85 percent), and whites—were much more likely to know about school choice options. Similarly, A area students were less likely than students from B households to submit on-time applications during the 2010–11 school year student assignment process.

JCPS offers parents multiple ways of learning about school choices, and high shares of parents reported receiving schooling information in multiple ways. Some of the most popular were brochures (56 percent), the district's website (51 percent overall, but only 42 percent of households in A areas), and talking with JCPS staff (50 percent). The most popular source of information for all parents—and particularly certain groups—was talking to parents of other JCPS students (62 percent of all respondents and 67 percent of parents in B areas). Parents in B areas reported using each source of information at a higher rate than parents in A areas; corresponding patterns were found between parents of non-FRL- and FRL-eligible students. These gaps, like the differential knowledge of school choice options described above, are similar in other districts with choice-based student assignment.

Encouragingly, the vast majority of respondents reported that the information they received about school choice options was somewhat or very helpful (75 percent). This was particularly true for economically advantaged households (81 percent). At the same time, one-ninth of all respondents—and higher shares of

TABLE 11.2 Factors impacting school choice

	Educational program (%)	Test scores (%)	Percentage of low-income students (%)	Student racial diversity (%)	Child care options (%)	Availability of transportation (%)	Location (%)
Overall	96	89	49	68	51	78	80
Household area							
A	97	91	58	77	61	86	80
B	96	89	43	62	44	72	80
Race/ethnicity							
White	96	87	39	58	40	70	79
Black	97	93	59	80	62	87	82
Other	96	89	66	79	71	87	77

Note: Percentages are of respondents reporting a 5, 6, or 7 on a scale where 1 is not at all important and 7 is extremely important.

A (13 percent) and FRL-eligible households (14 percent)—reported not receiving any information.

School choice policies are complicated, in part, because people weigh different things in evaluating how a school will fit their children. Unsurprisingly, virtually all of the JCPS respondents rated the school's educational program as an important consideration. A lesser percentage—but still high—believed that test scores were important (see table 11.2). More parents said they considered these academic factors than any other. White parents and those living in B areas were less concerned than nonwhite and A area parents about aspects of student body composition. They were also less concerned with pragmatic considerations: the availability of transportation and child care. As would be expected, child care was a higher priority in school choice for low-income families and those with children in lower grades. However, there were smaller differences among importance of location by student grade level. Finally, location was not as important for parents whose children did not ride a bus or rode the bus for at least an hour every day.

STUDENTS' PERCEPTIONS ABOUT DESEGREGATION

Amid all the controversy about the future of diversity in Louisville schools and the changes in the local plan imposed by the 2007 Supreme Court decision, we wondered whether students' experiences and attitudes had changed. With the cooperation of JCPS, we administered a student survey in January 2011 via an online survey tool. The district drew a representative sample of 1,292 high school juniors to include approximately one-fifth of its junior population (6,334). Because of some mixed-grade classes, a small percentage of students were not juniors. All of the high schools in the district participated in the study, proportionally represented in the sample. We obtained 1,095 completed surveys, a response rate of 85 percent. The respondents included 326 African Americans, 633 whites, 35 Asian Americans, 57 Latinos, and 101 students who identified themselves as from an "other" race or as multiracial.[21] Students were assured that their responses would be confidential and anonymous.[22]

The results are a strong reflection of the views of students nearing the end of high school and thinking about their experiences and their futures. This survey certainly does not show that all of the city's racial/ethnic problems have been solved in the schools or that perfect equality and harmony have been achieved. (Anyone who is familiar with the history of American race relations and the struggles across the country over the achievement gap knows that the United States still has far to go.) Its central finding, however, is that there have been solid accomplishments in the region's schools, that large and usually similar majorities of black and white students believe that growing up in diverse schools has been an advantage for their future in some important respects. Most students have a teacher who cares about them, most have been strongly encouraged to go to college and hope to attend a four-year school, and most have taken college entrance exams. Many students, both black and white, are taking demanding honors and college credit courses, though the percentages are not equal.

Perhaps the most encouraging evidence is that the students see how the schools are preparing them for the kind of society in which they are going to live and work. They feel comfortable in interracial settings, are able to discuss controversial racial and social issues, have deeper understanding of other groups, and are willing to work in diverse settings. In fact, there is good evidence here that integrated schools prepare young people for a successfully integrated life. As they think about a time in the future when they will make their own decisions, many express a preference for a diverse college, a diverse workplace, and living in a diverse neighborhood. They strongly relate these preferences to their schooling experience.

In today's economy, highly valued employees have not only the "hard" skills of math and understanding the substance of their job but increasingly the "soft" skills such as relating to others, working effectively in group settings, and being a contributor to or leader of collaborative tasks. There is considerable evidence in this survey that Louisville area students are convinced that they have acquired some valuable skills and understandings for their future lives. Certainly this bodes well for institutions and employers in the region and for the likelihood that all groups will be able to work together with understanding in the search for solutions to the community's problems.

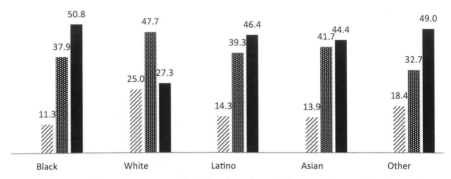

The Jefferson County Public Schools have implemented policies to produce diverse schools for 35 years. If you could advise the school district, what would recommend for the future?

⬚ Drop desegregation goals and policies

▦ Continue present desegregation efforts

■ Put more effort into policies for diversity and equal treatment

FIGURE 11.1. Jefferson County Public School students' advice on future diversity efforts, 2011 (from Diversity Assessment Questionnaire, question 46).

Since today's high school juniors will soon be voters, it seemed like a good idea to ask them not only what they had experienced but also what they thought should be done in the future. Like the parents in our other survey, these students were overwhelmingly but not unanimously committed to desegregation efforts. Just 19.9 percent thought that the district should "drop desegregation goals and policies." This included one white student in four and one African American student in nine (see figure 11.1). Surprisingly in a community where there is a debate over the possibility of doing much less to desegregate, two out of five students favored strengthening "policies for diversity and equal treatment." Though black students are often said to have borne the largest burden of integration, they are the most in support of putting more effort into diversity and equal treatment policies.

CONCLUSION

The greater Louisville community has shown a strong and consistent commitment to diverse schools, with a long tradition of adopting desegregation policies, which it has modified over time to provide more school choice and satisfy parents. The district's legal struggle to defend this commitment ended with a serious Supreme Court defeat in 2007 that forced it to draw up a new plan. The many changes this meant for local families, plus a less than perfect start-up, prompted serious criticism. However, there are major positive findings about the attitudes of parents and the experiences and plans of students that reaffirm the efforts of the school district and community to combine school choice and diversity. At the same time, significant numbers of parents expressed both concerns about the district transportation system's unnecessarily long trips and scheduling failures and a desire to have diversity closer to home. These concerns influence support for the plan and spurred the school board to order a review of the plan and its transportation system in 2011. In early 2012 the district adopted minor changes as a result and is continuing to study further changes.

There is strong approval of using diversity guidelines in the choice process but also a strong desire to honor individual preferences. Fortunately, this is not a serious problem in practice. For instance, in 2010, 83 percent of first grade applicants who submitted their form on time got their first choice, and many were perfectly willing to choose diverse schools. Eighty-seven percent of applications were submitted on time. Yet the fact that gaps exist between different groups in knowledge about choice options and submitting on-time applications suggests the need for more district outreach to parents. Further, a number of schools are not within the diversity guidelines of having 15–50 percent enrollment of students from Area A households.

Parents also expressed an extremely strong preference for having choice among schools. Since each local school cannot offer as big a variety of well-developed programs as the district as a whole, this will inevitably mean a considerable transportation network and disappointment for some who do not get their top choice or choices.

Though the Latino population of the county is still modest, the demographic trends in the state and the region make clear that it will rapidly grow. Good planning must consider Latinos in a serious way and include preparations for dealing with the cultural and linguistic issues they will bring to the county. The survey data show that Latino parents and students strongly support diverse education. This may help Louisville avoid the problem in much of the country of Latinos being highly segregated in weak schools.

It is still early in the implementation of the newest version of JCPS's choice-based integration policy, begun in 2012. This chapter illustrates some of the challenges of designing choice systems that further integration in the post–*Parents Involved* landscape. Both politically and legally, JCPS must continue to assert that the denial of some parent choices in the name of diversity will benefit all children and the community. Improving the educational options and performance of all schools might be an important part of such a strategy. Other efforts might include reconnecting with housing integration efforts, which might lead to reduced transportation needs and more integrative school choices by parents.

NOTES

This chapter is drawn from G. Orfield and Frankenberg, "Experiencing Integration in Louisville: How Parents and Students See the Gains and Challenges." After these surveys were conducted and reported to the school board and the public in metropolitan Louisville, the authors, together with Bruce Wicinas from Berkeley, prepared a plan for the board to continue to improve the district's desegregation efforts. Much of the new plan was adopted by the school board in 2012 and an effort to force the district to return to neighborhood schools was defeated in the Kentucky Supreme Court in September 2012.

1. *Green et al. v. County School Board of New Kent County, Virginia, et al.*

2. Pairing schools and changing the boundaries of adjacent school zones, for example, tend to concentrate desegregation efforts along current racial boundaries and leave large patterns of segregated white and nonwhite schools, fostering white flight from the small areas of integrated schools and speeding resegregation. The most stable plans are those that produce relatively equal racial distributions of students across metropolitan housing market areas. See Clotfelter, "Private Schools, Segregation, and the Southern States"; G. Orfield, *Must We Bus?: Segregated Schools and National Policy*; G. Orfield and Eaton, *Dismantling Desegregation: The Quiet Reversal of* Brown vs. Board of Education.

3. See examples at http://theintegrationreport.wordpress.com/2010/09/22/issue-27/. This is in stark contrast to Wake County, a North Carolina city with a similar voluntary desegregation history, where in 2009 antidiversity candidates won all four board seats on the ballot. Wake County's diversity policy, however, has limited parental choice.

4. Gallup Poll data in Schuman et al., *Racial Attitudes in America: Trends and Interpretations.*

5. Gallup Poll data in Orfield, "Public Opinion and School Desegregation," 62.

6. Data from annual Phi Delta Kappa / Gallup Surveys in ibid., 61.

7. Ibid., 65.

8. Harris Surveys in ibid., 63.

9. Maconahay and Hawley, "Reaction to Busing in Louisville: Summary of Adult Opinions in 1976 and 1977."

10. McDonald and Wade, "Whites Divided over Plan to End Forced Busing."

11. Wilkerson, "Student Assignment Survey: Summary of Findings."

12. For more sampling details, see G. Orfield and Frankenberg, "Experiencing Integration in Louisville."

13. Kifer, "Student Assignment Survey Elementary School Results: Jefferson County Public Schools."

14. Linn and Welner, eds., *Race-Conscious Policies for Assigning Students to Schools: Social Science Research and the Supreme Court Cases.*

15. Wilkerson, "Student Assignment Survey."

16. In 2008, 87 percent of parents agreed with the following statement: "Students should be allowed to transfer, no matter what the reason, as long as there is a seat for the student in the school to which he/she wishes to transfer."

17. See, e.g., Bushaw and Lopez, "Betting on Teachers."

18. This question was asked only of those who reported that they were somewhat or very familiar with the district's current student assignment plan.

19. The mean bus time is almost fifty minutes, which is influenced by a handful of extremely high values.

20. See, e.g., Fuller, Elmore, and Orfield, eds. *Who Chooses? Who Loses?: Culture, Institutions, and the Unequal Effects of School Choice.*

21. Seventy-one students checked more than one racial/ethnic category.

22. For more information on the development of this survey, see Kurlaender and Yun, "Is Diversity a Compelling Educational Interest?: Evidence from Louisville," 117–19.

Conclusion

A Theory of Choice with Equity

Gary Orfield and Erica Frankenberg

Choice sounds good but can mean a myriad of very different things. There are choices that produce life-changing gains and bad choices that seem good but lead to disaster. The idea that any kind of choice will produce good results is something no parent or teacher would suggest. Similarly, there are markets that have powerful and creative results, like the computer market, and markets that are profitable but destructive, such as those for cigarettes, gambling, and illegal drugs. Wise choices in good educational markets can increase opportunity, but betting the future of students in devastated communities on the idea that offering any kind of unregulated choice should be the top priority in educational reform is absurd. The central challenges of policy making are to clarify what we mean by *choice,* to create the conditions under which wise choices can be made, and to provide educational opportunities that are truly worth choosing. At a time when American education seems stuck and needs to be stronger and American society is increasingly nonwhite and unequal, we have to get this right. Fortunately, we have models that have produced clear benefits in the past, which we can use to construct a more powerful theory of choice and determine the policies that will make it real.

All major choice theories claim to expand opportunity for those previously locked into inadequate schools. Choice is a potentially powerful force that can disrupt patterns of school opportunities for good or for ill. Different forms of choice lead to very different results. Because differing approaches are based on fundamentally different assumptions about how choice works, it is important to clarify the theory and specify the policies needed to make choice function as a real tool for expanding equity. It is clear from the studies in this book and other research reviewed here that the integration theory offers the greatest promise and the pure market theory the most serious risks for disadvantaged students.

Choice policies must be constructed around an adequate understanding of how choice actually works. The history of failures and successes should guide policy. Choice systems that ignore social stratification have failed because they fundamentally misconstrue both the choices the market provides and the ability of people in a very unequal society to make equal use of choice. Unrestricted choice systems tend to further intensify inequality. Integrated schools are better for both individuals and communities. We have learned, through half a century of often painful experience, what conditions of choice systems increase equity, bring people together in positive ways, and expand opportunity. The fact is that most of our political leaders and some of the most important philanthropists have been ignoring these realities for several decades and that theories about perfect markets continue to be used to expand poor choice systems, making challenging the premises of current policy and broadening the debate over choice all the more important. The reality is that the civil rights choice policies worked—not perfectly, but much better than the alternatives. The simplistic version of choice that assumes that something lacking all of the essential elements of a market will produce better and more equitable schooling in a stratified society is wrong. In our society, the experience of many failures of unregulated markets has produced powerful regulations to assure safety and quality and protect the environment. Schools are very complex and important institutions that offer limited choice and need regulation to guarantee good and fair choices.

This chapter reviews the basic lessons of the experiences and research reported in this book and outlines the argument for the integration theory of choice.

WHAT IS SCHOOL CHOICE?

Calling something *school choice* only signifies that it will give some people another option or options under some circumstances. The options may be better or worse or not real options at all. Choice may be genuinely available to all or realistically available to only a few. There is nothing inherent in school choice that guarantees that the choice will be real and feasible or the new options better than (or even as good as) the assigned school in the regular public system. Research clearly shows this.

Contemporary choice advocates tend to see choice of any sort as better than none, despite the fact that the most highly regarded schools are often in areas with little or no choice. Choice is not an educational treatment, only a system of decentralized management. The market theory of choice assumes that nonpublic or quasi-public options and institutions are better by definition than public ones and that individuals will come up with better options regardless of the conditions under which choice is offered. This presupposes that there are good choices, that information is rich and fairly distributed, and that the most disadvantaged families and those with far more resources and contacts will equally understand and have access to the best choices. Market theory assumes that when some people have a chance to exit the weakest schools, those schools will not get worse for the students left behind but will improve because of competition. It presupposes that schools will not block choices and that students can get to schools of choice on their own. Only if all of these circumstances were true would choice be fair.

However, research shows that this set of assumptions has no basis in fact. The theory is based on a deductive model that does not fit observed reality. Many of its advocates are not interested in research or facts but believe this theory so intensely that they denounce anyone who challenges it regardless of evidence. Its first premise—that markets, or even anything with a few marketlike features, are better than nonmarkets by definition—is unexamined. However, schools are not interchangeable or readily understood commodities. The idea that markets will produce both efficiency and equity for the disadvantaged derives from the ideological assumption that private action is inherently better than public decisions and that access to choices makes things fair. In reality, school choices are sometimes better and sometimes worse. More-privileged families clearly make better use of choice opportunities and have much better information about them. Without offsetting policies, choice can easily increase stratification, adding more privilege for the privileged, and undermining diverse communities. Schools and public school districts can lose good students and funding while being locked into fixed costs that do not decline with enrollment. They may also lose support and reputation, which may doom the remaining students to an even more dismal set of opportunities. Obviously, a much more complex theory is needed.

The basis of much of the enthusiasm about choice is a radically simplified view of both society and institutions. It reflects a major stream in American political and social thought—the idea of individualism and individual rights, fiercely embraced even in a society that has dismissed blacks, American Indians, Mexicans, Asians, and, of course, women as groups so inferior that they could not be given full rights. The idea that the fundamental rights are negative rights, protecting individuals from actions of government, is at the core of the Bill of Rights and American political thought. The ideas of the self-made man, of the Horatio Alger stories, of the great entrepreneur, of families immigrating and working hard to become part of the American mainstream are fundamental in American political and social discourse. And, of course, many families have transformed their future through hard work and education, but both the opportunities and the successes are strongly linked to race. The discourse of individualism fits well with the assumptions of market choice advocates, which may explain market choice's popularity, but it overlooks the structural aspects of society that still limit the opportunities of many from historically disadvantaged groups. This ideology ignores another major stream of American thought, reflected in the Declaration of Independence's insistence that "all men are created equal" and the constitutional changes engendered by the end of the Civil War, such as the 14th Amendment's guarantee to the former slaves that all would enjoy "equal protection of the laws." This is a positive right of a historically oppressed group. America strongly emphasizes individualistic beliefs, particularly in conservative periods, but they have, of course, always been in tension with the reality of a society deeply divided by race/ethnicity, color, and, sometimes, language.

A central idea of the civil rights movement and much of civil rights law—and other laws designed to change the status of groups that had been subordinated in society—was that trying to solve structural inequalities by dealing with one individual case at a time could not work because of a multitude of prejudices, stereotypes, different starting points, institutions and practices that perpetuated inequality, and the practical impossibility of processing millions of cases. Creating meaningful rights, in this theory, required systematic action to dismantle institutional barriers and to cope with societal fears and prejudices. Inequality was deeply embedded and could only be overcome by recognizing the rights of historically excluded groups and changing institutional practices. To those who embraced the civil rights analysis, the idealized version of markets seemed a subterfuge serving to perpetuate and even legitimate inequality. It was not that civil rights advocates were opposed to choices for families about their children; it was that they wished choice to be used in ways that would prevent further segregation and insure that segregated nonwhite families had access to better schools. Their experience was that individual choice without equity policies reflected and perpetuated racial/ethnic inequality.

INACCURATE ASSUMPTIONS OF SCHOOL CHOICE

Since market theory often amounts to a series of conclusions spun out from the basic claim that markets are inherently superior, its advocates have often seen no need to look closely at how choice works. Forgetting the history of choice policies in our country and ignoring research from other nations showing that unrestricted choice produces unequal, segregated schools that reinforce the underlying stratification of society, policy makers have been swept up in the faith in markets to solve deeply embedded educational and societal problems. This is not research—this is theology. Too often critics are assailed as if they were heretics.

Assuming that the preconditions for a true market exist in spite of essential ones being obviously absent confuses the public, misleads policy makers, and fails to equalize opportunity. It seems as if the more times researchers produce evidence that this blind faith is misguided and that the results dramatically diverge from the theory, the more adherents repeat the theory. To simply accept dogma inconsistent with evidence is to needlessly risk the possibility of increasing inequity for the students who most need opportunity.

Unfortunately, true educational reform cannot be accomplished by repeating a mantra and pretending a market exists. That approach merely treats predictable and serious inequality as if it were the result of free choice in a fair, equitable setting, shifting the blame from society to those who choose among limited, confusing choices and diverting attention from both the real quality of the choices and the processes for choosing. In an era of conservative social policy, large majorities of whites have come to believe that discrimination no longer limits the choice of minorities in some crucial respects. In the most recent Gallup Poll on the subject, in 2009, for example, 82 percent of whites agreed that blacks had just as good a chance as whites to receive a job for which they were qualified.[1] If one assumes that equal opportunity already exists, it is reasonable to think that choice mechanisms will be fair without special provisions. If, on the other hand, as research consistently shows, many forms of discrimination and unequal connections and information are still pervasive, then we have to build a better theory.

Policy discourse in the United States has slipped from what conditions to impose to make choice fair to the belief that unrestricted choice will now produce results fundamentally different from those in the past. Choice theory needs to be revised to incorporate the lessons of history and of current experience.

IF SCHOOL CHOICE IS SO POWERFUL, WHY DON'T PRIVILEGED CLASS AND RACIAL GROUPS USE IT IN THEIR COMMUNITIES?

If lack of choice is the cause of educational stagnation and choice is a powerful instrument for school improvement, why don't the communities with the most power use it? There is abundant evidence that parents in these communities want the best possible education for their children. The fact that the issue of choice rarely arises among them means that these very concerned parents and their leaders see something else as much more important. That something is creating schools that are very successful and strongly connected to opportunities for higher education. They have the best, most experienced teachers, the strongest peer competition and support, the highest test scores and college-going rates, and the best reputations. Few of these schools are either schools of choice or outside the community's regular school system. They are serving affluent, largely suburban communities. Getting disadvantaged students into the best public schools of more-affluent and white communities was a central goal of the civil rights movement. It is not a serious goal of the choice movement. The dominant argument of choice proponents, often borrowing terminology from the civil rights era, is that giving poor families a charter school choice is somehow the equivalent of letting more-affluent families choose their schools through the housing market. But affluent families, at least if they are white (since housing discrimination is still severe), have the ability to choose very good public schools. The supposedly just substitute is usually a segregated, high-poverty charter school that is as weak as the local public school but presented as better merely because it is not part of a public school system.

The elite in our country may think individual choice in educational markets is a great thing for poor minority kids in city neighborhoods, yet they are rarely willing to allow choice for all in their schools or housing markets. Members of this group have, of course, exerted choice by deciding where to live, but this choice is quite deliberately not open to most. Elite communities tend to tightly regulate both their schools and their housing markets, to exclude all but the most affluent families, and their school systems typically offer little or no choice. The housing markets in more-affluent areas exclude the vast majority of potential residents through regulations that limit the acceptable types of housing stock and drive up the costs of housing. Given the prohibition against building affordable housing in the great majority of those communities, they basically prohibit access to their schools to all but a small minority of high-income or high-wealth families. This helps to perpetuate residential segregation and typically results in segregated schools, especially when school district boundaries overlap with municipal boundaries.[2] Many of these regulations may be largely invisible to those who are able to choose to live in such communities. Because such communities do not have to pay many of the costs created by concentrations of low-income families, they can focus great resources on their schools. They have well-resourced public systems that are like elite private schools in their class and race composition. The availability of such options to affluent families helps explain the fact that only about 2 percent of American students attend nonreligious private schools and that religious schools have little presence in more-affluent areas. State referenda to allow school vouchers have suffered sizable defeats in many such communities any time they have been on the ballot.[3]

The most widely announced goal of educational choice programs has been to give real choices to those who have had none because of their poverty or minority status and the weak school districts they live in. Charter school and voucher advocates have used this to justify their demands for public funds and to defend the exceptionally high level of segregation of black students in charter schools. This is also why choice programs have been overwhelmingly concentrated in central cities and poor communities with weak school districts.[4] The largest voucher programs have been, for example, in two large central cities with declining public school enrollment, Cleveland and Milwaukee. Yet evidence shows no academic gains from voucher programs and that even when such a program is oversubscribed, those students who are selected to receive vouchers may not persist in their new schools, if they matriculate at all.[5]

Those who say they want poor children to have the kinds of choices their children have should be challenged to share their own good schools and confront the systemic inequities that still exist in our public schools. Schools are so dramatically unequal within most metropolitan areas that simply observing classes at the same grade level and in the same subject in a poor urban high school and an affluent suburban school usually shocks a neutral observer.[6] Students receiving exceptionally high grades in urban schools are usually performing at a level that would be only average in an excellent suburban school and are sadly unprepared for a competitive college, regardless of their personal intelligence and dedication.[7] Much of the choice movement is about symbolic options. It might provide a quick hope for parents frustrated with their district school but may make little, if any, improvement in a child's long-term future. Yet advocates hold up the very act of exercising this choice as a major solution for problems of unequal opportunity.

Making choice real and beneficial will require serious leadership and policy changes. We need to expand the choices to include the schools that already work in communities where children are educated as creative analytic citizens, not drilled incessantly in tests on basic skills. Choice could be a much more powerful treatment if it included the truly good choices. One of the things the Berkeley, California, school district realized was that in order for its choice policy to produce integration in a community with many highly educated parents, all schools had to be viable choices for all sectors of the community.[8] Otherwise, some schools might not have been selected, and some students would have been mandatorily reassigned to such undesirable alternatives.

WHY UNCONTROLLED CHOICE STRATIFIES

Despite its potential drawbacks, choice with civil rights offers the only possible way, in our segregated society, for many black and Latino students to access schools that can develop their talents and connect them with powerful opportunities. Even at its best, choice by itself is inadequate, since there must be policies to upgrade or reorganize schools that no one chooses. As anyone who has looked at the housing markets in poor neighborhoods knows, market mechanisms by themselves do not break downward cycles.[9]

The incentives for choice providers differ in charter school or voucher plans and school district choice plans. The latter often include an explicit commitment to diversity. State legislation for charter schools, however, often provides little or no guidance regarding integration, and funding structures can incentivize their accepting more local students in segregated communities.[10] When choice providers have no obligation to educate all students, unlike school districts, or pursue integration, it is understandable that choice policies often result in segregation and the exclusion of expensive-to-educate special education and English-Language Learner (ELL) students. This is true in spite of the potential advantages of charters, which are often able to accept students across district boundary lines. As choice grows—and we think it is here to stay—federal, state, and local policies that affect many types of school choice must be revisited to mitigate its stratifying effects. Charters, which are an increasingly significant part of publicly supported American education, should build on the lessons of good magnet schools, and their federal and state aid should be conditioned on compliance with civil rights policies.

One of the central assumptions about choice is that everyone will know about all the available options and how to assess the appropriateness for their children. But it is clear that this assumption does not reflect reality. The chapters about Louisville and Hartford describe two contexts in which care has been taken to try to combat the gaps in information dissemination and use, but even in these cases serious gaps persist. In Louisville, despite widespread support for the integration plan, black and poor residents were more likely to not know about their options, to use fewer information sources, and to submit choice applications late (see chapter 11). Not surprisingly, they were less likely than more-advantaged residents to get their first-choice school. These problems are far more prevalent in schools without extensive outreach and information efforts like those communities have. It is also likely easier for larger entities like school districts to inform the community of school options than is the case for separate charter or voucher-accepting schools. Other research has shown how schools design their marketing deliberately to attract desired groups of students to apply.[11] It would be a useful step if some of the funders of the charter school movement would pay for parent information offices and publications and websites in English and locally prominent languages to tell parents about the available charter options in their metro area and give them contact information and application forms.

Knowledge that choice options exist is one important aspect of the selection process, but knowledge about what selection to make is both equally essential and even more elusive. In chapter 10, Jack Dougherty and his colleagues describe their efforts to help Hartford residents make school choices using several commonly considered characteristics. They even included a more sophisticated measure of academic quality, trying to strengthen information for parents. The Hartford research echoes other studies showing that racial views often lead some choosers to select weak schools.[12] Choice is premised on the assumption that families can adequately judge educational quality, but experience suggests the opposite. Even Hartford's innovative attempt shows that facts like the digital divide may limit the reach and ultimate usefulness of such tools.

Physical isolation in housing markets segregated by race and class is a fundamental reason why choice is necessary and attractive but also why choice alone will not solve the intractable problem of segregation. Segregation has locked many students into clearly inferior schools that have had weak records for many years. These schools are in communities that more-affluent families see as inferior and, sometimes, dangerous. Teachers are often quick to leave when other options are available. If children in these schools are to have access to better ones—and not simply rely on the limited hope that a substantially better school will move into their neighborhood—they need not only permission to transfer to another school but the means to get there. While middle-class, two-parent families are often able to either drive their children to a more distant school or pay for transportation, many poor and working-class families simply cannot. In most U.S. cities, public transportation is too limited, too unreliable, and, increasingly, too costly for many families. Further, if a school—as is the case for a concerning percentage of charters—does not provide subsidized school lunches, something that about half of American families are now eligible for, it is not a real option for these students.

School choice isn't a choice if you can't get to the school you want. Most American students—most of whom are suburban or live in a smaller city or town—go to school on school buses. A choice program that does not provide transportation not only has a built-in class bias and a racial bias (given segregated housing and the bad and increasingly costly public transit systems in many cities) but may also increase stratification by allowing those with means to exit and forcing those without means to stay behind. Running a choice program that lets families with resources for their own transportation participate while excluding less affluent others turns a policy that could create more equal opportunity into a mockery. It is like offering a lovely park on the other side of a river with no bridge.

HOW STRUCTURING CHOICE MATTERS
FOR INTEGRATION

A successful theory of choice must come to terms with the evidence that unconstrained individual choice is likely to produce inequitable results because of the many ways in which educational markets fundamentally differ from pure markets, including that different groups of parents have different levels of information and understanding about the system. Criticizing the market theory does not mean disagreeing that choice can be a powerful force in education. How powerful and equitable choice is depends largely on the policies underlying it. To be successful, choice programs in a deeply stratified society must not ignore inequalities of knowledge and social capital that expand the opportunities of those who start ahead.

Choice, though often provided in an inadequate way, should not be abandoned. Its power can be focused and channeled. To start, we must more holistically assess the context within which parents are making choices and how we can offer truly meaningful options accessible to all parts of the community. As this book has shown, the types of choice offered determine whether the lofty promises of choice advocates come close to being realized. Interdistrict desegregation programs, for example, use choice as a means to offer city students (albeit a limited number) the opportunity to attend well-financed suburban schools with strong peer groups that can change their life chances. A well-organized, integrated International Baccalaureate magnet school in the middle of a ghetto or barrio neighborhood can be a pathway to a strong college and a different life. There must be policies that can make choice a force for expanding opportunity and diversity. There must be bridges for all.

Choice is often disappointing, creating the illusion of opportunity without the reality. Knowing about the history of choice, however, should make policy makers and educators more aware that the individualistic model assumes a level playing field that does not exist. The early 1960s experience of freedom of choice and open enrollment made this clear. The more unrestricted choice is, the more likely it is to be unfair. A society with extremely unequal income and education and communities where those with the most and the fewest resources are physically separated, often in separate schools and school districts, simply does not have the preconditions of fair market competition. It is wrong to think of choice as genuinely free when these conditions and policies to create more equal opportunities do not exist.

Magnet schools and controlled choice arose from the realization that policies explicitly designed to use choice as a means to create diversity, not as an end in itself, could significantly offset the built-in inequalities of a stratified society. The basic ideas were to assure that there were meaningful choices and to greatly increase parent information and recruitment. In other words, policy makers understood that the conditions the market system is premised on were lacking. By creating what were often highly desirable new specialized schools, the magnet school movement provided all families options that had not existed before.

These policies, at their best, created specialized schools that were stably integrated without the coercion of either families or teachers. In this system, the central idea was not that choice was an educational treatment in itself but that the students gained from integration under positive conditions and from unique educational programs. The basic goal was not to maximize choice but to create a system of incentives and controls that would use choice to create diverse schools, widely acceptable to all, through voluntary means. This meant, of course, that not everyone could get their first choice (impossible in any case because of issues such as school capacity) and that when the demand did not create a desirable and lasting racial equilibrium, recruitment and reserved seats would adjust the system to result in the desired and educationally positive mix of students. Magnet schools were often in African American and Latino areas, to create an incentive for whites and Asians to come into these communities and, in the process, to break stereotypes about neighborhoods.

When conservative courts and presidential administrations dropped desegregation requirements and some magnet schools ended their desegregation goals and strategies, resegregation often occurred. Schools in nonwhite areas began to lose white demand and to resegregate as they no longer held seats for whites. Class diversity also decreased, and magnet schools became much like traditional segregated neighborhood schools. On the other hand, schools with intense white demand experienced the opposite transition, meaning that nonwhites became more isolated and marginal in these schools. Both trends resulted in a loss of substantial, stable diversity and the gains that it had produced.[13] This is why educators need a new policy to help communities learn the lessons of Berkeley, Louisville, and other places that have found ways to remain integrated even in the face of the obstacles created by the Supreme Court.

AN INTEGRATIVE THEORY OF CHOICE

Most choice advocates have ignored a key goal of the Supreme Court's *Brown v. Board of Education* decision and the civil rights movement: the creation of successfully integrated schools to train students equally and prepare them to live and work in a multiracial society. Since there is compelling evidence that integrated schools create major gains in both test scores and life chances for minority students and important gains for white students, it seems fair to add these outcomes as major positives for integrated schools, even if the current policy focus is only on educational gains measured in test and graduation results.[14]

To come up with the best guidance for the future, it is sometimes important to look back over options in many settings, to select what has worked best, and to think about ways to adapt those successes to conditions that may have changed. It is clear that market-based choice systems have provided no significant educational test score gains and actually intensified racial segregation. The integration theory, as applied in magnet and controlled choice transfer programs (within and between districts), includes basic civil rights requirements and offers the most viable and successful model for choice programs. The problem is how to take a model developed four decades ago in the midst of a major struggle for civil rights and the integration of blacks and apply it to today's situation, in which there is no comparable social movement, the Supreme Court has become an obstacle instead of a support, and the country is more profoundly multiracial and increasingly multilingual. What is needed is a broadened and updated integration theory along with legal and policy principles that could make it work. The federal government and major foundations, which have not funded serious research on race relations within schools since the 1970s, need to make this a priority, as the nation's schools are becoming primarily nonwhite and ever more segregated and unequal. Some parts of the answer are evident or are suggested in the studies in this book and other recent research. Some are still to be discovered, and many experiments are clearly called for. The basic principles, however, can be simply set out.

We have, over the past half century, gone through a full cycle of choice strategies, and we have learned a great deal though research and experience. For example, not having a specific plan for integration means implicitly accepting spreading segregation, driven by unequal knowledge of the choice system and its options, accompanied by racial stereotypes.[15] Assuming that people have adequate and reasonably equal knowledge about schools and choice systems means accepting increased stratification without recognizing its source. To fairly offer truly free choices, there must be a clear and central intention to do that, a direct facing of inequalities that perpetuate segregation, and a prohibition on choices that make segregation worse.

Since the market theory of choice rests on demonstrably wrong assumptions and has produced no significant evidence of either educational or social advantages, it should be rejected. While choice can never be truly equitable, choice that is well implemented within the integration theory has important advantages at both the individual and the community level. It often offers students locked in extremely unequal schools access to considerably better schools and, sometimes, to schools that serve elite families and are most connected with college and very different life chances. At the community level, schools that are integrated without coercion, under circumstances broadly acceptable to all groups, create an unusual opportunity to socialize students across the lines of race and class into an extremely diverse society, which will give them skills, knowledge, and sensitivities often invaluable in adult life and in the functioning of major community and public institutions. The advantages of desegregated settings are not automatic and can be lost or minimized. On the other hand, they can be intensified by applying well-developed methods and creating positive conditions inside diverse schools.[16]

As this book comes to its finish, it is important to state as clearly as possible the basic argument of the integration theory of choice during a period when many of the earlier insights about it have been ignored. The basic argument is as follows:

1. Choice is not the basic objective; it is a tool for pursuing a more fundamental objective—equalizing opportunity across lines of social cleavage.
2. The fundamental goal of choice is to overcome through voluntary means the systemic inequality embedded in segregated neighborhood schools.

3. Racial and class integration will enhance opportunity, and the schools will be an important tool to offset deep social divisions.

4. Choice must offer schools that are substantially better than impoverished and segregated neighborhood schools.

5. There must be major efforts to offset the inequality of knowledge about the choice process and the choices of schools.

6. There must be a clear goal of diversity and policies to offset the normal tendency of choice to stratify.

7. Obvious barriers to choice, such as lack of transportation or linguistic or special education programs needed by groups of students, must be eliminated.

8. The choice plan must produce a lasting, substantial level of integration to achieve its goals.

9. Policies known to protect and enhance the individual and community gains of diversity should be an integral part of a choice plan.

10. This approach should continue until it overcomes the external conditions that make the market model fail.

A basic principle of the integration theory of choice is that segregation is systematically unequal and that integrated schools, diverse in both race and class, are inherently better for the possibilities and average outcomes of students. The underlying social and economic realities are that intensely minority-segregated schools have less advantaged students, are far less able to attract and hold excellent teachers, offer a less challenging curriculum taught in classes with less prepared students and teachers, are more exposed to instability of enrollment and violence, and are far less respected and connected to college and job opportunities. They also cannot adequately prepare students to live and work effectively in a multiracial society.

It is true, of course, that some segregated schools overcome some of these disabilities, usually with extraordinary leadership and faculties dedicated to this mission, and that diverse schools often fail to realize the full potential of their diversity. But the general patterns are powerful. Getting students into schools with much richer possibilities is an essential first step; whether or not those possibilities are realized depends upon the degree to which diverse groups are treated positively within the school and, of course, the degree to which the students and their families take advantage of their new opportunities.

YES, BUT IS IT FEASIBLE?

The integration theory of choice has compelling advantages, but one could reasonably ask: "Is it politically possible?" One of the important lessons of history is that the magnet school movement was widely popular and many communities adopted its ideas without coercion, even as it was part of court-ordered desegregation plans in many others. In communities where magnets have been established for some time, many schools have developed strong reputations and lend strength to often-troubled school districts with weak neighborhood schools. Though the Barack Obama administration (like prior administrations) has done little to encourage this, there are many communities eager to receive federal funds to create new magnet schools. In late 2011, the Justice and Education Departments issued long-delayed policy guidance affirming the importance of integration and assuring school officials that they still had broad legal latitude to implement the kinds of initiatives discussed in this book.[17] Though there is always pressure in any choice system from people who do not get their top selection, experience shows that integrative choice gives a great many people choices that would not otherwise have existed: schools with a kind of stable and substantial diversity that is broadly acceptable across racial/ethnic lines. One could reasonably say that the courts, not politics, have undermined choice systems that are possible—even popular—and have clear benefits for many students and their communities. The negative leadership of conservative courts and administrations has invalidated viable methods of applying the integration theory of choice.

What has been sadly lacking is political leadership to pursue this effective method of choice. The decisions of the Bill Clinton and Obama administrations to largely ignore issues of desegregation and to embrace charter schools, disregarding the history of freedom of choice and the magnet experience, mean that there has been no serious recent national discussion of the conditions under which choice fosters equity and those under which it reflects and reinforces inequality and segregation.

The United States today is a multiracial society with profound inequality and few policies of any importance to equalize educational opportunity and prepare the rising generations to live, work, and govern successfully across deep lines of separation.[18] The mandatory policies of racial change that transformed the South in the civil rights era have been largely abandoned, and the growth of separation, hastened by many current choice policies, threatens our common future. The integration theory of choice is not a panacea, but it does channel the power of choice in ways that avoid increasing stratification and can contribute significantly both to real opportunities for the most excluded groups and to a more integrated, successful society for all.

This book was written not to suggest ending school choice but to expose the lost opportunities in current practices and to show a path in which choice does what both liberal and conservative advocates say they are committed to—expand opportunities for students in the most inferior and unequal public schools. There is justice in the often savage critiques of our many inferior segregated schools.

The worst outcome would be to create a parallel system of inferior segregated schools that sapped funding from the remaining neighborhood schools, call it choice, and congratulate ourselves on solving a problem. Unregulated choice tends to comfort the privileged, take pressure off demands for change in the larger system, protect more-affluent schools from any change, and offer illusory opportunities to the poor, blacks, and Latinos. This is happening in some of our communities. We can do much better.

A vigorous system of choice observing basic principles of equity and civil rights can provide life-changing opportunities and contribute to the health of communities. We need a system of choice that includes the schools attended by more-privileged students in metropolitan housing markets. Those isolated affluent white and Asian children need to prepare for the diverse nation they will live and work in and to share the rich opportunities they have been given. We need citywide and metro schools of choice with special educational offerings and outreach. If we clarify what we want, understand the preconditions of fair and successful outcomes, and put the policies that foster them into operation, we will make our society fairer and more successful. If we do not, we will continue the practice of recent decades—offering choices that are far from equal in systems that lack the basic elements of fairness and blaming poor students and families for not achieving equally. We have done much better in the past, the conditions for better outcomes are clear, and we must choose to do better again.

NOTES

1. Gallup, "Race Relations."

2. Shapiro, *The Hidden Cost of Being African American: How Wealth Perpetuates Inequality*; Harris and McArdle, *More than Money: The Spatial Mismatch between Where Homeowners of Color in Metro Boston Can Afford to Live and Where They Actually Reside*.

3. Bulman and Kirp, "The Shifting Politics of School Choice," 46–47.

4. A majority of charter schools (56 percent) are in either a large or a small city, according to National Center for Education Statistics definitions. Only 30 percent of traditional public schools are in central cities. See Frankenberg, Siegel-Hawley, and Wang, "Choice without Equity: Charter School Segregation."

5. Hochschild and Scovronick, *The American Dream and the Public Schools*.

6. See, for example, Kozol, *Shame of the Nation*; Ryan, *Five Miles Away, a World Apart: One City, Two Schools, and the Story of Educational Opportunity in Modern America*.

7. Willingham, Pollack, and Lewis, "Grades and Test Scores: Accounting for Observed Differences"; Carnevale et al., "Role of Tests in College Admissions: Evaluating Skills for Higher Education," notes that "students in high-poverty schools (those where more than 75 percent of students receive free or reduced-price lunch) who received mostly 'A's' in English got about the same reading score on the SAT as did 'C' and 'D' students in the most affluent schools" (2).

8. See chapter 3.

9. See, e.g., Massey and Denton, *American Apartheid: Segregation and the Making of the Underclass*, on the creation of ghettos.

10. Siegel-Hawley and Frankenberg, "Does Law Influence Charter School Diversity? An Analysis of Federal and State Legislation."

11. Lubienski, "School Competition and the Emergence of Symbolism in a Market Environment."

12. Clotfelter, *After* Brown: *The Rise and Retreat of School Desegregation.*

13. Orfield, "Reviving the Goal of an Integrated Society: A 21st Century Challenge."

14. Wells and Crain, "Perpetuation Theory and the Long-Term Effects of School Desegregation"; Linn and Welner, eds., *Race-Conscious Policies for Assigning Students to Schools: Social Science Research and the Supreme Court Cases.*

15. Brief Amicus Curiae of the American Psychological Association in Support of Respondents in *Parents Involved in Community Schools v. Seattle School District No. 1 et al.* and *Crystal D. Meredith v. Jefferson County Board of Education et al.*

16. Frankenberg and Orfield, *Lessons in Integration: Realizing the Promise of Racial Diversity in American Schools.*

17. U.S. Department of Justice Civil Rights Division and U.S. Department of Education Office for Civil Rights, "Guidance on the Voluntary Use of Race to Achieve Diversity and Avoid Racial Isolation in Elementary and Secondary Schools."

18. The census estimated that a majority of babies born in 2009 were nonwhite. Yen, "Census Shows Whites Lose US Majority among Babies."

Achieve Hartford. "Overview." 2010. www.achievehartford.org/about_ach.php.

Alexander v. Sandoval, 532 U.S. 275 (2001).

American Civil Rights Foundation v. Berkeley Unified School District, A121137 No. RG0692139 (Cal. Ct. of Appeal 1st District, March 17, 2009).

Andre-Bechely, L. "Finding Space and Managing Distance: Public School Choice in an Urban California District." *Urban Studies* 44:7 (2007): 1355–76.

Anrig, G. "An Idea Whose Time Has Gone: Conservatives Abandon Their Support for School Vouchers." *Washington Monthly* (April 2008): 29–33.

Anyon, J. "Social Class and School Knowledge." *Curriculum Inquiry* 11:1 (1981): 3–42.

Applebome, P. "In a Mother's Case, Reminders of Educational Inequalities." *New York Times,* April 27, 2011. www.nytimes.com/2011/04/28/nyregion/some-see-educational-inequality-at-heart-of-connecticut-case.html.

Aspen Associates Inc. *Minnesota Voluntary Public School Choice: 2005–2006.* Prepared for the Minnesota Department of Education. January 30, 2007. http://search.state.mn.us/.

Associated Press. "State Orders Detroit to Close Half Its Schools." February 21, 2011. www.cbsnews.com/2100-201_162-20034397.html.

Ave, M. "East Tampa Magnet Schools May Close." *St. Petersburg Times,* October 28, 2004.

———. "Few Pick Schools, So Far." *St. Petersburg Times,* January 7, 2004.

Balfanz, R., and N. Legters. "Locating the Dropout Crisis: Which High Schools Produce the Nation's Dropouts." In *Dropouts in America: Confronting the Graduation Rate Crisis,* ed. G. Orfield. Cambridge, MA: Harvard Education Press, 2004.

Ballou, D., E. Goldring, and K. Liu. "Magnet Schools and Student Achievement." National Center for the Study of Privatization in Education, Teachers College, Columbia University. March 2006. www.ncspe.org/publications_files/OP123.pdf.

Bartels, L. *Unequal Democracy: The Political Economy of the New Gilded Age.* New York: Russell Sage Foundation, 2008.

Bass, J. *Unlikely Heroes*. New York: Simon and Schuster, 1981.

Becker, H., K. Nakagawa, and R. Corwin. "Parent Involvement Contracts in California's Charter Schools: Strategy for Educational Improvement or Method of Exclusion?" *Teachers College Record* 98 (Spring 1997): 511–36.

Belk v. Charlotte-Mecklenburg Board of Education, 269 F.3d 305 (4th Cir. 2001).

Bell, C. "Real Options: The Role of Choice Sets in the Selection of Schools." *Teachers College Record*, January 9, 2006. www.tcrecord.org, ID Number: 12277, accessed July 13, 2009.

———. "Space and Place: Urban Parents' Geographical Preferences for Schools." *Urban Review* 39:4 (November 2007): 375–404.

Bennett, J. "Brand-Name Charters." *Education Next* 8:3 (Summer 2008): 28–34.

Berkeley Unified School District. "Information on Berkeley Unified's Student Assignment Plan: BUSD Student Assignment Plan/Policy." www.berkeleyschools.net/infor mation-on-berkeley-unifieds-student-assignment-plan/.

———. *Integration of the Berkeley Elementary Schools: A Report to the Superintendent*. Berkeley: Berkeley Unified School District, 1967.

Berry v. School District of Benton Harbor, 56 F. Supp. 2d 866 (W.D. Mich., 1999).

Betts, J. R., L. A. Rice, A. C. Zau, Y. E. Tang, and C. R. Koedel. *Does School Choice Work? Effects on Student Integration and Achievement*. San Francisco: Public Policy Institute of California, 2006.

Betts, J., A. C. Zau, and L. A. Rice. *Determinants of Student Achievement: New Evidence from San Diego*. San Francisco: Public Policy Institute of California, 2003.

Bhattacharjee, R. "Budget Cuts Result in Reduced School Bus Services." News Updates. *Berkeley Daily Planet*, June 26, 2009.

Biegel, S. "Court-Mandated Education Reform: The San Francisco Experience and the Shaping of Educational Policy after *Seattle-Louisville* and *Brian Ho v. SFUSD*." *Stanford Journal of Civil Rights and Civil Liberties* 4 (2008): 159–213.

Bifulco, R., C. D. Cobb, and C. Bell. "Can Interdistrict Choice Boost Student Achievement? The Case of Connecticut's Interdistrict Magnet School Program." Occasional Paper No. 167. New York: National Center for the Study of Privatization in Education, 2008.

Bifulco, R., H. Ladd, and S. Ross. "The Effects of Public School Choice on Those Left Behind: Evidence From Durham, North Carolina." *Peabody Journal of Education* 84 (2009): 130–49.

Blank, R. *Educational Effects of Magnet High Schools*. Madison, WI: National Center on Effective Secondary Schools, 1989.

Blank, R. K., R. A. Dentler, D. C. Baltzell, and K. Chabotar. *Survey of Magnet Schools: Analyzing a Model for Quality Integrated Education*. ED 236304. Final report of a national study for the U.S. Department of Education. Washington DC: James H. Lowry and Associates, 1983.

Blank, R., R. Levine, and L. Steele. "After Fifteen Years: Magnet Schools in Urban Education." In *Who Chooses? Who Loses?: Culture, Institutions, and the Unequal Effects of School Choice*, ed. B. Fuller, R. F. Elmore, and G. Orfield, 154–72. New York: Teachers College Press, 1996.

Board of Education of Oklahoma City Public Schools v. Dowell, 498 U.S. 239 (1991).

Bobo, L., H. Schuman, and C. Steeh. "Changing Racial Attitudes toward Residential Integration." In *Housing Desegregation and Federal Policy,* ed. J.M. Goering, 152–69. Chapel Hill: University of North Carolina Press, 1986.

Bodzin, S. "Chilean Students Taking to Streets against 'Pinochet's Education.'" *Christian Science Monitor,* August 11, 2011.

Boger, J., and G. Orfield, eds. *School Resegregation: Must the South Turn Back?* Chapel Hill: University of North Carolina Press, 2005.

Booher-Jennings, J. "Below the Bubble: 'Educational Triage' and the Texas Accountability System." *American Educational Research Journal* 42 (Summer 2005): 231–68.

Booker, K., S. Gilpatric, and T. Gronberg. "The Effect of Charter Schools on Traditional Public School Students in Texas: Are Children Who Stay Behind Left Behind?" *Journal of Urban Economics* 64:1 (2008): 123–45.

Borman, K., T. Eitle, D. Michaels, D. Eitle, B. Shircliffe, R. Lee, and S. Dorn. "Accountability in a Post-desegregation Era: The Continuing Significance of Racial Segregation in Florida's Schools." *American Educational Research Journal* 41 (2004): 605–31.

Boston Consulting Group. "The State of Public Education in New Orleans 2007." June 1, 2007. www.bcgperspectives.com/content/articles/organization_public_sector_public _education_new_orleans_2007/.

Bower, C. "Clayton Students Walk Out to Back Transfer Program." *St. Louis Post-Dispatch,* May 19, 2004.

Bowles, S., and H. Gintis. *Schooling in Capitalist America: Education Reform and the Contradictions of Economic Life.* New York: Basic Books, 1976.

Bowman, K.L. "Pursuing Educational Opportunities for Latino and Latina Students." *North Carolina Law Review* 88:3 (March 2011): 911–91.

Braddock, J. "Looking Back: The Effects of Court-Ordered Desegregation." In *From the Courtroom to the Classroom: The Shifting Landscape of School Desegregation,* ed. C. Smrekar and E. Goldring, 3 18. Cambridge, MA: Harvard University Press, 2009.

Brantlinger, E. *Dividing Classes: How the Middle Class Negotiates and Rationalizes School Advantage.* New York: Routledge Falmer, 2003.

Bridge, R.G., and J. Blackman. *Family Choice in Schooling* (R-2170/4). Vol. 4 of *A Study of Alternatives in American Education.* Santa Monica: Rand Corporation, 1978.

Brief Amicus Curiae of the American Civil Liberties Union et al. in Support of Respondents in *Parents Involved in Community Schools v. Seattle School District No 1 et al.* and *Crystal D. Meredith v. Jefferson County Board of Education et al.* (Nos. 05–908, 05–915) (127 S. Ct. 2738, 2007).

Brief Amicus Curiae of the American Psychological Association in Support of Respondents in *Parents Involved in Community Schools v. Seattle School District No. 1 et al.* and *Crystal D. Meredith v. Jefferson County Board of Education et al.* (Nos. 05–908, 05–915) (Sp. Ct., 2006).

Brief Amicus Curiae of the 553 Social Scientists in Support of Respondents in *Parents Involved in Community Schools v. Seattle School District No 1 et al.* and *Crystal D. Meredith v. Jefferson County Board of Education et al.* (Nos. 05–908, 05–915) (Sp. Ct., 2006).

Briggs v. Elliott, 132 F. Supp. 776 (E.D.S.C., 1955).

Brown v. Board of Education, 347 U.S. 483 (1955).

Brown v. Board of Education, 349 U.S. 294 (1954).

Bryk, A.S., P.B. Holland, and V.E. Lee. *Catholic Schools and the Common Good*. Cambridge, MA: Harvard University Press, 1993.

Buckley, J., and M. Schneider. *Charter Schools: Hope or Hype?* Princeton: Princeton University Press, 2007.

Bulman, R.C., and D.L. Kirp. "The Shifting Politics of School Choice." In *School Choice and Social Controversy: Politics, Policy and Law,* ed. S.D. Sugarman and F.R. Kemerer, 36–67. Washington DC: Brookings Institution Press, 1999.

Bureau of Equal Educational Opportunities, Massachusetts Department of Education. *Schools and Programs of Choice: Voluntary Desegregation in Massachusetts*. Boston: Edco Learning Center, 1977.

Bush, G.W. "Cleveland Voucher Program." News release. August 26, 1999.

———. First State of the Union address. February 27, 2001. *Congressional Record* 147, H43.

Bushaw, W.J., and S.J. Lopez. "Betting on Teachers." *Phi Delta Kappan* 93:1 (September 2011): 9–16.

Bush v. Holmes, 919 So. 2d (2006).

California Department of Education DataQuest. www.cde.ca.gov/ds/sd/cb/dataquest.asp.

California School Finder. www.schoolfinder.ca.gov.

California Teachers Association. "Why Isn't Kindergarten Mandatory in California?" *California Educator* 10:5 (February 2006). http://legacy.cta.org/media/publications/educator/archives/2006/200602_cal_ed_features06.htm, accessed May 18, 2012.

Carnevale, A., R. Fry, E. Haghighat, and E.W. Kimmel. "Role of Tests in College Admissions: Evaluating Skills for Higher Education." In *Achieving Inclusion in Higher Education,* report to Educational Testing Service Board of Trustees. Princeton, NJ: Educational Testing Service, 1998.

Carnoy, M., R. Jacobsen, L. Mishel, and R. Rothstein. *The Charter School Dust-Up: Examining the Evidence on Enrollment and Achievement*. New York: Teachers College Press, 2005.

Carr, M., and M. Ritter. *Measuring the Competitive Effect of Charter Schools on Student Achievement in Ohio's Traditional Public Schools*. Paper submitted to the National Center for the Study of Privatization in Education. NY: Columbia University Press, 2007. www.ncspe.org/publications_files/OP146.pdf, retrieved December 10, 2009.

Carr, S. "Charter Numbers Expected to Grow; 19 Groups Apply to Operate 24 Schools." *Times-Picayune,* September 2, 2009, National edition, 1.

———. "Recovery School District to Lay Off Dozens of Teachers Today." *Times-Picayune,* August 3, 2009. www.nola.com/news/index.ssf/2009/08/recovery_school_district_to_la.html, accessed December 17, 2009.

Carter, K., and A. Fenwick. "Charter X: What's in a Name?" July 30, 2009. http://columbia.news21.com/2009/indexc065.html?p=1909, accessed December, 9 2009.

Carter, S.C. *No Excuses: Lessons from 21 High-Performing, High-Poverty Schools*. Washington DC: Heritage Foundation, 2000.

Cech, J. "Catholic Closures Linked to Growth of City Charters." *Education Week* 27:1 (February 13, 2008).

Center for Educational Reform. "National Charter School and Enrollment Statistics 2010." www.edreform.com/2012/01/26/national-charter-school-and-enrollment-sta tistics-2010/, accessed May 14, 2012.

Center for National Policy Review, Catholic University Law School. *Why Must Northern School Systems Desegregate? A Summary of Federal Court Decisions in Recent Cases.* Washington DC: Center for National Policy Review, 1977.

Center for Research on Educational Outcomes. *Multiple Choice: Charter School Performance in Sixteen States.* Palo Alto: Stanford University, 2009. http://credo.stanford. edu/reports/MULTIPLE_CHOICE_CREDO.pdf, retrieved November 2, 2009.

Cerve, K. "Riverview Charter School Approves New Lottery Enrollment Plan." Island Packet Online, May 14, 2010. www.islandpacket.com/2010/05/14/1240691/riverview-charter-school-approves.html, accessed April 9, 2012.

Charles, C. Z. "Can We Live Together? Racial Preferences and Neighborhood Outcomes." In *The Geography of Opportunity: Race and Housing Choice in Metropolitan America,* ed. X. de Sousa Briggs, 45–80. Washington DC: Brookings Institution, 2005.

Chavez, L., and E. Frankenberg. "Integration Defended: Berkeley Unified's Strategy to Maintain School Diversity." Los Angeles. Civil Rights Project / Proyecto Derechos Civiles at UCLA, 2009. http://civilrightsproject.ucla.edu/research/k-12-education/ integration-and-diversity/integration-defended-berkeley-unified2019s-strategy-to-maintain-school-diversity.

Christenson, B., M. Eaton, M. S. Garet, L. C. Miller, H. Hikawa, and P. DuBois. *Evaluation of the Magnet Schools Assistance Program, 1998 Grantees.* Washington DC: U.S. Department of Education, Office of the Under Secretary, 2003. http://www2.ed.gov/ rschstat/eval/choice/magneteval/finalreport.pdf.

Chubb, J. E. "America's Public Schools: Choice Is a Panacea." *Brookings Review* 8:3 (Summer 1990): 4–12.

Chubb, J. E., and T. M. Moe. *Politics, Markets, and America's Schools.* Washington DC: Brookings Institution, 1990.

City of Berkeley Planning and Development Department. "City of Berkeley 2009–2014 Housing Element," ch. 5: "Objectives, Policies and Actions." www.ci.berkeley.ca.us/ contentdisplay.aspx?id=484, accessed November 12, 2008.

Clinton, W. J. Eighth State of the Union address. January 27, 2000. Transcript available at www.washingtonpost.com/wp-srv/politics/special/states/docs/sou00.htm.

Clotfelter, C. T. *After* Brown: *The Rise and Retreat of School Desegregation.* Princeton: Princeton University Press, 2004.

———. "Private Schools, Segregation, and the Southern States." *Peabody Journal of Education* 79:2 (2004): 74–97.

Clotfelter, C., H. Ladd, and J. Vigdor. "Teacher-Student Matching and the Assessment of Teacher Effectiveness." *Journal of Human Resources* 41 (2006): 778–820.

Cobb, C., and G. Glass. "Ethnic Segregation in Arizona Charter Schools." *Education Policy Analysis Archives* 7:1 (January 14, 1999): 1–34. http://epaa.asu.edu/epaa/v7n1/, accessed December 9, 2009.

Coleman, J., E. Campbell, C. Hobson, J. McPartland, A. Mood, F. Weinfeld, and R. York.

Equality of Educational Opportunity. Washington DC: Government Printing Office, 1966.

Coleman, J., T. Hoffer, and S. Kilgore. "Cognitive Outcomes in Public and Private Schools." *Sociology of Education* 55:2–3 (1982): 65–76.

Coleman, J.S., S.D. Kelly, and J.H. Moore. *Trends in School Segregation, 1968–1973.* Washington DC: Urban Institute, 1975.

ConnCAN. "About Us." 2011. www.conncan.org/aboutus.

Cookson, P. *School Choice: The Struggle for the Soul of America Education.* New Haven: Yale University Press, 1994.

Coons, J.E., and S.D. Sugarman. *Education by Choice: The Case for Family Control.* Berkeley: University of California Press, 1978.

Coyne, C. "Reputations and Realities: A Comparative Study of Parental Perceptions, School Quality, and the SmartChoices Website." Unpublished senior research project, Trinity College, April 2010. www.trincoll.edu/depts/educ/css/research.html.

Crain, R., R. Miller, J. Hawes, and J. Peichert. "Finding Niches: Desegregated Students Sixteen Years Later—Final Report on the Educational Outcomes of Project Concern, Hartford, Connecticut." New York City: Institute for Urban Education, Teachers College, Columbia University, 1992.

Crain, R.L., and J. Strauss. *School Desegregation and Black Educational Attainment: Results from a Long-Term Experiment.* Baltimore: Johns Hopkins University Center for the Social Organization of Schools, 1985.

Cullen, J.B., B.A. Jacob, and S.D. Levitt. "The Impact of School Choice on Student Outcomes: An Analysis of the Chicago Public Schools." *Journal of Public Economics* 89:5–6 (June 2005): 729–60.

Darling-Hammond, L. *The Flat World and Education: How America's Commitment to Equity Will Determine Our Future.* New York: Teachers College Press, 2010.

Davis v. East Baton Rouge Parish School Board et al., C.A. No. 56–1662 (M.D. La., 1999).

Days, D., III. "The Other Desegregation Story: Eradicating the Dual School System in Hillsborough County, Florida." *Fordham Law Review* 61 (October 1992): 33–38.

DeFour, M. "ACLU Alleges Milwaukee Voucher Program Discriminates against Disabled Students." *Wisconsin State Journal,* June 7, 2011.

Diamond, J.B. "Still Separate and Unequal: Examining Race, Opportunity, and School Achievement in 'Integrated' Suburbs." *Journal of Negro Education* 75 (Summer 2006): 495–505.

Dickman, A.M., S.A. Kurhajetz, and E.V. Dunk. *Choosing Integration: Chapter 220 in the Shadow of Open Enrollment.* Milwaukee: Public Policy Forum, 2003.

Dillon, S., and D.J. Schemo "Charter Schools Fall Short in Public Schools Matchup: U.S. Reports Findings of Study in 5 States." *New York Times,* November 23, 2004.

Dingerson, L. "Narrow and Unlovely." *Rethinking Schools Online* 21 (Summer 2007): 1–8.

District of Columbia Public Charter School Board. "Find a Charter School." www.dcpubliccharter.com/SearchSchools.aspx.

District of Columbia Public Schools. "Find a School." http://dcatlas.dcgis.dc.gov/schoolprofile.

Dougherty, J., J. Wanzer, and C. Ramsay. "*Sheff v. O'Neill:* Weak Desegregation Remedies and Strong Disincentives in Connecticut, 1996–2008." In *From the Courtroom to the Classroom: The Shifting Landscape of School Desegregation,* ed. C. Smrekar and E. Goldring, 103–27. Cambridge, MA: Harvard Education Press, 2009.

Dougherty, J., D. Zannoni, M. Chowan, C. Coyne, B. Dawson, T. Guruge, and B. Nukic. "How Does Information Influence Parental Choice? The SmartChoices Project in Hartford, Connecticut." Occasional Paper No. 189, National Center for the Study of Privatization in Education. May 2010. www.ncspe.org/publications_files/OP189.pdf.

Douglas, D. *Reading, Writing and Race: The Desegregation of Charlotte's Schools.* Chapel Hill: University of North Carolina, 1995.

Dreier, P. J., J. H. Mollenkopf, and T. Swanstrom. *Place Matters: Metropolitics for the Twenty-First Century,* 2nd ed. (rev.). Lawrence: University Press of Kansas, 2004.

Eaton, S. E. *The Children in Room E-4: American Education on Trial.* Chapel Hill, NC: Algonquin Books, 2006.

———. *The Other Boston Busing Story.* New Haven: Yale University Press, 2001.

———. "Slipping toward Segregation." In *Dismantling Desegregation: The Quiet Repeal of* Brown v. Board of Education, ed. G. Orfield and S. Eaton, 207–39. New York: New Press, 1996.

Eaton, S. E., and G. Chirichigno. *METCO Merits More: The History and Status of METCO.* Cambridge, MA: Charles Hamilton Houston Institute, 2011.

Eaton, S. E., and E. Crutcher. "Magnets, Media, and Mirages." In *Dismantling Desegregation: The Quiet Repeal of* Brown v. Board of Education, ed. G. Orfield and S. Eaton, 265–89. New York: New Press, 1996.

Education Matters! "Highlights from the Regional School Choice Application Process." June 24, 2010. http://archive.constantcontact.com/fs031/1102778616856/archive/1103503 763732.html.

Education Sector. "Growing Pains: Scaling Up the Nation's Best Charter Schools." Washington DC: Education Sector, 2009.

Eisenberg v. Montgomery County Public Schools, 197 F.3d 123 (4th Cir. 1999).

Engberg, J., D. Epple, J. Imbrogno, H. Sieg, and R. Zimmer. "Bounding the Treatment Effects of Education Programs That Have Lotteried Admission and Selective Attrition." New York: National Center for the Study of Privatization in Education, 2011.

eSchool News. "Race to the Top Program Spurs School-Reform Debate." July 28, 2010. www.eschoolnews.com/2010/07/28/race-to-the-top-program-spurs-school-reform -debate/, accessed December 7, 2010.

Farley, J. E., and G. D. Squires. "Fences and Neighbors: Segregation in 21st-Century America." *Contexts* 4:1 (2005): 33–39.

Federal Interagency Forum on Child and Family Statistics. "Language Spoken at Home and Difficulty Speaking English." In *America's Children: Key Indicators of Well-Being, 2011.* www.childstats.gov/americaschildren/famsoc5.asp.

Fenwick, A. "The Door-to-Door Salesman." July 30, 2009, http://columbia.news21.com /2009/index8ee8.html?p=2270, accessed December 9, 2009.

———. "Finding Zion." July 30, 2009. http://columbia.news21.com/2009/indexc13a.html ?p=2280, accessed December 9, 2009.

———. "The Wisdom of the Marketplace." July 30, 2009. http://columbia.news21.com/ 2009/index3309.html?p=3119, accessed December 9, 2009.

Ferguson, B., and K. Royal. "Admission Requirements and Charter Schools." Center for Action Research on New Orleans School Reforms, November 2009.

Finnegan, K., N. Adelman, L. Anderson, L. Cotton, M. B. Donnelly, and T. Price. "Evaluation of Charter Schools Program: 2004 Final Report." U.S. Department of Education, Policy and Programs Study Service, 2004.

Fitzgerald, J. "Checking In on Charter Schools: An Examination of Charter School Finances." Minnesota 2020 Report, June 2009.

Florida Department of Education. "Grading Florida's Public Schools, 2009–10." http:// schoolgrades.fldoe.org/pdf/0910/Guidesheet2010SchoolGrades.pdf, accessed May 14, 2012.

Florida Department of Education, Division of Accountability, Research and Measurement. www.fldoe.org/arm/.

Folger, J. K., and C. B. Nam. *Education of the American Population.* Washington DC: U.S. Bureau of the Census, 1967.

Forman, J., Jr. "The Secret History of School Choice: How Progressives Got Here First." *Georgetown Law Journal* 93:4 (2005): 1287–387.

Fossey, W. R. "School Choice in Massachusetts: Will It Help Schools Improve?" EdD dissertation, Harvard University, 1993.

Frahm, R. A. "Charter Schools: A Debate over Integration and Education." *Connecticut Mirror,* February 24, 2010. www.ctmirror.org/story/charter-schools-debate-over-inte gration-and-education.

Frankenberg, E. "America's Diverse, Racially Changing Schools and Their Teachers." EdD dissertation, Harvard University, 2008.

———. *Boston's METCO Program: Lessons for Hartford.* Washington DC: Poverty Race and Research Action Council, 2007.

———. "The Demographic Context of Urban Schools and Districts." *Equity and Excellence in Education* 42:3 (2009): 255–71.

———. *Improving and Expanding Project Choice.* Washington DC: Poverty Race and Research Action Council, 2007.

———. "The Segregation of American Teachers." *Education Policy Analysis Archives* 17:1 (January 9, 2009). http://epaa.asu.edu/epaa/v17n1/, accessed July 22, 2009.

Frankenberg, E., and C. Le. "The Post–*Parents Involved* Challenge: Confronting Extralegal Obstacles to Integration." *Ohio State Law Journal* 69:5 (2008): 1015–72.

Frankenberg, E., and C. Lee. "Charter Schools and Race: A Lost Opportunity for Integrated Education." *Education Policy Analysis Archives* 11:32 (2003). http://epaa.asu.edu/ ojs/article/view/260/386.

Frankenberg, E., and G. Orfield, eds. *Lessons in Integration: Realizing the Promise of Racial Diversity in American Schools.* Charlottesville: University of Virginia Press, 2007.

———, eds. *The Resegregation of Suburban Schools: A Hidden Crisis in American Education.* Cambridge, MA: Harvard Education Press, 2012.

Frankenberg, E., and G. Siegel-Hawley. "The Forgotten Choice: Magnet Schools in a

Changing Landscape." Los Angeles: Civil Rights Project/Proyecto Derechos Civiles at UCLA, 2008.

———. "Overlooking Equity: Charter Schools and Civil Rights Policy." Los Angeles: UCLA Civil Rights Policy, 2009. www.civilrightsproject.ucla.edu/research/deseg/equity-overlooked-report-2009.pdf.

Frankenberg, E., G. Siegel-Hawley, and J. Wang. "Choice without Equity: Charter School Segregation." *Education Policy Analysis Archives* 19:1 (2011). http://epaa.asu.edu/ojs/article/view/779/878.

Franko, K. "Schools Boost Efforts to ID Fake Student Addresses." *Washington Times,* February 27, 2011. www.washingtontimes.com/news/2011/feb/27/schools-boost-efforts-to-id-fake-student-addresses/.

Freeman, C., B. Scafidi, and D. Sjoquist. "Racial Segregation in Georgia Public Schools, 1994–2001: Trends, Causes and Impact on Teacher Quality." In *School Resegregation: Must the South Turn Back?*, ed. J. Boger and G. Orfield, 148–63. Chapel Hill: University of North Carolina Press, 2005.

Freivogel, W. "St. Louis: The Nation's Largest Voluntary School Choice Plan." In *Divided We Fail: Coming Together through Public School Choice,* ed. R. Kahlenberg. New York: Century Foundation Press, 2002.

Friedman Foundation for Educational Choice. "Milton Friedman on Vouchers." Transcript of CNBC interview, March 24, 2003. www.edchoice.org/The-Friedmans/The-Friedmans-on-School-Choice/Milton-Friedman-on-Vouchers.aspx.

Fuller, B., R. F. Elmore, and G. Orfield, eds. *Who Chooses? Who Loses?: Culture, Institutions, and the Unequal Effects of School Choice.* New York: Teachers College Press, 1996.

Fuller, B., K. Gesicki, E. Kang, and J. Wright. "Is the No Child Left Behind Act Working? The Reliability of How States Track Achievement." Working paper 06–01. Berkeley: Policy Analysis for California Education, 2006.

Galatzan, T. "A Wave of Affiliated Charters: What Does It Mean?" *Galatzan Gazette,* May 10, 2012. www.galatzangazette.com/home1/2012/5/10/a-wave-of-affiliated-charters-what-does-it-mean.html.

Gallup. "Race Relations." www.gallup.com/poll/1687/Race-Relations.aspx, accessed July 5, 2011.

Gamoran, A. "Student Achievement in Public Magnet, Public Comprehensive, and Private City High Schools." *Educational Evaluation and Policy Analysis* 18 (1996): 1–18.

Gándara, P. "Latinos, Language, and Segregation." In *Integrating Schools in a Changing Society: New Policies and Legal Options for a Multicultural Generation,* ed. E. Frankenberg and E. DeBray, 265–78. Chapel Hill: University of North Carolina Press, 2011.

Gates, B. Remarks at the National Charter Schools Conference, Chicago, June 29, 2010.

Glenn, C., C. McLaughlin, and L. Salganik. *Parent Information for School Choice: The Case for Massachusetts.* Boston: Center on Families, Communities, Schools and Children's Learning, 1993.

Godwin, R. K., and F. R. Kemerer. *School Choice Tradeoffs: Liberty, Equity and Diversity.* Austin: University of Texas Press, 2002.

Goldring, E., and C. Smrekar. "Magnet Schools: Reform and Race in Urban Education." *Clearing House* 76:1 (September–October 2002): 13–15.

———. "Magnet Schools and the Pursuit of Racial Balance." *Education and Urban Society* 33:1 (2000): 17–35.

Goldstein, E. "To Choose or Not to Choose: Sheena Iyengar Shakes Up Psychology." *Chronicle Review,* March 14, 2010, B6–B10.

Grady, S., and S. Bielick. *Trends in the Use of School Choice: 1993 to 2007.* NCES 2010–004. Washington DC: National Center for Education Statistics, Institute of Education Sciences, U.S. Department of Education, 2010.

Granovetter, M. "The Strength of Weak Ties." *American Journal of Sociology* 78:6 (1973): 1360–80.

GreatSchools. "Compare Schools near an Address." www.greatschools.org/, accessed August 1, 2010.

Green, P., and J. Mead. *Charter Schools and the Law: Establishing New Legal Relationships.* Norwood, MA: Christopher Gordon, 2004.

Green et al. v. County School Board of New Kent County, Virginia, et al., 391 U.S. 430 (1968).

Greenberg, J. *Crusaders in the Courts: Legal Battles of the Civil Rights Movement.* New York: Twelve Tables Press, 2004.

Greene, J. "Choosing Integration." In *School Choice and Diversity: What the Evidence Says,* ed. J. Scott, 36–41. New York: Teachers College Press, 2005.

Griffin v. County School Board of Prince Edward County, 377 U.S. 218 (1964). Oral arguments available at www.oyez.org/cases/1960–1969/1963/1963_592/.

Grutter v. Bollinger, 539 U.S. 306 (2003).

Hamilton, L., and K. Guin. "Understanding How Families Choose Schools." In *Getting Choice Right: Ensuring Equity and Efficiency in Education Policy,* ed. J. Betts and T. Loveless, 40–60. Washington DC: Brookings Institution, 2005.

Hampel, P. "Districts Vote to Extend Desegregation Program." *St. Louis Post-Dispatch,* June 23, 2007, A12.

Harrington, J., and D. Cameron. "Pockets of Severe Poverty Intensify and Spread around the Tampa Bay Area." *Tampa Bay Times,* November 7, 2011.

Harris, D. "Lost Learning, Forgotten Promises: A National Analysis of School Racial Segregation, Student Achievement, and 'Controlled Choice' Plans." November 29, 2006. Center for American Progress. www.americanprogress.org/issues/2006/11/lostlearning.html, accessed July 25, 2009.

Harris, D. J., and N. McArdle. *More than Money: The Spatial Mismatch between Where Homeowners of Color in Metro Boston Can Afford to Live and Where They Actually Reside.* Cambridge, MA: Harvard Civil Rights Project, 2004.

HartfordInfo. "Digital Access in the Hartford Region." 2009. www.hartfordinfo.org/issues/wsd/Education/wsd_internet_access.asp, accessed May 14, 2012.

———. "National Assessment of Adult Literacy: State and County Estimates of Low Literacy." www.hartfordinfo.org/issues/wsd/Literacy/wsd_010109.asp, accessed May 14, 2012.

Harvey, J., and P. Hill. "Doing School Choice Right: Preliminary Findings." Center on Reinventing Public Education, April 2006.

Hastings, J., and J. Weinstein. "Information, School Choice, and Academic Achievement: Evidence from Two Experiments." *Quarterly Journal of Economics* 123:4 (2008): 1373–414.

Heaney, G. W., and S. Uchitelle. *Unending Struggle: The Long Road to an Equal Education in St. Louis.* St. Louis: Reedy, 2004.

Hendrie, C. "In Indianapolis, Nashville, a New Era Dawns." *Education Week* 17:42 (1998): 8–9.

Henig, J. "The Local Dynamics of Choice: Ethnic Preferences and Institutional Responses." In *Who Chooses? Who Loses?: Culture, Institutions, and the Unequal Effects of School Choice,* ed. B. Fuller, R. F. Elmore, and G. Orfield, 95–117. New York: Teachers College Press, 1996.

———. *Rethinking School Choice: The Limits of the Market Metaphor.* Princeton: Princeton University Press, 1994.

———. "What Do We Know about the Outcomes of KIPP Schools?" East Lansing, MI: Great Lakes Center for Education Research and Practice, November 2008.

Henig, J., and J. MacDonald. "Locational Decisions of Charter Schools: Probing the Market Metaphor." *Social Studies Quarterly* 83:4 (2002): 962–80.

Hernandez, A. "Berkeley Schools Redraw Plan for Integration." *Daily Californian,* February 5, 2004.

Herscher, E. "Berkeley Plans to Overhaul Public Schools." *San Francisco Chronicle,* October 18, 1993.

Hess, F. M. "Race to the Top? The Promise—and Challenges—of Expanding the Reach of Charter Schools." American Enterprise Institute, April 6, 2009. www.aei.org/article/education/k-12/race-to-the-top-the-promise--and-challenges--of-expanding-the-reach-of-charter-schools/.

Higgins, M., and F. Hess. "Learning to Succeed at Scale." *Journal of School Choice* 3:1 (2009): 8–24.

Hillsborough County Public Schools. "School District of Hillsborough County Plan Development for Acquiring and Maintaining Unity Status." Approved November 2000.

———. "Tools for Maintaining Integrated School Systems." Undated planning document.

Hobday, M., G. Finn, and M. Orfield. "A Missed Opportunity: Minnesota's Failed Experiment with Choice-Based Integration." *William Mitchell Law Review* 35:3 (2009): 936–76.

Hochschild, J. L., and N. Scovronick. *The American Dream and the Public Schools.* New York: Oxford University Press, 2003.

Holley-Walker, D. "The Accountability Cycle: The Recovery School District Act and New Orleans' Charter Schools." *Connecticut Law Review* 40:1 (November 2007): 125–63.

Holme, J. J. "Buying Homes, Buying Schools: School Choice and the Social Construction of School Quality." *Harvard Educational Review* 72:2 (2002): 177–205.

Holme, J. J., and A. S. Wells. "School Choice beyond District Borders: Lessons for the Reauthorization of NCLB from Interdistrict Desegregation and Open Enrollment Plans." In *Improving on No Child Left Behind,* ed. Richard Kahlenberg. New York: Century Foundation, 2008.

Holtz, D. "Berkeley Hopes to Woo Whites to City Schools." *San Francisco Chronicle,* December 16, 1989.

Hoxby, C. "Achievement in Charter Schools and Regular Public Schools in the United States: Understanding the Differences." December 2004. www.innovations.harvard. edu/cache/documents/4848.pdf.

Hughes, D. *Designing Effective Google Maps for Social Change: A Case Study of Smart-Choices.* September 2009. www.devlinhughes.com/SmartChoices.

Ihlanfeldt, K. R. "Exclusionary Land-Use Regulations within Suburban Communities: A Review of the Evidence and Policy Prescriptions." *Urban Studies* 41:2 (2004): 261–83.

Institute on Race and Poverty. "The Choice Is Ours: Expanding Educational Opportunity for All Twin Cities Children." May 2006. www.irpumn.org/uls/resources/projects/ CIYFinalReport_topost.pdf.

———. "A Comprehensive Strategy to Integrate Twin Cities Schools and Neighborhoods." October 2009. www.irpumn.org/uls/resources/projects/Regional_Integration_Draft_3_-_Long_Version.pdf.

———. "Failed Promises: Assessing Charter Schools in the Twin Cities." November 2008. www.irpumn.org/uls/resources/projects/2_Charter_Report_Final.pdf.

———. "The State of Public Schools in Post-Katrina New Orleans: The Challenge of Creating Equal Opportunity." May 2010. www.irpumn.org/uls/resources/projects/ the_state_of_schools_in_new_orleans.pdf.

Iyengar, S., and M. Lepper. "When Choice Is Demotivating: Can One Desire Too Much of a Good Thing?" *Journal of Personality and Social Psychology* 79:6 (2000): 995–1006.

Jefferson County Public Schools. "It's Unanimous! School Board Votes to Approve New Student Assignment Plan." May 29, 2008. www.jefferson.k12.ky.us/News/Archive/ spotlight/assignment.pdf.

Kahlenberg, R. *All Together Now: Creating Middle Class Schools through Public School Choice.* Washington DC: Brookings Institute, 2001.

Kahneman, D., and A. Tversky, eds. *Choices, Values, and Frames.* New York: Cambridge University Press, 2000.

Karp, S. "One in 10 Charter School Students Transfers Out." November 9, 2010. www.catalyst-chicago.org/news/2010/11/09/one-in-10-charter-school-students-transfers-out.

Keyes v. Denver School District No. 1, 413 U.S. 189 (1973).

Khadduri, J., L. Buron, and C. Climaco. "Are States Using the Low Income Housing Tax Credit to Enable Families with Children to Live in Low Poverty and Racially Integrated Neighborhoods?" Prepared by Abt Associates Inc. for the Poverty and Race Research Action Council and the National Fair Housing Alliance. July 28, 2006. www. prrac.org/pdf/LIHTC_report_2006.pdf.

Kifer, E. "Student Assignment Survey Elementary School Results: Jefferson County Public Schools." Washington DC: Georgetown College, Center for Advanced Study of Assessment, April 2008. www.courier-journal.com/assets/B2105798415.pdf.

Kimberley, M. "Hedge Fund–Funded Charter School Lobby Buys Elections, Destroys Education." *Black Agenda Report,* September 16, 2010. www.commondreams.org/ view/2010/09/16-2.

KIPP Believe College Prep Charter School Website, Section on How to Enroll, available at www.kippbelieve.org/06/5enrol.cfm (accessed 12/3/09).

Kleitz, B., G. Weiher, K. Tedin, and R. Matland. "Choice, Charter Schools, and Household Preferences." *Social Science Quarterly* 81:3 (2000): 846–54.

Koretz, D. M. *Measuring Up: What Educational Testing Really Tells Us.* Cambridge, MA: Harvard University Press, 2008.

Koski, K., and J. Oakes. "Equal Educational Opportunity, School Reform, and the Courts: A Study of the Desegregation Litigation in San Jose." In *From the Courtroom to the Classroom: The Shifting Landscape of School Desegregation,* ed. C. Smrekar and E. Goldring, 71–102. Cambridge, MA: Harvard Education Press, 2009.

Kozol, J. *The Shame of the Nation: The Restoration of Apartheid Schooling in America.* New York: Crown, 2005.

Kurlaender, M., and J. Yun. "Is Diversity a Compelling Educational Interest?: Evidence from Louisville." In *Diversity Challenged: Evidence on the Impact of Affirmative Action,* ed. G. Orfield and M. Kurlaender, 111–41. Cambridge, MA: Harvard University Press, 2001.

Lacireno-Paquet, N. "Do EMO Operated Charter Schools Serve Disadvantaged Students? The Influence of State Policies." *Education Policy Analysis Archives* 12:26 (June 15, 2004): 1–22. http://epaa.asu.edu/epaa/v12n26/, accessed December 12, 2009.

Lankford, H., S. Loeb, and J. Wyckoff. "Teacher Sorting and the Plight of Urban Schools: A Descriptive Analysis." *Educational Evaluation and Policy Analysis* 24 (2002): 37–62.

Lankford, H., and J. Wyckoff. "Why Are Schools Racially Segregated? Implications for School Choice Policies." In *School Choice and Diversity: What the Evidence Says,* ed. J. Scott, 9–26. New York: Teachers College Press, 2005.

Lareau, A. *Home Advantage: Social Class and Parental Intervention in Elementary Education.* New York: Falmer Press, 1989.

Lee, R. S., K. Borman, and W. Tyson. "Florida's A+ Plan: Education Reform Policies and Student Outcomes." In *Education Reform in Florida: Diversity and Equity in Public Policy,* ed. K. Borman and S. Dorn, 241–80. Albany: State University of New York Press, 2007.

Lewis, A. *Portrait of a Decade: The Second American Revolution.* New York: Bantam Books, 1965.

Lieberson, S. *A Piece of the Pie: Blacks and White Immigrants since 1880.* Berkeley: University of California Press, 1981.

Linn, R. L., and K. G. Welner, eds. *Race-Conscious Policies for Assigning Students to Schools: Social Science Research and the Supreme Court Cases.* Washington DC: National Academy of Education, 2007.

Liu, A., and A. Plyer. *The New Orleans Index Anniversary Edition: Four Years after Katrina.* Washington DC: Brookings Institution, January 2009. www.brookings.edu/reports/2007/08neworleansindex.aspx, accessed December 9, 2009.

Logan, J., D. Oakley, and J. Stowell. "School Segregation in Metropolitan Regions: The Impacts of Policy Choices on Public Education." *American Journal of Sociology* 113 (May 2008): 1116–44.

Louisiana Charter School Association. "2009 Louisiana Legislative Session: Bills to

Watch." http://lacharterschools.org/index.php?option=com_content&task=view&id =54&Itemid=92, accessed December 17, 2009.

Louisiana Department of Education. www.doe.state.la.us/.

Lubienski, C. "Marketing Schools: Consumer Goods and Competitive Incentives for Consumer Information." *Education and Urban Society* 40:1 (2007): 118–41.

———. "The Politics of Parental Choice: Theory and Evidence on Quality Information." In *School Choice Policies and Outcomes: Empirical and Philosophical Perspectives,* ed. W. Feinberg and C. Lubienski, 99–119. Albany: State University of New York Press, 2008.

———. "School Competition and the Emergence of Symbolism in a Market Environment." In *To Educate a Nation: Federal and National Strategies of School Reform,* ed. C. F. Kaestle and A. E. Lodewick, 257–80. Lawrence: University Press of Kansas, 2007.

Lubienski, C., C. Gulosino, and P. Weitzel. "School Choice and Competitive Incentives: Mapping the Distribution of Educational Opportunities across Local Education Markets." *American Journal of Education* 105 (August 2009): 601–47.

Macey, E., J. Decker, and S. Eckes. "The Knowledge Is Power Program (KIPP): An Analysis of One Model's Efforts to Promote Achievement in Underserved Communities." *Journal of School Choice* 3 (2009): 212–41.

Maconahay, J. B., and W. Hawley. "Reaction to Busing in Louisville: Summary of Adult Opinions in 1976 and 1977." Durham, NC: Duke University Center for Policy Analysis, 1979.

Madison, J., J. Jay, and A. Hamilton. *Federalist Papers.* http://constitution.org/fed/federa 00.htm.

Manning v. School Board of Hillsborough County, 24 F. Supp. 1277 (U.S. Dist. for the M.D. Fla., 1998).

Manning v. School Board of Hillsborough County, 244 F. 3d 927 (11th Cir. Fla., 2001).

Manno, B., G. Vanourek, and C. Finn. "Charter Schools: Serving Disadvantaged Youth." *Education and Urban Society* 31: 4 (August 1999): 429–45.

Massey, D. S., and N. A. Denton. *American Apartheid: Segregation and the Making of the Underclass.* Cambridge, MA: Harvard University Press, 1993.

Mathews, J. "Inside the Bay Area KIPP Schools." *Washington Post,* September 19, 2008.

McDonald, S., and S. Wade. "Whites Divided over Plan to End Forced Busing," *Louisville Courier-Journal,* October 27, 1991.

McEwan, P. J., M. Urquiola, and E. Vegas. "School Choice, Stratification, and Information on School Performance: Lessons from Chile." *Economía* 8 (Spring 2008): 1–27.

McMurry, M. "Minnesota Education Trends, 2000 to 2005." *Minnesota State Demographic Center Population Notes,* September 2006. www.demography.state.mn.us/documents/ MinnesotaEducationTrends20002005.pdf, accessed April 26, 2007.

Metz, M. *Different by Design: The Context and Character of Three Magnet Schools.* New York: Routledge, 1986.

Mickelson, R. A. "The Incomplete Desegregation of the Charlotte-Mecklenburg Schools and Its Consequences." In *School Resegregation: Must the South Turn Back?,* ed. J. Boger and G. Orfield, 87–110. Chapel Hill: University of North Carolina Press, 2005.

———. "Twenty-First Century Social Science Research on School Diversity and Educational Outcomes." *Ohio State Law Journal* 69 (2008): 1173–228.

Mickelson, R., M. Bottia, and S. Southworth. *School Choice and Segregation by Race, Class, and Achievement.* Boulder, CO: National Education Policy Center, 2008. http:// epsl.asu.edu/epru/documents/EPSL-0803-260-EPRU.pdf, retrieved August 18, 2008.

Milem, J. F. "The Educational Benefits of Diversity: Evidence from Multiple Sectors." In *Compelling Interest: Examining the Evidence on Racial Dynamics in Colleges and Universities,* ed. M. Chang, D. Witt, J. Jones, and K. Hakuta, 126–69. Palo Alto: Stanford University Press, 2003.

Milliken v. Bradley, 418 U.S. 717 (1974).

Minow, M. *In Brown's Wake: Legacies of America's Educational Landmark.* New York: Oxford University Press, 2010.

Minutes of the School Support Committee, April 26, 2004. City of Temple Terrace, Florida.

Miron, G., and C. Nelson. *What's Public about Charter Schools? Lessons Learned about Choice and Accountability.* Thousand Oaks, CA: Corwin, 2002.

Miron, G., J. Urschel, W. Mathis, and E. Tornquist. "Schools without Diversity: Education Management Organizations, Charter Schools, and the Demographic Stratification of the American School System." Boulder and Tempe: Education and the Public Interest Center and Education Policy Research Unit, 2010. http://nepc.colorado.edu/files/EMO-Seg.pdf.

Molnar, A., G. Miron, and J. Urschel. *Profiles of For-Profit Educational Management Organizations: 2008–09.* Boulder and Tempe: Education and the Public Interest Center and Education Policy Research Unit, Arizona State University, 2009. http://epicpolicy.org/publication/profiles-profit-emos-2008–09.

Monroe #1 Boards of Cooperative Educational Services. "The History of Project U-S, June 1963–June 2005." 2005.

———. Newsletters from February 2006, February 2007, June 2008, and September 2008.

———. "Policy, Urban-Suburban Interdistrict Transfer Program Parent Commitment." June 2005.

———. "Urban-Suburban Interdistrict Transfer Program Student Enrollment, 2002–2009." 2009.

———. "Urban-Suburban Parent-Student Handbook." 2007.

———. "Urban-Suburban, Planning for Participation." 2007.

Morgan v. Hennigan, 379 F. Supp. 410 (D.C. Mass., June 21, 1974).

Morland, K., S. Wing, A. Diez-Roux, and C. Poole. "Neighborhood Characteristics Associated with the Location of Food Stores and Food Service Places." *American Journal of Preventive Medicine* 22:1 (January 2002): 23–29.

Moua, W. "Are Hmong Students Making the Grades?" *Twin Cities Daily Planet,* March 25, 2008.

Mozdzer, J. "Hartford's School 'Choice' Program Outlined; Some Parents Disappointed." *Hartford Courant,* September 26, 2008.

Nathan, J. *Charter Schools: Creating Hope and Opportunity for American Education.* San Francisco: Jossey-Bass, 1996.

Nathan, J., and J. Ysseldyke. "What Minnesota Has Learned about School Choice." *Phi Delta Kappan* 75:9 (May 1, 1994): 682–88. www.jstor.org/stable/20405203.

National Alliance for Public Charter Schools. *Top Ten Charter Communities by Market Share—Fourth Annual Edition.* Washington DC: National Alliance for Public Charter Schools, 2009.

National Assessment of Educational Progress. "NAEP State Comparisons" database. http://nces.ed.gov/nationsreportcard/statecomparisons/.

National Center for Education Statistics. Common Core of Data. http://nces.ed.gov/ccd/.

———. *NAEP 2008: Trends in Academic Progress, Reading 1971–2008, Mathematics 1973–2008.* Washington DC: Institute of Education Sciences, U.S. Dept. of Education, April 2009.

———. Schools and Staffing Survey. http://nces.ed.gov/surveys/sass/.

New Orleans Parents Organizing Network. *The New Orleans Parents' Guide to Public Schools,* 3rd ed. New Orleans: New Orleans Parents Organizing Network, 2009.

Newsweek. "America's Best High Schools 2010." June 13, 2010. www.newsweek.com/feature/americas-best-high-schools.html.

Ni, Y. *Are Charter Schools More Racially Segregated than Traditional Public Schools?* Policy Report 30, Education Policy Center. East Lansing: Michigan State University, 2007.

1991 Omnibus K–12 Education Finance Bill. House File 700 / Senate File 467, *Laws of Minnesota 1991,* chapter 265, article 9, section 3.

Olszewski, L. "Integration Phase-Out in Berkeley Schools: Neighborhoods Prepare for End of System." *San Francisco Chronicle,* December 19, 1994.

———. "School Choice Delivers in Berkeley: Most Children Get Into the Campuses Parents Had Picked." *San Francisco Chronicle,* March 18, 1995.

Oluwole, J., and P. Green. "Charter Schools: Racial Balancing Provisions and *Parents Involved.*" *University of Arkansas Law Review* 61 (2008): 1–52.

Orfield, G. "Conservative Activists and the Rush toward Resegregation." In *Law and Social Reform,* ed. Jay P. Heubert, 39–87. New Haven: Yale University Press, 1999.

———. *Must We Bus?: Segregated Schools and National Policy.* Washington DC: Brookings Institute, 1978.

———. "Public Opinion and School Desegregation." *Teachers College Record* 96:4 (1995): 654–70.

———. *Public School Desegregation in the United States, 1968–1980.* Washington DC: Joint Center for Political Studies, 1983.

———. *The Reconstruction of Southern Education: The Schools and the 1964 Civil Rights Act.* Hoboken, NJ: John Wiley and Sons, 1969.

———. "Reviving the Goal of an Integrated Society: A 21st Century Challenge." Los Angeles: Civil Rights Project / Proyecto Derechos Civiles at UCLA, 2009.

———. "Schools More Separate: Consequences of a Decade of Resegregation." Cambridge, MA: Civil Rights Project, 2001.

———. "Segregated Housing and School Resegregation." In *Dismantling Desegregation: The Quiet Repeal of* Brown v. Board of Education, ed. G. Orfield and S. Eaton, 291–330. New York: New Press, 1996.

———, ed. *Symposium on School Desegregation and White Flight.* Washington DC: Notre Dame Center for Civil Rights and Center for National Policy Review, 1975.

Orfield, G., and S. E. Eaton. *Dismantling Desegregation: The Quiet Reversal of* Brown vs. Board of Education. New York: New Press, 1997.

Orfield, G., and E. Frankenberg. "Experiencing Integration in Louisville: How Parents and Students See the Gains and Challenges." Los Angeles: Civil Rights Project / Proyecto Derechos Civiles at UCLA, 2011. http://civilrightsproject.ucla.edu/research/k-12-education/integration-and-diversity/experiencing-integration-in-louisville-how-parents-and-students-see-the-gains-and-challenges/louisville_finalV3_12711.pdf.

———. "The Last Have Become First: Rural and Small Town America Lead the Way on Desegregation." Los Angeles: Civil Rights Project / Proyecto Derechos Civiles at UCLA, 2008.

Orfield, G., and M. Kurlaender, eds. *Diversity Challenged: Evidence on the Impact of Affirmative Action.* Cambridge, MA: Harvard Education Publishing Group, 2001.

Orfield, G., and C. Lee. Brown *at 50: King's Dream or* Plessy's *Nightmare.* Cambridge, MA: Civil Rights Project at Harvard University, 2004.

———. *Historic Reversals, Accelerating Resegregation and the Need for New Integration Strategies.* Los Angeles: Civil Rights Project / Proyecto Derechos Civiles at UCLA, 2007.

———. *Racial Transformation and the Changing Nature of Segregation.* Cambridge, MA: Civil Rights Project at Harvard University, 2006.

———. *Why Segregation Matters: Poverty and Educational Inequality.* Cambridge, MA: Civil Rights Project at Harvard University, 2005.

Orfield, G., and S. F. Reardon. "Race, Poverty, and Inequality." In *New Opportunities: Civil Rights at a Crossroads,* ed. S. M. Liss and W. L. Taylor. Washington DC: Citizens' Commission on Civil Rights, 1994.

Orfield, G., G. Siegel-Hawley, and J. Kucsera. *Divided We Fail: Segregated and Unequal Schools in the Southland.* Los Angeles: Civil Rights Project / Proyecto Derechos Civiles at UCLA, 2011.

Orfield, M. *Minority Suburbanization, Stable Integration, and Economic Opportunity in Fifteen Metropolitan Regions: A Report by the Institute on Race and Poverty to the Detroit Branch NAACP.* Minneapolis: Institute on Race and Poverty, 2006.

Orfield, M., and T. F. Luce Jr., eds. *Region: Planning the Future of the Twin Cities.* Minneapolis: University of Minnesota Press, 2010.

Orfield, M., B. Gumus-Dawes, T. F. Luce Jr., and G. Finn. "Neighborhood and School Segregation." In *Region: Planning the Future of the Twin Cities,* ed. M. Orfield and T. F. Luce Jr. Minneapolis: University of Minnesota Press, 2010.

Palmer, E. A. *"The Choice Is Yours" after Two Years: An Evaluation.* Prepared by Aspen Associates Inc. for the Minnesota Department of Education. December 2003. http://education.state.mn.us/MDE/StuSuc/EnrollChoice/ChoiceYours/index.html.

Parents Involved in Community Schools v. Seattle School District No. 1, 551 U.S. 701 (2007).

Parker, W. "The Color of Choice: Race and Charter Schools." *Tulane Law Review* 75:3 (2001): 563–630.

———. "The Future of School Desegregation." *Northwestern University Law Review* 94:4 (Summer 2000): 1157—227.

Payne, C., and T. Knowles. "Promise and Peril: Charter Schools, Urban School Reform, and the Obama Administration." *Harvard Educational Review* 79:2 (Summer 2009): 227–39.

Peterson, P. E. "School Choice: A Report Card." *Virginia Journal of Social Policy and the Law* 6:1 (Fall 1998): 47–80.

Pettigrew, T. F., and L. R. Tropp. *When Groups Meet: The Dynamics of Intergroup Contact.* Philadelphia: Psychology Press, 2011.

Pfeiffer, D. *The Opportunity Illusion: Subsidized Housing and Failing Schools in California.* Los Angeles: Civil Rights Project / Proyecto Derechos Civiles at UCLA, 2009.

Pierce v. Society of Sisters of the Holy Names of Jesus and Mary, 268 U.S. 510 (1925).

Powell, J., J. Blackborby, J. Marsh, K. Finnegan, and L. Anderson. *Evaluation of Charter School Effectiveness.* Menlo Park, CA: SRI International, 1997.

powell, j.a. "Towards an 'Integrated' Theory of Integration." In *School Resegregation: Must the South Turn Back?,* ed. J. Boger and G. Orfield. Chapel Hill: University of North Carolina Press, 2005.

Prevention Institute for the Center for Health Improvement. "Nutrition Policy Profiles: Supermarket Access in Low-Income Communities." May 2002. www.preventioninstitute.org/CHI_supermarkets.html.

Price, H. D. "Race, Religion, and the Rules Committee: The Kennedy Aid-to-Education Bills." In *The Uses of Power: Seven Cases in American Politics,* ed. A. F. Westin, 1–72. New York: Harcourt Brace, 1962.

Proctor, M. "Brandon Deserves to Vote on Its Future." *St. Petersburg Times,* February 6, 1988.

Quigley, B. "New Orleans' Children Fighting for the Right to Learn, Part 1." *Truthout Report,* August 12, 2007. www.truthout.org/article/bill-quigley-part-i-new-orleans-children-fighting-right-learn, accessed December 2, 2009.

Raffel, J. *Historical Dictionary of School Segregation and Desegregation: The American Experience.* Westport, CT: Greenwood Publishing Group, 1998.

Reardon, S., and J. Yun. "Integrating Neighborhoods, Segregating Schools: The Retreat from School Desegregation in the South, 1990–2000." In *School Resegregation: Must the South Turn Back?,* ed. J. Boger and G. Orfield, 51–69. Chapel Hill: University of North Carolina Press, 2005.

Reed v. Rhodes, 422 F. Supp 708, 796–97 (N.D. Ohio, 1976), aff'd, 662 F. 2d 1219 (6th Cir., 1981).

Renzulli, L., and L. Evans. "School Choice, Charter Schools, and White Flight." *Social Problems* 52:3 (2005): 398–418.

"Report and Recommendation," *Manning v. School Board.* U.S. Dist. for M.D. of Fla. August 26, 1997.

Riley, N. S. "'We're in the Venture Philanthrophy Business.'" The Weekend Interview. *Wall Street Journal,* August 28, 2009.

Ripley, R., and G. A. Franklin. *Congress, the Bureaucracy, and Public Policy,* 5th ed. Pacific Grove, CA: Brooks/Cole, 1991.

———. "Interest Groups and the Policy Making Process: Sources of Countervailing Power in America." In *The Politics of Interests,* ed. M. P. Petracca. Boulder, CO: Westview Press, 1992.

Ritholtz, B., and A. Task. *Bailout Nation: How Greed and Easy Money Corrupted Wall Street and Shook the World Economy*. New York: John Wiley and Sons, 2009.

Ritter, J. "Across USA, Steps Forward and Steps Back—Indianapolis: A System That Seems to Be Working." *USA Today*, May 12, 1994, 9A.

Robelen, E. "KIPP Student-Attrition Patterns Eyed." *Education Week* 26:41 (2007): 1–16.

Roberts, S. "Segregation Curtailed in U.S. Cities, Study Finds." *New York Times*, January 30, 2012.

Rouse, C. E., and L. Barrow. "School Vouchers and Student Achievement: Recent Evidence, Remaining Questions." *Annual Review of Economics* 1 (2009): 17–42.

Rumberger, R. W., and G. Palardy. "Does Resegregation Matter?: The Impact of Social Composition on Academic Achievement in Southern High Schools." In *School Resegregation: Must the South Turn Back?*, ed. J. Boger and G. Orfield, 127–47. Chapel Hill: University of North Carolina Press, 2005.

———. "Does Segregation Still Matter? The Impact of Social Composition on Academic Achievement in High School." *Teachers College Record* 107:9 (September 2005): 1999–2045.

Rury, J. L., and A. Saatcioglu. "Suburban Advantage: Opportunity Hoarding and Secondary Attainment in the Postwar Metropolitan North." *American Journal of Education* 117:3 (May 2011): 307–42.

Ryan, J. *Five Miles Away, a World Apart: One City, Two Schools, and the Story of Educational Opportunity in Modern America*. New York: Oxford University Press, 2010.

Salganik, L. H. "Apples and Apples: Comparing Performance Indicators for Places with Similar Demographic Characteristics." *Educational Evaluation and Policy Analysis* 16 (1994): 125–41.

Saltman, K. "The Rise of Venture Philanthropy and the Ongoing Neoliberal Assault on Public Education: The Case of the Eli and Edythe Broad Foundation." *Workplace* 16 (2009): 53–72.

Saporito, S., and D. Sohoni. "Coloring outside the Lines: Racial Segregation in Public Schools and Their Attendance Boundaries." *Sociology of Education* 79:2 (2006): 81–105.

Schelling, T. *Micromotives and Macrobehavior*. New York: W. W. Norton, 1978.

Schofield, J. W. "Review of Research on School Desegregation's Impact on Elementary and Secondary School Students." In *Handbook of Research on Multicultural Education*, ed. J. A. Banks and C. A. McGee Banks, 635–46. New York: Macmillan, 1995.

School District of Hillsborough County. "Plan for Maintaining a Unitary School System." Tampa, FL: Hillsborough County Public Schools, November 14, 2000.

Schuman, S., C. Steeh, L. Bobo, and M. Krysan. *Racial Attitudes in America: Trends and Interpretations*. Cambridge, MA: Harvard University Press, 1997.

Schwartz, B. *The Paradox of Choice: Why More Is Less*. New York: Ecco, 2004.

Schwartz, R. B., M. A. Robinson, M. W. Kirst, and D. L. Kirp. "Goals 2000 and the Standards Movement." Brookings Papers on Education Policy 3 (2000): 173–14.

Schwarzler, J. "Official Google Blog: Statistics for a Changing World: Google Public Data Explorer in Labs." March 8, 2010. http://googleblog.blogspot.com/2010/03/statistics-for-changing-world-google.html.

Schweitzer, S. "Critics Scorn New Desegregation Plan." *St. Petersburg Times,* March 17, 2000.

——. "Distrust Surrounds School Vote." *St. Petersburg Times,* November 21, 2000.

Scott, J. "The Politics of Venture Philanthropy in Charter School Policy and Advocacy." *Education Policy* 23:1 (2009): 106–36.

——. "School Choice as a Civil Right: The Political Construction of a Claim and Implications for School Desegregation." In *Integrating Schools in a Changing Society: New Policies and Legal Options for a Multiracial Generation,* ed. E. Frankenberg and E. DeBray, 32–52. Chapel Hill: University of North Carolina Press, 2011.

Scott, J., and C. DiMartino. "Public Education under New Management: A Typology of Educational Privatization Applied to New York City's Restructuring." *Peabody Journal of Education* 84 (2009): 432–52.

Scott S. Cowen Institute for Public Education Initiatives at Tulane University. *Public School Performance in New Orleans: A Supplement to the 2008 State of Public Education in New Orleans Report.* New Orleans: Cowen Institute, 2009.

Shapiro, T. *The Hidden Cost of Being African American: How Wealth Perpetuates Inequality.* New York: Oxford University Press, 2004.

Sheff v. O'Neill, 678 A.2d 1267 (Conn., 1996).

Shelly v. Kraemer, 334 U.S. 1 (1948).

Siegel-Hawley, G. "City Lines, County Lines, Color Lines: An Analysis of School and Housing Segregation in Four Southern Metropolitan Areas, 1990–2010." PhD dissertation, University of California, Los Angeles, 2011.

Siegel-Hawley, G., and E. Frankenberg. "Reviving Magnet Schools: Strengthening a Successful Choice Option." Los Angeles: Civil Rights Project/Proyecto Derechos Civiles at UCLA, 2012.

——. "Does Law Influence Charter School Diversity? An Analysis of Federal and State Legislation." *Michigan Journal of Race and Law* 16:2 (2011): 321–76.

Sinclair, W. "Desegregation's Quiet Success." *Washington Post,* June 17, 1978.

Slater, D. "The Integration Calypso." *East Bay Express,* April 30, 1993.

Slavin, R. E. *Student Team Learning: A Practical Guide to Cooperative Learning,* 3rd ed. Washington DC: National Education Association, 1991.

SmartChoices. "About This Website." http://SmartChoices.trincoll.edu/about.html, accessed May 14, 2012.

Smith, A. *An Inquiry into the Nature and Causes of the Wealth of Nations.* Originally published 1776; repr. Chicago: Encyclopedia Britannica Great Books of the Western World, 1952.

Smrekar, C., and E. Goldring. *School Choice in Urban America: Magnet Schools and the Pursuit of Equity.* New York: Teachers College Press, 1999.

Snorten, C. *An Analysis of the Effects of the Indianapolis Public Schools Desegregation Court Order, 1981–1982 through 1991–1992.* Bloomington: Indiana University, 2005.

Solochek, J. S. "Critics Say Florida Lawmakers Are Too Cozy with Charter Schools." *St. Petersburg Times,* December 18, 2011.

Southern Education Foundation. *A New Diverse Majority: Students of Color in the South's Public Schools.* Atlanta: Southern Education Foundation, 2010.

———. *New Orleans Schools Four Years after Katrina: A Lingering Federal Responsibility.* Atlanta: Southern Education Foundation, 2009.

State of Minnesota Office of the Legislative Auditor. "Evaluation Report: Charter Schools." June 2008.

Steele, L., and M. Eaton. "Reducing, Eliminating, and Preventing Minority Isolation in American Schools: The Impact of the Magnet Schools Assistance Program." Report prepared for the Office of the Under Secretary, U.S. Department of Education, by the American Institutes for Research. Washington DC: U.S. Department of Education, Office of the Under Secretary, 1996.

Steele, L., and R. Levine. "Educational Innovations in Multiracial Contexts: The Growth of Magnet Schools in American Education." Washington DC: U.S. Department of Education, Office of the Under Secretary, 1994.

Sullivan, N. V., and E. S. Stewart. *Now Is the Time: Integration in the Berkeley Schools.* Bloomington: Indiana University Press, 1970.

Sunderman, G. L., J. S. Kim, and G. Orfield. *NCLB Meets School Realities: Lessons from the Field.* Thousand Oaks, CA: Corwin, 2005.

Swann v. Charlotte-Mecklenburg, 402 U.S. 1 (1971).

Swanson, C. "Sketching a Portrait of Public High School Graduation: Who Graduates? Who Doesn't?" In *Dropouts in America: Confronting the Graduation Rate Crisis,* ed. G. Orfield. Cambridge, MA: Harvard Education Press, 2004.

Tefera, A., G. Siegel-Hawley, and E. Frankenberg. "School Integration Efforts Three Years after *Parents Involved.*" Los Angeles: Civil Rights Project / Proyecto Derechos Civiles at UCLA, 2010.

Thernstrom, A., and S. Thernstrom. *No Excuses: Closing the Racial Gap in Learning.* New York: Simon and Schuster, 2003.

Thevenot, B. "New Orleans Charter School Operator Plans Expansion." July 24, 2009. www.nola.com/education/index.ssf/2009/07/kipp_schools_a_leading_charter.html, accessed December 8, 2009.

Torregano, M., and P. Shannon. "Educational Greenfield: A Critical Policy Analysis of Plans to Transform New Orleans Public Schools." *Journal for Critical Education Policy Studies* 7:1 (June 2009): 320–40.

Trent, W. "The Continuing Effects of the Dual System of Education in St. Louis." *Journal of Negro Education* 66:3 (1997): 336–40.

Tuttle v. Arlington County School Board, 195 F.3d 698 (4th Cir. 1999).

Tuzzolo, E., and D. Hewitt. "Rebuilding Inequity: The Re-emergence of the School-to-Prison Pipeline in New Orleans." *High School Journal* 90:2 (December 2006–January 2007): 59–68.

United Teachers of New Orleans (UTNO), Louisiana Federation of Teachers (LFT), and the American Federation of Teachers (AFT). "'National Model' or Flawed Approach? The Post-Katrina New Orleans Public Schools." New Orleans: UTNO, LFT, and AFT, 2006.

U.S. Census Bureau. "Current Population Survey," "Survey on Internet and Computer Use," question HENET3. October 2007. Downloaded from HartfordInfo, "Digital

Access in the Hartford Region." www.hartfordinfo.org/issues/wsd/Education/wsd_internet_access.asp, last updated August 2, 2011.

————. "DP-3: Profile of Selected Economic Characteristics, Census 2000 Summary File 3." American FactFinder. http://factfinder2.census.gov.

————. *Statistical Abstract of the United States: 2012.* www.census.gov/compendia/statab/.

U.S. Commission on Civil Rights. *Southern School Desegregation 1966–67.* Washington DC: U.S. Commission on Civil Rights, 1967.

U.S. Department of Education. *Evaluation of the Public Charter Schools Program: Final Report.* Prepared by SRI International for Department of Education. 2004. www.ed.gov/rschstat/eval/choice/pcsp-final/finalreport.pdf, accessed April 30, 2007.

————. "Fiscal Year 2011 Budget Summary: Section III. A. Elementary and Secondary Education: Magnet Schools Assistance." February 1, 2010. www2.ed.gov/about/overview/budget/budget11/summary/edlite-section3a.html#magnet, accessed March 9, 2010.

————. "Magnet Schools Assistance Program." *Federal Register* 75:42 (March 4, 2010): 9777–80. http://www2.ed.gov/legislation/FedRegister/other/2010–1/030410a.html.

————. "President Obama, Secretary Duncan Announce Race to the Top." *Homeroom,* July 24, 2009.

U.S. Department of Education, Office for Civil Rights. Civil Rights Data Collection. http://ocrdata.ed.gov/.

U.S. Department of Justice Civil Rights Division and U.S. Department of Education Office for Civil Rights. "Guidance on the Voluntary Use of Race to Achieve Diversity and Avoid Racial Isolation in Elementary and Secondary Schools." December 2, 2011. http://www2.ed.gov/about/offices/list/ocr/docs/guidance-ese-201111.html.

US News and World Report. "America's Best High Schools." December 9, 2009. www.usnews.com/articles/education/high-schools/2009/12/09/americas-best-high-schools-gold-medal-list.html.

Vaznis, J. "Charter Schools See More Attrition: Fewer Students Are Graduating, Union Study Finds." *Boston Globe,* September 16, 2009. www.boston.com/news/local/massachusetts/articles/2009/09/16/charter_schools_see_more_attrition_union_study_finds/, retrieved October 1, 2009.

Viadero, D. "Study Casts Doubt on Strength of Charter Managers: Author Says Final Text Eased Negative Findings on CMOs." *Education Week* 29:14 (December 9, 2009): 1, 13.

Vigue, D. I. "Metco Students May Be Ousted from Lynnfield." *Boston Globe,* March 2, 1999, section A, 1.

Walford, G. "Diversity, Choice, and Selection in England and Wales." *Educational Administration Quarterly* 33:2 (1997): 158–69.

Walton Family Foundation, "Education Reform: Overview." www.waltonfamilyfoundation.org/educationreform, accessed June 5, 2012.

Wanzer, J., H. Moore, and J. Dougherty. "Race and Magnet School Choice: A Mixed-Methods Neighborhood Study in Urban Connecticut." Unpublished paper delivered at the American Educational Research Association meeting, March 28, 2008. www.trincoll.edu/depts/educ/css/research/Wanzer_etal_AERA08.pdf.

Warner, J. "Why Are the Rich So Interested in Public-School Reform?" *Time,* December

9, 2011. http://ideas.time.com/2011/12/09/why-are-the-rich-so-interested-in-public-school-reform/.

Washington Post. "Obama Delivers Remarks on Education at National Urban League: Speech Transcript." July 29, 2010. http://projects.washingtonpost.com/obama-speeches /speech/346/.

Weaver, T. "Controlled Choice: An Alternative School Choice Plan." *ERIC Digest* 70 (June 1992), ERIC identifier: ED344342. www.ericdigests.org/1992–4/choice.htm.

Weiher, G. *The Fractured Metropolis: Political Fragmentation and Metropolitan Segregation.* Albany: State University of New York Press, 1991.

Weinberg, M. *A Chance to Learn: A History of Race and Education in the United States.* New York: Cambridge University Press, 1977.

Weiss, B. J., ed. *American Education and the European Immigrant: 1840–1940.* Champaign: University of Illinois Press, 1982.

Wells, A. S. "African-American Students' View of School Choice." In *Who Chooses? Who Loses?: Culture, Institutions, and the Unequal Effects of School Choice,* ed. B. Fuller, R. F. Elmore, and G. Orfield. New York: Teachers College Press, 1996.

———. "Beyond the Rhetoric of Charter School Reform: A Study of Ten California School Districts." Los Angeles: UCLA Charter School Study, 1998.

———. "The 'Consequences' of School Desegregation: The Mismatch between the Research and the Rationale." *Hastings Constitutional Law Quarterly* 28:4 (2001): 771–97.

———. *Time to Choose: America at the Crossroads of School Choice Policy.* New York: Hill and Wang, 1993.

Wells, A. S., B. J. Baldridge, J. Duran, C. Grzesikowski, R. Lofton, A. Roda, M. Warner, and T. White. *Boundary Crossing for Diversity, Equity and Achievement: Interdistrict School Desegregation and Educational Opportunity.* Cambridge, MA: Charles Hamilton Houston Institute for Race and Justice, Harvard Law School, 2009.

Wells, A. S., B. Baldridge, J. Duran, R. Lofton, A. Roda, M. Warner, T. White, and C. Grzeskowski. "Why Boundaries Matter: A Study of Five Separate and Unequal Long Island School Districts." Final report to the Long Island Index. July 2009. www.longis-landindex.org/fileadmin/Reports_and_Maps/Other_Research/2009_Why_Boundaries_Matter_UNABRIDGED.pdf.

Wells, A. S., and R. L. Crain. "Perpetuation Theory and the Long-Term Effects of School Desegregation." *Review of Educational Research* 64:4 (1994): 531–55.

———. *Stepping Over the Color Line: African-American Students in White Suburban Schools.* New Haven: Yale University Press, 1997.

———. "Where School Desegregation and Choice Policies Collide: Voluntary Transfer Plans and Controlled Choice." In *School Choice and Diversity: What the Evidence Says,* ed. J. Scott, 59–76. New York: Teachers College Press, 2005.

Wells, A. S., and E. Frankenberg. "The Public Schools and the Challenge of the Supreme Court's Integration Decision." *Phi Delta Kappan* 89:3 (2007): 178–88.

Wells, A. S., J. J. Holme, A. T. Revilla, and A. K. Atanda. *Both Sides Now: The Story of School Desegregation's Graduates.* Berkeley: University of California Press, 2009.

Wells, A. S., and A. Roda. "'Colorblindness' and Free-Market School Choice Policies: Political Rhetoric, Educational Research, and Racial Segregation." Forthcoming.

Welner, K., and K. Howe. "Steering Toward Separation: The Evidence and Implications of Special Education Students' Exclusion from Choice Schools." In *School Choice and Diversity: What the Evidence Says,* ed. J. Scott, 93–111. New York: Teachers College Press, 2005.

Welter, R. *Popular Education and Democratic Thought in America.* New York: Columbia University Press, 1962.

Wilkerson, T. "Student Assignment Survey: Summary of Findings." Report to Jefferson County Public Schools. Louisville, KY: Wilkerson and Associates, 1996.

Willie, C., and M. Alves. *Controlled Choice: A New Approach to School Desegregated Experience and School Improvement.* New England Desegregation Assistance Center. Providence, RI: Brown University, 1996.

Willie, C. V., R. Edwards, and M. J. Alves. *Student Diversity, Choice and School Improvement.* Westport, CT: Bergin and Garvey, 2002.

Willingham, W. W., J. M. Pollack, and C. Lewis. "Grades and Test Scores: Accounting for Observed Differences." *Journal of Educational Measurement* 39:1 (Spring 2002): 1–37.

Wirt, J., S. Choy, S. Provanski, and G. Hampden-Thompson. *The Condition of Education 2005.* NCES 2005–094. Washington DC: U.S. Department of Education, National Center for Education Statistics, 2005.

Wisconsin Advisory Committee to the United States Commission on Civil Rights. *Impact of School Desegregation in Milwaukee Public Schools on Quality Education for Minorities—15 Years Later.* Washington DC: U.S. Civil Rights Commission on Civil Rights, 1992.

Wright et al. v. Council of the City of Emporia et al., 407 U.S. 451 (1972).

Yen, H. "Census Shows Whites Lose US Majority among Babies." June 23, 2011. http://abcnews.go.com/Politics/wireStory?id=13909607#.T2dFsGJWp6o.

Yu, C., and W. L. Taylor. eds. *Difficult Choices: Do Magnet Schools Serve Children in Need?* Washington DC: Citizens' Commission on Civil Rights, 1997.

Zelman v. Simmons-Harris, 536 U.S. 639 (2002).

Zickuhr, K., and A. Smith. "Digital Differences." Pew Internet and American Life Project. April 13, 2012. http://pewinternet.org/Reports/2012/Digital-differences/Overview/Digital-differences.aspx.

Zimmer, R., B. Gill, K. Booker, S. Lavertu, T. R. Sass, and J. Witte. "Charter Schools in Eight States: Effects on Achievement, Attainment, Integration, and Competition." Santa Monica, CA: Rand Corporation, 2009.

CONTRIBUTORS

GARY ORFIELD is a professor of education, law, political science, and urban planning at the University of California, Los Angeles. His research interests are civil rights, education policy, urban policy, and minority opportunity. He was a cofounder and director of the Harvard Civil Rights Project and now serves as codirector of the Civil Rights Project / *Proyecto Derechos Civiles* at UCLA. His central interest has been the development and implementation of social policy, with a focus on its impact on equal opportunity for success in American society.

ERICA FRANKENBERG is an assistant professor in the Department of Education Policy Studies in the College of Education at the Pennsylvania State University. Her research interests focus on racial desegregation and inequality in K–12 schools, and the connections between school segregation and other metropolitan policies. Prior to joining the Penn State faculty, she was the research and policy director for the Initiative on School Integration at the Civil Rights Project / Proyecto Derechos Civiles at UCLA. She received her doctorate in educational policy at the Harvard University Graduate School of Education.

OTHER AUTHORS

MAHAM CHOWHAN received her bachelor's degree in economics from Trinity College in 2010 and conducted the quantitative analysis of SmartChoices user statistics.

COURTENEY COYNE received her bachelor's degrees in educational studies, Hispanic studies, and international studies from Trinity College in 2010 and transcribed and coded parent interviews for the SmartChoices project.

BENJAMIN DAWSON received his bachelor's of science degree in economics from Trinity College in 2011 and conducted the quantitative analysis of SmartChoices user statistics.

JACK DOUGHERTY, an associate professor of educational studies, works with undergraduate researchers through the Cities, Suburbs, and Schools Project at Trinity College. His current book project, *On the Line: How Schooling, Housing, and Civil Rights Shaped Hartford and Its Suburbs,* is available at http://OnTheLine.trincoll.edu.

COURTNEY GRZESIKOWSKI received her EdM in sociology and education with a concentration in education policy from Teachers College, Columbia University, in 2011. Her research interests include educational equity, teacher quality, policy reform, mixed methods, school desegregation, and intercollegiate athletics. She currently works for a nonprofit organization in New York City.

BARIS GUMUS-DAWES previously worked for the Institute of Race and Poverty after having worked with a number of Twin Cities organizations. She has served as a policy analyst for the Minnesota Housing Partnership and as a research associate for Ameregis Inc. Gumus-Dawes holds a PhD in sociology from Yale University and a master's degree in economics from the University of Cambridge.

TEHANI GURUGE received her bachelor's degree in economics from Trinity College in 2011 and conducted the quantitative analysis of SmartChoices user statistics.

THOMAS LUCE, the research director of the Institute on Race and Poverty, has a thirty-year record of research on economic development and fiscal issues in American metropolitan areas. Most recently he coauthored *Region: Planning the Future of the Twin Cities.* Luce received his BA from Swarthmore College and has an MS from the University of London and a PhD in public policy from the University of Pennsylvania.

JENNIFER MORLEY is a sociologist of education who focuses on issues including school choice, multicultural education and cultural competence, and urban educational constructs. She is also a practitioner, overseeing new grant-funded programs in the Magnet Schools and Programs Office of a large Florida school district. Morley has a BA in psychology, a dual MA in secondary education and interdisciplinary social sciences, and a PhD in curriculum and instruction from the University of South Florida.

BEGAETA NUKIC received her bachelor's degree in mathematics and educational studies from Trinity College in 2011. She helped train and organize student researchers and interviewed parents and guardians for the SmartChoices project.

MYRON ORFIELD is the executive director of the Institute on Race and Poverty at the University of Minnesota Law School, a nonresident senior fellow at the Brookings Institution in Washington DC, and an affiliate faculty member at the Hubert H. Humphrey Institute of Public Affairs. He teaches and writes in the fields of civil rights, state and local government, state and local finance, land use, questions of regional governance, and the legislative process.

BARBARA SHIRCLIFFE is an associate professor of the social foundations of education at the University of South Florida. As a historian of education, her research interests include the history of education; school policy; school desegregation; school community relations; and the effects of class, race, and gender in structuring policy and outcomes.

GENEVIEVE SIEGEL-HAWLEY is an assistant professor at Virginia Commonwealth University. Her research examines the impact of segregation and resegregation in American schools and explores viable policy options for a truly integrated society.

MIYA WARNER is a doctoral student in sociology and education at Teachers College, Columbia University. Her research focuses broadly on the influence of policy on educational equity and access. She is also a research associate for the Center for Understanding Race and Education (CURE) at Teachers College.

AMY STUART WELLS is a professor of sociology and education and the director of the Center for Understanding Race and Education (CURE) at Teachers College, Columbia University. She was also the director of the Building Knowledge for Social Justice Project (2009–11) at the Ford Foundation. Her research and writing have focused broadly on issues of race and education and more specifically on educational policies such as school desegregation, school choice, charter schools, and tracking and how they shape and constrain opportunities for students of color.

DIANE ZANNONI, a professor of economics at Trinity College, consulted on the Smart-Choices research design and supervised the quantitative analysis.

INDEX

management organizations), 140–41, 166–68, 176, 182n42, 189; EMOs (educational management organizations), 182n42, 201; and HCPS, 104; and interdistrict transfer programs in general, 189, 191, 201, 202–3; nonprofit management, 8, 19; for-profit management, 8, 19, 168

mandatory desegregation, 12–13, 15, 17, 24, 26, 28; and BUSD, 70, 72–73; and Hartford (Conn.) schools, 221; and HCPS, 91, 93–94, 96; and integration theory, 58, 60–61, 268; and JCPS, 240–41, 243; and traditional American education, 41–42

mandatory education, 8, 41

Manning v. School Board of Hillsborough County, 93

marketing. *See* recruitment

market theory, 28–29, 31, 37–39, 42–55, 255–263, 265–66; assumptions of, 45–46, 55, 62–63, 262, 266; and efficiency, 42–43, 45, 47, 49, 54–55, 257; and Hartford (Conn.) schools, 221; and HCPS, 90–91; integration theory compared to, 38–39, 45, 56–59, 61–63, 266–67; and interdistrict transfer programs in general, 188, 190, 199–206, 202–3, 209, 211, 215; and "invisible hand," 43–44; limits to, 9, 46–55, 259–261; and magnet programs/schools in general, 108; and monopoly power, 43–46; and social stratification, 50, 54, 63, 256–58, 261–64

Massachusetts, 13, 143n15, 214. *See also* Boston (Mass.) schools

math achievement/proficiency, 111–12, 193, 251; and New Orleans schools, 171, *172, 173, 174, 175;* and Twin Cities schools, 149–150, *150,* 158n18

media, 19, 219, 226–27, 241–43

Medicaid, 7

METCO (Metropolitan Council for Educational Opportunity), 25, 194–96, 198–99, 207, 212, 214

metropolitan areas, 15–17, 24–25; and BUSD, 76, 78; and charter schools, 131, 136, 140; and Hartford (Conn.) schools, 111, 219–221, 223, 225–26; and HCPS, 30, 89–105; and integration theory, 60, 269; and interdistrict transfer programs in general, 31, 189, 195, 208–9, 212–13; and JCPS, 32, 238, 242, 254n2; and market theory, 51–53, 261–62; and New Orleans schools, 160–62, 172, 177–79; and Twin Cities schools, 31, 145–

157, 147, 150. See also names of other metro areas

Metro Tampa schools. *See* Hillsborough County Public Schools (HCPS)

Michigan, 21, 135, 138–39. *See also names of Michigan cities*

middle class, 5, 7, 14–15, 19–20, 123, 178; and integration theory, 59–61; and market theory, 50, 52–53, 263

midwestern states, 135–36

Milliken v. Bradley, 13, 41, 57, 92, 190

Milwaukee (Wis.) schools, 13, 17, 107, 196, 201, 209, 210, 212–13, 260; Chapter 220 program, 196, 210, 212; Parents Concerned about Chapter 220, 212; Public School District, 212–13

Minneapolis (Minn.) schools, 11, 146, 148–49, 151, 153, 155–56; Choice Is Yours Program (CIY), 149–150, *150,* 152–53, 158n22, 197, 208, 210–11, 214; Hmong International Academy, 151; and interdistrict transfer programs, 194, 197, 201, 206, 208, *209,* 210–11, 214; Lucy Laney Elementary School, 151; Public School District, 208; WATS (Wide Area Transportation System), 210; Western Metro Education Program, 210. *See also* Twin Cities schools

Minnesota, 19, 25, 145–46, 152–54, 183n52; Department of Education, 208; Integration Revenue Program, 152–53, 155. *See also* Twin Cities schools; *names of Minnesota cities*

minority schools/students, 3, 5, 7, 10–11, 13, 15–16, 18, 21, 28, 31, 40; and BUSD, 82; and charter schools in general, 130–31, 135–37, *137,* 140; and Hartford (Conn.) schools, 220, 222–23, *222,* 228, 234–35; and HCPS, 90, 93, 96–97, 100, 102–3; and integration theory, 39, 55, 60–61, 265, 267; and interdistrict transfer programs in general, 197, 199, 212; and JCPS, 243, 247; and magnet programs/schools in general, 111, 114, 116, 118, 124n13; and market theory, 37, 45–46, 53, 259–260; and Twin Cities schools, 156. *See also names of minority groups*

Minow, Martha, 26

Missouri, 132, 196, 213. *See also* St. Louis (Mo.) schools; *names of other Missouri cities*

mobility, social, 40, 63, 101; and interdistrict transfer programs in general, 188, 197–99

mobility rates, 79–80, 86, 149, 171–74, 227

Moe, Terry M., 23, 46